REDUCING POVERTY IN AMERICA

To my wife, Lynne,
without whose support
this book would not have been

edited by

MICHAEL R. DARBY

REDUCING POVERTY IN AMERICA

VIEWS AND APPROACHES

SAGE Publications
International Educational and Professional Publisher
Thousand Oaks   London   New Delhi

Copyright © 1996 by Sage Publications, Inc.

For information address:

SAGE Publications, Inc.
2455 Teller Road
Thousand Oaks, California 91320
E-mail: order@sagepub.com

SAGE Publications Ltd.
6 Bonhill Street
London EC2A 4PU
United Kingdom

SAGE Publications India Pvt. Ltd.
M-32 Market
Greater Kailash I
New Delhi 110 048 India

Printed in the United States of America

Library of Congress Cataloging-in-Publication Data

Main entry under title:

Reducing poverty in America: Views and approaches / edited by Michael
R. Darby.
        p.   cm.
    Includes bibliographical references and index.
    ISBN 0-7619-0006-3 (cloth: alk. paper).—ISBN 0-7619-0007-1
(pbk.: alk. paper)
        1. Poverty—United States. 2. Poor—United States. 3. Public
welfare—United States. 4. Full employment policies—United States.
5. Occupational training—United States. 6. Education—United
States. 7. United States—Social policy—1993- 8. United States—
Economic policy—1993- I. Darby, Michael R.
HC110.P6R43   1996
362.5′0973—dc2095-35748

This book is printed on acid-free paper.

98 99 10 9 8 7 6 5 4 3 2

Sage Production Editor: Diana E. Axelsen
Sage Typesetter: Andrea D. Swanson

Contents

Acknowledgments

This book grew out of a unique gathering of scholars, business executives, government officials, and community activists in Los Angeles in January 1993. The organizers were concerned that poverty lay at the roots of the 1992 Los Angeles riots and that—unlike a generation earlier—we must reduce poverty to ensure that such a disaster does not occur again. This Conference on Reducing Poverty in America was unique because the organizers were also committed to bringing together the best minds representing the full range of thought on the issues. As a result, analysts with different politics and philosophies found themselves truly joined on the issues.

It fell to Michael R. Darby, who had chaired a program committee also including Professors William Ouchi, Alfred E. Osborne, Jr., and James Q. Wilson, to select the best papers and work with the authors to create a balanced, readable book that could reach a much wider audience.

The moving spirit behind both the conference and this book was B. Kipling Hagopian, General Partner of Brentwood Associates, a Los Angeles venture capital firm. In addition to conceiving the idea, Mr. Hagopian was chairman of the Organizing Committee, which also included former Senator John V. Tunney (vice-chairman), Joseph E. Alibrandi, Jeffrey C. Barbakow, Michael Burns, Christopher C. DeMuth, Robert A. DeWitt, David Fisher, Sidney Harman, Anderson School, Dean J. Clayburn LaForce, Gerald L. Parsky,

Timothy M. Pennington III, Richard J. Riordan (currently mayor of Los Angeles), Dorothy Tucker, and Jack F. Walker.

The conference was presented by the John M. Olin Center for Policy in UCLA's John E. Anderson Graduate School of Management, in association with the American Enterprise Institute for Public Policy Research, the UCLA Institute for Industrial Relations, and the UCLA Center for the Study of Urban Policy.

Financial support was provided by "patrons" (contributions of $10,000 or more) Aurora Capital Partners, L.P.; Brentwood Associates; Ernst & Young; Foothill Group, Inc.; Jacobs Family Foundation; Latham & Watkins; Litton Industries, Inc.; National Medical Enterprises, Inc.; The Riordan Foundation; and Whittaker Corporation; "sponsors" (contributions of $5,000 or more) ARCO Foundation; Bank of America; Brobeck, Phleger & Harrison; The Capital Group, Inc.; Easton, Inc.; Gibson, Dunn & Crutcher; Hagopian Family Foundation; Harman International Industries, Inc.; Alexander and Adelaide Hixon; Management Compensation Group Incorporated; Paul, Hastings, Janofsky & Walker; Prudential Securities; Salomon Brothers, Inc.; Sutro & Co., Inc.; Times Mirror Corporation; Trust Company of the West; and various individuals.

We are also indebted to the public relations firm, GCI, Spindler and to Paul Spindler for the donation of his time and staff to create broad awareness of the Conference; and to Richard Rice and Donald Spector for the donation of advertising and graphic design services.

PART I

Poverty and the Underclass

1

Facing and Reducing Poverty

Michael R. Darby

As we approach the end of the 20th century, the reality is that millions of people in America are poor. Being poor hurts. By itself, poverty diminishes the quality of life. But poverty is often accompanied by an array of other problems, some of which may be causes of poverty and others that are the consequence of being poor. When we see a poor child, we know that he or she deserves a chance for a better life. The central reality that millions are poor in our rich nation motivates us to wrestle with numbers that are far from firm and to search for cures. We do so even in the knowledge that some initiatives will prove tragic in practice for the poor people involved in the demonstration projects that are the governmental equivalents of pharmaceutical clinical trials. Some help, some hurt, some have no effect. The other authors in this volume struggle with the question of what we should do about poverty. In this introductory chapter, I shall return shortly to that central question and their answers to it. Before doing so, however, I believe it is important to consider the politics of poverty and how those politics have been allowed to systematically distort the official data on poverty. These data are so distorted that they cannot tell us whether and by how much we have progressed since the War on Poverty was launched by President Lyndon B. Johnson some three decades ago.

3

The Politics of Poverty Statistics

The reality is that millions of people are poor, and another reality is that there is no firm basis to say just how many millions there are. For several years, I had the honor to oversee the Census Bureau and see firsthand the efforts that went into the preparation of the annual poverty reports and supplements that together are the basis for much of what we know about the incidence of poverty in America. The Census Bureau employees preparing those reports are dedicated, able professionals, but they are constrained by their political masters in both the White House and Congress to report numbers with known flaws long after those flaws have been demonstrated to the economic and statistical communities.

In 1963, it fell to Mollie Orshansky at the U.S. Department of Agriculture to define who was poor and who was not, so that speeches could be prepared to launch the War on Poverty. Consider her dilemma: There was no agreed basis for doing what was her job to do. For some people, poor people were the bottom 10%—or 15% or 20%—of the income distribution. But defining those who are poor as a fixed percentage of Americans definitely would not do because with such a definition, the poverty rate would always be the same no matter what government accomplished. She was to create a number based on 1963 conditions that could be extrapolated forward to show how many people were lifted out of poverty by the War on Poverty.

The collective memory of the federal statistical agencies tells us that she computed what it would cost in 1963 to buy food for an adequate but far from lavish diet and proposed that the poverty line should be drawn on the assumption that this cost was one quarter of the family budget. Eventually, her proposal and the resulting statistics reached the president. He did not believe that it was politically acceptable to launch a war on poverty that was aimed at some 30% of the U.S. population. Thus, the word came down, and the poverty line was defined as three, not four, times Mollie Orshansky's basic food budget. The poverty lines for different-sized families were then extrapolated forward and backward by using the Consumer Price Index (CPI) reported by the Bureau of Labor Statistics (BLS). When someone says that 36 million Americans lived in poverty in 1991 (U.S. Department of Commerce, 1992a), they are referring to Census Bureau estimates based on these extrapolated poverty lines and money incomes reported in the Current Population Survey.

Such a definition of poverty may be arbitrary, but it could still be useful as a yardstick against which to judge progress or its lack in reducing poverty in America. Two major factors have made this yardstick grow through time, however.

First, the CPI measure was fundamentally flawed until 1982, overmeasuring actual inflation by as much as two or three percentage points in some years of high inflation until it was redefined. This partial double counting of inflation was popular with such groups as Social Security recipients and union members operating under CPI-indexed contracts because it increased their incomes. As a result, when the BLS corrected the CPI, it did not correct it retrospectively. Thus, past benefits and, incidentally, the poverty lines, which were arbitrarily moved up in real (deflated) terms during the 1970s and early 1980s, were left uncorrected. The resulting poverty lines were closer to Mollie Orshansky's than LBJ's: Effectively, the percentage in poverty was increased by the enlarged yardstick. This may seem like a niggling statistical point, but raising the hurdle eliminated statistically much real progress made against poverty in the 1970s and early 1980s (see Figure 1.1). Correcting for this error as is done in the unpublicized supplements to the poverty reports (e.g., U.S. Department of Commerce, 1992b) results in a statistically accurate picture of more substantial progress against poverty, until the 1979-1983 recessions.

Second, welfare benefits were generally cash payments in 1963 when the poverty line was first drawn. Now some two thirds of benefits are in noncash form such as food stamps or Medicaid and thus do not affect officially measured poverty. That is, these major programs that have substantially improved living conditions among those who are poor and near poor are simply not counted in the official definition of poverty. The Census Bureau also reports substantially lower poverty rates when the value of noncash benefits is added into the income definition. Combining the two corrections as is also done in Figure 1.1 lowers the official poverty numbers and rates by some 40% in recent years. I believe that these long overdue corrections are important to understand what progress has been made against poverty. If we do not know what is going on, how can we expect to judge accurately the effectiveness of prior programs and make decisions that will actually reduce poverty?

Why, we must ask, have those corrections not been made and the distorted numbers dropped from the public debate? First, advocates of poor people are strongly opposed to any corrections that might reduce their perceived constituency. They make it clear to the White House that the president will be pilloried in the press if such a change is permitted—the president will be portrayed as a heartless person who wants to sweep poverty under the rug. It is probably rare to find individuals close to the president who believe that doing the right thing with the statistics is more important than avoiding bad publicity. So the order is passed by a senior White House official and the Census Bureau career staff is thwarted in its efforts to report the facts as honestly and objectively as possible.

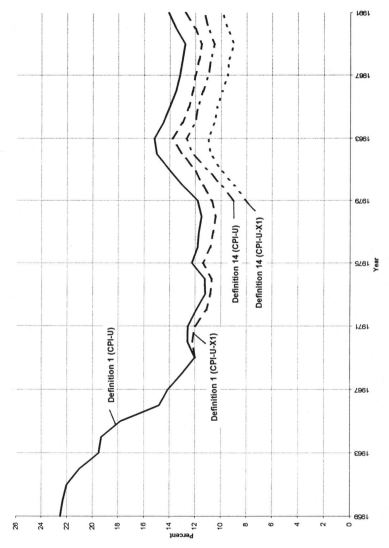

Figure 1.1. Poverty Rates by Definition of Income and Type of Deflator (1959 to 1991)

SOURCE: U.S. Department of Commerce, (1992b), p. xxiii.
NOTES: Definition 1: Cash income only. Definition 14: Cash income less taxes plus noncash income and benefits (e.g., food stamps, school lunches, and subsidies).

6

Things are not hopeless. The supplements to the poverty reports are still published, and serious analysts can dig out the real numbers, although in less detail than would otherwise be the case. If this is an isolated distortion, we probably should not be concerned. I believe that this probably is an isolated area. I know of no other area of direct White House interference with the federal statistical system. Nonetheless, I must confess that when I read a quantitative analysis of poverty, I find myself asking whether the author or authors are using known distorted or real statistics and, if so, whether this is done from ignorance, cynically to make a point, or simply in despair of trying to correct a long-standing error.

An Overview of the Volume

However much poverty there actually is, Americans want to reduce it as much and as fast as possible and are not content with the current state of affairs. Cynics tell us that poor people are always with us and that we can do more harm than good with well-intentioned but inevitably futile attempts to cure the incurable. The remainder of this book brings together some of the leading scholars of poverty to see what can be done to reduce poverty and its correlates and to see what approaches are blind alleys.

The good news is that liberals and conservatives seem to be talking to and learning from each other. The issues between the two are being joined, and both sides of the debate are turning to empirical data to resolve those issues. This sometimes leads to confusion when social scientists and policy analysts who are identified with a particular political side, after studying the evidence, seem to adopt a position identified with the other political side. This type of confusion is a good sign, however, because it means that serious quantitative research is being done and being taking seriously—seriously enough to change opinions that for so long have appeared more akin to religious faith than substantive propositions about how people behave. Substantive propositions are subject to being refuted by the data, but if they are supported by the data, they have the advantage of being useful to formulate policy that actually works as intended.

The bad news is that there do not seem to be any programs that really reduce poverty in a cheap and effective way. There seem to be some programs that do not work. Others seem modestly successful at meeting limited objectives in a cost-effective way. Most observers would say that those programs are well worth pursuing or even enlarging. But no programs seem to be on the horizon that will fundamentally and dramatically reduce the incidence of poverty in the United States.

In part, this may reflect a fundamental truth that some people are poor because they lack the capacity to attain the levels of education and training required to earn what the rest of us would consider an adequate standard of living in the United States at the end of the 20th century. But there is an apparently much larger group of people who could—given the training, education, and will—earn enough to support themselves and perhaps others adequately and who still do not do so. It would be wonderful to be able to transform these people into more productive, and happier, citizens. The ability to do this wholesale seems to be lacking, and even the effective programs are very much retail, working one by one individual.

A fundamental issue running throughout this volume is whether we are trying to reduce the incidence of poverty defined as low income or reduce the incidence of welfare dependency or whether the real problem is how to save the children otherwise doomed to a self-reproducing underclass. In Chapter 2, Douglas Besharov goes over the "facts" of poverty in the national data relative to the distinct though related concepts of poverty, welfare dependency, and the underclass. Reading this chapter brings one quickly up to speed on the basic statistical knowledge on which much of the rest of the volume rests, directly or indirectly.

A number of the authors of this volume—particularly the black authors— believe that there is an underclass culture that inherently value-free governmental programs are powerless to address. These authors see that only a revival of community values, possibly a religious revival, can abort the cycle of failure and despair in black inner-city neighborhoods. Clearly, under the U.S. Constitution, government cannot be expected to lead a religious revival, but it can be asked to not interfere with those community-based programs that are rooted in religious belief in the worth of the individual.

Many people think that the distinction between those who are poor and those in the underclass culture, in which acts destructive of oneself and others are condoned, is a matter of splitting hairs. If any such illusion survives a reading of Besharov's recitation of the national facts, it is shattered by the paradox raised in Chapter 3 by David Hayes-Bautista: California's Latino population does not display the behavioral problems associated with poverty nationally. In fact, although Latinos work hard and live admirable lives, they are still quite often poor.

Whether the anomalous Latino results reflect a mixed population in transition from poor immigrants to American mainstream is not clear. It is clear that solutions to poverty for one social group may completely miss the sources of poverty experienced by other social groups. This much we can learn from the stubborn facts of the case.

The other six parts of this volume represent the best thought of 18 distinguished social scientists and policy analysts on how best to go about actually reducing poverty, welfare dependency, the underclass, or some combination of these related but distinct social ills. The organization is straightforward. Part II lays out three broadly different visions of how to approach these goals. Parts III, IV, V, and VI then examine in considerable depth four separate areas of focus in antipoverty efforts: education, community empowerment, job training, and social interventions. Last, Part VII relates the state of knowledge reflected in this volume to the broader issues raised in Part II.

APPROACHES TO REDUCING POVERTY

To be more specific, in the opening chapter of Part II, Christopher Jencks advocates welfare reforms that treat more realistically the abilities of welfare mothers to support themselves and their children. Charles Murray argues that the real problem is not poverty per se but the behaviors—particularly having children without being prepared to care for them—that are at the core of the idea of the underclass. In reading these chapters together, it does seem that cumulative evidence on the limited successes of past programs has reduced the distances between left and right and enhanced the support for some form of negative income tax or earned income tax credit.

Glenn Loury, himself an economist, believes that social scientists generally—and Jencks and Murray in particular—place entirely too much emphasis on the marginal incentives controlled by government and entirely too little on "the disintegration of urban black society," which he sees as largely independent of marginal incentives. The differences between Murray and Loury may be less than meet the eye, however, as both stress the necessity for a cultural, indeed moral, renaissance for poor urban blacks. Nonetheless, Loury sees such a renaissance as essentially based within these communities, while Murray stresses the larger context of American society.

IMPROVING SCHOOLING FOR THE POOR

The level of education in a country is probably the best predictor of that country's relative income internationally. If we apply that international lesson within the United States, it seems that improving the quantity and quality of education is the best single program for increasing incomes in general and especially for those who are poor. In Chapter 7, John Chubb and Terry Moe argue that, surprisingly, private schools do better than public schools not only at improving the average quality of schooling but also at reducing inequality in schooling, because they are less likely to sidetrack the poorest students in dead-end tracks. Indeed, they find that the higher average quality of education received in private schooling is almost entirely because of superior outcomes for the lower half of the ability distribution. To the extent that poorer students are learning more, they are likely to stay in school longer as well.

Albert Shanker, president of the American Federation of Teachers, confronts head-on Chubb, Moe, and other proponents of parental choice in education. He argues that the quality differences are not significant except that public schools have allowed students to choose easier classes. Thus, quality can be best achieved by imposing more rigorous standards. Shanker believes that our society must put a greater premium on successful school performance if students are to be motivated to achieve. I note that most recent economic studies indicate that returns to education, particularly higher education, have been increasing substantially during the last decade or two.

EMPOWERING PEOPLE: POLITICS AND MARKETS

Empowerment of poor people to change their lives may be the most important avenue besides schooling for reducing poverty. Three chapters examine different types of empowerment. Ernesto Cortés, a disciple of the late Saul Alinsky, discusses political organization and process as a means of improving the lives of those in poverty both directly and through their transforming effect on their lives. John Weicher presents the market-based program that he developed with Jack Kemp at the Department of Housing and Urban Development to transform poor people into property owners who control their own lives and have the opportunity to prosper. Robert Woodson reports on spontaneous leaders who develop within poor neighborhoods and challenge those who measure their success by how many poor people are dependent on them. He believes that this inherent competition leads to discrediting programs with great success records compared with conventional programs, on the grounds that they involve uneducated and/or charismatic leaders and place emphasis on religious belief.

JOB TRAINING: FROM WELFARE TO PAYROLLS

Job training is often advocated as a magic bullet to cure poverty and welfare dependence. During the 1992 campaign, President Clinton seemed to advocate linking eligibility for welfare to participation in a job training program. In Chapter 12, Judith Gueron lays out a meticulous evaluation of what can realistically be expected of job training efforts. She points out that many mothers on welfare have little economic incentive to become employed even after they have completed job training programs—these programs are more effective at increasing work than reducing poverty.

Lawrence Mead emphasizes that few poor adults work regularly. He believes that this lack of work, rather than their inability to earn much more than they receive from welfare, is the primary reason for their poverty. He advocates enforcement of work or job training requirements as a condition of welfare. He admits that work enforcement tests have not indicated much reduction in welfare rolls, but he points out that work requirements do reduce government costs, thus making higher benefit levels possible. More important, for Mead, increased work effort of participants ties them into the social structure of the rest of American society. Accordingly, he also advocates creating incentives for nonworking men to become employed.

Margaret Simms takes some issue with Mead's analysis in Chapter 14. She points particularly to the difficulty in predicting what would be the work experience of those who are not working by extrapolating from the possibly very different group of working poor people. She emphasizes a special role for business as a partner with government and labor.

REDUCING POVERTY
THROUGH SOCIAL INTERVENTION

Historically, social intervention has been advocated to break the vicious cycle of poverty. Head Start has been singled out for political support by both parties. Edward Zigler, the father of Head Start, and Sally Styfco discuss the successes and failures of early childhood intervention and report that Head Start is not so universal a success as it has been claimed but that some Head Start programs are truly effective and others could be made more so through proper attention to the lessons of experience. They believe that if the lessons of the Head Start program are taken seriously, an improved Head Start program would be a proper model for the entire system of early childhood services. They envision a dovetailed, three-stage intervention system beginning prenatally with a parent-child program that phases into a preschool program for children at age 3 and, in turn, a continuing program covering kindergarten through third grade.

Leslie Lenkowsky reviews the broader record of social intervention programs aimed at prevention and rehabilitation of poor persons. He argues that these programs have been pursued for some two centuries with little evidence of effectiveness and that the same thrust is the basis of the new "services strategy" aimed at intervening to save the children "at risk" for a life of poverty and at changing the behavior of poor people so that they achieve self-sufficiency. Lenkowsky observes that these programs are often extremely expensive per poor person because they involve large expenditures for professional staff. In the past, efforts along these lines were largely discredited because their proponents promised results far beyond what could be delivered. He hopes that we do not repeat that mistake. In addition, he sees the need to accept the ineffectiveness of most of the programs tested and to identify and figure out how to replicate the exceptions.

REFLECTIONS ON REDUCING POVERTY IN AMERICA

In the final three chapters of this volume, three very different, very distinguished observers of our society reflect on the current state of knowledge as reflected in this volume and on the prospects for reducing poverty in America. The rapprochement that seems incipient among the poverty specialists writing the earlier chapters is not reflected in their discussion.

James Johnson sees the emerging synthesis of mainstream liberal and conservative thought as basically missing the point. He sees poverty as a result of the capitalist system and particularly of the increased emphasis on free markets during the Reagan and Bush administrations. He proposes a heuristic model that incorporates additional relationships and hypotheses than those considered elsewhere.

Ben Wattenberg looks at the politics of the 1992 presidential election and stresses the importance of President Clinton's "no more something for nothing" welfare proposals. He sees welfare reform as fundamental both as a normative test and as a positive predictor of President Clinton's prospects for reelection in 1996.

In the closing chapter, James Q. Wilson turns to the cultural side of poverty. It is not just getting the incentives right, he tells us—we must also reverse a fundamental deterioration in our standards of how people must behave. We are so afraid of being judgmental that we fail to use judgment. This theme echoes issues raised in various ways in other chapters such as those by Murray, Loury, and Woodson.

References

U.S. Department of Commerce, Bureau of the Census. (1992a, August). *Poverty in the United States: 1991* (Current Population Reports, Series P-60, No. 181). Washington, DC: Government Printing Office.

U.S. Department of Commerce, Bureau of the Census. (1992b, August). *Measuring the effects of benefits and taxes on income and poverty: 1979-1991* (Current Population Reports, Series P-60, No. 182-RD). Washington, DC: Government Printing Office.

Poverty, Welfare Dependency, and the Underclass

Trends and Explanations

Douglas J. Besharov

My role in this chapter is to set the stage for the discussions that follow by providing a road map of contemporary poverty. As neutrally as I can, I will present what we know about the shape of poverty and the factors that contribute to it. Because my space is limited, I can present only a partial picture of what is happening.

As the title of this chapter suggests, there are three perspectives or ways to examine poverty. First, we can consider the people whose income falls under the government's official poverty line. Second, we can consider those who are on welfare, especially those who seem to be caught in all but permanent welfare dependency. Third, we can consider those who are part of what some observers call the "underclass," that is, those poor people whose poverty is aggravated by growing concentrations of socially pathological behaviors.

The Official Poverty Line

Since 1963, the federal government has maintained an official poverty line. Persons or families whose annual incomes fall below it are officially considered poor by the federal government. The poverty line was originally created by Mollie Orshansky at the U.S. Department of Agriculture (USDA). On the assumption that food expenditures account for 33% of a family's budget, she set the poverty level at three times the cost of what the USDA called the lowest-cost "nutritionally adequate" diet. Every year since then, the poverty line has been adjusted upward for inflation. In 1992, the poverty line was $7,202 for one person, $9,212 for a family of two, $11,280 for a family of three, $14,463 for a family of four, and so on (U.S. House of Representatives, 1992, Appendix J, Table 1, p. 1272).

The official poverty line has many weaknesses that I do not have time to discuss in this chapter. Suffice it to say that because of the poverty line's shortcomings, many means-tested federal programs of assistance to the "poor" do not use the poverty line to determine eligibility for benefits. Food stamp eligibility, for example, is set at 130% of the poverty line; Medicaid for pregnant women and children under 6 is set at 133% of the poverty line.

Despite its many weaknesses, the official poverty line is the most widely used measure of poverty trends because it provides a reasonably accurate picture of relative changes in the condition of Americans who are disadvantaged. One caveat: The data we have on poverty are almost entirely based on reports from poor persons themselves. It is widely agreed that as much as 20% of income among those who are poor is not reported. Moreover, the Census Bureau has great difficulty even finding some of the persons who are the most disadvantaged, especially black men. Therefore, any discussion of poverty statistics has to be taken with due care.

One other point: I know that many people prefer the term *Latino*. Because I am using data published by the Census Bureau, however, for technical clarity I will use its terminology, that is, *Hispanic*.

With this understanding, let's look at poverty trends during the past 30 years. As Figure 2.1 shows, between 1959 and 1973 there was a sustained and substantial reduction in the number of people living in poverty, from about 22% of the population to about 11%. But the figure also portrays the central conundrum of poverty policy. In explaining his economic philosophy, President John Kennedy used to say that "a rising tide raises all boats." That used to be true, as Figure 2.1 indicates.

Sometime in the 1970s, however, something changed—and the connection between economic growth and reductions in poverty was broken, as Figure 2.1 also indicates. Progress against poverty all but ended, although the gross

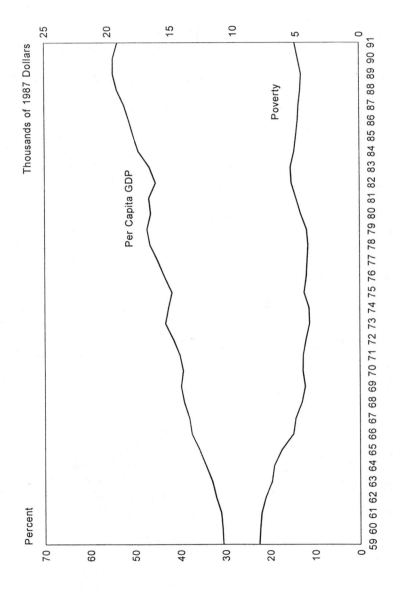

Figure 2.1. Poverty Rate and GDP (1959-1991)
SOURCES: Economic Report of the President (1992); U.S. Department of Commerce (1992b, Table 2).

domestic product (GDP) continued to rise on a per capita basis. Deciding what happened is central to deciding what type of antipoverty program to have.

Welfare Recipiency

I mentioned that many means-tested federal programs do not use the official poverty line to determine eligibility. In fact, and contrary to widespread belief, not all poor people are on Aid to Families With Dependent Children (AFDC). Actual eligibility for welfare benefits is established by the states, and it varies substantially.

As Figure 2.2 indicates, only about 56% of all families with incomes under the poverty line were on welfare in 1991. Most of these were headed by a single or separated mother who was not working. Of all poor families, only about 20% had one member who worked full-time for the full year.

As Figure 2.3 indicates, as of August 1992, almost 13 million people were on welfare. Most startling, in just more than 2 years (from July 1989 to November 1991), caseloads rose by 24%. Today, one in seven American children is on welfare, at a combined federal, state, and local annual cost of $22 billion. Nationally, the average monthly maximum AFDC payment is $372. Food Stamps is also an important income support program—for the working poor as well as for AFDC families. About 25 million people received food stamps in 1992, at a cost of $20.5 billion.

There is also an important racial and ethnic dimension to welfare recipiency. In 1990, 40% of those on welfare were blacks, who make up 12% of the general population; 17% were Hispanics, who compose 8% of the general population. Of perhaps even greater significance, 33% of all black children are on welfare right now, as are 21% of Hispanic children. That is in contrast to only 6% of white children. (See Figure 2.4.)

Explanations

What's happening? Why has poverty proved so intransigent in the face of continued economic growth? To begin to understand, it helps to disaggregate the basic poverty statistic to see how different groups are doing. There are many ways to divide the poverty population. A relatively simple but actually quite revealing way is to consider the experiences of three groups:

1. older persons, that is, individuals 65 or more years old;
2. children, that is, individuals under 18; and

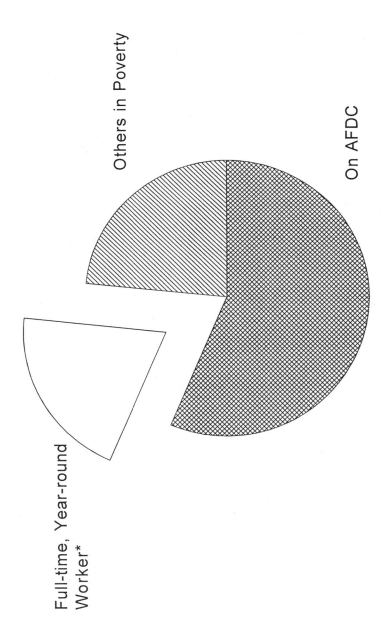

Others in Poverty

On AFDC

Full-time, Year-round
Worker*

Figure 2.2. Families in Poverty (1991)

SOURCES: U.S. Department of Commerce (1992b, Tables C, 14); U.S. House of Representatives (1992, p. 660).
NOTE: *Families in poverty in which at least one person worked full-time, year-round.

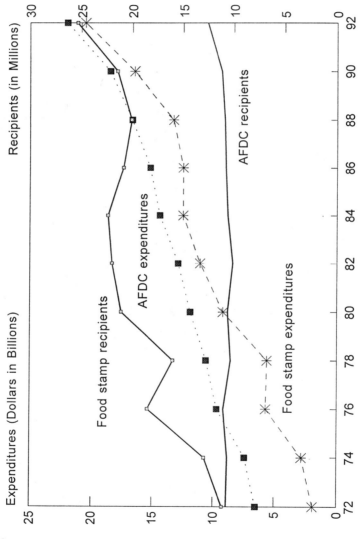

Figure 2.3. Trends in AFDC and Food Stamps: Benefits and Recipiency (1972-1992)
SOURCE: U.S. House of Representatives (1992, Sec. 7 and Appendix P).

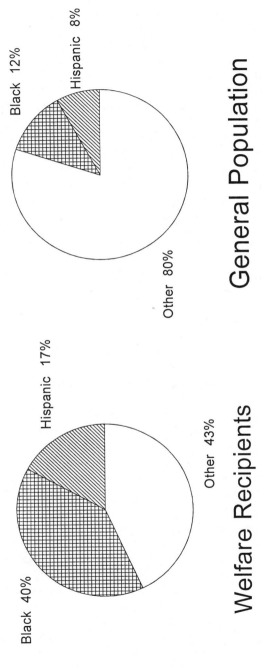

Welfare Recipients   General Population

Percent of children on welfare in 1990: 33% of blacks,
21% of Hispanics, and 6% of whites

Figure 2.4. Welfare by Race (1990)
SOURCES: Department of Health and Human Services, unpublished data; U.S. House of Representatives (1992, Sec. 7, Table 29).

3. unrelated individuals, that is, "persons 15 years and over (other than inmates of institutions) who are not living with any relatives" (U.S. Department of Commerce, 1992b, p. A-9).

As Figure 2.5 indicates, the poverty rate for older persons and for unrelated individuals continued to decline after 1973 when the overall poverty rate began to rise, although at a slower pace. The poverty rate for children, however, began to climb after 1969. In the last 22 years, the poverty rate for children has increased by more than 50%.

Liberals often say that poverty could be reduced by throwing money at it. That is certainly what happened in regard to older persons. But it was a lot of money. In 1991, Social Security expenditures for Old Age and Survivors Insurance and Disability Insurance benefits were $269 billion, about 5% of the GDP (U.S. House of Representatives, 1992, Sec. 3, Table 7, p. 85).

Poverty among unrelated individuals fell for a different reason: declining marriage rates among the relatively more affluent. In the 1950s, marriage rates were as high or higher than at any time in U.S. history. Those who were not married tended to be among the most economically disadvantaged, as reflected in Figure 2.5. In the last 30 years, however, there has been a marked decline in marriage among higher-income Americans. An increased proportion of affluent women are not marrying at all, and many others are delaying marriage (see Figures 2.6 and 2.7). As a result, the basic social and demographic composition of "unrelated individuals" has changed, which, in turn, has lowered the poverty rate for this group.

This dynamic is important to an understanding of poverty because its obverse can be observed in the poverty rate for children, who, more and more, are members of two low-income groups: relatively young, two-parent couples and single mothers. To understand what is happening to these two groups, I want to describe five parallel—and interacting—developments:

1. the decline in low-wage jobs,
2. the impact of immigration,
3. the decline in labor force participation and work effort,
4. the breakdown of traditional family structures, and
5. drugs.

Low-wage jobs. In the last 20 years, there have been major changes in the economy, especially a pronounced decline in earnings after 1979, as indicated by Figure 2.8. This figure portrays a clear stagnation of wages. Much of the decline (as opposed to the failure to rise) can be explained by sharply increasing health care costs (as well as other fringe benefits). Many factors are feeding this decline. Among the most prominent are weaker unions,

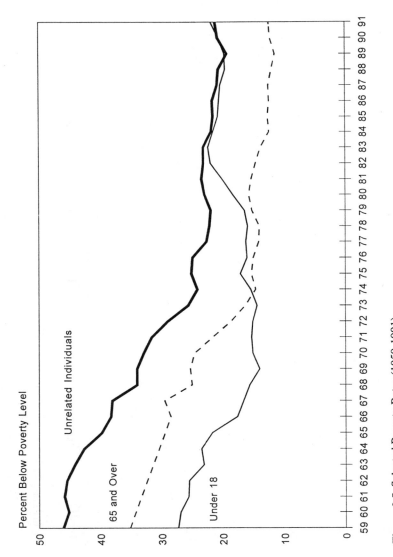

Figure 2.5. Selected Poverty Rates (1959-1991)
SOURCE: U.S. Department of Commerce (1992b, Tables 2 and 3).

21

22

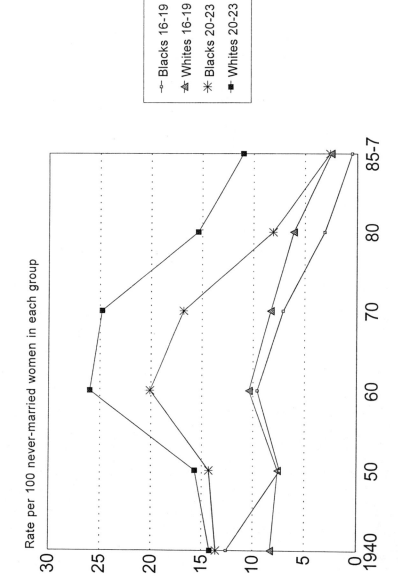

Figure 2.6. Marriage Rates of Women Ages 16-23 (1940-1987)
SOURCE: Mare and Winship (1991, pp. 183-184).

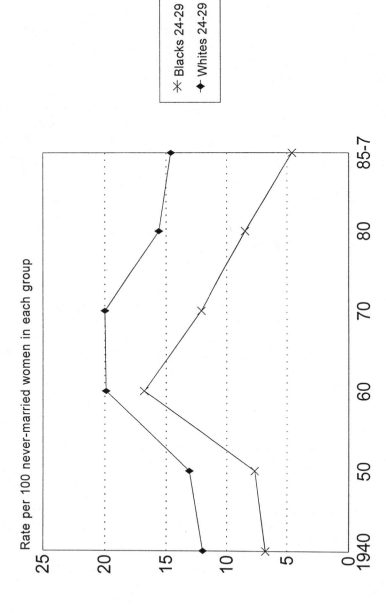

Rate per 100 never-married women in each group

✳ Blacks 24-29
◆ Whites 24-29

Figure 2.7. Marriage Rates of Women Ages 24-29 (1940-1987)
SOURCE: Mare and Winship (1991, pp. 183-184).

23

stronger international competition, changing technologies, and a larger service sector—all of which tend to weaken the demand for low-skilled *male*
workers.

Immigration. Second, immigration has had a pronounced—and dual—effect
on low-wage workers. At least in the short run, immigration tends to lower
entry-level wages as the newcomers compete with those already here. In addition,
there appears to be a leapfrogging effect, with new immigrants actually doing
better than natives. Both these processes are reflected in Figure 2.9.

Labor force participation. The third factor explaining declining economic
fortunes is that work effort is down among men—but not among women, as
shown in Figure 2.10. Again, however, I emphasize the difficulty of distinguishing between cause and effect. Work effort went down before earnings,
but clearly, there is an interactive relationship between the two.

The media often treat the issue of nonwork in racial terms. And, certainly,
when one looks at Figure 2.11, which shows men with no income by race, one
sees a large racial disparity. As Figures 2.12 and 2.13 reveal, however, with
a control for educational attainment, labor force participation, if anything, was
higher in 1988 for blacks in all but one group—male high school dropouts. I
will further discuss this serious problem shortly.

Family structures. The fourth major explanation of poverty increases is the
change in family structure. For 30 years, out-of-wedlock birth rates have been
steadily increasing (see Figure 2.14). Between 1960 and 1989, the rate of
out-of-wedlock births among single women almost doubled. Because the
number of single women has also grown, the number of children born out of
wedlock tripled, from 225,000 children to about 1 million. One in four
American children is now born out of wedlock.

Out-of-wedlock birth rates have been rising consistently for both whites
and Hispanics. The rate for blacks jumped 38% in the 1950s and then declined
almost 20% between 1960 and 1985. But it is again rising fast; the increase
between 1985 and 1989, 4 short years, almost entirely offset the earlier,
25-year decline. All three rates are now at their all-time highs (see Figures
2.15 and 2.16).

Many attribute this increase in out-of-wedlock births, and family breakdown
in general, to the poor economic condition of young men, especially young black
men. As is apparent from the figures, however, the rate of out-of-wedlock births
rose before unemployment went up and earnings went down.

Whatever the cause, the economic impact of this rise in out-of-wedlock
births is clear. As Figure 2.17 shows, median income for all American families

text continued on page 35

Index Level

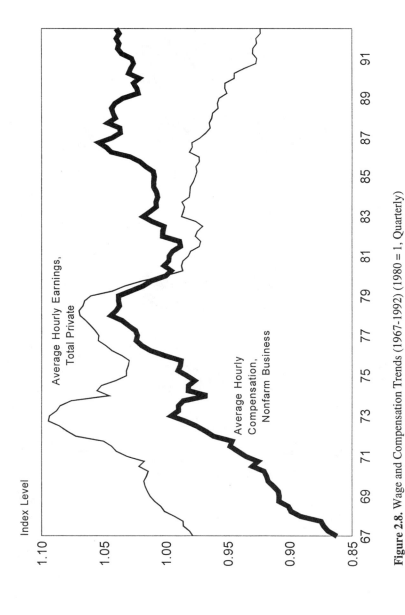

Figure 2.8. Wage and Compensation Trends (1967-1992) (1980 = 1, Quarterly)

SOURCES: M. Kosters, American Enterprise Institute, January 1993; U.S. Bureau of Labor Statistics.
NOTE: Data are adjusted for inflation using the Consumer Price Index (CPI).

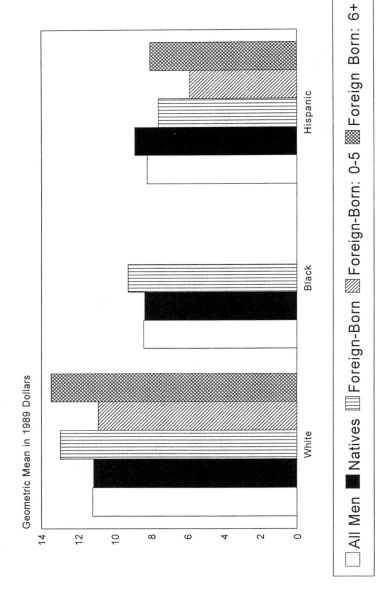

Figure 2.9. Hourly Pay of Men (1989)
SOURCE: Sorensen and Enchautegul (1992).

26

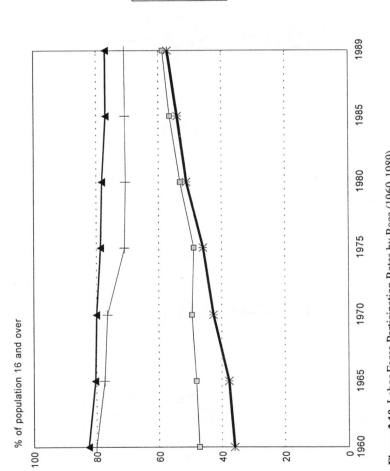

% of population 16 and over

▲	White Men	
+	Black Men	
✳	White Women	
▣	Black Women	

Figure 2.10. Labor Force Participation Rates by Race (1960-1989)
SOURCE: U.S. Department of Commerce (1971, 1980, 1991).

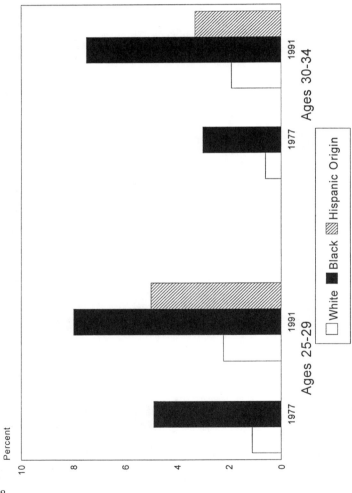

Figure 2.11. Men With No Income (1977, 1991)
SOURCE: U.S. Department of Commerce (1992a, Table 29).

28

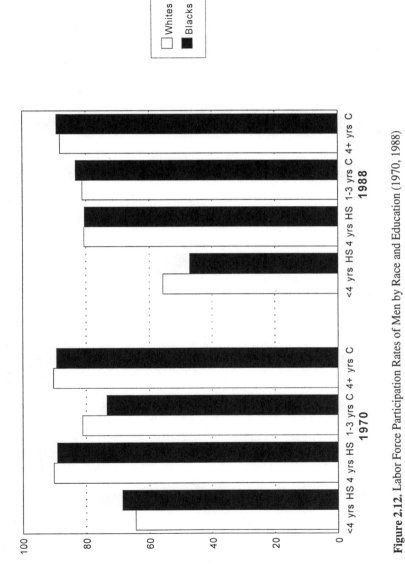

Figure 2.12. Labor Force Participation Rates of Men by Race and Education (1970, 1988)

SOURCE: U.S. Bureau of Labor Statistics (n.d., unpublished tabulations from the Current Population Survey, March 1970 and 1988).
NOTES: Figures for 1970 include men 18 years old and older; 1988 figures include men 16 years and over. Figures for 1970 blacks are for nonwhite men.

30

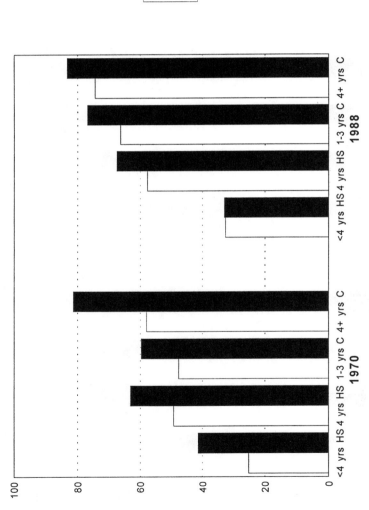

Figure 2.13. Labor Force Participation Rates of Women by Race and Education (1970, 1988)

SOURCE: U.S. Bureau of Labor Statistics (n.d., unpublished tabulations from the Current Population Survey, March 1970 and March 1988).

NOTES: Figures for 1970 include women 18 years old and older; 1988 figures include women 16 years old and older. Figures for 1970 blacks are for nonwhite women.

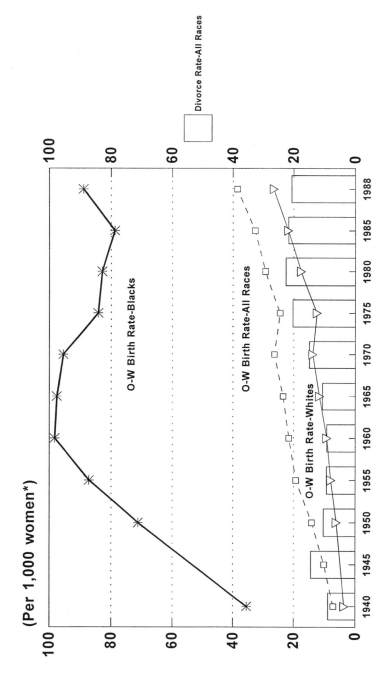

(Per 1,000 women*)

Figure 2.14. Out-of-Wedlock Birth and Divorce Rates (1940-1988)

SOURCES: U.S. Department of Commerce (1975, Series B28-35, p. 52; Series B216-220, p. 64); U.S. Department of Commerce (1992c, Tables 89 and 127).
NOTE: *Unmarried for out-of-wedlock rates and married for divorce rates.

31

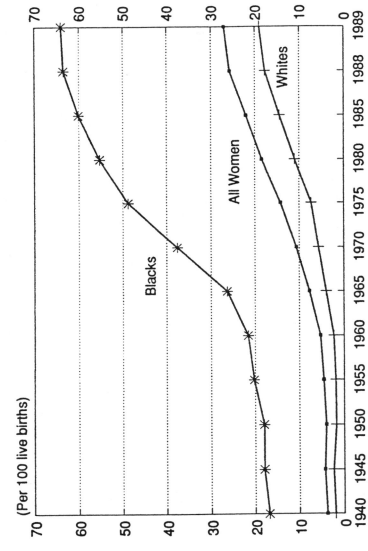

Figure 2.15. Out-of-Wedlock Birth Ratios (1940-1989)

SOURCES: U.S. Department of Commerce (1975); U.S. Department of Commerce (1992c).
NOTE: Pre-1970 figures for blacks include all nonwhite races.

32

(thousands)

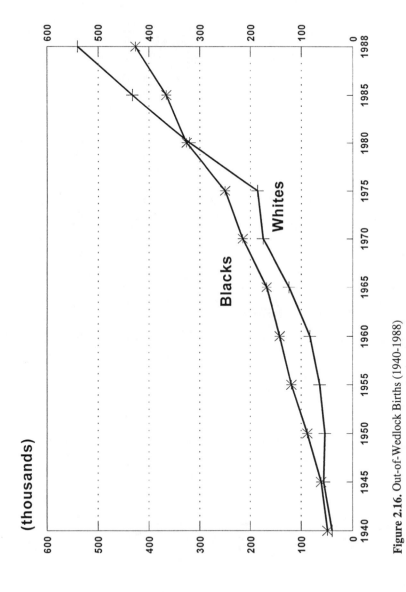

Figure 2.16. Out-of-Wedlock Births (1940-1988)

SOURCES: U.S. Department of Commerce (1975); U.S. Department of Commerce (1992c).
NOTE: Pre-1970 figures for blacks include all nonwhite races.

33

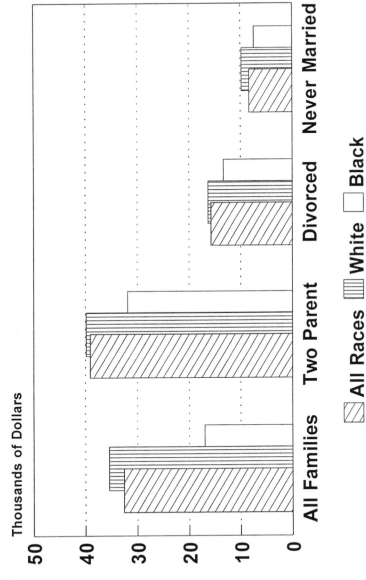

Figure 2.17. Median Family Income of Households by Race and Marital Status (1990)
SOURCE: U.S. Department of Commerce (1991a, Table 6, pp. 45-60).

is $32,551. For two-parent families, it is $39,076. But for families headed by a divorced women, it is $15,762, and for families headed by a never-married mother, it is $8,337. Note, also, that racial differences tend to disappear when family structure is taken into account.

About 50% of all unwed teen mothers go on welfare within 1 year of the birth of their first child; 77% go on within 5 years, according to the Congressional Budget Office (see Congress of the United States, 1990, Table 13, p. 52). According to Zill, Moore, Nord, and Stief (1991) of Child Trends, 43% of long-term welfare recipients (on the rolls for 10 years or more) started their families as unwed teens (p. 32).

A mother's age and marital status at the birth of her first child are stronger determinants of welfare dependency than is her race. One year after the birth of their first child, white and black unmarried, adolescent mothers have about the same welfare rate. After 5 years, black mothers have a somewhat higher rate (84% versus 72%), but various demographic factors such as family income, educational attainment, and family structure account for this relatively small difference.

This continuing increase in out-of-wedlock births is reflected in rising AFDC rolls, which are higher than at any time in U.S. history. In August 1992, almost 13 million people were on welfare. As mentioned earlier, in just over 2 years (from July 1989 to November 1991), caseloads rose by 24%. Much of this increase, of course, is the result of a weak economy (see Figure 2.18). However, careful research by a number of analysts indicates that as much as half of the increased caseload has been caused by the growth in female-headed households and, particularly, the growth of out-of-wedlock births among young, disadvantaged women. For example, Gabe (1992) of the Congressional Research Service found that the rise in never-married mothers accounted for more than 70% of the additional 400,000 welfare families found in a Census Bureau survey between 1987 and 1991 (p. 23). (Gabe's statistic cannot be applied to the whole AFDC increase because the Census survey he used misses about half of all welfare families.)

Drugs. Finally, one cannot consider contemporary poverty without mentioning drug and alcohol abuse and the toll that it takes on the most disadvantaged people. Figures 2.19 and 2.20 show that although reported drug use among middle-class Americans is declining, use by the inner-city disadvantaged persons has become more severe.

The social and economic implications of heavy drug use are illustrated by Figure 2.21, which shows that between 1985 and 1987, about 30% of all black male residents of the District of Columbia were arrested, and by Figure 2.22, which shows a 50% increase in the number of children in foster care since

text continued on page 41

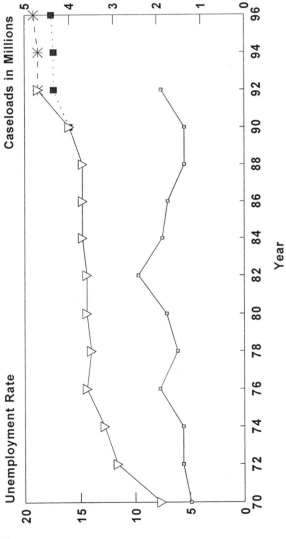

Figure 2.18. AFDC Caseloads and Unemployment Rates (1970-1996)
SOURCES: Economic Report of the President (1992, Table B-36); U.S. House of Representatives (1992, Sec. 7, Table 22).

36

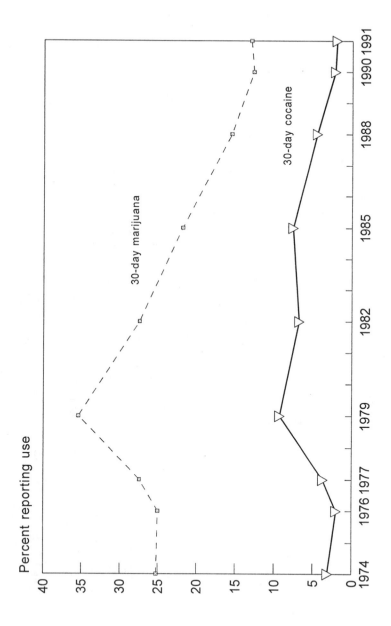

Figure 2.19. Household Drug Use Down: National Household Survey, 30-Day Prevalence Rates for 18- to 25-Year-Olds (1974-1991)

SOURCE: U.S. Department of Health and Human Services (1974-1991).

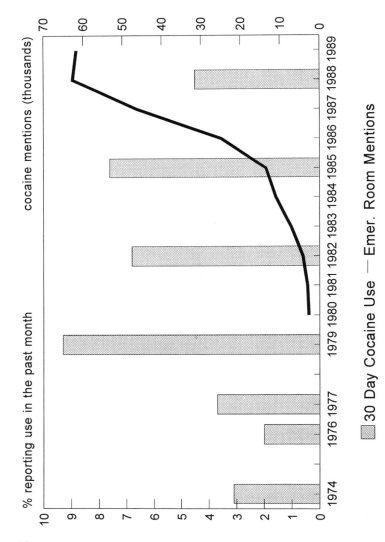

Figure 2.20. Reported Cocaine Use Declining, While Emergency Room Mentions on the Rise (1974-1989)

SOURCES: U.S. Department of Health and Human Services (1974-1991); U.S. Department of Health and Human Services (n.d.).

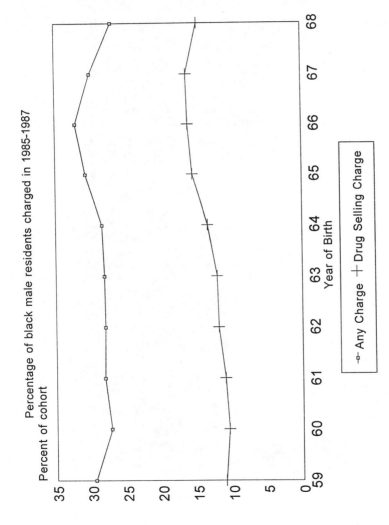

Figure 2.21. Risks of Arrest for Black Male Residents in Washington, D.C., by Year of Birth and Type of Charge (1985-1987)

SOURCE: District of Columbia Pretrial Services Agency as cited in Reuter, Macoun, and Murphy (1990). Reprinted by permission of author.

40

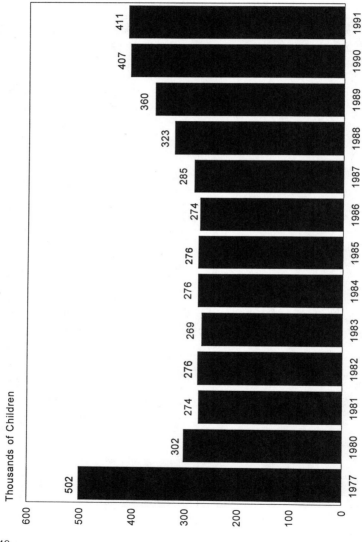

Figure 2.22. Children in Foster Care (1977-1991)

SOURCES: U.S. House of Representatives (1992, Table 23, p. 903); for 1977, C. Gershenson, Center for the Study of Social Policy (personal communication, n.d.).

1985. Most of these additional children are drawn from the r[...] minority communities of inner cities.

Recommendations

Many people will argue about which of the foregoing factors is the most important in explaining poverty. My own sense is that they all interact and that underlying many of them has been a fundamental shift in values concerning work, family, and personal responsibility. In any event, for policy making, I do not think that we need to be obsessed with developing mathematically precise explanations for the causes of poverty. As long as we have the right factors in our sights and have a rough idea of their relative importance, we can address them, as long as we do so with the requisite caution.

The four areas in which we should be looking for solutions are these:

- Better schooling and vocational education
- Contraception
- Welfare reform
- Taking back the inner city

BETTER SCHOOLING AND VOCATIONAL EDUCATION

In recent years, it has become fashionable to talk about "making work pay." Usually, however, this is proposed in the context of income support programs, with calls to raise welfare payments, expand the Earned Income Tax Credit, create a child allowance, and, most recently, to provide "child support assurance." All of these ideas, unfortunately, address only the symptoms of the problem. They do not raise the earnings of those who are poor; they only make them more dependent on government support. That is why my own preference is to increase the earning *capacity* of young people. As Figure 2.23 shows, when one controls for education, income differences across the races are substantially reduced.

The young people we are most concerned about are caught in a cycle of underinvestment in themselves. The central antipoverty question is how to break that cycle. Somehow, schools and other social institutions (including families) need to give these young people a better education and a sense of opportunity. Again, some will say the issue is money. But my own opinion is that the problem is deeper, as reflected in Figure 2.24, where we see that a 25-year rise in education spending per pupil has had no discernible impact on SAT scores.

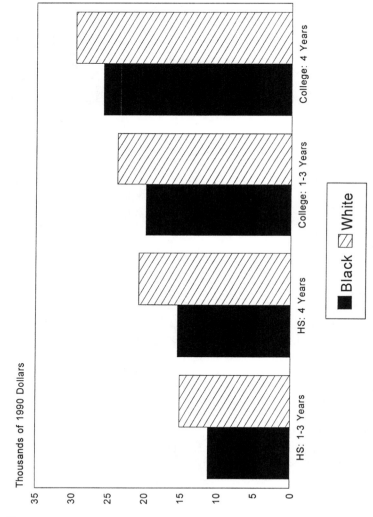

Figure 2.23. Median Earnings, Men Ages 25-34, by Education (1990)
SOURCE: U.S. Department of Commerce (1991b, Table 29).

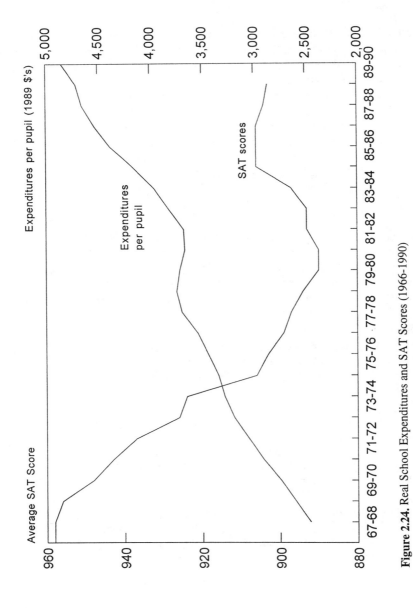

Figure 2.24. Real School Expenditures and SAT Scores (1966-1990)

SOURCE: National Center for Education Statistics (1991, Tables 119 and 154).
NOTE: Current expenditures in 1989 dollars per pupil in average daily attendance in public elementary and secondary schools.

CONTRACEPTION

Many experts debate the reasons why disadvantaged young people have children whom they cannot support without government help. But there is little disagreement that having children can make it many times more difficult to escape poverty.

Certainly some of these pregnancies are planned, but many others are not, as witnessed by the high abortion rate among teenagers portrayed in Figure 2.25. We need to develop and encourage *both* more abstinence among young people and better contraceptive practices.

Norplant and Depo-Provera are both promising additions to the range of contraception options available to U.S. women. Many have already criticized them because they may be used to coerce poor women into having fewer children. I think this fear is not well-founded and that in fact, the poor will welcome these new technologies—if for no other reason than because they are an alternative to sterilization (see Figure 2.26).

WELFARE REFORM

Welfare dependency has taken on a life of its own. We have to change the nature of welfare, at least for teen mothers. I do not expect dramatic change; the welfare system is like a massive oil tanker, which needs 5 miles to turn around. Nevertheless, some cautious changes are needed.

We often hear that about half of all new recipients are off the rolls within 2 years. This is true—but only because of the high turnover among short-term recipients. At any one time, about 82% of all recipients are in the midst of spells that will last 5 years or more. And about 65% are caught up in spells of 8 or more years (see Figure 2.27).

During his presidential campaign, President Clinton pledged "the end of welfare as we know it." He promised to

> provide people with the education, training, job placement assistance and child care they need for two years—so that they can break the cycle of dependency. After two years, those who can work will be required to go to work, either in the private sector or in meaningful community service jobs. (Cited in U.S. Department of Health and Human Services, 1994, p. 1)

The bulk of long-term welfare recipients are unmarried mothers, most of whom had their first baby as unwed teenagers. These young mothers have poor prospects to begin with and have further limited their life chances by systematically underinvesting in themselves—by dropping out of school, by

text continued on page 49

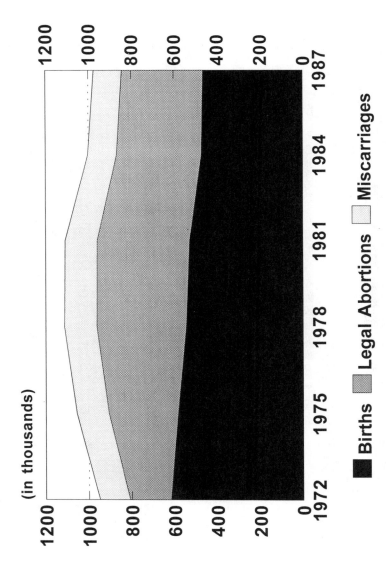

(in thousands)

Figure 2.25. Births, Abortions, and Miscarriages Among Women Ages 15-19 (1972-1987)
SOURCE: Henshaw (1992, p. 1).

45

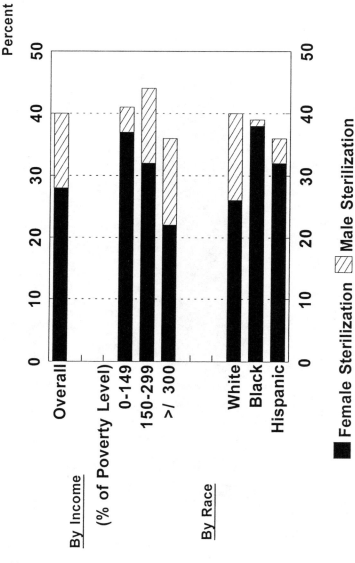

Figure 2.26. Combined Sterilization: Women Ages 15-44 and Their Partners (1988)
SOURCE: Mosher (1990, p. 201).

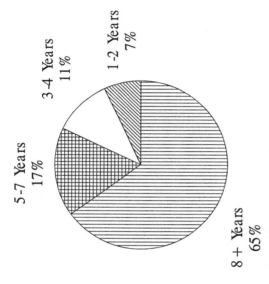

5-7 Years
17%

3-4 Years
11%

1-2 Years
7%

8 + Years
65%

48% of people who enter AFDC in any one year are off within 2 years, but 65% of recipients at any point in time are on for 8 or more years

Figure 2.27. Persons on AFDC at a Point in Time by Length of Spell (Multiple Spell Analysis)
SOURCE: Bane and Ellwood (1983), cited in U.S. House of Representatives (1993, Table 40, p. 715).

Figure 2.28. Recipients Who Will Have AFDC Spells of 10 or More Years, by Marital Status at Beginning of First Spell

SOURCE: Ellwood (1986, Table IV-1), cited in U.S. House of Representatives (1993, Table 42, p. 718).

having a baby out of wedlock, and by not working. As a result, they do not have the education, practical skills, or work habits needed to earn a satisfactory living (see Figure 2.28).

Steady increases in unwed parenthood among ill-prepared young people pose the central challenge to contemporary efforts to fight poverty. It is within this context that the fight over how to implement Clinton's campaign promise is waged.

Those recipients motivated to improve their life situations, such as most divorced mothers, will probably do well under Clinton's plan. But to make a real dent in welfare dependency, Clinton's program will have to apply to unwed mothers, who form the bulk of long-term welfare recipients.

This will not be easy. Years of inactivity leave their mark. Even in a strong economy, breaking patterns of behavior that took a lifetime to establish can take years. Richly funded demonstration programs, for example, find it exceedingly difficult to improve the ability of these women to care for their children, let alone to become economically self-sufficient. Earnings improvements in the realm of 6% are considered successes for poorly educated young mothers who have sporadic work histories. (Most programs do not even try to work with the young fathers.)

California's welfare-to-work program is a case in point. In 1985, the state established the Greater Avenues for Independence Program (GAIN), an education and training project for welfare recipients. A six-county evaluation using random assignment to experimental and control groups found that for single parents, average yearly earnings increased by only $271. (Total yearly earnings averaged $1,902). The county with the greatest impact on earnings (Riverside) was able to raise earnings by about $1,000, but average total earnings were still less than $2,500—not nearly enough to lift these single mothers off welfare. In fact, welfare rolls declined only 7% in Riverside and a disappointing 3% in the other counties (Riccio & Friedlander, 1992, p. x, Table 1).

This does not mean that all young mothers should be placed in traditional community service jobs. Many have enormous problems that will prevent them from satisfying even this minimal obligation (e.g., see Figure 2.29). These young people may need a modern version of the 19th-century settlement house, in which counseling, education, enriched child development services, and other activities to structure otherwise idle time are all provided under one roof. The base for such a program could be the expanded Head Start program that everyone seems to support. In fact, Head Start professionals even have a name for this approach; they call it "two-generational" programming.

Those young people who had children out of wedlock—with no means to support them and largely unprepared to care for them—have demonstrated that *on their own,* they do not make the wisest decisions. Their lives desper-

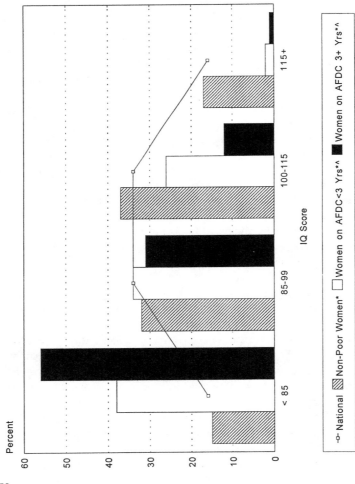

Figure 2.29. Selected IQ Scores by Poverty Status and Welfare Receipt

SOURCE: Zill, Moore, Nord, and Stief (1991, Table 16).
NOTE: *Scores represent Armed Forces Qualification Test scores calibrated on the same scale as the IQ test. ^Out of the 5 years preceding survey.

ately need the structure that only the larger society can provide. Participation mandates such as those President Clinton has proposed could end welfare as we know it—for the good of society, the children, and, yes, the mothers.

TAKING BACK THE INNER CITY

Finally, for the very poorest persons living in inner cities, we need a neighborhood-based strategy. People need to be reasonably safe from crime if they are to be economically active. Moreover, in some neighborhoods, there seems to be a contagious spread of socially harmful behaviors.

Some experts have a name for these communities: "underclass neighborhoods." Sawhill (1989) and her colleagues at the Urban Institute define such neighborhoods as having high incidences of school dropouts, female-headed families with children, welfare dependency, and joblessness or irregular employment among adult men. Technically, high incidences signify rates at least one standard deviation above the U.S. mean. In 1980, this meant that the underclass neighborhoods had welfare rates of 34% (compared with 8% nationwide), male nonemployment of 56% (compared with 31% nationwide), and high school dropout rates of 36% (compared with 13% nationwide), with 60% of all households headed by women (compared with 19% nationwide).

Using this definition, they found that the number of people living in underclass neighborhoods increased more than threefold between 1970 and 1980 (see Figure 2.30). Drugs and AIDS are two of the major problems that have to be addressed. (See Figures 2.31 and 2.32.)

But here, I can only emphasize the difficulty of doing something constructive. Surely we must act, but just as surely we should do so with a keen appreciation of our ignorance about what *might* (notice I do not say *will*) work.

Conclusion

In this chapter, I have laid out an outline of the facts that the other authors of this volume address. I hope that I have provided both an overview of poverty and a template against which their proposals can be compared.

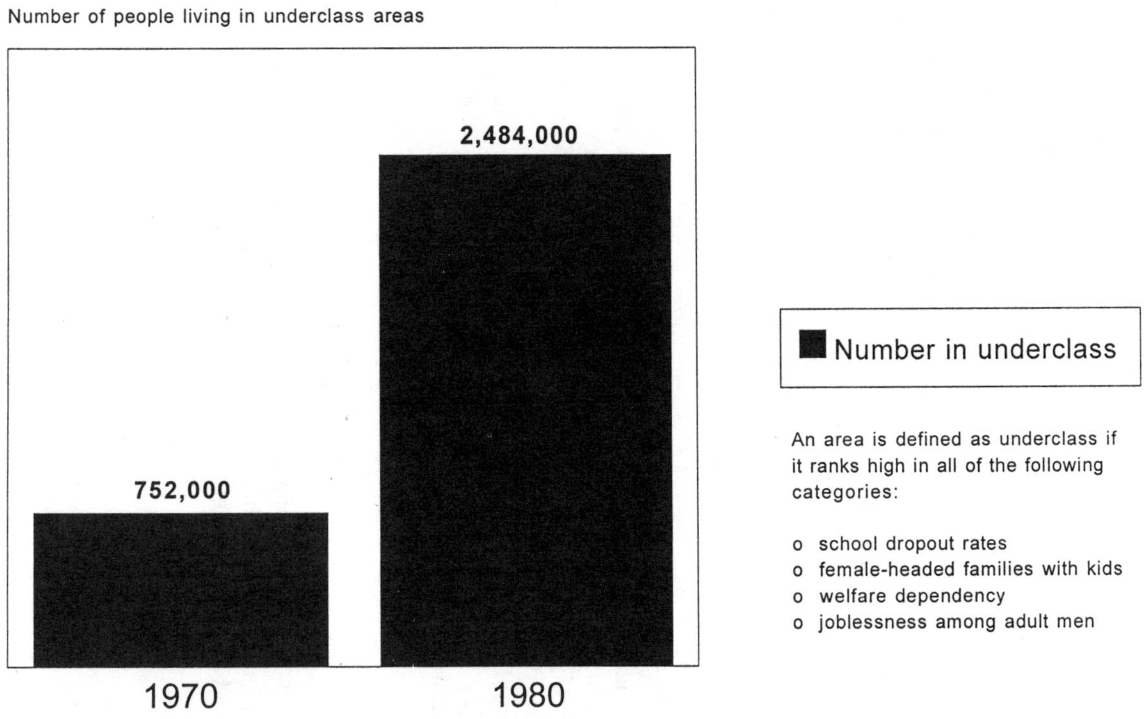

Number of people living in underclass areas

Number in underclass

An area is defined as underclass if it ranks high in all of the following categories:

o school dropout rates
o female-headed families with kids
o welfare dependency
o joblessness among adult men

752,000

2,484,000

1970

1980

Figure 2.30. Underclass Populations (1970, 1980)
SOURCE: Sawhill (1989).

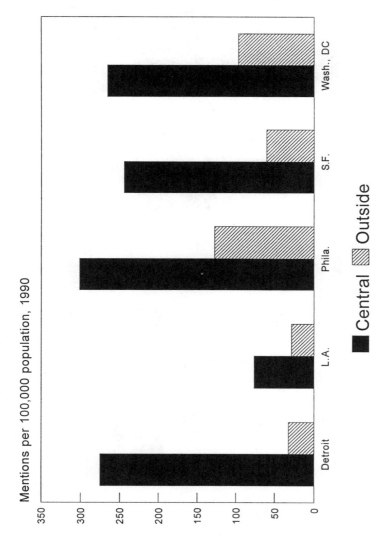

Figure 2.31. Cocaine Emergencies Concentrated in Central Cities (1990)

SOURCE: Reuter, Ebenor, and McCaffrey (1993). Reprinted by permission of author. Unpublished data from Drug Abuse Warning Network (U.S. Department of Health and Human Services).

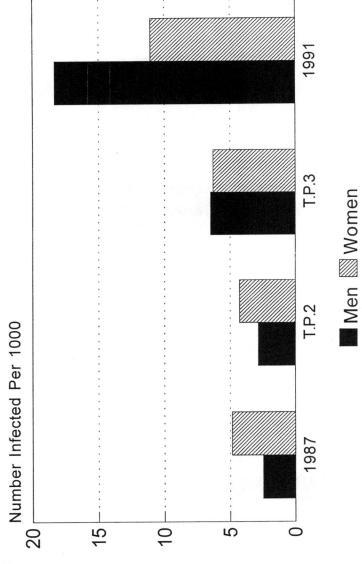

Figure 2.32. HIV Infection in Urban Adolescents (1987-1991)

SOURCE: D'Angelo, Geston, Brasseux, Guagliardo, and Shaffer (1992).

NOTE: T.P. = Time Period.

References

Bane, M. J., & Ellwood, D. T. (1983, June). *The dynamics of dependence: The routes to self-sufficiency* (Paper prepared for the U.S. Department of Health and Human Services under Contract No. 100-82-0038). Cambridge, MA: Urban Systems Research and Engineering.

Congress of the United States. (1990, September). *Sources of support for adolescent mothers.* Washington, DC: Congressional Budget Office.

D'Angelo, L. J., Geston, P. R., Brasseux, C. O., Guagliardo, M. F., & Shaffer, N. (1992). *A longitudinal study of HIV infection in urban adolescents.* Washington, DC: Children's National Medical Center and Atlanta, GA: Centers for Disease Control.

Economic report of the president. (1992, February). Washington, DC: Office of the President of the United States.

Ellwood, D. T. (1986). *Targeting "would-be" long-term recipients of AFDC* (Paper prepared for the U.S. Department of Health and Human Services under Contract No. 100-84-0059). Princeton, NJ: Mathematical Policy Research.

Gabe, T. (1992, December 9). *Demographic trends affecting Aid to Families With Dependent Children (AFDC) caseload growth* (CRS Report to Congress). Washington, DC: Library of Congress, Congressional Research Service.

Henshaw, S. (1992, April 2). *U.S. teenage pregnancy statistics.* New York: Alan Guttmacher Institute.

Mare, R., & Winship, C. (1991). Socioeconomic change and the decline of marriage for blacks and whites. In C. Jencks & P. E. Peterson (Eds.), *The urban underclass* (pp. 183-184). Washington, DC: Brookings Institution.

Mosher, W. D. (1990). Contraceptive practice in the United States, 1982-1988. *Family Planning Perspectives, 22*(5), 198-205.

National Center for Education Statistics. (1991). *Digest of education statistics, 1990* (NCES 91-660). Washington, DC: U.S. Department of Education.

Reuter, P., Macoun, R., & Murphy, P. (1990). *Money from crime: A study of the economics of drug dealing in Washington, D.C.* Santa Monica, CA: RAND.

Riccio, J., & Friedlander, D. (1992, May). *GAIN: Program strategies, participation patterns, and first-year impacts in six counties.* New York: Manpower Demonstration Research Corporation.

Sawhill, I. V. (1989, Summer). The underclass: An overview. *The Public Interest, 96,* 3-15.

Sorensen, E., & Enchautegul, M. (1992). *Immigrant male earnings in the 1980's: Divergent patterns by race and ethnicity.* Washington, DC: Urban Institute.

U.S. Bureau of Labor Statistics. (n.d.). [Unpublished tabulations from the Current Population Survey, March 1970, 1988]. Unpublished data.

U.S. Department of Commerce, Bureau of the Census. (1971, 1980, 1991). *Statistical abstract of the United States* (Annual). Washington, DC: Government Printing Office.

U.S. Department of Commerce, Bureau of the Census. (1975). *Historical statistics of the United States: Colonial times to 1970.* Washington, DC: Government Printing Office.

U.S. Department of Commerce, Bureau of the Census. (1991a, May). *Marital status and living arrangements: March 1990* (Current Population Reports, Series P-20, No. 450). Washington, DC: Government Printing Office.

U.S. Department of Commerce, Bureau of the Census. (1991b). *Money income of households, families, and persons in the United States: 1990* (Current Population Reports, Series P-60, No. 174). Washington, DC: Government Printing Office.

U.S. Department of Commerce, Bureau of the Census. (1992a). *Money income of households, families, and persons in the United States: 1991* (Current Population Reports, Series P-60, No. 180). Washington, DC: Government Printing Office.

U.S. Department of Commerce, Bureau of the Census. (1992b, August). *Poverty in the United States: 1991* (Current Population Reports, Series P-60, No. 181). Washington, DC: Government Printing Office.

U.S. Department of Commerce, Bureau of the Census. (1992c). *Statistical abstract of the United States: 1992.* Washington, DC: Government Printing Office.

U.S. Department of Health and Human Services. (1974-1991). *National household survey on drug abuse: Main finding* (Selected years). Washington, DC: Author.

U.S. Department of Health and Human Services, Assistant Secretary of Planning and Evaluation. (1994). *Work and Responsibility Act of 1994: Detailed summary.* Washington, DC: Author.

U.S. Department of Health and Human Services. (n.d.). *Drug abuse warning network* [Data system]. Washington, DC: Author.

U.S. House of Representatives, Committee on Ways and Means. (1992). *1992 Green book: Overview of entitlement programs.* Washington, DC: Government Printing Office.

U.S. House of Representatives, Committee on Ways and Means. (1993). *1993 Green book: Overview of entitlement programs.* Washington, DC: Government Printing Office.

Zill, N., Moore, K. A., Nord, C. W., & Stief, T. (1991, February 25). *Welfare mothers as potential employees: A statistical profile based on national survey data.* Washington, DC: Child Trends.

Poverty and the Underclass
Some Latino Crosscurrents

David Hayes-Bautista

Discussions of poverty frequently focus on single black mothers and their families, but the poverty rate is also high among the rapidly growing Latino population. In this brief chapter, I shall focus on some elements we need to look at as we try to develop policy for poverty, particularly in California and in other western states with a large Mexican-origin Latino population. We will see a picture that is a little different from that presented in Chapter 2—a picture that I think can enrich this debate. Besharov discusses the sorts of individual behaviors involved in poverty. I shall present some data that show that this connection between individual behavior and poverty is compounded by other things as well.

Figure 3.1 gives an idea of why this is important. The population in California has been changing quantitatively during the past few years. In 1970, one could speak of a majority population and minorities. By 1990, the Anglo population was a bare majority and by the year 2000 will be itself a minority. The growth in what I call the "emergent majority" population is driven by a tremendous increase in the Latino and Asian populations and some modest increase in the black population as well. Clearly, we need to consider—if

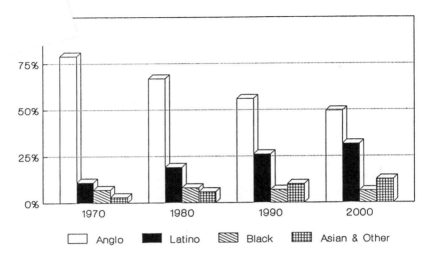

Figure 3.1. Changes in Ethnic Composition: California (1970-2000)

SOURCES: California Employment Development Department (1986); U.S. Department of Commerce (1991); Latino Futures Research Group.

this is half the population—what are its behaviors and how do we as a society respond?

First, let's look at some of these behaviors. Figure 3.2 shows the population in poverty by ethnicity in California in 1989. Latinos have the highest percentage of the population living in poverty of any group.

Now let's look at male labor force participation, low rates of which are normally a precursor to poverty (see Figure 3.3). For 1990, Latinos had the highest labor force participation of any group. If we were to examine this same labor force participation longitudinally from 1940 to 1990, we would notice that Latino participation has consistently been the highest of any group.

If we look at where people are employed, there is again a trend: Latinos are more likely than any other group to be employed by the private sector. Latinos are also the least likely to be employed in the public sector. Thus, when we talk about poverty and labor force participation, it is true that working is a necessary, but I think not a sufficient, condition for nonpoverty. Clearly, Latinos work hard; just as clearly, they live in poverty.

Now, the issue of welfare dependency is a hotly debated issue. There are no good (at least to my knowledge) comprehensive data sets. We have some small snapshots that suggest that at least we need to reexamine facile correlations. In considering California data for 1990 on AFDC recipients by

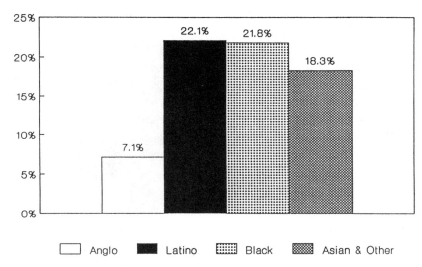

Figure 3.2. Percentage Below Poverty by Ethnicity: California (1989)
SOURCE: CPS (1990).

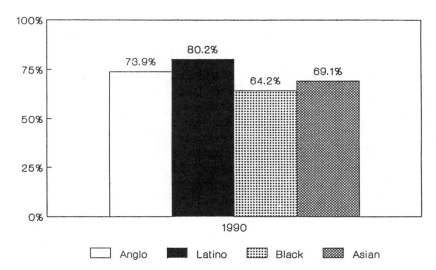

Figure 3.3. Labor Force Participation: Male, 16+, California (1990)
SOURCE: CPS (1991).

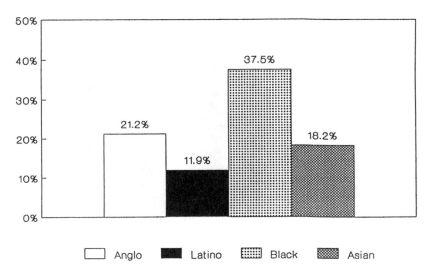

Figure 3.4. AFDC Enrollment as Percentage of Poverty Population: California (1990)
SOURCE: California Department of Social Services (1991).

ethnicity as a percentage of that population who lives in poverty, we notice that Latinos have the lowest participation rate (see Figure 3.4). Many Latinos live in poverty, so this low rate does translate to some sizeable absolute numbers, but the relative participation is perhaps not what we think it is.

Another way of looking at this is to examine unearned income received. For persons ages 20 to 24, Latinos actually received the fewest unearned dollars in 1985 per capita (Hayes-Bautista, Schink, & Chapa, 1986). Again, this is not definitive or conclusive, but I think it is suggestive that we need to reevaluate this issue.

Now, let us consider an important type of household: couples with children, the classic anti-Murphy Brown household. In California during 1990, Latinos were more likely than any other group to have a household headed by a couple—the American ideal: mom and dad, brother and sister, dog Spot, cat Puff, the picket fence, the lawn, and everything else (see Figure 3.5).

In fact, if we were to look at this longitudinally from 1940 to 1990, we would see some interesting trends. To begin with, the rate of household formation of couples with children for all groups went up during the postwar period and has been going down since. Now in this period, Latinos have consistently been most likely to have households composed of couples with children (California Employment Development Department [CEDD],

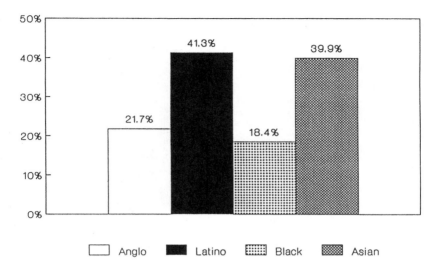

Figure 3.5. Couples With Children Households: California (1990)
SOURCE: U.S. Department of Commerce (1991, STF3).

1986).But before we start to think that here is the magic answer, note that this percentage has gone down for all groups. Latinos are not immune to the larger social pressures that grind away families.

A look at just the children themselves, that is, the type of family in which they live, shows that Latino children are just about as likely as Anglo and Asian children to be raised in couple-headed households (CEDD, 1986). These figures indicate that the household structure seems to be strong. In support of this conclusion, Latinos have one of the lowest rates of placement in foster care per 1,000 children (Figure 3.6). Again, this provides an indication that these families must be working in some fashion.

Yet a lot of these kids are poor, and we need to discuss these questions. For example, in Chapter 2, Besharov indicates that the best antipoverty for children is a stable, intact family. But the Latino population has some pretty stable, pretty intact families, yet they are poor. So, again, stable, intact families are wonderful; however, I think they are a necessary but not a sufficient condition for moving folks out of poverty.

Education is the Achilles' heel of Latino policy. Yet a survey comparing the high school graduation rates of first-generation Latino immigrants in California with the second and the second with the third generation (that is, the grandchildren of immigrants) showed a tremendous increase generation

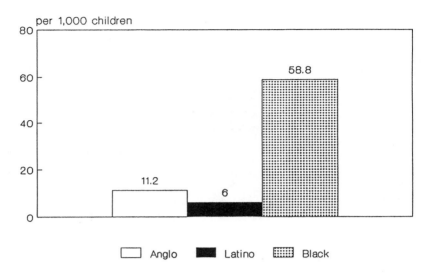

Figure 3.6. Placement in Foster Care per 1,000 Children: Los Angeles County (1992)
SOURCE: Los Angeles County Department of Children Services (1992).

by generation in educational levels (Figure 3.7). Now, there is still a gap with Anglos in this sample, but I think it is clear that Latinos do get educated.

Now, let us turn to some health data that I think are rather interesting. Take, for example, the figures on life expectancy at birth in Los Angeles County. An Anglo baby at birth can expect to live 75.1 years. A Latino baby can expect to live 79.4 years, about 4.3 years longer than an Anglo baby (Los Angeles County Department of Health Services [LACDHS], 1991). This is a startling contrast with Hobbesian images of poor people's lives: poor, nasty, brutish, and short.

Vital statistics data, or actuarial data, also show a different picture. Let us consider the overall age-adjusted death rate for the Anglo, Latino, black, and Asian populations. The Latino rate is about 30% lower than for Anglos, about half that of blacks, and is exceeded only slightly by Asians (LACDHS, 1991).

One of the classic indicators of poverty is the percentage of babies born at low birth weight. Latinos actually have a slightly lower rate of low birth weight babies than Anglos. In fact, Latinos have the lowest rate of any group in Los Angeles County (LACDHS, 1991). This is consistent with state and national level data.

The indicator we all tend to worry about most is infant mortality. In Los Angeles County in 1990, Latinos had substantially lower infant mortality than Anglos and blacks (LACDHS, 1991; see Figure 3.8). This may be unique to

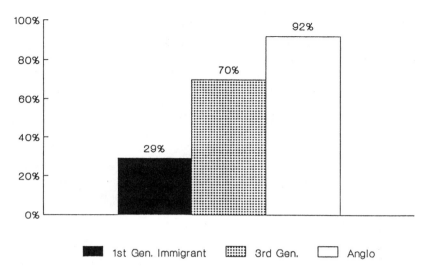

Figure 3.7. C.I.P. Sample High School Graduation by Generation: California (1990)
SOURCE: UCLA CSRS.

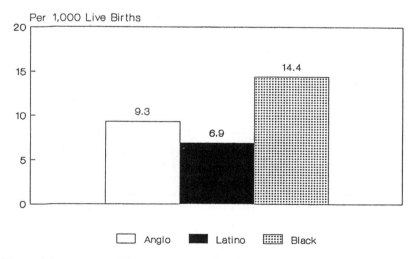

Figure 3.8. Infant Death Rate by Ethnicity: Los Angeles County (1990)
SOURCE: Los Angeles County Department of Health Services (1991, p. 34).

Los Angeles County, however. In California as a whole, Latino infant mortality is only about 10% lower than that of Anglos, as opposed to being 25% lower than Anglo infant mortality in Los Angeles County (California Department of Health Services, 1991).

Those birth outcome data are unexpected and are called an "epidemiological paradox." Here is a population that lives in poverty, has low levels of education (among first-generation immigrants), suffers from terrible access to care, yet has spectacular birth outcomes. The question is, how do we explain this? The answer is, we can't. We call it a paradox and don't understand it, but the profiles are both consistent and stable.

For age-adjusted drug-related deaths for California, Latinos have a slightly lower rate of drug-related deaths than Anglos. In Los Angeles County, Latino drug babies are born at half the rate of Anglo drug babies. Clearly, there is drug use for all three groups. Anglo, Latino, and black drug use all could come down quite a bit. But the issue is not the out-of-control issue for Latinos that tends to be depicted on television.

Additional individual behaviors show similar patterns. For example, a recent statewide survey indicated that Latinas are less likely than non-Latinas (this includes Anglos, blacks, and Asians) to be current smokers and that when Latinas do smoke, they smoke the least. In addition, regarding statewide drinking patterns, Latinas are more likely to be abstainers than non-Latinas and much less likely to be frequent drinkers than non-Latinas.

For age-adjusted weapon-related deaths, from 1985 to 1989, the Latino and Anglo rates were virtually interchangeable until 1988. Then in 1988, the Latino rate started to rise (California Department of Health Services, 1991; see Figure 3.9). This may be a 1-year variation or the beginning of a trend; but this rate has been stable and probably surprisingly, given the popular image of Latinos of drugs, gangs, and crime. Yet when we look at the outcomes—the drug babies and the death rates—a different type of profile begins to emerge, somewhat at odds with the public perception.

I hasten to add that we need much more data. Now, just so I don't paint a wonderful glowing picture with no problems, I point out that we do need to look at some problems, such as the situation of Latino health. Although the Latino population is a low-mortality population, it is an extremely high-morbidity one. For example, data from Orange County show that the morbidity rate for Latinos for cysticercosis, malaria, and shigellosis are extremely elevated. These are public health diseases that one can contract regardless of how good one's individual behavior is, because these are environmentally induced diseases that unfortunately require public intervention. And I think that is where the key is.

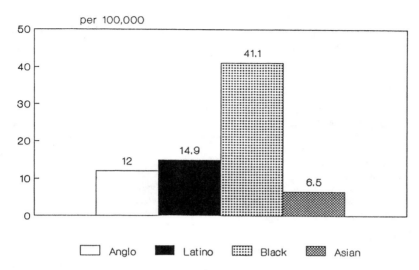

Figure 3.9. Weapon-Related Deaths, Age-Adjusted: California (1989)
SOURCE: California Department of Health Services, (1991, p. 28).

The urban underclass model has tended to be used quite a bit to create policy for the urban poor. I am not so sure that it is the most helpful model in California. As we have seen, Latinos tend to present a somewhat different profile. In comparing Latino behavior with the urban underclass model, I believe that the urban underclass model is too narrow to be usefully applied in California and probably anywhere in the West. Nor am I sure how useful it is for other populations outside the West. The underclass model tends to focus on individual behavior and tends not to look at the larger structural issues that clearly, at least for Latino populations, are equally as important. There is a tendency to demonize people who are poor as sexually loose—and all the rest of that litany. This blaming allows us to just step away and feel that somehow those who are poor are not quite like us.

As we look at the Latino data, I'm not so sure we want to demonize. That approach unfortunately tends to polarize the policy debate: When we argue whether a population is morally good or morally bad, we tend to get away from the issue of what is happening in poverty and the economy. I fear that the continued use of this model, particularly in Los Angeles, in the postriot era, risks the loss of economic opportunity that can be obtained. The growth of minority-owned businesses in Los Angeles County has been extremely high during the past 20 years. This presents a real opportunity. If we focus on dysfunction, we might lose sight of the opportunity. I hope this chapter provides a more comprehensive picture and raises a few issues that should form part of this debate.

References

California Department of Health Services, Health Data and Statistics Branch. (1991). *The year 2000 national health objectives: California's experience.* Sacramento: Author.

California Employment Development Department. (1986). *Socio-economic indicators, California: 1940-1990.* Sacramento: Health and Welfare Agency.

Hayes-Bautista, D. E., Schink, W. O., & Chapa, J. (1986). *The burden of support: Young Latinos in an aging society.* Stanford, CA: Stanford University Press.

Los Angeles County, Department of Health Services, Data Collection and Analysis. (1991). *Los Angeles County vital statistics: 1987.* Los Angeles: Author.

U.S. Department of Commerce, Bureau of the Census. (1991). *1990 census of population.* Washington, DC: Government Printing Office.

PART II

Approaches to Reducing Poverty

Can We Replace Welfare With Work?

Christopher Jencks

Sooner or later, every discussion of poverty in America comes back to the topic of welfare. This is not, I think, because welfare actually plays a major role in creating or perpetuating poverty in this country. Discussions of poverty tend to focus on welfare because at a superficial level anyway, it is a subject on which we all agree. We all hate it. Liberals hate welfare because the system treats applicants like criminals and does not give them enough money to support their children. Conservatives hate it because the system costs the taxpayers money, discourages work, and encourages what they see as dependency.

Grassroots hostility to the present welfare system has led state legislators, Congress, and the president to propose major changes in the system. Many states have trimmed benefits for parents receiving Aid to Families With Dependent Children (AFDC), for childless adults receiving General Assistance (GA), or both. But by far the biggest proposed changes are to put time limits on welfare and the Republican proposal to eliminate any legal "entitlement" to benefits.

A 2-year limit would be the most radical change in AFDC since Congress established the program in the 1930s. More than half the people currently

AUTHOR'S NOTE: A much earlier version of this chapter appeared with the title "Can We Put a Time Limit on Welfare?" in *The American Prospect,* 1992, Fall, No. 11, pp. 32-40.

69

receiving AFDC have been on the rolls more than 2 years. As a crude first approximation, therefore, we can assume that a 2-year limit would cut the number of recipients by at least half. If we exempted the disabled from the time limit, however, the reduction would be somewhat smaller. If we exempted those with infants, it would be smaller yet. Still, a 2-year limit would be a big change.

Is Dependency the Problem?

A time limit on AFDC appeals to many conservatives because they think it would solve the problem of long-term dependency. This claim is hard to assess empirically because it is difficult to be sure what *dependency* really means. Almost all of us depend on other people for money. Some of us depend on our employers, some of us depend on our parents, some of us depend on our spouses, and some of us depend on our government. In some sense, therefore, we are all dependent. I know no evidence that depending on the government has significantly worse psychological effects than depending on your parents, your spouse, or even your employer. If you interview female welfare recipients, one of the things they often mention as a good feature of welfare—and they don't mention many—is that it frees them from having to depend on men, whom they have found to be extremely unreliable. Older persons say the same thing about social security: It frees them from dependence on their children. What looks like the worst form of dependency to people with better choices is likely to look like the best form to those with fewer choices.

I think what we really mean when we talk about welfare making people dependent is that it makes them childlike. The government does something for them, but they do nothing in return. That makes it hard for us to treat welfare recipients with respect, which in turn makes it hard for them to retain their self-respect. Nonetheless, we have little evidence that collecting welfare is worse for the recipients than the other options now open to them. People who have spent a long time on welfare have more psychological problems than people who have never been on welfare, but that is mainly because people with psychological problems have trouble getting off welfare.

I am not sure that people really want to know whether welfare harms recipients, but if they do, they need to make comparisons that are not contaminated by selection bias. We know, for example, that single mothers are somewhat more likely to collect welfare in high-benefit states than in low-benefit states. Thus, if welfare actually harms recipients, single mothers as a group should exhibit less self-confidence, less self-respect, and worse mental health in high-benefit states than in low-benefit states. Children of single parents should also have more problems if they live in high-benefit states. Such a pattern would strongly support the conservative view that cutting benefits is good for single mothers and their children. But nobody has shown this yet.

Many conservatives and some liberals also think that welfare is addictive. The idea is that people get hooked on welfare just the way they get hooked on drugs. Once they have become habituated to getting a check from the government, they are less willing to take a job, even if a good one comes along. I know no solid evidence for this, either. If welfare were addictive, we would expect a large fraction of those who get benefits to stay on the rolls as long as they legally can. That is not the case. Most people who go on welfare get off in less than 2 years. Of course, some return again. That could be evidence of addiction, but it could also mean they lost their job, had another baby, or broke up with the man on whose income they had been depending.

Some people do stay on welfare for a long time, however, and because they are on for a long time, they account for a large fraction of the total welfare caseload at any given moment. Are these long-term recipients truly addicted to welfare, or are they just people with especially severe physical, mental, or emotional problems, who have unusual difficulty finding an employer or a lover to support them? If they were really addicted, we would expect them to remain on the rolls as long as they were legally eligible. They would, in other words, usually stay on the rolls until their youngest child left home or reached the age of 18. In reality, 89% of all welfare recipients leave the rolls before they become legally ineligible (D. Ellwood, personal communication).

The reason most single mothers leave welfare before their children reach 18 is no secret. Older children require less supervision, so their parents can work without having to pay for child care. In addition, older mothers can earn significantly more than young mothers, even if they have no work experience.

The reason it takes welfare recipients a long time to get off the rolls is also pretty obvious, at least if you ask them. A single mother has to find a relatively good job to end up better off than she would be on welfare. In Pennsylvania, a fairly typical state, a welfare mother with two children got about $7,500 in cash and food stamps plus a Medicaid card in 1994 (U.S. House of Representatives, 1994, p. 335). That was not enough to live on. But if she could get some extra money from her family, from her boyfriend, or from working in the informal economy, she could usually keep her family together and a roof over her head.

Now suppose she worked 35 hours a week, was unemployed 10% of the time, and earned $5 an hour. After subtracting social security, she would end up with about $7,600 in an average year, which is just what she had before.

If she applied for the Earned Income Tax Credit (EITC) and food stamps, she could get another $3,900. But that would not necessarily mean she is better off than she was on welfare, because she must now pay for child care, medical care, getting to work, and whatever clothes she needs for her job. If she had significant medical expenses, she usually could not afford to work. Even if she had no major medical expenses, she would come out ahead only if she could find cheap, reliable child care—which usually means child care from a relative. Otherwise, she would be better off collecting welfare and working occasionally at off-the-books jobs. In most cases, that would be true even if she could earn $6 or $7 an hour in her regular job.

What Does It Cost to Raise Children?

Although I have not been able to find any evidence that collecting welfare is worse for the recipients than the other options now open to them, this idea is now so widely accepted that we have to treat it as a political fact, regardless of whether it is true. In politics, therefore, the question is no longer *whether* we should try to cut the welfare rolls, but *how* we should try to do so.

Conservatives have traditionally used two tactics for cutting the welfare rolls. First, they have tried to keep benefits as low as possible to encourage more single mothers to accept low-wage jobs. Second, they have tried to make collecting welfare as onerous and humiliating as possible, on the reasonable assumption that if you make welfare unpleasant, more recipients will decide to take jobs. Clinton's alternative was to stop cutting benefits and humiliating recipients and instead put a time limit on the program. On its face, this seems like a more humane approach. But what happens at the end of 2 years?

Contrary to what many liberals claim, the big obstacle to making single mothers economically self-sufficient is seldom a shortage of jobs. During recessions, of course, jobs are hard to find. But during economic recoveries, minimum-wage jobs become easier to find, although that was less true from 1992 to 1995 than in earlier upturns. The problem is that a minimum-wage job will not make a single mother economically self-sufficient.

There is endless controversy about how much money single mothers need to make ends meet. Some conservative legislators and absent fathers seem to imagine that single mothers can live on air. Liberals have been somewhat more realistic, but not much. In large part, this is because we all take official income statistics too literally.

In 1992, for example, the official poverty line for a family of three was just over $11,000. When the Census Bureau interviewed the heads of three-person families, one out of every nine reported an income below $11,000 (U.S.

Department of Commerce, 1993, Table 20). Most observers, both liberal and conservative, conclude from this that families can survive on a subpoverty budget. I believe that conclusion is wrong.

Start with a simple fact. The Census Bureau also conducts a Consumer Expenditure Survey, which asks families how much they spend on different items. About a sixth of all households reported incomes below $10,000 for 1990. These low-income households reported incomes averaging only $5,900. Yet these same households reported *expenditures* averaging $12,600. Those who reported incomes below $5,000 reported that they spent as much as those who reported incomes between $5,000 and $10,000 (U.S. Bureau of Labor Statistics, 1992).[1]

Where did these low-income households get the money to buy $12,600 worth of goods and services? The short answer is that we do not know. Some of these households drew down their savings, but most had no savings on which to draw. Some were borrowing against future income. Some undoubtedly had unreported income, although eliminating those who failed to answer all the income questions does not do much to bring their income and expenditures into line. A few probably overreported their expenditures. Some were single adults whose budget deficit was made up by a live-in boyfriend or girlfriend whose presence they did not report.

Even expenditure surveys often underestimate the real cost of survival. Many poor families with low cash expenditures survive only because they also get a lot of goods and services for which they do not have to pay cash. Some get food stamps, housing subsidies, or medical care from the government. Some get free housing because they work as janitors, caretakers, or tenant farmers or because they live with relatives. Some ride to work with a friend or get free child care from a relative. No survey provides a full accounting of what poor families consume.

Kathryn Edin's interviews with Chicago welfare mothers confirm this judgment. She found that although the typical mother got less than $5,000 a year in cash from AFDC, the women all supplemented their checks in various ways. Some had unreported jobs. Some got money from their families or boyfriends. None of them lived on their checks alone. Even if we ignore the value of their free medical care and housing subsidies, almost all were consuming goods and services worth at least $8,000 a year, and the average was around $11,000 (Edin & Jencks, 1992). As Table 4.1 indicates, the picture was similar in Cambridge, Massachusetts, and Charleston, South Carolina, in 1991-1992.

Let there be no misunderstanding. Edin found no one who was living high on the hog. Most were desperately poor. Some had to skip meals or settle for rice and beans near the end of the month. Others had no heat in the winter or

TABLE 4.1 Monthly Income and Expenditures of Welfare Mothers in Chicago, Charleston, and Cambridge

	Chicago (1988-1990)	Charleston (1991-1992)	Cambridge (1991-1992)
Cash expenditures (including food stamps)			
10th percentile	626	539	642
90th percentile	1,247	1,360	1,298
Mean	915	875	940
Mean income by source			
AFDC	336	195	493
Food stamps (face value)	208	223	138
SSI and foster care	31	75	62
Unreported work	144	68	76
Friends, relatives, and absent fathers	162	299	126
Illegal activities	43	4	30
Other sources[a]	42	15	34
Total	966	881	960
Sample size	61	46	45
Percent in subsidized housing	48%	42%	71%

SOURCE: K. Edin, unpublished data (1988-1992).
a. Student loans and grants, private charity, and other public assistance sources.

no telephone. Even the most prosperous recipients lived on tighter budgets than most people have ever lived on, even as graduate students. Nor is it hard to see why. Most were, in fact, supporting their entire families on less monthly income than graduate students get to support themselves alone.

If these mothers had been working regularly, their expenses would have been even higher, because they would have needed more and better clothes, more transportation, and more child care. A reasonable guess is that the average mother would have needed $15,000 worth of goods and services each year to maintain her family's current level of consumption if she had been working. At today's prices, the figure would be even higher.

When Edin went looking for single mothers who supported themselves entirely by working, she found few who consumed less than $15,000 worth of goods and services. That does not mean, of course, that they were all earning $15,000 from their jobs. Many were combining their regular earnings with money from their families, boyfriends, or second jobs. Others got food, housing, or transportation they did not pay for, just as welfare mothers did. But few were consuming less than $15,000 worth of goods and services per year, and hardly anyone who worked was consuming less than $11,000 worth of goods and services. These figures were even higher in Cambridge and Charleston.

TABLE 4.2 Mean Earnings of Women Aged 18 to 34 Who Worked Full-Time
Throughout 1990, by Age and Education

	Age	
Years of School	18 to 24	25 to 34
No high school	—	$11,832
Some high school	$11,033	$13,825
High school graduate	$13,385	$17,026
Some college	$14,487	$20,872

SOURCE: U.S. Department of Commerce (1991, Tables 29 and 30).
NOTE: The sample size in the empty cell is too small to yield reliable estimates.

How Can Single Mothers Find Enough Money?

To earn $15,000 a year, a woman who works 40 hours a week must earn
almost $7.50 an hour. The minimum wage is currently $4.25 an hour, and
although many liberals want to raise it, there is no serious support for pushing
it above $5 an hour. By working regularly at $5 an hour, a person can earn
just over $10,000 a year before taxes and deductions. Furthermore, most
$5-an-hour jobs involve a lot of layoffs and short weeks, so even if an
unskilled single mother is trying to work regularly, she cannot count on doing
so. We therefore have to assume that many single mothers will earn only
$8,000 or $9,000 in a good year, and even less during recessions.

Census data confirm that few welfare mothers are likely to earn $15,000 a
year. Most welfare mothers are under the age of 35, and only a few have
attended college. Table 4.2 shows what women with these characteristics
typically earned if they worked full-time throughout 1990. High school
graduates over the age of 25 averaged $17,000 a year, but nearly half earned
less than $15,000. High school dropouts did far worse, as did younger women.
Although these figures cover 1990, real wages for women without college
degrees have not risen since then. Indeed, most evidence suggests that they
have fallen.

The averages in Table 4.2 cover only women who worked full-time throughout
the year. That means they overestimate welfare mothers' potential earnings,
because those who worked regularly were the women whom some employer
valued enough to employ steadily. Few women who currently collect welfare
will fall into this class.

If AFDC recipients all spent 2 years getting additional education and
training, their potential earnings would rise, but here again we need to be
realistic. Table 4.2 shows that high school graduates earned 20% to 25% more
than high school dropouts in 1990 and that women with some college eventually

earned 20% to 25% more than high school graduates. But it does not follow that 2 years of training could boost AFDC recipients' potential earnings by 20% to 25%.

High school graduates come from more advantaged families than dropouts; they are better at reading, math, and other subjects when they enter high school; and they are less likely to have been in trouble with the school authorities or the police. The same logic applies when comparing students who attended college for a couple of years with those who merely finished high school. Although there is no consensus about how much of the apparent effect of schooling reflects this selection process, most estimates suggest that adjusting for biases of this type cuts the apparent returns to schooling by at least a quarter.

We must also remember that single mothers are seldom in a position to give as much time to their studies as the average high school or college student gives, so additional schooling is likely to do them less good. Realistically, therefore, we should probably not expect 2 years of either formal schooling or job training to raise welfare recipients' earning power by more than 10% or 15%. My reading of the literature on job training also supports this conclusion.

I am not saying no one can devise a program that will raise welfare mothers' potential earnings enough to make them economically self-sufficient. I am saying that neither our experience with public education nor our experience with job training programs for welfare mothers suggests that we currently know how to do this on a large scale. We should keep trying. We can do better. But when we think about changing the welfare system, we should recognize that programs with effects this large will be the exception, not the rule.

If time limits are to be implemented, therefore, we need to find a way of closing the gap between what single mothers can earn and what they need to support their families. Otherwise we are likely to end up with hundreds of thousands of homeless families instead of the tens of thousands we have now. Even worse, we will force more mothers to abandon their children, re-creating the very problem we invented AFDC to solve in the 1930s. To avoid all this, we will have to provide single mothers who work in minimum-wage jobs with both free medical care and something like $5,000 worth of other resources every year to supplement their wages. In years when the labor market is slack, the figure will have to be even higher.

Conservatives want absent fathers to come up with this money. That is certainly a good ideal. Even if the cost of pursuing absent fathers exceeds the amount collected, harassing them will make men in general more cautious about fathering children they cannot support. Until the 1960s, a lot of young men used condoms because they knew an unplanned pregnancy meant a

TABLE 4.3 Employment Status and Earnings of Men Aged 18 to 34 in 1990, by Education and Race

Age and Race	No High School	Some High School	High School Graduate
Percentage of 25- to 34-year-old men with no earnings in 1990			
White	16.0	6.8	3.9
Hispanic[a]	8.9	9.3	6.3
Black	52.1	24.0	9.4
Mean earnings of 25- to 34-year-old men who worked			
White	12,837	16,108	22,312
Hispanic[a]	12,344	14,808	17,861
Black	—	10,935	15,888
Percentage of 25- to 34-year-old men who worked full-time, year-round			
White	49.5	54.5	72.1
Hispanic[a]	55.9	58.5	66.0
Black	—	40.9	61.8
Mean earnings of 18- to 24-year-old men			
All men with earnings	$8,800	$6,879	$11,186
Full-time, year-round workers	12,710	14,613	15,829

SOURCE: U.S. Department of Commerce (1991).
NOTES: The data do not cover men living in prisons or other institutions, members of the armed forces, men who are homeless, or men living in conventional households whose presence was not reported by the household head. The sample sizes in the empty cells are too small to yield reliable estimates.
a. Hispanics can be of any race, but most call themselves white.

shotgun marriage. Now that parents no longer pressure expectant couples to marry, we need some other way of encouraging men to use birth control. If they know that having a child out of wedlock will either cost them a lot of money or lead to a lot of grief when they cannot pay, condom sales should edge upward. But the absent fathers of today's welfare children do not have anything like enough money to fill the gap between what single mothers can earn and what they need to support their children. If a mother of two is earning $9,000 a year, an absent father will typically have to come up with another $6,000 to balance her budget. Child support orders seldom require absent fathers to pay out more than 30% of their income. That means an absent father has to earn at least $20,000 a year before his payments reach $6,000. Although the average American man who worked in 1990 earned $27,000, the fathers of children who get AFDC earned far less.

Men with children on AFDC are mostly young and poorly educated. In addition, nearly half are black, which has a far larger negative effect on men's earnings than on women's earnings. As Table 4.3 indicates, a large minority of such men did not work at all during 1990, and the proportion who did not work would be even higher if we included men who were in jail, in mental hospitals, homeless, or not enumerated by the Current Population Survey because they were living with someone who did not report their presence.

Table 4.3 also shows the mean earnings of the groups most likely to have fathered children currently on welfare. Only white high school graduates over the age of 25 averaged more than $20,000 in 1990, and even in this group almost half earned less than $20,000. Men who had not finished high school, had not reached their late 20s, or were not white all averaged less than $20,000, so their child support payments would have averaged less than $6,000. Indeed, because most child support orders require men to pay less than 30% of their income, and because even a revamped enforcement system will never be completely effective, the fraction of all fathers who would actually contribute as much as $6,000 a year will be quite small.

When single mothers with low-wage jobs do not have enough money to pay their bills, some can move in with their parents, siblings, or friends. Unfortunately, sharing space tends to create a lot of conflict among the adults involved. As a result, only a minority seem able to sustain such relationships over the long run. Many single mothers with budget deficits therefore end up sharing their bed—and their bills—with a boyfriend. These boyfriends may not contribute much, but they usually contribute something.

Casual boyfriends help single mothers survive with less public support than they would otherwise need, but it does not follow that public policy should encourage women to depend on them. Such a policy often pushes women into abusive relationships. It also leads to more pregnancies, more abortions, and more unwanted children. Indeed, such arrangements can be so unsatisfactory that some single mothers prefer prostitution, which can be less emotionally demanding and usually brings in more money.

Public Support for Single Mothers

To free single mothers from having to depend on ne'er-do-well men, I fear we will have to turn to the solution conservatives hate the most, namely using tax dollars to make up part of the difference between what unskilled single mothers can earn and what they need to support their families.

The simplest way to do this is through the EITC, which gives employed parents with children a refundable credit when their earnings are unusually low. At the moment, the EITC is quite attractive to legislators, because it helps only those who work. In addition, it mostly lowers tax revenues rather than increasing expenditures, which looks good in the newspapers. But even if Congress does not scale back the EITC, it will never be enough to allow all women with minimum-wage jobs to support their children. We also need to provide all working families with medical insurance, subsidize child care for working parents with preschool children, and rethink our approach to housing subsidies.

When we think about housing, we need to recognize that there are times when parents' interests differ from their children's interests. This is especially true when parents decide where to live. Historically, federal housing subsidies went mainly to build large, publicly owned projects reserved entirely for those who were poor. Rents in these projects were limited to 25% or 30% of the tenant's reported income, which was often very low. This policy was, in effect, a way of bribing poor parents to live near other poor parents. That was good for more affluent families, but it has had terrible effects on many children of poor families, who grow up in communities in which crime is a way of life and hardly anyone does schoolwork.

In the 1970s, the government moved away from publicly owned projects and began subsidizing tenants in private housing, in which they usually have somewhat more affluent neighbors. But most of this housing is still located in relatively poor neighborhoods, and most blacks also end up in overwhelmingly black neighborhoods. A child-oriented housing policy should give low-income parents stronger incentives to move to better neighborhoods, in which their children would be safer and would attend better schools. Chicago's *Gautraux* program, initiated as a result of a court order designed to eliminate racial segregation in the city's housing programs, has been doing this for many years and has yielded impressive benefits for children. It is important to recognize, however, that a program of this type will work only if it actively encourages poor mothers to move to better areas. Otherwise, most mothers will stay where their friends are, regardless of the long-term consequences for their children.

If we did all these things, any single mother who worked regularly would be able to make ends meet, even if she held only a minimum-wage job. If she got child support, she might even be able to take her children to a movie now and then. But these programs do not help single mothers who cannot find steady work. What are we to do for them? The only feasible solution seems to be some type of subminimum-wage public employment program that would guarantee single mothers some earnings and thus allow them to qualify for other work-related benefits.

Setting up a program that allowed all working single mothers to make ends meet would not be cheap. A 2-year limit on AFDC would save perhaps $13 billion a year, but there were 7.7 million families headed by women with children under the age of 18 in 1990, and 4.3 million of them reported incomes below $15,000 (U.S. Department of Commerce, 1991). Raising all these families' incomes to $15,000 a year would cost about $33 billion, even if we did not give any benefits to anyone else. If we want all these families to get goods and services worth $15,000 while at the same time ensuring that everyone has a significant incentive to take a better job, we also have to give some benefits to people who earn more than $15,000. By the time we are done, such a program could easily raise government expenditures by $30 to $50 billion. If we extend benefits to children in two-parent households, the bill could be even higher, as it usually is in Europe.

Why should a program that asks more people to work end up demanding more money from taxpayers? We know that several million single mothers are currently getting by on low-wage jobs that pay less than $15,000 a year. Why can't we just insist that welfare mothers do the same thing? The answer is that single mothers with low-wage jobs currently survive by making arrangements that we cannot expect all mothers to make. One lives with her mother. Another has a boyfriend who beats her up but whom she does not throw out because he also helps pay the rent. A third sometimes works as a prostitute at the hotel where she cleans. A fourth leaves her children home alone after school because she cannot afford paid child care. We cannot create a system that assumes all working mothers will make such arrangements, although we know that some now do so. If we try, a lot more single mothers will be unable to make ends meet, and we will end up with more families in shelters and more abandoned children in foster care. Yet as soon as we construct a system that allows a woman with a minimum-wage job to pay her bills without depending on anyone else, a lot more women will choose to exercise this option. The woman who now lives with her mother will move out, and the woman whose boyfriend beats her up will kick him out. The prostitute will turn fewer tricks, and the woman who works until 5:00 p.m. will get paid child care. Single mothers' lives will be a lot better, but there will probably be more of them, and taxes will certainly have to be slightly higher.

My rough guess is that a program of the type I have sketched would raise the nation's tax burden 1%, from 34% to 35% of the gross domestic product. That is a lot in today's political climate. We must therefore ask whether America could make a more gradual transition from today's welfare system to a new system based on the expectation that women should work. Can we devise a strategy that involves spending a few billion dollars in the first year, slightly more the second year, and so forth?

Such a strategy is certainly feasible in theory. The problem is that we will need to keep the present welfare system intact until *after* we have created a viable alternative for mothers who take low-wage jobs. Until the 1994 elections, Congress had been moving in this direction, gradually expanding benefits for working poor people while doing little for welfare recipients. Now it is moving in the opposite direction. Yet if we could create a system that rewarded work, the politics of helping the poor would be transformed. Americans are quite willing to help people who are trying to help themselves. But we can keep moving in this direction only if both liberals and conservatives recognize the long-term benefits of a system that allows single mothers to combine wages with government benefits.

To achieve that end, liberals must join conservatives in trying to make sure that mothers who work end up better off than mothers who do not work. If liberals fail at that, as they have during the past half century, the public will continue to see welfare as a menace, and it will continue to punish legislators who appear intent on making it more generous.

Conservatives must do their share as well. First, they have to recognize that it costs far more to support a family than anyone currently admits. Second, they have to admit that there is no practical way of ensuring that all families have two parents. Third, they need to recognize that in a competitive labor market, a lot of women will earn very modest wages. That means we can never hope to eliminate all government support for single mothers unless we are willing to let a lot of children starve. Instead, we will have to move toward a system in which work and welfare go together, with government benefits made contingent on doing an appropriate amount of paid work.

Note

1. These statistics are for what the survey calls "consumer units," not households, but in 97% of all households, the two concepts are identical.

References

Edin, K. (1988-1992). [Income and expenditures of welfare mothers]. Unpublished data from interviews.

Edin, K., & Jencks, C. (1992). Reforming welfare. In C. Jencks (Ed.), *Rethinking social policy* (pp. 204-236). Cambridge, MA: Harvard University Press.

U.S. Bureau of Labor Statistics. (1992). *Consumer expenditure survey: Quarterly data from the interview survey* (Report 833). Washington, DC: U.S. Department of Labor.

U.S. Department of Commerce, Bureau of the Census. (1991). *Money income of households, families, and persons in the United States: 1990* (Current Population Reports, Series P-60, No. 174). Washington, DC: Government Printing Office.

U.S. Department of Commerce, Bureau of the Census. (1993). *Money income of households, families, and persons in the United States: 1992* (Current Population Reports, Series P-60, No. 184). Washington, DC: Government Printing Office.

U.S. House of Representatives, Committee on Ways and Means. (1994). *1994 green book: Overview of entitlement programs.* Washington, DC: Government Printing Office.

5

Reducing Poverty and Reducing the Underclass

Different Problems, Different Solutions

Charles Murray

The topic of this volume is how to reduce poverty. But let us begin by confronting a few realities. What really prompted the conference from which this volume grew is not that roughly 15% of Americans live below the poverty line but that a riot occurred in South-Central Los Angeles in the spring of 1992. This suggests to me the possibility that "poverty" may not really be what is on people's minds. In his presenatorial incarnation, when he was one of the most perceptive social scientists in the country, Daniel Patrick Moynihan (1968) wrote of the aftermath of the riots of the 1960s, when white confusion and white guilt created a "near-obsessive concern to locate the 'blame' for poverty, especially Negro poverty, on forces and institutions outside the community concerned" (p. 33). I am not saying whites have nothing to feel guilty about; I am saying, however, that policy made on the basis of white guilt has a long and consistent history of wrongheadedness.

A second reality is that the dominant white reaction to the 1992 Los Angeles riot is not a desire to reduce poverty but increasing worry about the black underclass. Sometimes this worry takes the form of fear and resentment. As evidence for that, note the behavior of both major party presidential candidates throughout the fall 1992 campaign. Both knew from their focus groups that to mention the rioters with sympathy and a promise of large programs for the inner city was a surefire recipe for losing the election. But fear and resentment are not the only motivators for the worry. Many Americans—a substantial majority, I suspect, although I lack the numbers to prove it—do not believe that poverty caused the riot in South-Central L.A. To them, the violence and the looting of the riot are an extension of the continuing breakdowns of family, community norms, and civility that have constituted the trajectory of the black inner city for almost three decades now. Let me say clearly at the outset that I broadly share this position. Any proposed new strategy for dealing with poverty must do one of two things. Either it must demonstrate why this widely held view is incorrect and that simply reducing poverty will also cause these other problems to diminish, or it must confront the question not only of how to reduce poverty but also of how to reduce the underclass.

My purpose in this chapter is twofold. My substantive objective is to disentangle these two quite different issues of reducing poverty and reducing the underclass. I also have a therapeutic purpose in mind, which I will try to serve by being blunt. The dialogue about social problems in this country is beset with hypocrisy, albeit hypocrisy that is often well intended, and it has to stop. It will do us all good to start saying more plainly what is on our minds.

Poverty: The Easy Problem

Poverty has in recent years been to policy analysis what damnation is to a Baptist preacher. For more than three decades now, ever since Harrington (1962) published *The Other America* and Mollie Orshansky (in the U.S. Department of Agriculture) invented the poverty line, progress or retrogression in American social policy has been measured against this benchmark. Few goals have been more highly valued than to "bring people above the poverty line." To be below the poverty line has, in the eyes of many people, been sufficient proof that a person requires government help.

There are three reasons for this preoccupation with poverty. One is that deficits in material resources are visible. We can see, paint, photograph, televise, and videotape sunken cheeks and tattered clothes. Furthermore, problems that really have little to do with poverty manifest themselves as poverty. Let me take as an example the run-down public housing block with broken windows, pools of urine in the stairwells, graffiti on the walls, and children playing untended in a compound littered with trash. The cause of these conditions is not necessarily poverty. In communities around the world that are incomparably poorer than South-Central L.A., one may find poor people living in tidy huts, with neatly tended compounds and children playing peacefully under the watchful eye of adults. The causes of the broken windows and the urine and the untended children are other deficits, no less serious than poverty—indeed, often *more* serious than poverty. But the manifestation of these deficits looks like poverty.

This points to the second reason why money has taken on such a central place in our thinking about social problems. These symptoms can be eradicated, at least temporarily, by money. We can hire glaziers to install new glass, cleaning crews to hose down the stairwells, and teachers to staff day care centers for the children. It is harder to figure out how to deal with the other deficits that may be the underlying causes, and so we tend to take the easy way out, pretend that the problem is poverty, and then look for ways to get rid of the poverty. Remember the old saying—if the only tool you have is a hammer, everything begins to look like a nail. Money is our hammer.

The third reason why poverty looms so large is semantic. The word *poverty* carries with it an implication of threats to survival. Without food, people starve to death. Without shelter, they perish of exposure. The state of being "in poverty" is loosely identified with a state of being at risk of life and health. The plight of the street people offers an apt illustration. The street people *are* in the streets and *do* appear to be in danger of starving—and they are also "in poverty." I, in my role as hard-hearted conservative, can come along and point out that the street people constitute a small fraction of the people labeled "homeless" and that homeless people constitute a small fraction of the people under the poverty line. I may analyze the data on why people live in the streets and demonstrate beyond empirical question that the reason why people live in the streets in a place like Calcutta (i.e., they have no way to make enough money to afford housing) applies to only a small fraction of the street people in the United States, large proportions of whom actively resist efforts to place them in residential shelters. I may then conclude, with evidence and logic on my side, that the problem of street people and the problem of poverty are separate, that the means for solving one are unrelated to the means for solving the other. But for most people, I will be unpersuasive. They will see the street people and try to think of ways of reducing poverty.

When we bring this complex set of feelings to the American context, we also have to deal with the official poverty line, which raises another set of problems. The poverty line had a half-baked rationale when it was first created in the early 1960s, and things have only gotten worse since. It is easy to subject both the original poverty line and its subsequent implementation to ridicule. Let me give just one brief example: The poverty line for a family of four is the same everywhere in the country. In 1991, the poverty threshold for a family of four was a few dollars less than $14,000 (U.S. Department of Commerce, 1992b, Table A-3)—and it makes no difference whatsoever to the definition of whether you are "living in poverty" if you are trying to raise that family of four in South-Central L.A. or in my Iowa hometown. From any detached perspective, this is cuckoo. Anyone who has lived in small-town America knows of people who technically live under the poverty line but are doing fine. In some cases, they are elderly people who long since paid off the mortgage on their home and are getting by on social security—but in a small town in Iowa, that is enough. In some cases, they are two-parent families in which the father and mother own their own home and a car, make $18,000 a year, but have four children, which puts them technically under the poverty line. Are these people low-income? Of course. Do they have to economize, get by with few luxuries? Yes. But are they living in poverty in any meaningful sense of the word? No. Or suppose we go to the South Bronx and find a family that makes $18,000 but has only three children. They are *not* living in poverty, according to the official definition, which is just as misleading.

Another large difficulty with the poverty figures is that they are based on income as it is reported to an interviewer dispatched by the Bureau of the Census as part of its monthly Current Population Survey. I suppose it is cynical of me to assume that income might not be accurately reported to a representative of the U.S. government, but there is evidence that—shocking, shocking—such is the case. This is probably true for all income groups, but it seems to be most unequivocally true for low-income groups. Let me refer you, for example, to the 1992 edition of the *Statistical Abstract of the United States* (U.S. Department of Commerce, 1992c, Table 692), which summarizes the results of the Consumer Expenditure Survey. Down at the bottom of this long table is a breakdown of income and expenditures by income quintile. In the bottom quintile of income, which includes all of the poverty population and all of the near-poverty population, the mean income was only $5,637—a low income indeed. But this same population of people reported total expenditures that averaged $12,908. This is not a population that has access to credit cards or to large credit lines in their bank accounts. Yet somehow they were spending more than twice what they supposedly took in. The precise effects of this underreporting are impossible to calculate from the data at hand, but this much seems to be a conservative conclusion: Poverty numbers based on reported income do not accurately reflect the monetary resources available to some significant portion of the people whom we are counting as poor.

Technically, then, I should be able to demonstrate beyond reasonable argument that when we talk about poverty in the United States, the numbers that the government supplies and the actual number of people living in destitution are far different. Probably (I have to be fuzzy on this point, because no one really knows), there are far fewer truly poor people than the government statistics suggest. But having done all that, what would I have accomplished, except to convince most of my readers that I am trying to avoid confronting the poverty problem by statistical flimflam? The distinguished historian Gertrude Himmelfarb (1984) put the issue memorably in her history of the concept of poverty:

> Whatever progress has been charted on the graph of "progress and poverty," it is poverty that still strikes the eye and strikes at the heart. It is as if the modern sensibility can only register failure, not success, as if modernity has bequeathed to us a social conscience that is unappeasable and inconsolable. (pp. 533-534)

I have gone on at such length about the concept of poverty because I think that the focus on poverty is a fundamental error in thinking about American social policy. Poverty is not what ails us. But I am also convinced that the country will never be able to think clearly about the real problems of constructing a happy, vital society until the poverty issue has been put aside. We must reach a state of affairs in which the dialogue begins from a common agreement that everyone in the country can, if he or she behaves with a modicum of sense, have enough material resources to live a decent existence.

A Way to End Involuntary Poverty

There is, in fact, a way to reach that state of affairs. It is not politically feasible. I do not present it with the slightest hope that I am introducing a solution, because the first criterion of any solution is that it be politically feasible. Nonetheless, the nation does have the resources to achieve an end to involuntary poverty. I have decided after long equivocation that I support it, and I will therefore put it forward. It is a specific form of the negative income tax (NIT).

The late Nobel laureate economist George Stigler first mentioned an NIT in an article published in 1946. The essence of the plan is simplicity itself: The government establishes a minimum income and, if your taxable income for the year falls below that sum, you get a check for the difference. The NIT got more attention in 1962, when another Nobel laureate, Milton Friedman, endorsed it in *Capitalism and Freedom*. Friedman did not propose the NIT with much enthusiasm, because he foresaw that it would have a number of undesirable consequences, but he thought it would be better than the system we had.

In the 1960s, the NIT was enthusiastically adopted by Great Society planners as a way to end poverty once and for all, and from this enthusiasm grew the largest controlled social science experiment in history, the Income Maintenance Experiment, in which thousands of families in several American cities were made eligible for the NIT for several years. A form of the NIT was embodied in Richard Nixon's Family Assistance Program. But the reform impulse of the late 1960s and early 1970s soon faded, and the results from the Income Maintenance Experiment indicated that the negative effects of the NIT on work effort and family breakup were substantial. The idea faded from view.

It is just as well that the NIT was not enacted then, for the government would probably have made a hash of it. Critics of the NIT, including myself, have always had this scenario in mind: We enact the NIT. Everyone in the country has a guaranteed income. But the month after the NIT goes into effect, it becomes apparent that many people are still homeless, have no money left for food, are still neglecting their children, and are otherwise experiencing the symptoms that in recent decades have been glibly associated with poverty. And that same month, the federal government would begin a new food stamp program, a new public housing program, a new day care program—rebuilding the federal crazy quilt of social programs on top of the NIT. We would be worse off.

There is, however, a way of preventing this from happening through a constitutional amendment that would fundamentally restructure the relationship of the federal government to individuals. I am not a constitutional expert, so the wording surely is faulty, but the sense of the amendment I propose for the Constitution is this:

> Congress shall establish a minimum cash income that shall be made available in equal amount and under equal terms to all citizens upon reaching the age of 18. With this exception, Congress shall make no law that uses federal funds directly or indirectly for grants of money, goods, or services to individuals.

In other words, the federal government would be taken entirely out of the business of taking money from one taxpayer to give to another taxpayer, *except* for the NIT. To give an idea of how fundamentally the amendment would alter the governmental landscape, Table 5.1 presents a partial listing of the programs that would disappear, along with the 1991 outlays in billions of dollars.

Other programs would also go—guaranteed student loans, for example, some other educational expenditures, the National Endowment for the Arts, and any of the other programs that give out money or services to individuals, or to organizations whose purpose is to provide services to individuals. Just the programs listed in Table 5.1 added up to $605.1 billion in 1991. The biggest item in the list is social security. I take it for granted (when I try to

TABLE 5.1 Major Transfer Payment Program

Program	1991 Outlays (in billions)
Social Security	$269.0
Medicare	$104.5
Medicaid and related health care services	$60.7
Means-tested income security (mostly AFDC and SSI)	$37.0
Veterans benefits and services	$31.3
Food and nutrition assistance (mostly food stamps)	$28.5
Unemployment insurance	$27.1
Housing assistance	$17.2
Farm income stabilization	$12.9
Social services	$11.5
Training and employment	$5.4

SOURCE: U.S. Department of Commerce, (1992c, Table 495).

imagine politicians taking this proposal seriously) that grandfather clauses would apply in a transitional period, with associated costs.

Because universal medical coverage seems to be an idea whose time has come, I will take as given that it must be part of the plan. But remember that $165.2 billion was spent on federal health programs in 1991 (U.S. Department of Commerce, 1992c, Table 495). Given a base of that magnitude, there are ways of arriving at universal medical coverage that do not cost a lot more than current expenditures. Rather than try to present a fully imagined plan that folds medical coverage into the NIT, which is far too ambitious for this chapter, let us assume that it will cost $200 billion, or about 20% more than we are currently spending. All the budget figures I use subsequently thus subtract that cost, leaving, in round numbers, a kitty of $400 billion to finance an NIT if one had existed in 1991. By the same token, keep in mind that the income floor for the NIT as I am about to present it does not have to be spent on medical care.

How high must the income floor be if we are to rid ourselves of poverty? In 1991, the poverty threshold for one unrelated individual was $6,932 (U.S. Department of Commerce, 1992b, Table A-3). We should consider the alternative of setting the floor even more generously, however, at half the median income. This has three attractions.

First, half the median income is clean and simple. It has that natural feel to it that Schelling (1960) has taught us is so necessary to reaching a compromise. By contrast, the official poverty line is, as I have discussed, a joke. Any other attempt to come up with a better poverty line will run into insuperable problems because poverty is, finally, an arbitrary concept. Second, half the median income has become a standard figure in social democratic circles both in the United States and Europe as representing an appropriate maximum for income inequality. The third attraction of setting the floor at half the median income is that the minimum income will go down when the median income goes down. The negative side effects of an NIT will be kept at an acceptable level by social pressures, not by laws. That is, it is appropriate that healthy working-age people who do not work despite the availability of jobs suffer social stigma as a result. One of the sources of such pressure is a broad social sensitivity to the idea that a guaranteed income is possible for unproductive people only because of the productive ones. If the median income of the working people of this country goes down, it might be psychologically useful—as well as ethically appropriate, in my view—that the monthly supplement checks go down too.

The main question is whether the economy can afford to pay the higher floor that half the median income represents. There are many ways to calculate median income. The most commonly used figure is per capita money income, which as of 1991 was $14,617 (U.S. Department of Commerce, 1992a, Table A). Using that definition, half the median income would thus be $7,308, about $400 more than the poverty line. I will use that figure, rounding it up to $7,500.

Could we afford a floor of $7,500? An examination of the income distribution for 1991 as published by the Bureau of the Census (U.S. Department of Commerce, 1992a, Table 25), using conservative assumptions, indicates that the amount required would be approximately $350 billion. It is a calculation built on estimates, however, involving not only people whose 1990 income was below $7,500 but also people whose 1990 income was above $7,500 but who would have fallen below it if federal transfer programs had not existed. The $350 billion estimate was intended to err on the high side, but it could conceivably be too low. A full-scale analysis would also have to worry about estimating the new costs produced by people who formerly worked but would stop working under an NIT. The budgetary issue is one of great complexity, to be examined by platoons of economists if the NIT were to be contemplated seriously. For now, the main point is this: Even given considerable uncertainty in the estimate of costs, a floor of $7,500 is not a pipe dream. It is extremely unlikely that the actual figure would come close to the more than $400 billion that the federal government spent in 1990 on the social programs that would be replaced by the NIT. If the poverty line were used as the floor, the cost would probably be well under $300 billion. Any of these scenarios leaves a great deal of money left for the transition costs without threatening to raise the net budget.

Under an NIT, the vast majority of working-age Americans would continue as before, paying withholding tax and getting refunds after submitting tax returns. People with no income at all would receive the mirror image of withholding: monthly checks consisting of $\frac{1}{12}$ of the floor. People with jobs paying less than the floor would have the reverse of withholding: monthly supplements to bring them up to the floor. People who got regular jobs paying more than the floor would stop getting supplements and begin paying withholding. People working off the books would continue to beat the system, as they do now.

No one should be under illusions about the consequences of implementing an NIT. We should expect it to have negative effects on the labor force supply, especially among young workers. Perhaps—the evidence from the income maintenance experiments is still under dispute—it would have negative effects on marital stability. And nothing in an NIT will prevent people from gambling away the rent money, having large numbers of babies that they cannot support adequately with the minimum income, or in other ways reducing themselves to penury.

Further, I should say clearly that the primary reasons I am in favor of such a system are not to reduce poverty. The great task for social policy in the 21st century, in my view, is to reconstitute the Jeffersonian state in a modern form—to revitalize Jeffersonian conceptions of freedom, of self-government, and of the pursuit of happiness. To me, the NIT is the trade-off that people such as me must be prepared to make to return the role of the federal government to something approaching its proper limits.

For purposes of this chapter, however, the NIT will highlight the reasons why such people are living in penury. Some may ask, "How can a person live on $7,500?" But that is not the right question. The right question is, "How can a person live on $7,500 in a society in which every other adult also has an income of at least that amount?" That answer is, "Easily." Just two people, whether husband and wife or a pair of roommates sharing expenses, will have a combined income of $15,000. Three individuals pooling their resources will have $22,500, and so on. I will return to some of the ways in which this situation might play out in socially desirable ways later in the chapter. For the time being, the great advantage of the NIT will be that when poverty still exists (as it will), we can put aside the distracting clutter of today's policy debates, stop expecting the federal government to take responsibility for fixing the remaining poverty, and focus on what needs to be done, and what should not be done, in dealing with the behaviors that produce poverty even when a minimum income exists. I am assuming that the residual problems of human suffering that remain will be large but that they will be returned to the only sphere in which we have a hope of handling those problems effectively: family, neighbors, and community.

Now back to reality. The program I have described is *not* politically feasible and will not be for the foreseeable future. The NIT still has a bad reputation from the Income Maintenance Experiment; the social security lobby will protect social security; the right will never support the NIT unless it is confident it will not become an add-on to other social programs; the left will never give up its right to create those social programs. But I have gone to some lengths to describe the program nonetheless, because it is economically feasible. The nation is rich enough to do two things simultaneously: give everyone in the country a clear opportunity to keep themselves above the poverty line and do so in a way that will fundamentally contract the federal government's intrusion into our personal and social life. It is a good idea—with downsides, I freely grant—but much better than the system we have now. I wish it could be made law.

The additional point is that poverty in the monetary sense is easy to reduce. All it requires is money. The U.S. government has lots of money. It squanders it, true, and we end up with a huge budget deficit. But it need not be so.

Reducing the Underclass: The Hard Problem

None of the foregoing has much to do with the underclass, because poverty is not the distinguishing feature of the underclass. Let us pause for a moment and consider what it is we are talking about when we use the term *underclass* and then think about how that population might be reduced.

The word *underclass* has come into common use only in the last decade, but the phenomenon it refers to is much older. Every society in history has had an underclass. The United States has always had one. We just didn't call it an underclass when I grew up. Like many people, I was raised to understand that there were two types of poor people. One class of poor people were never even called "poor." They didn't have much money, that's all. My own parents had been poor in this sense when they were growing up. But this class of poor people worked hard, raised their children, and were full-fledged members of the community. They did not have much money—but that did not really make them different from everyone else.

Then there was another set of poor people, just a few of them in my town. These poor people lacked more than money. They behaved differently from everyone else. Their homes were littered and unkempt. The men in the family were unable to hold a job for more than a few weeks at a time. The children were often neglected and badly behaved, creating trouble in school. Often the parents of the children were not married. Drunkenness and sexual promiscuity were common. So was crime, both minor and serious.

This type of behavior is what I mean by the term *underclass*—not just poverty, but a way of behaving. It is a distinction that has been made in many ways throughout the years—between the poor person and the pauper, between the deserving and the undeserving poor, between the people who can work and want to versus the people who can work but won't. Historically, the number of people who fit the description of what we now call the underclass was small, in the United States as elsewhere. There were many poor people—indeed, until recently in human history, almost everyone was poor—but even in our largest cities, only small pockets of people would fit the definition of an underclass. Then the underclass grew. You may refer to Besharov's Chapter 2 for a number of the quantitative measures of that growth and to Jencks's (1991) chapter in a recent collection of writings on the subject. Most of the growth seems to have occurred between the mid-1960s and the mid-1970s. Overall, the underclass is still not a large proportion of the population. Sawhill (1989) and her colleagues at the Urban Institute estimated that 1.1 million people lived in "underclass neighborhoods" as of 1980, and only a portion of those would qualify as "members" of the underclass. This underrepresents the problem insofar as many more people are affected by the underclass than are part of it, but it is well to keep the comparatively small raw numbers in mind. In a population of 250 million, each million is only $\frac{4}{10}$ of 1%.

I will focus on three types of people who constitute the core of the problem we refer to as underclass. My thesis is that we have no reason to believe that providing them with enough money to raise them above the poverty line will do much of anything about their behavior, nor will any policy strategy based on income transfers do much to counteract the dynamics we see at work in the inner city. The three types of people are the chronic criminal, the young man who is chronically out of the labor market, and the unmarried young woman who is chronically on welfare. The large reasons why I am so pessimistic about reducing their numbers or changing their behavior are, first, because the state of the art in social interventions has not yet figured out how to achieve such changes, no matter how much money we spend; and, second, because the three types of people are not scattered randomly through the country but are concentrated in communities in which they create a social milieu that feeds the very problem they represent. Consider the three types of people who make up the core of the underclass problem.

The chronic criminal. The criminal is one of the most thoroughly studied members of society. An accumulation of knowledge during more than a century of research has led to a number of findings that are no longer a subject of much scientific dispute among specialists, although they remain somewhat politically incorrect.[1]

A small proportion of criminals accounts for a large proportion of crime. The common finding is that approximately 5% to 7% of all people who are ever arrested account for about half of all arrests. This seems to hold true in countries with low crime rates, such as Scandinavia, and in countries with high ones, such as the United States. It seems to hold true in the same country through time—in the United States during the low-crime decade of the 1950s and during the high-crime decade of the 1970s.

These chronic criminals commit truly astonishing numbers of crimes, often numbering in the hundreds. They almost always begin in their teens and keep it up into their 20s, with the intensity of their activity then tapering off as they approach 30 and beyond.

Criminals tend to have low cognitive ability. Overall, the mean IQ of all criminals is about 10 points lower than that of the general population, which puts the average criminal at roughly the 25th percentile. The more chronic the criminal, the lower his or her IQ is likely to be. This statement holds true for whites and blacks alike (Wilson & Herrnstein, 1985, chap. 6).

Criminals tend to have other personality characteristics that make them difficult to mold into good citizens. Statistically, they tend to be aggressive, resistant to discipline, hyperactive, and impulsive. They tend to have shallow emotional attachments even to their families, attention deficits, and a lack of commitment to religious and social mores. Crime rates in general, and the behavior of the chronic criminal in particular, have little to do with the economy, either in macroeconomic terms (crime does not track with the national unemployment rate) or in microeconomic terms (personal histories of crime are not perceptibly related to economic deprivation). If we put together these pieces of knowledge about the criminal, bearing in mind that all of them are accentuated in chronic criminals, it is realistic to be pessimistic about the prospects for setting up a job program, a drug rehabilitation program, a literacy program, an NIT, or any other social intervention that will change their behavior.

Young men who are out of the labor force. The next classic member of the underclass is the young, healthy, low-income man who is out of the labor force—"not available for work," in the jargon. Unlike crime, this phenomenon is hard to measure. In years of high unemployment, it is virtually impossible to measure. How can one distinguish between young men who want to work but cannot find jobs versus young men who may say they want to work but really do not? Yet the phenomenon is nonetheless real, as we have found in the United States. It was exposed most clearly during the mid-1980s, when in the United States we had what the social scientists call "a natural experiment."

Until then, people who denied that an underclass existed had argued that virtually all poor young black men really *wanted* to work, but they could not get to the jobs because of lack of public transportation, or the jobs paid too little, or there simply were no jobs. During the mid-1980s, however, labor markets in many large American cities became tight, with low-skill jobs widely available at good pay at easily accessible locations. The effects of this tight labor market on the labor market behavior of young black men have been studied extensively, and the conclusions are clear. There was good news and bad news. The good news was that almost all young black men who wanted jobs got them. The *unemployment* rate of young black men in some inner cities went from nearly 40% to single digits (Freeman, 1991). The problem is that the unemployment rate is based on people who are looking for work. The bad news from the natural experiment was that this abundant availability of jobs had almost no effect on young black men who were *not* looking for work. In good years and bad, almost 30% of black men ages 16 to 24 with no more than a high school education are not employed and are not looking for work. And this figure is based just on men who are not in school, so they do not have school as a reason for being out. Few of them are physically disabled. And yet 3 out of 10 show no signs of wanting to participate in society in the simplest and most natural of all ways for a man to participate, by holding a job.[2]

Who are these men? One of the best windows on this question is provided by the National Longitudinal Survey of Youth, which picked more than 12,000 youths in the beginning of 1979 and has followed them ever since. As of the 1990 survey, they were ages 25 to 32. Among the men who had been out of the labor force for at least half of 1989, for reasons other than school or being unable to work, 61% had never been married (compared with only 33% of the other men), 53% of them had dropped out of high school, and 36% came from the bottom decile in cognitive ability.[3]

I should add that eventually most of these men will get in the labor market. By the time he reaches his 30s, a man finds that street life and its hustles are a younger man's game. It is no longer as easy to persuade a young woman to support him on her welfare check. Perhaps he has been to jail and decided that crime is not worth the risk. But although he then gets into the labor market, he has already missed his chance. He comes to the labor market with no skills and no work record, and he is consigned to the margins of the economy for the rest of his life. The damage has been done. And meanwhile, the next generation of young men, having grown up in a world in which their role models were the men who got by without having to hold a job, are repeating the mistakes of their older brothers and fathers.

But why is this happening? Historically, almost all young men have been socialized so that they do not commit crimes when they grow up. Historically, almost all young men have reached adolescence understanding that work is central to a man's life, and that not to work is in some important sense not to be a man. Why is it that in the late 20th century in the United States—and, for that matter, in many European countries—young men are growing up so different? The answer is surely complicated and involves changes in the economy, demographics, and the rest. But in addition to these explanations that social scientists have generally preferred to investigate, I propose that both the crime statistics and the labor dropout statistics tell us what happens when boys grow up in communities in which there are no fathers. This leads me to the third and most important indicator of a growing underclass: the proportion of babies who are born to unmarried women—what we in the United States call the "illegitimacy ratio."

Unmarried mothers on welfare. Notice that I am not talking about all forms of single parenthood. I am not talking about the children of divorced mothers, for example, nor the children of widows. I focus on illegitimacy rather than on the more general phenomenon of one-parent families because in a world in which all social trends are ambiguous, illegitimacy is less ambiguous than other forms of single parenthood. It is a matter of degree. Of course, some unmarried mothers are excellent mothers and some unmarried fathers are excellent fathers. Of course, some divorced parents disappear from the children's lives altogether, and some divorces have more destructive effects on the children than a failure to marry would have had. Being without two parents is generally worse for the child than having two parents, no matter how it happens. But illegitimacy is the purest form of being without two parents— legally, the child is without a father from day one; he or she is often without one practically as well.

Call it what you will, in the United States we have witnessed a catastrophe in poor communities. This emerges most obviously in the statistics on blacks, who are disproportionately poor. In 1960, fewer than 22% of black children were born to single women. This percentage was comparatively high even then and was the cause of much concern. But to think of it another way, more than 78% of all black children in 1960 were born to two parents, which meant in turn that the two-parent family, complete with father, was visible, common, and even the norm in black communities. By 1970, 38% of black births were to single women; by 1980, 55%. By the time of the most recent figures for 1992, 68%—two out of every three black children—were illegitimate. Meanwhile, the rate for whites had been growing even faster proportionately, but from a much smaller base of 2% in 1960 to 23% in 1992 (National Center for Health Statistics, 1994, Table 14).

The sharp rise is only half of the story. The other and equally important half is that illegitimate births are not scattered evenly among the population. In this, press reports can be misleading. There is much publicity in the United States about the movie star who deliberately decides to have a baby on her own, but this is a comparatively rare event. The increase in the proportion of illegitimate births is strikingly concentrated within poor communities. Thus, in the black inner city with its high concentrations of poverty, the illegitimacy ratio is even higher than the 68% I just mentioned. In New York, Milwaukee, and most other cities that have reported such data, the proportion of black children born to single women in the inner city is in excess of 80% (National Center for Health Statistics, 1994, Table 14).

Lest you think that this is an exclusively black phenomenon, let me point out that it applies to whites as well. Let us return to the National Longitudinal Study of Youth and talk exclusively of whites. Among white mothers who were not below the American poverty line in the year prior to birth, only 6% of children were illegitimate. Among white mothers who *were* poor in the year prior to birth, 46% of the births were illegitimate. For reasons that we must begin to understand and discuss more openly, illegitimacy in the United States and apparently elsewhere has been characterized by two disturbing facts: It has risen extremely rapidly, and this rise has been extremely concentrated among women in the lowest socioeconomic classes.[4]

As always when talking about these sensitive issues, let me be as clear as possible about what I am and am not saying. I am not upset about people who have sex before marriage. I am not bemoaning welfare cheats or welfare mothers who should be forced to work—in fact, there is a lot more working going on among welfare mothers than we commonly realize. Instead, I am arguing that it is a bad thing when large proportions of women within a given community have babies without being married, and my reasons for this conclusion are practical.

One of these reasons is that women who have babies out of wedlock tend to make worse mothers than women who have babies within wedlock. This is predictable. Although there are many individual exceptions, the acts of having a child out of wedlock and of going on welfare both have a self-selection component. Regarding statistical tendencies, the woman who has the foresight to use birth control and a sense of the solemnity of motherhood that leads her to want to avoid getting pregnant until she gets married is likely to be a more responsible and more intelligent person than the young woman who does not share either that foresight or sense of solemnity. The mother who wants to stay off welfare and is able to pull off that challenging feat is statistically likely to be a different type of person than the mother who goes on welfare—in pride, industriousness, ingenuity, and the maturity and seriousness with which she approaches the job of mothering her children. And these logical expectations are reflected in what actually happens to children.

To illustrate, let me take just one example, but one of the most thoroughly documented ones. The women in the National Longitudinal Study of Youth that I cited earlier, now in their late 20s and early 30s, have already had a large proportion of the children who will be born to that sample, and the study has had the opportunity to examine the home environments in which their children are growing up. These environments are characterized using an index developed by Bradley and Caldwell (1981; see also Bradley, Caldwell, & Rock, 1988; Caldwell & Bradley, 1984) called Home Observation for Measurement of the Environment (HOME) for the purpose of identifying and describing the homes of infants and young children who were at risk of developmental disabilities. It consists of several dozen items, varying according to the age of the child, tapping into such things as emotional responsivity, intellectual stimulation, style of restriction and punishment, maternal involvement, and the like. The index has been validated across ethnic groups and even cross-nationally.

The results put the importance of poverty versus family structure into perspective. Poverty indeed does have a role in determining home environments, but the effects of poverty are much different for married women and unmarried welfare mothers and mothers who have never been on welfare. Here, for example, is the mean percentile on the HOME index for children in homes where the family is below the poverty line:

47th percentile, for legitimate children born to parents with no history of welfare

40th percentile, for illegitimate children born to a mother with no history of welfare

30th percentile, for illegitimate children born to a mother who went on welfare after the child was born but did not become a chronic recipient

24th percentile, for illegitimate children born to a mother who is a chronic welfare recipient

Poverty was significant—add 12 percentiles onto each of the above scores to get the results for the same categories for families who were not in poverty—but it was far from the whole story.

These averages do not convey the true dimensions of the problem, however. Children are remarkably resilient and can survive a wide variety of environments more or less intact. But beyond a certain point, it is difficult for even the most resilient child to thrive. Let us then consider for a moment the children in the bottom 5% on the HOME scale—in other words, those in the most deprived environments. They are not necessarily deprived of money, because few items in the HOME scale are dependent on money—but deprived of stimulation, warmth, consistent discipline, and an organized environment within which the world can make sense and the child can learn to understand the world. If parenting were random, a child would have a 1 in 20 chance of being born into the bottom 5%. With that in mind, consider the implications that a child born to a married mother and father, with no history of welfare—nothing more extraordinary than that—risked only 1 chance in 42 of growing up in such an environment. If, on the other hand, the child were born to a single woman who became a chronic welfare recipient (meaning essentially that she remained on welfare at least 5 years), the child's odds of growing up in that bottom 5% were greater than 1 in 6. The odds that the child in a chronic welfare family would be in the bottom quartile of home environments was greater than 1 in 2.

These numbers about index scores, means, and percentiles are bloodless representations of a tragic reality. When the single parent is unmarried, immature, on welfare, with an absentee father who is in any event as poorly equipped to be a parent as the mother, the single-parent family tends to be a disastrous place to bring up children—not in subtle ways, but in ways that produce the most horrendous forms of emotional and social maldevelopment. I am speaking of bad parenting with consequences up to and including death.

Let me try hard to be understood correctly. I am not saying that *poor* women tend to be bad mothers. Poor women have been wonderful mothers throughout history—or, more precisely, the overwhelming majority of mothers throughout history have been poor. I am saying that young, emotionally immature, uneducated women without husbands tend to be bad mothers. Too many of their children are poorly nourished not because there is no money for food but because the mothers do not know how, or do not make the effort, to feed them nutritious diets. Too many of these children come to school or preschool not knowing how to talk in complete sentences, without the most basic vocabulary, without the most basic social skills—not because the mother had to be away from home working but because of the ways the mother has treated them, or failed to treat them, when she has been around. Too many reach school unable to function in a cause-and-effect world because they have been accustomed from birth to a chaotic world in which rules and expectations change unpredictably from moment to moment.

I could provide additional references and numbers if there were those who wanted them. The real problem is a matter not of data, however, but of courage. For years, all that has been necessary to get a sense of the dimensions of the problem of bad parenting among welfare mothers in the inner city is to talk with the police, social workers, and preschool and elementary school teachers who must deal with these problems from day to day. Social scientists and politicians have squirmed endlessly to avoid confronting reality, because of all the politically incorrect things to say, one of the most incorrect is this: The main problem is not poverty. The problem is not even remotely related to the Murphy Browns of the world. The main problem is that large numbers of unmarried young women who are unequipped to be parents are having babies anyway and being rotten parents. The problem is not scattered evenly throughout society but is concentrated among blacks in the inner city.

Another of the practical reasons for worrying about concentrations of illegitimate births is that communities need fathers. For many years, this is an argument that few intellectuals in the United States were willing to accept. One of the side effects of the feminist movement in the United States, despite its many positive accomplishments, was a period in the 1970s and 1980s when men were not highly regarded. "Why should it be a 'problem' that a woman has a child without a husband?" they used to ask. Why isn't a single woman perfectly capable of raising a healthy, happy child, if only the state will provide a decent level of support so that she may do so? Why is raising a child without marrying any different from raising a child after a divorce? Men are still not highly regarded in some intellectual circles, but the scholarship of the last several years has made it difficult to continue repeating these questions.

There is still much to be learned about what happens in communities in which there are almost no fathers playing their traditional roles. It is, after all, something genuinely new under the sun. Human societies have not operated this way hitherto. Let me give my reading on the basis of the fragments of information we do have, emphasizing that some of it is interpretive:

The clichés about role models are true. Children grow up making sense of the world around them in light of their own experience. Little boys do not naturally grow up to be responsible fathers and husbands. They do not naturally grow up knowing how to get up every morning at the same time and go to work. They do not naturally grow up thinking that work is not just a way to make money but a way to hold one's head high in the world. And most emphatically of all, little boys do not reach adolescence naturally wanting to refrain from sex, just as little girls do not become adolescents naturally wanting to refrain from having babies. On all of these dimensions and many more, boys and girls grow into responsible parents and neighbors and workers because they are imitating the adults around them.

That is why single parenthood is a problem for communities, and that is why illegitimacy is the most worrisome aspect of single parenthood. Children tend to behave as the adults around them behave. A male child with no father, living in a neighborhood with no fathers, judges by what he sees. You can send in social workers and schoolteachers and clergy to tell a young man that when he grows up he should be a good father to his children, but he does not know what that means unless he has seen it.

In communities without fathers, the children tend to run wild. The fewer the fathers, the greater the tendency. "Run wild" can mean such simple things as young children having no set bedtime. It can mean their being left alone in the house at night while the mother goes out with her boyfriend. It can mean an 18-month-old toddler allowed to play in the street. And it also seems to mean a generation of children who tend to be unusually aggressive and violent. This again is especially true of boys who, without fathers, reach the turmoil of adolescence, when boys are naturally barbarians anyway. Boys have to be taught to be civilized, and we are learning that a father's discipline is often crucially important in that process.

The key to understanding what all this means for the underclass is not the individual case but the community. If a boy grows up in a home without a father, but he grows up around friends who have fathers, much of what they learn is visible to the boy without a father as well. In a situation in which large proportions of an entire community lack fathers, the problems multiply. Thirty years ago, there was hardly a poor neighborhood in urban America in which children did not still see plentiful examples of good fathers around them. Twenty years ago, the balance had already shifted in many poor neighborhoods. For the last 10 years, there are no good exceptions. The father has become scarce in every low-income community in the country, and we are paying a terrible price.

There has been some progress in coming to grips with the problem. Ten years ago, I could not have written the preceding paragraphs without being called a racist. Today, at least some people can read them without drawing that conclusion. Perhaps the greatest sign of progress is that one no longer hears so much cant about the extended black family. As most of you know, it was popular for many years to argue that the black family in the United States had a different tradition from the white family. The extended family—meaning grandparents and aunts and uncles—had a much larger role in black culture, it was argued, and the lack of a biological father in the home did not mean that the child lacked male role models. But in the last few years, social scientists have stopped talking so blithely about the extended family in black culture because, slowly but surely, people have begun realizing that the argument about the extended family becomes a cruel joke—because when there is no marriage in one generation, grandfathers and uncles too become scarce in the next generation. If there is no marriage in the next generation as well, they vanish. Marriage is just as necessary for extended families as for nuclear families.

THE LIMITS OF INTERVENTIONS

Given this view of the situation, what is there to be done through policy? Broadly speaking, all social programs for dealing with the underclass may be divided into three categories: sustenance, opportunity, and remediation.

Sustenance programs consist of programs such as AFDC, food stamps, and public housing. No one expects them to solve the problem of the underclass. They are no more than holding actions even in the view of their proponents. Their opponents, of whom I am one, think they actually contribute to the problem.

Opportunity programs are simple in theory, and we once had high hopes for them. People are held back by lack of opportunity; therefore, all we need to do is mount programs that put an opportunity—a chance to get job training, a chance to go to college—on the table, and we can then watch eager applicants take advantage of these opportunities. Opportunity programs are among the most attractive to me, but people who have looked closely at their results have sharply downgraded their expectations when it comes to the underclass. In part, this reflects America's success. It has not been headlined, but since the early 1960s, the United States has been extraordinarily successful in recruiting the most able young people, whatever their race, sex, or income, into college. As far as anyone can tell, there is simply not a sizable population of highly talented young people out there who are prevented from fulfilling their potential because of lack of opportunity. This does not mean that such individual cases do not remain, and providing a chance for the able and deserving is one of the best things that any of us can do for our fellow citizens. I encourage such efforts. They do not, however, represent the answer to the underclass.

It has become increasingly apparent that if social programs are to be used to make inroads into the underclass, they must be essentially remedial. The remediation can be as prosaic as remedial reading for an eighth grader who cannot read, as complicated as teaching someone to get up at the same time every morning and go to work, or as poignant as having to teach a young mother that it is a good thing to smile and talk to her baby while changing the baby's diapers. But one way or another, a wide variety of deficits have to be made up. Many of these ultimately involve making up for things that in the ordinary course of events are expected to be provided by fathers and mothers and neighbors.

What are the practical limits of such interventions? What is the best-case scenario? I think the information for a pretty good answer to that question is already available. During the last 30 years, we have tried hundreds, probably thousands, of interventions on a demonstration basis. Many of these have been generously funded. Many strategies have been tried many times, each attempting to improve on the weaknesses of earlier attempts. Many have been rigorously evaluated. My own reading of this literature is that it points to a depressing conclusion. The practical limits of remediation are quickly reached.

Once again, I recognize I am beating upwind, for among the advocates of social programs, the current wisdom is that we now know that certain things do work. It has almost become a mantra: "We know Head Start works. We know Job Corps works." Commentary on the problems of the black inner city also has recently begun to assume that certain solutions *will* work, if only we do the obvious thing and try them. Thus, one often reads op-ed columns in which it is assumed that of course black teenage girls would have fewer babies, if only they have access to better sex education, or that of course the rate of black teenage dropout from the labor force will go down, if only jobs are made available. This self-assurance is invincibly ignorant of history. The effects of such programs have been assessed, we have a rich and reasonably consistent body of results, and those results are not consistent with the optimism.

Head Start is a striking example. Let me begin by saying that I think a good preschool is generally a good thing for the same reason that kindergarten is a good thing, and I am in favor of providing good preschools for disadvantaged children. But Head Start is discussed not just as a nice thing to do for children but as an example of what we can do to make progress in the inner city. The reality is that no program of the 1960s has been more often evaluated, more thoroughly, than Head Start—a synthesis by Hubbell (1983) annotated 1,500 studies. This work has produced a few broad conclusions. One is that Head Start programs, properly implemented, can enhance some aspects of social development and school performance. These effects are spotty, and when they occur they fade, disappearing altogether after about 3 years. All in all, Head Start is not exactly a failure (it is still a nice thing to do for kids), but neither is there any reason to believe that anything will change in the inner city, if only Congress fully funds Head Start.

But don't we know that Head Start reduces delinquency and unemployment and pregnancies in later life? No. We have a handful of experimental programs that have made such claims with varying degrees of evidence to back them up, but none of them bear much resemblance to Head Start. By far the best known of these is the Perry Preschool Program from Ypsilanti, Michigan, which had 58 youngsters and a control group of 65. (Let us pause for a moment and consider what would happen to someone who tried to claim that an intervention strategy did *not* work on the basis of one program with 58 youngsters.) Perry Preschool had four teachers each year, and in any given year, these four teachers together were dealing with no more than a total of 24 children—a 1:6 ratio. The teachers were handpicked, highly trained, and motivated. They received further extensive training in the special curriculum adopted for the program. In addition to the daily preschool time, the program included a 1½-hour home visit to each mother each week of the program (see Berrueta-Clement, Schweinhart, Barnett, Epstein, & Weikart, 1984).

The first salient point is thus that Perry Preschool was a handcrafted little jewel that the federal government cannot conceivably replicate nationwide—

not because there is not enough money (although that is part of it), but because of the nature of large programs. Bureaucracies give you Head Starts, not Perry Preschools. The other salient point has to do with outcomes. Perry Preschool is the chief source of the claim that preschool intervention can reduce high school dropout, unemployment, delinquency, and pregnancies. Yet when the program's 58 children were assessed at age 19, 33% had dropped out of high school, 41% were unemployed, 31% had been arrested, and the 25 girls had experienced 17 pregnancies (Berrueta-Clement et al., 1984). All of these were evidence of success because the rates for the control group were even worse, but it is not the sort of success that the advocates of Head Start can afford to describe explicitly.

Like Head Start, Job Corps has been evaluated many times through the years. When the results have been aggregated across all centers, they have usually shown modest gains in average earnings—a matter of a few hundred dollars per year. When evaluators examine individual centers, anecdotal evidence indicates that some work better than others. The best ones have a demanding workload, strict rules of behavior, and strict enforcement (which means that many of the entrants never finish the course). Or in other words, Job Corps works for young people who are able to get up every morning, stick with a task, accept a subordinate relationship, and work hard. These people also tend to do well without Job Corps. Not even the best Job Corps center has a good track record with young people who cannot make themselves get up every morning, get discouraged easily, get mad when someone tells them what to do, and take a nap when no one is watching. But the latter describes characteristics of chronically unemployed persons.

We have a great deal of experience with jobs programs that try to deal with those who are chronically unemployed and inner-city youths who have never held jobs. After 12 years in which social programs have been unpopular, it is easy to forget how massive those jobs programs were. At its height in the late 1970s, the programs under the Comprehensive Employment and Training Act (CETA) had an annual budget equivalent to $19 billion in 1990 dollars (Murray, 1984, p. 83). The evaluations of CETA are in, and the consensus conclusion was that it had some positive impact on women, but not on men.[5] This is consistent with findings from other, small-scale demonstration projects such as those conducted by the Manpower Demonstration Research Corporation and early results from the evaluation of the Job Training Partnership Act. Unfortunately, the failure to affect men is decisive, because a core problem in the inner city is that men are not assuming their role in the community as husbands, fathers, and providers.

Let me try to moderate the "nothing works" versus "yes they do" terms in which the effects of social programs are too often debated. Local programs, especially those run by the people who had the idea in the first place, sometimes work. Programs to help those who are helping themselves sometimes work. Workfare programs in small towns and rural areas sometimes work. The most uniformly poor track records, coming exceedingly close to the blanket generalization, "nothing works," may be grouped into two categories: large federal programs intended to change behavior (as opposed to doling out commodities or cash) and any program, small or large, local or federal, trying to change the behavior of a clientele that is not already socialized to norms of working-class and middle-class society. Federal programs to help the urban underclass are especially vulnerable to failure on both counts.

There is this additional, unhappy, but factually accurate point to be made: The three categories of people who are at the core of the underclass—chronic criminals, chronic dropouts from the labor force, and chronic welfare mothers—are among the hardest to educate, train, and socialize to the requirements of the workplace and bring the fewest personal assets in both personality and cognitive skills to whatever intervention might be tried. Whether these deficits come from nature or nurture is irrelevant; everything we know from social interventions indicates that by adolescence, the personality and cognitive traits in question are for practical purposes hard-wired.

In sum: We do not know how—let me repeat and italicize those words, *we do not know how*—to change the behavior of significant proportions of the people who fall under the rubric of the "urban underclass" through program interventions, no matter how much money we spend. The truth is unpalatable, the attempts to wiggle away from it have been resourceful, not to say inventive, but here it is, in the words of Rossi (1987), one of the nation's most highly respected experts on program evaluation:

> A review of the history of the last two decades of efforts to evaluate major social programs in the United States sustains the proposition that over this period the American establishment of policy makers, agency officials, professionals and social scientists did not know how to design and implement social programs that were minimally effective, let alone spectacularly so. (p. 4)

There is a glimmer of optimism, insofar as intentions to develop precisely the program that has the best chance: locally inspired, tailored to local conditions, run by people who had the idea in the first place. My purpose is not to get people to do nothing. Instead, I harp on the difficulties of doing good not out of pure cussedness, nor a desire to be the one who correctly predicts disaster. Rather, if I am right—if remediation, however expensively funded, is not going to make much of a dent in the underclass—then every day that we fail to recognize that fact is a day wasted. If I am right, then we are going to have to contemplate the prospect of much more radical changes in outlook than we have been accustomed to.

SO WHAT IS TO BE DONE?

It is precisely because I believe that radical changes are eventually going to have to be considered that I bothered to present the idea of the negative income tax. In beginning the discussion of solutions, it is worth a few moments to think about how such an unthinkably radical change might succeed in reducing the underclass.

Let us begin with the teenage girl in the inner city. The current system tells her: "You have nothing now and no prospects for the future. If you engage in sex, which is fun, and happen to have a baby, who is lovable, the consequence will be that you also get a cash income and an apartment and free medical care for you and the baby, plus some other things." The NIT tells her: "When you reach the age of 18, you will have $7,500. You may spend it on clothes, movies, a place of your own, a trip to the beach, tuition at secretarial school, or a boyfriend. Or you can have a baby and spend it on diapers." These will not be just words. There will be some girls in the neighborhood who have reached their 18th birthdays and had a baby anyway and some who have not. The differences between their lives will be there for their younger sisters to see, and they will be large. Sex will still be fun and babies will still be endearing under the NIT, and births to single women will not drop to zero. But under the NIT, young women in the inner city will have a substantial, tangible, near-term incentive not to have the first baby. This is a fundamental change.

For girls under 18, the world changes even more radically. They get nothing. They have to go to their parents (who are eligible for the income floor) or to the father of the baby, who is eligible if he is over 18. This brings us to the young men, who for the first time now have something to lose by fathering babies.

To get the NIT, you have to be part of the tax system. To be part of the tax system means you can be located. To the young man, the NIT says: "When you reach the age of 18, you will have $7,500. You may spend it on whatever you wish—except for that part that is garnished for child support." Once again, these will be more than just words. There will be boys in the neighborhood who by the time they are 18 are liable to child support for two or three children and will have little left over. It is a no-win comparison with the boys who are not so encumbered. For those who wanted to use their NIT to go to school and better themselves, that option is foreclosed altogether. For those who were looking forward to doing nothing and collecting their $7,500, that option too is foreclosed. For those who go into crime—well, nothing is stopping the unencumbered young man from getting his $7,500 and supplementing it via crime too, if he is so inclined. There is no scenario in which the young man saddled with child support, or the threat of it, does not pay some sort of significant price in comparison with his peers who are not so saddled. This too will be visible to younger brothers.

I began with the problem of illegitimate children because nothing in the inner city will measurably improve until that problem diminishes and the formation of families begins anew. But many of the effects of the NIT in the inner city will be much more uncomplicatedly positive.

The NIT will mean that all youngsters who graduate from high school will know that they can continue the education for which they are qualified, whether a 4-year university or vocational training. They can fully afford a state school on $7,500. Although they cannot afford Yale, they make it a lot easier for Yale to make up the difference by bringing $7,500 to the table. Furthermore, children will know from kindergarten on up that these opportunities are before them, and the prospect of opportunity may reasonably be expected to affect their behavior as children.

The NIT will mean that every American who is civilized enough to make friends and pool resources can afford a decent place to live, good food, and the amenities. No one will *need* to live a life of poverty. The ticket out of poverty will be a modicum of friendly, socialized behavior. If one accepts that everyone not clinically disturbed has the free will to shape his or her own behavior to that extent, poverty will become literally a choice.

I will not try to spin out this scenario any further. It should already be clear that to some extent, I put a misleading title on this chapter. The solution to the poverty problem, in the form of an NIT, might actually do something to diminish the size of the underclass as well. But because the enactment of an NIT is so politically unlikely, let me turn to what I see as the more immediate nature of the change that must occur in social policy if the trends in the inner city are to have any hope of turning around.

I am generally in favor of programs that decentralize decisions—programs that empower people, to use the fashionable phrase. I am in favor of parents choosing schools and schools choosing among applicants, of public housing beneficiaries choosing their own apartments and landlords choosing among prospective tenants, and of people in the neighborhood deciding whether the young man down the street who has been arrested for mugging gets put back on the street or in jail. I think social networks and vital neighborhoods arise naturally from a situation in which the government ensures that people are prevented from bonking each other on the head, and people are otherwise left free—and thereby obligated—to earn their own place in their own neighborhoods by their behavior.

These are general principles, however. Let me close by drawing together a number of strands in this chapter and stating as baldly as I can how I see the nature of the solution to the underclass and the prerequisites for realizing that solution.

In my view, the disappearance of the two-parent family in the inner city is the central dynamic sustaining the underclass. The solution to the problem of the underclass ultimately lies in restoring a situation in which almost all women either get pregnant after they get married or get married after they get pregnant—and, correlatively, in which people who have babies have gone through a self-selection process that is more likely to lead to situations in which the mother and father are prepared to fill the roles required of them. When a young woman does get pregnant with no partner to take joint responsibility for the child, the solution lies in restoring a secondary self-selection process, whereby the only single mothers who choose to keep their babies instead of getting an abortion or giving the child up for adoption tend to be (a) women who can support the child themselves or (b) women who have enlisted the support of others—usually their own parents. Either way, this secondary self-selection screen at least increases the chances that the baby will thrive.

People do not need lessons in how to bring this state of affairs about. It has been a primary function of community life everywhere and throughout history, as close to a cultural constant as the human race has exhibited: Somehow, widely disparate social and cultural systems have managed to erect customs and sanctions ensuring that almost all children born to the tribe have two adults prepared to take responsibility for the upbringing of that child. These sanctions have generally consisted of two sorts. It has been economically punishing to have a child without a husband, because a single woman with a child is not a functional economic unit, and it has been socially punishing. The social stigma has in itself been related to the economic, however. Communities have understood without having to be taught that they cannot afford economically to have large numbers of single women with children.

Seen in this light, the evil of the current welfare system is not that it bribes women to have babies. Wanting to have babies is natural for young women who have reached puberty. Wanting to have sex is natural for both young women and young men who have reached puberty. The evil is that the current system enables men to father babies and enables women to bear them without the usual societal restraints. Its most direct effect is to soften the economic punishment. Its secondary effect is to undermine the contrary lessons that parents try to teach—many of them no longer apply, once the economic rules have been changed. Its tertiary effect is to undermine the foundation for the stigma, because the community no longer has to deal with the immediate economic effects of illegitimacy. In other words, the rules and sanctions lose their power because day-to-day reality no longer validates them.

These effects of the welfare system are not amenable to change. There are no incremental ways to alter the welfare system so that it no longer enables young women to have babies without husbands, and getting rid of the welfare system is out of the question. But the elites who run this country can change their minds about whether having children out of wedlock is appropriately stigmatized.

What difference will that make? Let me ask another question. What would people have said 20 years ago if I had asked what difference it would make if the elites changed their minds about whether smoking in public was appropriately stigmatized? What in fact happened, far in advance of the laws that trailed in the wake of the changed elite wisdom, were huge changes in behavior. If you want to associate with the upper socioeconomic classes in America today, you had better be prepared to refrain from smoking while in their presence. They are tolerant to a fault about all sorts of things, but they will not stand for smoking.

Until the same type of change is made in the elites' stance toward the behaviors we now call "dysfunctional" in the underclass—until the elites are willing to look down on them—the debate about policy will continue to be confined to the margins of the problem. Readers will see what I mean as they watch the welfare reform debate unfolding. But ironically, if the elites once again are willing to look down on such behaviors, it is also probably true that the need for major policy changes would be importantly diminished. Social stigma is one of the most powerful forces extant. It cannot be faked, however. It has to arise out of an authentic consensus among the forces that run society that certain things are not done. After several years of circling around this most difficult issue, this is the formulation I find most compelling. It has just two premises.

First premise: Having a baby is about the most important thing that any human being does.

Second premise: To bring a baby into the world when one is not intellectually, emotionally, and financially prepared to care for it is wrong. Not just ill-advised. Not just inimical to the mother's long-term self-interest. It is irresponsible. It is wrong.

Almost everyone agrees with me on the first premise. The second usually arouses consternation. People want to agree with me, of course, in broad terms. After all, I am told, no one is *endorsing* the idea of young women

having babies they are not prepared to care for. Everyone agrees that it is a
. . . bad idea . . . for a woman to do so—for the woman too, one must
remember, not just the baby. What most people are unable to do is to spit out
those three one-syllable words, *it is wrong.* The day that they can will be the
day that we can begin to hope that the social tragedy represented by the
American underclass will at last begin to ebb.

Notes

1. The best one-volume source for a review of the literature on the topics discussed in this section is Wilson and Herrnstein (1985).

2. Calculations are from my analysis. These consisted of 30% who had dropped out and never gone further and 23% who had eventually passed a high school equivalency exam (GED). As Cameron and Heckman (1993) have demonstrated, however, the labor market behavior and outcomes of GED people are much more like those of people who never go back to school than they are like those of high school graduates.

3. Figures are based on my analysis.

4. Figures are based on my analysis.

5. The best longitudinal studies of CETA, commissioned by the U.S. Department of Labor (1987), are gathered in *Evaluation Review.*

References

Berrueta-Clement, J. R., Schweinhart, L. J., Barnett, W. S., Epstein, A. S., & Weikart, D. P. (1984). *Changed lives: The effects of the Perry Preschool Program on youths through age 19.* Ypsilanti, MI: High-Scope Educational Research Foundation.

Bradley, R. H., & Caldwell, B. M. (1981). The HOME inventory: A validation of the preschool scale for black children. *Child Development, 52,* 708-710.

Bradley, R. H., Caldwell, B. M., & Rock, S. L. (1988). Home environment and school performance: A ten-year follow-up and examination of three models of environmental action. *Child Development, 59,* 852-867.

Caldwell, B. M., & Bradley, R. H. (1984). *Home observation for measurement of the environment.* Little Rock: University of Arkansas Press.

Cameron, S. V., & Heckman, J. J. (1993). The nonequivalence of high school equivalents [Part 1]. *Journal of Labor Economics, 11*(1), 1-47.

Freeman, R. B. (1991). Employment and earnings of disadvantaged young men in a labor shortage economy. In C. Jencks & P. E. Peterson (Eds.), *The urban underclass* (pp. 103-121). Washington, DC: Brookings Institution.

Friedman, M. (1962). *Capitalism and freedom.* Chicago: University of Chicago Press.

Harrington, M. (1962). *The other America.* New York: Macmillan.

Himmelfarb, G. (1984). *The idea of poverty: England in the early industrial age.* New York: Knopf.

Hubbell, R. (1983). *A review of Head Start since 1970.* Washington, DC: U.S. Department of Health and Human Services.

Jencks, C. (1991). Is the American underclass growing? In C. Jencks & P. E. Peterson (Eds.), *The urban underclass* (pp. 28-100). Washington, DC: Brookings Institution.

Moynihan, D. P. (Ed.). (1968). *On understanding poverty.* New York: Basic Books.

Murray, C. (1984). *Losing ground: American social policy 1950-1980.* New York: Basic Books.

National Center for Health Statistics. (1994). Advance report of final natality statistics, 1992 [Special issue]. *Monthly Vital Statistics Report, 43*(5).

Rossi, P. (1987). The iron law of evaluation and other metallic rules. In J. Miller & M. Lewis (Eds.), *Research in social problems and public policy* (Vol. 4, pp. 3-20). Greenwich, CT: JAI.

Sawhill, I. V. (1989, Summer). The underclass: An overview. *The Public Interest, 96,* 3-15.

Shelling, T. (1960). *The strategy of conflict.* Cambridge, MA: Harvard University Press.

Stigler, G. (1946). The economics of minimum wage legislation. *American Economic Review, 36,* 358-365.

U.S. Department of Commerce, Bureau of the Census. (1992a). *Money income of households, families, and persons in the United States* (Current Population Reports, Series P-60, No. 180). Washington, DC: Government Printing Office.

U.S. Department of Commerce, Bureau of the Census. (1992b). *Poverty in the United States: 1991* (Current Population Reports, Series P-60, No. 181). Washington, DC: Government Printing Office.

U.S. Department of Commerce, Bureau of the Census. (1992c). *Statistical abstract of the United States: 1992.* Washington, DC: Government Printing Office.

U.S. Department of Labor. (1987, August). *Evaluation review* (Vol. 11). Washington, DC: Author.

Wilson, J. Q., & Herrnstein, R. J. (1985). *Crime and human nature.* New York: Simon & Schuster.

A Dissent From the Incentive
Approaches to Reducing Poverty

Glenn C. Loury

I no longer believe that we social scientists and policy analysts—even as distinguished a group as assembled for this volume—are going to find the solutions to the problems of poverty. Rather, solutions, if any are to be had, must be fashioned out in the communities and in the lives of the individuals who are subject to some of these forces and conditions that we are so discussing.

I confess to being pessimistic about the prospects that social science analyses can ultimately contribute very much here. This is not to say that the effort to evaluate the effects of programs or to do research on the causes of unemployment, teenage motherhood, drug addiction, and the like should be abandoned. Billions have been spent on such work since the advent of the Great Society, which, among other things, created a huge demand for the services of academic economists, statisticians, sociologists, and others to chronicle and analyze the effects of government efforts to help people who are poor. We have learned much, although we remain ignorant about even more. But my point is not to disparage the often ingenious efforts of analysts to fathom the intricacies of human motivations, of bureaucratic machinations, or of structural transformations. Rather, I question whether the prospect of real improvement in the conditions under which those who are poor are living depends much at all on the answers to the types of questions that social scientists are inclined to pose.

In Chapters 5 and 4, respectively, we have typical examples of the scholarship of the right and left among social scientists addressing poverty issues. In essence, these two scholars are arguing about whether the core of the problem is that people do not know how to live, as Murray maintains in Chapter 5, or that people simply do not have enough money, as Jencks urges in Chapter 4. A commonsense observation of the world around us suggests that both are true.

I cannot agree with Murray when he states,

> We must reach a state of affairs in which the dialogue begins from a common agreement that everyone in the country can, if he or she behaves with a modicum of sense, have enough material resources to live a decent existence. (p. 86, this volume)

Translation: The poverty problem is driven entirely by the behavioral failing of poor people.

Why must we all sign off on this rather extreme view before useful dialogue can begin? How will our assent to this proposition lead to a solution to the problem of poverty? Suppose one grants, for the sake of argument, that Murray's assertion is valid. What exactly are its policy implications—to do nothing and wait for people to reform themselves? This type of ideological posturing is not helpful. Murray complains in his chapter that the strictures of political correctness prevent candid discussion of the real bases for the problems of persons who are poor. This has sometimes been true, although that is increasingly less the case. In any event, the flaw in his passage quoted above is not that it is *politically* incorrect but rather that it is most likely just plain wrong and leads nowhere.

On the other hand, Jencks seems determined to ignore entirely the behavioral element—the extent to which many poor people are implicated, through their own freely chosen acts, in their condition and that of their children. There is no mention of these factors in his chapter. His analysis is essentially a counting exercise—how much money does it appear that a mother living alone with two children needs to live "decently" in urban America, compared with how much she might be expected to earn in a minimum-wage job. He notes that the numbers do not add up. She cannot earn enough, net of the costs of child care, transportation, and so forth, to live reasonably well. So, Jencks concludes that it is unreasonable to expect welfare reform to reach the point of demanding self-sufficiency from its recipients after a short time (say 2 years) without a massive and quite expensive program to supplement the earnings of all of the working poor.

Here I agree that we should ask Murray's implicit questions: If it is indeed impossible for an unskilled young woman without a husband to support herself and her children decently in our society, why does she choose to bear these children under such conditions? Is it the responsibility of society to provide her with an adequate provision without regard to whether she evidences a willingness to meet her own responsibilities? How shall we communicate to those prospective mothers and fathers the awesome consequences of their behavioral choices in such a way that they choose differently?

Jencks seems to have no taste, or stomach, for these questions, but they must be asked and answered. It is not acceptable that the behavioral underpinnings of the conditions in which many poor families are living be placed out of bounds and kept out of the discussion of policy. But being willing to entertain these questions is not the same thing as having answers to them. Moreover, social scientists are not necessarily the best people to provide answers. These are not, in the main, technical questions with answers to be derived from a thorough knowledge of statistical data. These problems will not be solved by retiring to a computer laboratory for the analysis of the latest reports of the Census Bureau.

The issues raised by behavioral dysfunction and the questions of who bears what responsibility in the face of that dysfunction are inherently political and moral questions for which the nation, as a political and moral community, must produce answers. To find these answers, we must have the will to examine ourselves, how we live, and what we value—and this self-examination must involve not just those who are poor, but all of us. As a number of social critics have recently emphasized, there is a relationship between the behavioral problems of people who are poor and the cultural crisis affecting the middle and upper classes in America, as evidenced by rising divorce rates, the spread of venereal diseases, the problems of the education system, increases in teen suicide and alcohol and drug abuse, problems with international competitiveness, and the like.

At issue here is people's capacity as a political and moral community to engage in an effective discourse about values and ways of living and to convey normative judgments that arise out of that discourse. I am dubious, for example, that it will ever again be possible for the federal government of the United States through the Congress or the executive branch to put the force of its enormous power behind the simple normative proposition that children ought not be born to parents prior to marriage. In the last quarter century, it has become increasingly more difficult for a public figure to give voice to this belief, one that not so long ago would have been universally regarded as appropriate. Consider the contempt with which elite opinion received the promotion of "family values" by Dan Quayle during the 1992 presidential campaign.

This is a curious situation. National campaigns have been aimed at some aspects of behavior, with positive results. Smoking, for example, has been successfully inveighed against during the last generation, with both public and private efforts. The national consciousness of environmental issues has been raised in recent decades, in part through the use of public rhetoric and exhortation. But efforts to shape private values about sexuality, marriage, and childbearing are far more contentious, raising ideological conflicts with feminist and gay rights advocates. And the tools available to policymakers to influence behavior in this area—taxes and transfer programs, mainly—seem to have little effect. We have seen a huge growth among blacks and whites in the incidence of teenage pregnancy and births out of wedlock during the last 30 years, but however one reads the evidence, it is difficult to attribute much of the change to the marginal incentives of tax and transfer programs. There is talk about increasing the tax exemption for families with children, but I know of no data to suggest that this would have any substantial impact on divorce or illegitimate birth rates.

Despite being an economist, a believer in the power of incentives to shape human behavior in the marketplace, I do not find this at all surprising. People do not construct their basic understandings of what is important in their lives by considering whether they will receive a few thousand dollars more if they embrace one way of life as opposed to another.

Hayes-Bautista presents some powerful data in Chapter 3 that underscore precisely what I am saying here. His figures demonstrate convincingly that the low-income Latino population of California cannot be accurately characterized as an "underclass" population. On one indicator of "behavioral pathology" after another, Latinos seemed to be doing as well, if not better, than Anglos. Those same figures, however, show dramatic variation across ethnic groups within the California population—blacks, whites, Asians, and Latinos—on the same indicators of pathology that Hayes-Bautista uses to show that Latinos are not doing too badly. There are huge differences between these population subgroups with respect to measures of mortality, labor force participation, drug use, and violence. Blacks fared much worse than did Latinos or Asians. Of course, no one believes that race per se is important here. But cultural differences that vary with race may be. The local culture that socializes an individual through childhood and adolescence into adulthood may have more impact on whether that person will perpetuate a drive-by shooting or end up addicted to crack cocaine than would any policy activity undertaken by a mayor, governor, or the president.

Stated directly and without benefit of euphemism, the conditions under which many people live today in poor black communities such as South-Central Los Angeles reveal as much about the disintegration of urban black society as they do about the indifference, hostility, or racism of white society. Institutional barriers to black participation in American life still exist, but they have come down considerably, and everybody knows it. Everybody also knows that other barriers have grown up within the urban black milieu (and not only there) in these last decades that are profoundly debilitating. These effects are most clearly manifest in patterns of behavior among young men and women in these communities—involving criminal offending, early unwed childbearing, low academic achievement, drug use, gratuitous violence, and guns—that destroy a person's ability to seize existing opportunity. These behaviors have to be changed if broadly gauged progress is to come.

Here the social scientists and the politicians have failed us. For the longest time, as Murray reminds us, it *was* forbidden to speak of the unraveling social fabric of ghetto life. This has changed in the last decade, with the discovery of the so-called black underclass, but the former conspiracy of silence has not been replaced with a meaningful discourse on how this broken world will be mended. Liberals, such as Jencks, have now acknowledged that behavioral problems are fundamental but insist that these problems derive ultimately from the lack of economic opportunities and will abate once "good jobs at good wages" are at hand. Conservatives, such as Murray, see the tragic developments in the inner cities as the unintended legacy of a misconceived welfare state. If the government would stop underwriting irresponsible behavior with its various transfer programs, they argue, poor people would be forced to discover the virtues of self-restraint.

These polar positions have something important in common. They both implicitly assume that economic factors lie behind the behavioral problems, even behaviors involving sexuality, marriage, childbearing, and parenting, that reflect people's basic understandings of what gives their lives meaning. Both points of view suggest that behavioral problems in the ghetto, or anywhere else for that matter, can be cured from without, by changing government policy, by getting the incentives right. Both smack of a mechanistic determinism, wherein the mysteries of human motivation are susceptible to calculated intervention. Both have difficulty explaining why some poor minority communities show a much lower incidence of these behavioral problems than others and are apparently less influenced by the same objective economic forces.

Moreover, these economic determinists' views of social disorder in the inner city lend themselves easily to the favored lines of political argument about social policy. Those who want the federal budget to shrink can cite the worsening conditions of the ghetto in the face of the growth in social spending during the last generation as evidence that the Great Society failed. Those who seek a middle way—the welfare reformers—can split the difference by talking about how the receipt of benefits must be accompanied by an acceptance of responsibility by poor persons, although the government must provide services that help poor persons accept their responsibilities.

These debates over policy on social spending are no doubt important, but there is something sterile and superficial about them. Ultimately, they fail to engage questions of personal morality, of character and values, and of moral leadership in the public sphere. Politicians and social scientists have had little to say in public about what is wrong with the way people in a particular community are living and what ways of life are better for them and their children. The view seems to be that in a pluralistic democracy, such discussions by public officials are inappropriate. Nor do the public schools teach that a specific way of living is virtuous, in part because we do not agree among ourselves about such matters. We give only muted public voice to the judgments that it is wrong to use drugs, to be sexually promiscuous, to be indolent and without discipline, to be disrespectful of legitimate authority, and to be unreliable, untruthful, and unfaithful. We no longer teach values to children but offer them "values clarification" instead, elevating process (how does one discover his or her own values?) over substance (what are the values that a "decent" person should embrace?)

The advocacy of a particularistic conception of virtuous living has vanished from American public discourse. And it is unthinkable that it would be evoked in the context of a discussion of race and social policy. Marriage as an institution is virtually dead in inner-city black communities. The vast majority of poor black children are now raised by a mother alone. But who will say that black men and women *should* get together and stay together more than they now do, for the sake of their children? Who will say that young people of any race *should* abstain from sexual intimacy until their relationships have been consecrated by marriage? These are, in this secular age, not matters for public policy. Most Americans believe that $1\frac{1}{2}$ million abortions a year are too many, constituting a moral problem for society, but the public discourse on this issue is dominated by the question of a woman's right to choose this morally problematic course. Nearly everyone prefers, on moral as well as pragmatic grounds, that 15-year-olds not be sexually active, but to publicly urge such a stance in response to an epidemic of sexually transmitted disease among young people is to invite ridicule. Government, it appears, must confine itself to dealing with the consequences of these matters not having been taken up elsewhere.

Evidently, we are going to have to look to the nongovernmental agencies of moral and cultural development in particular communities to take on some of the burden of promoting positive behavioral change. In every community are agencies of moral and cultural development that seek to shape the ways in which individuals conceive of their duties to themselves, their obligations to each other, and their responsibilities before God. The family and the church are primary among these. These are the natural sources of legitimate moral teaching—indeed, the only sources. If these institutions are not restored, the behavioral problems of the ghetto will not be overcome. Such a restoration obviously cannot be the object of programmatic intervention by public agencies. Rather, it must be led from within the communities in question, by the moral and political leaders of those communities. The bully pulpit of public leadership, however, *can* be used to encourage, rather than disparage, these private efforts at the inculcation of specific moral codes.

The mention of God may seem quaint or vaguely inappropriate for such an august academic volume, but it is clear that the behavior problems of the ghetto (and not only there) involve spiritual issues. A person's spiritual commitments influence that individual's understanding of parental responsibilities. No economist has yet to devise an incentive scheme for eliciting parental involvement in a child's development that is as effective as the motivations of conscience deriving from the parents' understanding that they are God's stewards in the lives of their children. The effective teaching of sexual abstinence or of the eschewal of violence is most naturally based on an appeal to spiritual concepts. The most effective substance abuse recovery programs are built around spiritual principles. The reports of successful efforts at reconstruction in ghetto communities invariably reveal a religious institution or set of devout believers at the center of the effort.

Although public policy should not reflect particular religious doctrines under the U.S. form of government, this is no reason to keep an understanding of the importance of spirituality out of public discussions of poverty. Everything worth talking about in public need not result in a government program or a federal statute! We should recognize the importance of the efforts in many communities to reconstruct systems of beliefs and values from which individuals derive meaning and around which people can organize their lives. From such conceptions of ultimate meaning do people derive their understanding of their fundamental responsibilities and their sense of their own worthiness.

PART III

Improving Schooling for the Poor

7

Politics, Markets, and Equality in Schools

John E. Chubb
Terry M. Moe

American education can be said to have two basic problems. The first is that students generally achieve too little. According to the National Assessment of Educational Progress (NAEP), the typical American high school student possesses only middle school knowledge and skills. According to the International Assessment of Educational Progress, the typical middle school student does not rank in the top 10 in mathematics or science when compared with 13-year-olds around the world. This problem—call it a problem of efficiency—is compounded by a second problem, a problem of equality. Students differ too much in what they achieve, with poor, black, and Hispanic students too often at the bottom. The United States sends a higher percentage

AUTHORS' NOTE: This chapter was previously published as "Politics, Markets, and Equality in Schools," by J. E. Chubb and T. M. Moe, in *The Service Productivity and Quality Challenge*, P. T. Harker, Ed. (pp. 435-469), Dordrecht, The Netherlands: Kluwer Academic Publishers, 1995. All rights reserved. Copyright © 1995 Kluwer Academic Publishers. Reprinted with permission. No part of the material protected by this copyright notice may be reproduced or utilized in any form or by any means, electronic or mechanical, including photocopying, recording or by any information storage and retrieval system, without written permission from the copyright owner.

of its students to college than most nations, and the best American students are as accomplished as any in the world. Yet a fifth of all big-city students fail to finish high school, roughly twice the national average. And despite considerable progress, black students trail white students by nearly 200 points on the SAT.

In a recent book, *Politics, Markets, and America's Schools* (Chubb & Moe, 1990), we proposed a reform to attack these problems fundamentally. We outlined a new system of public education based on market principles and implemented through a mechanism that is now usually called school choice. In essence, parents would be entitled to send their children to any school of their choice, at public expense, and schools would be encouraged to improve through competition with other schools for enrollment.

The reasoning behind this proposal was derived from our analysis of public and private education. Public schools are failing, we argued, because of the institutions that govern them. Driven by politics, institutions of direct demo- cratic control—school boards and district offices, state legislatures, the U.S. Congress, and their respective education departments—work to overwhelm public schools with bureaucracy and rob public schools of the autonomy that is the foundation for effective organization and performance. Market institu- tions, which control private schools, do the opposite. Bureaucracy has little place in a competitive environment that places a premium on responding to family needs and organizing to produce superior educational results. If the United States wants different—and better—public schools, it will need to control them with different institutions. The institutions that control public schools today, directly and from the top down, should have their authority severely limited, and new institutions that would control schools indirectly and from the bottom up—market institutions of choice and competition— should operate in their place.

The benefits of institutional reform, we argued, include not only greater effectiveness or efficiency but greater educational equality as well. Urban schools, attended disproportionately by poor and minority students and burdened disproportionately by politics and bureaucracy, are the schools most likely to change in an environment of school autonomy and parental choice. Flush with resources once consumed by oversized district offices and powers once exercised by unknowledgeable and distant authorities, urban schools should find their opportunities for innovation especially enhanced. Because of the density and diversity of city populations, urban families should find their selection of schools especially wide. Poor families would also gain effective access to a right—the right to choose their children's schools—that more affluent families have always exercised through residential decisions (or by opting for private schools) but that poor families have never been able to afford to use.

Still, we argued, equality requires more support than markets alone can provide. We therefore recommended an institutional structure in which market forces are carefully regulated. Our proposal, after all, was for a *public* system of educational choice—fully funded by the government and operated according to ground rules established by the government. Among them are these: Parents may not top off their public scholarship with private funds and thereby choose a more expensive education. Schools may not completely control their admissions, as every school is required to accept some students it would not admit voluntarily. And all parents, but especially poor parents, are to be assisted by public authorities in finding, evaluating, and applying to schools. We proposed, we thought, a system that would revolutionize public education and increase educational opportunity for all.

To judge from what our critics have said, however, our thinking was at least half wrong. Yes, a system of choice might reduce bureaucracy, enhance school autonomy, and strengthen the role of parents. It might even stimulate enough reorganization, innovation, and rededication within schools to nudge the average level of achievement across the nation upward. But whatever it might do in these regards, it would certainly do at too high a price, for it would certainly exacerbate inequality.

In a system of school choice, critics argue, some parents would inevitably be better choosers than others. Schools would inevitably prefer to admit the easy-to-educate rather than children who misbehave or have learning disabilities. Children with advantages, of parenting or of nature, would fill up the good schools, while disadvantaged children would be left behind in bad schools made even worse by the departure of the ablest students. White families would, of course, flee black and Hispanic families, and some black families would choose Afrocentric schools with dubious academic curricula. The rich would get richer, the poor would get poorer, and the shameful days of school segregation would return.

Of course, we disagree with this assessment. But in fairness to our critics, we must admit that our book was principally about efficiency or effectiveness, about the roots of poor performance in schools. We were concerned with issues of equality too, and we tried to address them adequately. Still, our analysis focused on efficiency. It traced the effect of schools on children—all children—to school organization, to the administrative environment that shapes the organization, and finally, to the institutions that determine how schools will be administered or controlled. Our empirical analysis did not examine in any depth or detail the distribution of student achievement or the causes of inequality. Perhaps most important, our analysis did not compare educational equality under political and market conditions.

Now, we would like to do just that. Specifically, we want to understand better what schools and school systems do to ameliorate inequality or to bring it about, and we want to consider whether political or market institutions are likely to differ on these scores. To help us, we have been analyzing a new longitudinal study of schools, students, and families—the National Education Longitudinal Study, 1988 (known as NELS:88)—that follows a national sample of approximately 25,000 students in roughly 1,000 schools from 8th grade in 1988 through 10th grade in 1990 (National Center for Education Statistics, 1990, 1992). The study uses many of the same survey items as the High School and Beyond Study and the Administrator and Teacher Survey, which provided the data for *Politics, Markets, and America's Schools.* NELS:88 is therefore especially appropriate for this follow-up research.

In this chapter, we want to summarize in a nontechnical way the results of our first cut into these new data and our first effort to think comprehensively about educational equality. (The technical results, too extensive for this volume, are available on request.) We divide our discussion into two logical parts: equality within schools and equality between schools. When you get right down to it, educational inequality has two basic sources in schooling— the different treatment of children within schools and the different treatment of children by different schools. Either way, if the treatment differs in quality, educational inequality will be produced. Political and market institutions, we find, are not similarly prone to produce such differences. Suffice it to say that this analysis finds little evidence that political institutions are better at promoting educational equality than market institutions are. Indeed, our preliminary results go consistently the other way.

Some Equality Standards

Before we consider how alternative institutions affect educational equality, we need to be clear what we mean by equality. We need to establish some equality standards against which institutions can be judged. Of course, this is no straightforward task. Equality can be defined in many different ways, and alternative conceptions of equality are regularly debated by democratic theorists, economists, and politicians—to name only some of the main contestants. We shall not venture any comprehensive definition of this complex concept but rather a set of standards that, taken together, form a loose hierarchy that builds from weaker forms of equality to stronger.

At the base of this hierarchy is the standard of *nondiscrimination*: Students should not be denied access to schools or programs within schools because of their race, ethnic background, sex, or economic class. This does not mean that all schools and programs will have representative distributions of blacks and whites, rich and poor, and so forth. This is not a standard of affirmative action.

The standard simply says that race, sex, and class shall not be explicit or—more likely—implicit criteria for access to education. For example, a black child might still be excluded from an accelerated math program because of low test scores, but he or she would not be excluded because, regardless of test scores, schools believe black children do not excel at math: The latter would constitute discrimination. In the analysis that follows, we focus on race and class discrimination because these are the lines along which American society is most sharply and permanently divided educationally and, in some consequence, politically and economically. Of course, racial discrimination is also unconstitutional in all public schools and in all private schools that want tax-exempt status—which means all but a handful.

Next up the hierarchy is the standard of *separate but equal.* In a nondiscriminating world, children of different racial, ethnic, and economic backgrounds are nevertheless going to end up in different schools and programs. Kids attend public schools in their neighborhoods and private schools of their choosing; they are not assigned to schools randomly. Within schools, kids choose different classes and programs. In addition, some kids qualify for gifted and talented programs, some for remedial programs, and some for nothing special at all. If children from different backgrounds are to have the chance to make equal educational gains, the disparate schools, programs, and classes in which they find themselves must provide equally good educational experiences. This means that the heavily minority urban school and the predominantly white suburban school must be places of similar quality, by whatever measures are relevant. It also means that the gifted and talented program, overpopulated with rich kids, and the remedial program, home to so many kids who are poor, must be equally well suited to helping their respective groups of children work up to their potential.

A tougher standard than separate but equal is what we call *equal opportunity.* If we envision a society in which children from different racial and economic backgrounds do not differ radically in high school and college graduation rates or in academic achievement, it may be inadequate merely to accept well-qualified black children in college prep programs—for their test scores are too often too low—or to ensure that the remedial classes poor children take are truly excellent—for they will never be as good as the advanced placement classes rich children take. If we are serious about equalizing educational outcomes, it may be necessary to expand the availability of the best educational opportunities and to ensure maximum feasible participation in them. This means that more children, of all backgrounds, will take high-level classes and follow the college track through high school. It also means that students of differing backgrounds—racial, economic, *and* academic—will attend classes together. Schools will be less likely to segregate kids by ability, because the opportunities are inherently limited for kids placed in slow groups. Schools will be more likely to operate heterogeneous classes in which swifter and slower children work side by side or even together. This arrangement not only expands educational opportunity but also increases the interaction of children from different backgrounds. It satisfies a standard that might also be called equal, not separate.

Satisfying even a tough opportunity standard, however, does not guarantee any reduction in the education gap that divides American society. The next standard begins to do so. Following Gutmann (1987), we call it the *quality threshold*. This standard of equality says that schools and school systems will ensure that the education of no child falls below a threshold necessary to participate effectively as a citizen. What this means precisely is open to debate. But what it means generally is that every child will leave school able to read, write, calculate, solve moderately complex problems, think about public affairs, and hold a job sufficient to avoid public dependence. It means at least a good high school education. This standard does not mean that there will not be huge gaps in ultimate educational attainment; some students will inevitably want more education than others—a Ph.D., an M.D., a J.D.—and not all students will be equally able at academics. But this standard is about more than opportunity. It judges schools by how its weakest or most disadvantaged students actually turn out.

The final and toughest standard is also about outcomes, but about outcomes for all. We call it *equal outcomes.* This standard says that if we are truly concerned about the wide disparity in academic achievement that follows class and racial lines, we ought to evaluate schools and school systems by the job they do in reducing this disparity. Take two schools that begin with similar distributions of children—equal numbers of slow, average, and bright children in each school. Then look at the distribution of academic achievement within each school when the children graduate. The school that is doing the better job for educational equality is the one with the tighter distribution, with the narrower gap between bright and slow. That school is providing more equal outcomes.

A school that provides equal outcomes, however, should not sacrifice educational excellence to do so. The education problems that the United States must address are twofold problems of equality and of efficiency. A school that provides equal outcomes could conceivably do so by holding down the achievement of the brightest students. Its distribution of achievement might then be narrow, but its average level of achievement might be quite low. The same problem might occur if a school placed too many poorly prepared children in an advanced classroom; well-prepared students might be held back. In the analysis that follows, we will be asking in various ways how schools measure up to our five standards of equality, but we will also be paying attention to their average level of performance—their effectiveness or efficiency.

Equality Within Schools

Critics of school choice have focused most of their attention on the disparities a marketplace might create from one school to the next. Yet critics of educational inequality more generally have focused as much or more attention on the disparities that exist within individual schools.[1] A school can create or exacerbate inequality in many ways. It can discriminate against children of certain races or ethnic backgrounds in assigning children to instructional groups or curriculum tracks. It can assign children to classes in a nondiscriminatory fashion—on the basis of test scores, for example—yet provide instruction of widely varying quality to different tracks or groups. Even if organized objectively, groups or tracks may separate children of different class or racial backgrounds so thoroughly that a school can become effectively segregated internally. In addition, a school may so limit the size of its high group or college track that all but the brightest children are denied educational opportunity.

Grouping and tracking are widespread practices in American education, so it is only reasonable to ask whether they contribute to the wide variation in student performance. As critics of these practices often point out, there is more variation in student achievement within American schools than there is on average between schools. It is no wonder, then, that the study of educational inequality has probably produced more research on grouping and tracking than on disparities between schools.[2] We, too, think that grouping and tracking practices deserve careful attention. But we think that existing research on the subject is deficient in one major respect. It has scarcely considered the roots of the practices to which so many critics strongly object. Could it be that the patterns of grouping and tracking found in public schools today are rooted in the institutional structure of which the schools are a part? Could it be that grouping and tracking, like other qualities of school organization that we have studied before, are institutionally determined?

That is our suspicion. But existing research provides few clues whether we are right. The problem is that research into the effects of tracking and grouping looks mostly at public schools, which are all governed by institutions of the same basic form.[3] If we want to know whether these important organizational practices are influenced by how schools are governed or controlled, we must consider how schools that are controlled differently deal with student diversity, too. From an institutional standpoint, the schools that differ most from public schools are private schools. Despite their enormous diversity—from secular independent schools connected to no larger entity to religious schools sometimes part of sizable systems—private schools differ from public schools fundamentally: Private schools are not controlled directly, from the top down, by democratic authorities; they are controlled indirectly, from the bottom up, by market forces.

In the analysis that follows, we compare the grouping and tracking practices of public and private schools. Such a comparison cannot tell us everything we might need to know to predict how a system of school choice would affect inequality within schools. Private education today serves only 12% of America's children and provides only a quarter of the country's schools. If all children and schools participated in a public educational marketplace, matters might be somewhat different than they are in private education now. Nevertheless, the best evidence we can possibly have of how schools would manage student diversity in a marketplace is to compare schools that are doing so now with schools that are managing subject to political control.

DIVERSITY WITHIN SCHOOLS

Generally speaking, schools are more likely to separate children into ability groups or curriculum tracks if the children in the school differ substantially in their prior achievement or capacity to learn. Schools run a greater risk of reinforcing or worsening inequality if their students are unequal to begin with. It is generally easier for schools to integrate children if the differences among them are not large.

Public schools might be expected to face more student diversity than private schools do because public schools typically enroll all children in a neighborhood, regardless of background, whereas private schools enroll children interested in education of a particular type. This expectation must be tempered, however, because choice operates in the public sector, too. Families base their residential choices on, among other things, the quality of neighborhood public schools and the cost of housing. This choice process sorts children into public schools by economic class and educational taste, much as an analogous choice process sorts children into private schools. It is an empirical question, then, whether public schools or private schools face more internal diversity.

In our analysis, we measured the diversity that typical public schools and private schools must manage.[4] We calculated the average standard deviation of public and private eighth graders on a number of dimensions of educational inequality. We found that the average public school does face more diversity than the average private school, but not dramatically more. On average, student bodies are 10% to 15% less diverse in private schools than in public schools. This means, for example, that in a public school, a lower-class student is somewhat more likely to be around a middle-class student, or that a student living with two married parents is somewhat more likely to interact with a student living with a single mother. The biggest difference between public and private schools is in parent income, for which there is 25% less diversity in private schools, presumably because most every parent in a private school must be able to afford the same tuition—high, low, or in between. A publicly funded system of school choice might reduce this source of homogeneity because ability to pay would not limit access to schools.

Interestingly, the dimension along which there is nearly the least difference between public and private schools is academic achievement. Students were given standardized tests in four subjects: reading, mathematics, history, and science. In our analysis, we considered the average standard deviations within schools of math scores—because math is where ability grouping most often takes place—and combined scores. For the most part, private schools are only slightly more homogeneous academically than public schools. Pending further analysis, we cannot say whether private schools have less internal inequality in student achievement because they admit slightly more homogeneous students or because they better organize themselves to reduce academic inequality. The important point at this juncture is that private schools, by virtue of the control they exercise over admission, face less diversity than public schools face, but not dramatically less. Residential sorting in the public sector is evidently rather powerful because public and private schools have fairly similar student bodies, as measured by a number of gauges of diversity.

This similarity can be seen in yet another way. We examined the distribution of public and private schools by the percentage of black students in their eighth grades. That examination revealed that the overwhelming majority of public and private schools are almost completely white—only 0% to 2% black. There are more private schools than public schools in this category, to be sure. But when we consider schools that are not homogeneously white— say, enrolling 3% black or more—public and private schools are similarly distributed. In each sector, such schools range fairly evenly from minority black to majority black enrollments.

ABILITY GROUPING

The primary way by which schools have long managed student diversity is to group children homogeneously by ability. This practice is said to facilitate instruction, as teachers can concentrate on material at one level of difficulty without worrying that the material is too hard for some or too unchallenging for others. Homogeneous grouping is also criticized for locking kids into achievement tracks that diverge unnecessarily. Children in the slower groups in elementary school are said to never catch up with the children in the higher groups because the instruction in the slower groups is simply not as ambitious or effective as that in the higher groups. Children in the slower groups are said to feel stigmatized by their placement. Rarely, critics say, do these children ever escape their low groups and enter a college prep track in high school (for critical reviews, see Oakes, 1985; Persell, 1977).

Slower children are better off, critics of grouping argue, in heterogeneous classrooms and ability groups in which they work side by side with swifter children on a common curriculum, only at a slightly slower pace. Instructional techniques such as "cooperative learning" are supposed to make it possible for slower children to succeed in heterogeneous groups and for swifter children to progress just as fast as they would in a homogeneous, accelerated group. Research on these claims is still far from definitive. And the effects of grouping, whether homogeneous or heterogeneous, depend on the particular ways in which grouping is implemented. For example, the inequality that homogeneous grouping may perpetuate can be overcome if group assignments are regularly reassessed and students reassigned. Nevertheless, research currently suggests that slower children are harmed by homogeneous grouping and that swifter children are served as well by heterogeneous groups as by homogeneous ones (see, e.g., research reviewed in Slavin, 1990). On grounds of equality, then, and perhaps efficiency, it appears that heterogeneous grouping is a better instructional strategy.

So, what is the preferred practice of American schools? In our analysis, we estimated the percentage of eighth graders grouped homogeneously for mathematics. In public as well as private schools, the overwhelming majority of students are still taught in homogeneous ability groups. Most schools separate kids into groups of slow, medium, and swift learners and risk the inequality in learning that may result thereby. There is a sharp difference, however, between public and private schools in the use of grouping. Private schools place 15 percentage points more students in heterogeneous groups than public schools do. About 30% of all private school kids take math in heterogeneous groups; only 15% of all public school kids do.

This difference also appears to operate independent of objective reasons for grouping. Our analysis divided students into schools that are above and below the population median in socioeconomic diversity—because socioeconomic status is a strong predictor of academic success. Presumably, schools will separate kids into homogeneous groups less often as their student bodies decline in diversity: The more similar students are, the less the need to separate them. To a slight extent, this turns out to be true. But for the most part, public and private schools exhibit different propensities to group heterogeneously, regardless of student diversity. Public schools almost invariably sort and separate kids into homogeneous ability groups; private schools are more willing to keep different children together.

Is this really a basic difference between public and private schools? Or does the difference have other explanations? To try to find out, we considered a number of alternative explanations simultaneously. We estimated a probit model designed to predict a student's math group, that is, whether the group is homogeneous or heterogeneous. We found that the type of group an eighth grader is in has many "causes," or at least is influenced in many ways. For example, a student is somewhat more likely to be placed in a homogeneous group (presumably a high one) if he or she comes from a family higher in socioeconomic status, has strong prior math grades, and is Asian. There is ever so slight evidence that black students are less likely to be grouped homogeneously.

But ultimately there are three strong influences on a student's group. First is the socioeconomic status of the school. Schools serving more affluent children are more likely to group homogeneously, presumably to provide high-level groups. Second, schools that are internally diverse, with wide variations in math achievement, are more likely to group homogeneously—although this may be an effect as well as a cause. Third, all things being equal, a child is much less likely to be grouped homogeneously—to be separated from children of different ability—in a private school than in a public school. For the average child, the probability of being grouped homogeneously for math is .829 in a public school but only .556 in a private school.

Of course, private schools may be less able to group homogeneously because they are smaller and do not have enough students to offer more specialized classes. In other words, private schools might group heterogeneously if they were larger. Let us ignore for now the question of why private schools are smaller—because perhaps they want to be small so they can avoid internal specialization—and just consider how public and private schools of similar size group children. We reestimated the probit model, adding a control for eighth-grade enrollment. We found that size matters but that public and private schools still differ. Allowing for school size, an average student has a 10% higher probability of being grouped homogeneously in a public school than in a private school.

Why do private schools show a greater willingness to keep children of different backgrounds together? We think there are two reasons, both rooted in basic differences between political and market institutions. The first has to do with the different structure of top-down control in the two institutions. Direct democratic control, as it is now structured, promotes the growth of bureaucracy around public schools. As we have argued, this bureaucracy generally tends to rob public schools of the autonomy that they need to exercise professional discretion and to organize themselves as effective educational teams. This bureaucracy also tends to do something very particular that affects how public schools deal with diversity. It prescribes how public schools deal with diversity. Public schools are required by law—federal, state, and local—to run various gifted and talented programs, enrichment programs, remedial programs, vocational programs, and numerous other programs. They are also required to use objective criteria—usually test scores—in assigning children to programs. A system of externally imposed rules determines how children will be organized and served.

There is more to this system, however, than the bureaucracy that implements it. The bureaucracy is not the source of the rules that limit how schools respond to diversity. The source is democratic authority, exercised by boards of education, state legislatures, and the U.S. Congress. As we observed in *Politics, Markets, and America's Schools,* this authority is exercised in a distinctive way. Groups that vie for control of public authority insist on nailing down their political victories in detailed legislation that makes it difficult for subsequent victors to influence how legislation is implemented. Groups want to limit discretion in schools not only because they distrust the professionals who work there but also because they want to guard against the uncertainty of what future political decisions may bring.

What this distinctive political process means for equality in public schools is that the public schools are likely to be required to provide different services to different students—even if everyone agrees this practice mainly accentuates differences. For example, there is broad agreement among educators that disadvantaged children are hurt more than helped by programs that pull them out of regular classrooms for remedial work. Yet the politics of "compensatory education" leads to demands for special treatment that can be easily monitored and documented—hence, veritable mandates for "pull-out" programs. If schools were free to help disadvantaged children however they saw fit, what would guarantee that those children would actually get something extra? The politics of compensatory education is a 30-year saga of ever tightening constraints. Although it is the classic case, it is not unrepresentative of the limitations that public schools face as they try to manage diversity. Public schools are effectively required to treat different children differently.

Private schools are generally not subject to such requirements. They are managed by administrative structures that do not grow out of public authority. There is no politics of comparable consequence, and there is no political uncertainty. The administrative structure exists to facilitate the voluntary relationships between individual schools and families—which is to say, it scarcely exists at all. On most matters, including the management of student diversity, private schools are far freer than public schools to organize as they see fit. Private schools may treat different students differently or they may try to treat all students the same. If they want to treat all students the same, private schools may design grouping practices to do so—or they may simply limit their enrollment to prevent grouping from being feasible or necessary.

How private schools manage diversity depends more on demands from families than on the requirements of bureaucracy, which brings us to a second important difference between educational markets and political institutions, as they are currently structured. In an educational market, parents shop for the school that they believe is right for their child. Placing the child in a particular school is the parents' way of getting "something special" for the child. The odds are great that this school will not be large in size offering different things to different people. In today's public system, parents do not have the opportunity to shop or choose among schools to nearly the degree that parents do in the private market. Children are assigned to public schools, and at least within legal jurisdictions, there is not supposed to be anything special about any schools. The schools are supposed to be the same. If public school parents want something special for their child, they must either work through the political process, which we just described, or they can apply pressure at the school site for special treatment. Public schools are likely to feel more direct pressure from parents than private schools do for the creation of ability groups and special programs and the placement of particular children in them.

Overall, then, we believe public and private schools show different propensities to separate children of different backgrounds because these schools belong to different institutional systems. Direct democratic control encourages the development of bureaucratic classification systems; market control discourages this. Market control also defuses pressure at the school site for special treatment; political control increases it. Despite these differences, educators in both sectors tend to group children homogeneously. But there is a substantially greater willingness in private schools to keep different children together, to give all kids the same educational opportunity.

THE OPERATION OF ABILITY GROUPS

Once schools decide to group kids by ability—and most schools do—there are still major steps schools can take to promote equality. They can ensure nondiscrimination in group placement. They can extend the opportunity to participate in accelerated groups to the largest number of students possible. They can work to provide an equally high quality learning experience in groups at every level.

In our analysis, we considered how public and private schools differ in all these regards. To begin, we found that private schools place more children— about nine percentage points more children—than public schools do in high math ability groups. Of course, private schools may have a higher percentage of very able students than public schools do. So we estimated a model of ability grouping in which the many influences on grouping can be compared. The model is a probit of the placement of a child into one of two categories, the high math group or a lower math group. The model ultimately revealed that the chances of being placed in a high group, all else being equal, are noticeably higher in private schools than in public. An average child has a .480 chance of being placed in a high group in a private school but only a .378 chance in a public school.

The model also provided some interesting information about how group placement decisions are apparently made. In all schools, public and private, ability grouping depends mostly on individual test scores and prior grades. In both public and private schools, there is evidence of affirmative action on behalf of black students. All things being equal, a black student is somewhat more likely than a white student to be placed in a high math group. Why this occurs is unclear. It may be that schools are more willing to give black children the benefit of the doubt in close cases because their scores are generally low and they are therefore underrepresented in high groups. Whatever the case, if we accept test scores and grades as valid placement criteria, there is no evidence of racial discrimination against black students in ability grouping.

Black and disadvantaged students enjoy another edge in high grouping as well. All things being equal, it is harder to get into a high group in a school in which there is lots of competition for spaces, in a school that is high on average in test scores or socioeconomic status. Minority and disadvantaged children tend to attend schools with less competition for high groups and thus, if qualified, are more likely than kids in more competitive schools to get a high placement. This, and the lack of blatant discrimination, does not mean that disadvantaged children are grouped ambitiously to any great degree; they still dominate the low groups. Our observation is simply that matters could be significantly worse.

In eighth grade—or actually just prior to it—schools make an additional grouping decision, a decision that can prove far more important than the assignment of students to ability groups. At this juncture, schools decide which students will take algebra during eighth grade and which students will wait until ninth grade or longer. The importance of this decision is that eighth-grade algebra tends to be a gatekeeper for the academic or college preparatory track in high school. Students who take algebra in eighth grade usually go on to take an accelerated sequence of mathematics classes through the 12th grade and to follow a curriculum aimed at attending a competitive 4-year college. In comparison, students who do not take algebra in eighth grade often take less mathematics and less advanced mathematics down the road and follow a general or vocational curriculum. Of course, the mathematics courses and high school curriculum that students take may be largely a reflection of student preparation or ability. But schools do make course assignments, and schools do have the option of ambitiously assigning students to challenging programs—or of letting students just slide by.

Public and private schools differ significantly in their willingness to place eighth graders in algebra. We found that 60% of private school students are placed in (full- or part-time) algebra, whereas only 42% of public school students are. We also found that this difference is a result of the schools and not of the students in them. We estimated a model of algebra enrollment that asked the following: Is the student taking algebra in eighth grade or not? The estimates indicate that an average child has a .568 chance of being placed in algebra by a private school but only a .401 probability in a public school— provided that algebra is offered in these schools as a separate course.[5] In all schools, placement is most powerfully influenced by math scores and socioeconomic status. As with ability groups, it is tougher, all things being equal, to get into algebra in an academically competitive school. And again, there is no evidence of racial discrimination. If anything, there is affirmative action (in both sectors) on behalf of blacks, Asians, and to a slight extent, Hispanics. All of these influences notwithstanding, there is strong evidence that private schools provide a sizable boost to algebra taking—and to enrollments in high math groups more generally.

Why might this be? One possibility is that in ways we simply have not measured, private school students are better prepared for algebra and accelerated math than public school students are. We cannot rule this explanation out completely. We controlled for the most direct evidence that schools have of math preparedness, however—prior math grades and math scores on standardized tests. We also controlled for a host of student background characteristics that might influence course assignments. And we allowed for competition within schools. In light of this, it seems unlikely that the 10- to 20-point placement probability differences for algebra and high math groups are all because of student differences.

We think the differences more likely derive from the organization of public and private schools and the institutional contexts in which these schools operate. Public schools are organized to be all things to all people, to treat different kids differently, and to meet the needs of many and varied constituents. This has come to mean schools that are internally differentiated with lots of programs, levels, and tracks. In such schools, it makes sense to offer different students different mathematics options in eighth grade—none better and none worse, all simply appropriate for different kids. Private schools tend to be more specialized or focused. They have a vision of what their graduates should achieve, and they try to do the same for all of their students. Private schools therefore tend to offer few electives and to keep all students on the same path, traditionally an academic one.

Public schools have differentiated organizations because they are subject to multiple layers of political control that impose bureaucratic complexity. Private schools tend to have simpler organizations because they lack political control and must instead meet the demands of clients. In education, the market test is easiest to meet with a coherent teamlike organization, not a loosely connected comprehensive one. Perhaps a private school could meet such a test by focusing on goals other than academic excellence—religion, for example—and placing nobody in algebra in eighth grade. But parents who are choosing schools generally seem to care about academic results. And a pretty good recipe for academic results is a rigorous academic curriculum. Academic opportunity, therefore, is more widely—and equally—extended in private schools than in public.

Now, it might still be that the differentiated approach to student organization is a sound and equitable one. It may be better for all students not to push slower learners into tough classes or to burden bright students with slower classmates. It may be better for all students if students are grouped by ability and are offered first-rate programs appropriate to their different levels of preparation. Because both public and private schools engage in a good deal of ability grouping, it is worth looking closely at the quality of the learning experience in different groups.

In our analysis, we looked at a number of indicators of educational quality contained in the student questionnaire. These indicators showed that at least in the eyes of students, the educational environment is better in private schools than in public. On every indicator, a higher percentage of private students than of public students gave highly favorable responses. On several questions bearing directly on the learning experience—for example, "the teaching is good" and "teachers are interested in students"—the differences seem substantial.

Using these indicators, we then looked at differences within schools. We estimated regression models of each measure of the learning environment in public and in private schools. The models predicted an individual student's response to each measure as a function of the average response of other students in the student's school, the student's own socioeconomic status, and the student's ability group in mathematics. The models enable us to estimate whether children in higher groups experience different learning conditions from children in lower groups, controlling for the average learning condition in each school and a proxy for the orientation of each child to learning—socioeconomic status. Estimating separate models for public and private schools enabled us to compare equality across sectors.

The results are not perfectly consistent. Generally, the educational conditions in high groups are more positive than they are in lower groups in both public and private schools. The differences between groups, however, are smaller than criticisms of grouping would lead one to expect. And the disparities are not generally greater within public schools than within private schools. On some indicators of educational conditions—for example, "teachers are interested in students" and teachers "put down" students—the higher and lower groups differ more in public schools than in private schools. On other indicators—for example, "teachers praise my efforts"—private ability groups are farther apart than public ability groups are. In both public and private schools, it seems, the best students have a *somewhat* better experience than average or worse students—when those schools use ability grouping.

Yet two differences between public and private schools do seem to exist. First, the educational conditions within all math ability groups are generally better in private schools than in public schools. Disparities exist within schools in both sectors, but conditions vary around higher means in private schools than in public schools. Second, in schools that serve mostly lower socioeconomic status students—a subject we examine closely in the final part of this chapter—the disparities in group conditions are significantly greater within public schools than within private schools. This finding echoes the results of earlier studies of Catholic schools serving poor families. For example, sociologists Coleman and Hoffer (1987) and Bryk, Lee, and Holland (1993) argue that the undifferentiated Catholic education program and philosophy produce a "common school" effect for children of differing backgrounds.

Why might public and private schools display their various internal differences? Researchers have put forward a number of explanations. We think that the institutions of public and private education provide important clues as well. Public schools, we proposed earlier, are bound by administrative constraints to operate different programs and tracks. They are not free to push all students into ambitious groups or to ignore objective indicators that suggest a different or lower placement. Private schools are free to do whatever is likely to satisfy parents and to use their best professional judgment in placing students. Private schools, as we have seen, still judge that many students are not up to the challenge of accelerated programs. But private schools also believe that the most ambitious placement feasible is the one that is likely to raise students to their full potential. Of course, getting kids to realize their potential is an attractive strategy for satisfying parents. Public schools want to satisfy parents, too. But they must also satisfy higher authorities who mandate how different students must be served. The result, we think, is a higher rate of ambitious placements in private schools.

As for differences in educational experiences within schools, we think institutions also hold part of the answer. Private schools have a powerful incentive to provide the children of all of their families the same educational quality: All parents are paying the same tuition and expecting the same quality. If it is within their power to provide equal quality, private schools will strive to do so. Public schools undoubtedly would like to do this also; parents voting and paying taxes are equally entitled to quality, too. The problem, we think, is that public schools are not as free as private schools to provide equal quality. In particular, public schools are not free to assign teachers to any class or group they please; collective bargaining agreements often give teachers the right to decline assignments—to teach difficult kids, for example—on the basis of seniority or to choose assignments, such as working with the gifted and talented. In general, public schools are not as free as private schools to shape their organizations or to determine the content of their educational programs. Another consequence of these limitations is that public schools cannot as easily as private schools guarantee equality to students, once students are separated.

HIGH SCHOOL TRACKING

Ability groups and class assignments in middle school are precursors of broader and more significant divisions in high school. After eighth grade, students are often organized into general programs of study or tracks that determine the amount and level of academic course work that students take until graduation. These tracks—most often labeled academic, general, and vocational—prepare children for different postgraduation experiences. Academic track students are readied for 4-year colleges or universities; students in other tracks are schooled for work or less academic forms of higher education, such as community colleges.

Tracking has been the target of enormous criticism because it is perceived to be discriminatory and detrimental to students in nonacademic tracks (see Oakes, 1985; Persell, 1977). Tracking has also been the subject of extensive research, especially by educational sociologists, who see a potentially strong link between tracking in schools and economic stratification in society (among many possible sources, see especially Alexander & Cook, 1982; Alexander, Cook, & McDill, 1978; Gamoran & DeMare, 1989; Heynes, 1974). That research has plainly shown that racial minorities and poor children are overrepresented in nonacademic tracks; it has not shown, however, that overrepresentation is the result of discrimination. Research has also documented wide gaps in achievement between students in different tracks, but it has not demonstrated that those gaps are caused or exacerbated by differences in educational quality between tracks. More troubling for tracking is that little evidence supports its supposed benefits: Average achievement seems to be no higher in tracked schools than in untracked ones. Evidence on all of these points, however, is quite debatable. The argument over the merits of tracking therefore rages on.

Our interest in the tracking debate derives from the possibility that schools in different institutional systems may have inherent tendencies to track differently. This is a vitally important consideration if we are concerned with improving schools—raising levels of educational achievement and reducing levels of inequality. If tracking, as it is practiced in public schools today, turns out to be inefficient, inequitable, or both, it is crucial to know why it is so widely practiced and how it can be changed. If high school tracking practices, like middle school grouping practices, have deep institutional roots, it may prove difficult to change tracking without changing institutions, too.

It is well known that private school students are more likely to enroll in an academic track than public school students are. Among 10th graders in the NELS:88 First Follow-up Survey (National Center for Education Statistics, 1992), well over half of all private school students are taking a college prep program, whereas only a third of public school students are.[6] In our analysis, we estimated a model that attempts to determine why. The model attempts to predict whether a student is in an academic track or not.

The model shows, first, that track placements work similarly to ability group decisions and class assignments in middle school. The strongest influence on track placement, by far, is prior academic achievement—measured in this analysis by eighth-grade tests in math, reading, science, and history. A student's socioeconomic status does have some impact, with higher-status children favored. But there is no evidence of racial discrimination against minorities. In fact, there is strong evidence (in both sectors) of affirmative action on behalf of black youngsters. All else being equal, a black child is more likely than a white child to be placed in an academic program. As with middle schools, there is also evidence that competitive high schools, those high in average test scores and socioeconomic status, make it tougher for kids to be placed in the top programs. This, too, may provide a boost for disadvantaged kids who are usually not in competitive schools.

Once all of this is taken into consideration, however, a strong private school effect still seems to remain. A child who is average on every variable specified in this model has only a .302 probability of being placed in an academic track in a public school but a .425 probability of being so placed in a private school. It is true that private school students may be more academically inclined than public school students are. But that greater inclination would have to manifest itself to private schools in subtle yet powerful ways, for the model allows for all of the indicators that schools are said to consider in placing students in tracks. It is therefore unlikely that the public-private difference in tracking probabilities is not due, in some large part, to differences between public and private schools. As we explained before, there are good reasons to expect private schools to be more ambitious in their grouping practices.

Of course, this difference does not mean that the private form of organization is superior on grounds of efficiency or equality. Private schools do extend the college prep opportunity to more students. But in so doing, they could compromise the quality of their advanced courses. Public schools might help children just as well or better than private schools do by offering quality instruction, tailored to different levels of preparation, to students in different tracks. In the analysis, we tried to explore these possibilities.

First, we compared educational conditions in academic and nonacademic track classes. The models that we employed are essentially the same as those that we used to compare conditions in eighth-grade ability groups. The results, however, are somewhat different. Again, there is a tendency for the educational experience to be better for students in academic classes than for students in nonacademic classes in both sectors. And again, differences in experiences are not as large as criticisms of tracking lead one to believe they should be. The disparities in educational experiences, however, are generally greater within public schools than within private schools.

ACHIEVEMENT CONSEQUENCES

The evidence we have seen so far indicates that private schools may do a better job than public schools of providing equal educational outcomes. Private schools strive to do this by offering relatively high proportions of their students the best academic opportunities without compromising the quality of those opportunities for anyone. We have also seen some evidence that for students who do not make it into top groups or programs, the experience may be somewhat better for private students than for public. Now, we want to see if these organizational differences have consequences for student achievement. To do so, we estimated an elaborate regression model of 10th-grade combined math and reading scores.[7] The determinants of achievement include prior (8th-grade) math and reading achievement, and prior history and science achievement, which we included as a proxy for academic ability more generally. The model also includes a generous set of controls for individual background—socioeconomic status, race, sex, and the number of parents in the home. In addition, the model allows for regional variations and for differences between urban, suburban, and rural settings. Finally, the model controls for differences in 8th-grade schooling—for students who switch between public and private schools at the start of high school.

All of the coefficients in the model behaved as expected. Achievement in 10th grade is best predicted by achievement in 8th grade. The coefficients of greatest interest to us are those distinguishing private schools from public schools and academic track students from nonacademic track students. These coefficients reveal three important things. First, private schools provide an independent boost to student achievement relative to public schools, after all else is considered. Second, academic track course work increases achievement beyond levels that would be expected from identical students doing nonacademic course work. And third, students in the academic track end up closer to their nonacademic track schoolmates in the private sector than in the public sector.

In general, we also find that academic track students do equally well, all else being the same, in public and private schools. In other words, by operating a more inclusive academic track, private schools do not compromise the education of their brightest students. Students in the more exclusive academic track in public schools perform no better. Because private schools are providing the highest academic opportunity to more students than public schools are, private schools are also boosting the achievement of more of their better students than public schools are.

SUMMARY

All things considered, the private sector seems to do a better job of promoting equality within schools than the public sector does. Both sectors seem to be nondiscriminating in their internal organizing decisions. But private schools maintain more equality when students are separated, and they succeed more in keeping diverse students together and in extending opportunity widely. Private schools also do a better job of maintaining a decent threshold of quality for students in the lower parts of the ability distribution.

The end result is that students in private schools are more likely to exhibit equal educational outcomes than students in public schools are.

Equality Between Schools

In *Politics, Markets, and America's Schools,* we argued that the quality of a school depends foremost on the quality of its organization—its focus, expectations, leadership, professionalism, and teamwork. Organization was the one overarching characteristic of schools that most influenced student achievement once student background characteristics were taken into account. School organization, we also argued, is strongly influenced itself—most strongly by what we called autonomy. The best predictor of the quality of school organization is the freedom of a school from bureaucratic authority. The freer schools are to staff their own organizations and to define their own educational programs, the more likely they are to be organized effectively. The ultimate problem for public schools, we argued, is that they are part of institutional systems that routinely function to deny schools autonomy and in turn to undermine their organizations and performance. Private schools enjoy an enormous advantage in this regard because the market system of which they are a part promotes autonomy and rewards effective organization and performance.

This does not mean, however, that private schools should consistently outperform public schools, because other factors are involved. Public schools, we observed, tend to be granted ample autonomy if they are part of suburban school systems, which are usually small, homogeneous, and relatively free of political conflict and uncertainty. Public schools can also be granted substantial discretion if the students they are educating do not have serious academic or behavior problems. By the same token, private schools can find themselves constrained by authorities if their students are unusually difficult. On average, then, we expect private schools to have greater autonomy than public schools and a greater chance for success. But we also expect the performance of public and private schools to vary a good deal and to overlap.

This hypothetical variation has important implications for the distribution of schools that might exist in a system of education based on school choice. As critics have observed, a choice system might concentrate difficult students in a limited number of schools and exacerbate inequality across the educational system. As they point out, our analysis shows that autonomy, organization, and, eventually, performance are influenced by the caliber of the students. A choice system might then breed differences between schools and make inequality worse.

We do not believe this would happen. In part, equality is a matter of system design. A system of school choice can be designed to protect or even promote equality between schools. As we have recommended, parents can be prohibited from adding to tuition payments made by the government. Schools can be required to accept certain numbers of educationally disadvantaged children. Parents can be assisted by the government in making informed school choices. Equality, however, is more than a matter of design. We also think it is a systemic characteristic, better protected by markets than by political institutions as we now know them.

In our view, the quality of a school is likely to depend foremost on its autonomy to solve its own problems and on the severity of the problems it must solve. In a market system, autonomy will generally be high. In a system of schools subject to direct democratic control, autonomy will vary with the structure of democratic institutions. Autonomy will generally be high in small, politically homogeneous systems and low in large, politically heterogeneous systems. All else being equal, autonomy will always be higher in market systems than in systems subject to direct political control. Overall, autonomy will tend to vary much more in political systems than in market systems because political institutions vary much more in basic structure than markets do. This is especially true in the United States, in which 15,000 school districts and 50 state governments create a literal multitude of institutional settings for schools.

If autonomy varies much more in political systems than in systems based on markets, then so, too, should school quality. Markets should exert a homogenizing influence on schools, providing relatively equal opportunities to schools to organize effectively and weeding out schools that do not organize effectively. Political institutions should present schools a wider variety of organizing situations—from highly constrained to relatively free—and should basically tolerate the operation of schools consistent with these constraints, regardless of their performance. Private schools should therefore vary less in quality than public schools do.

Except under one condition: If school choice worked to sort children into an array of schools that vary dramatically in student composition, then the homogenizing influence that markets exert on school organizations might be offset by the diversifying influence markets can exert on school enrollments. In a market system, every school would still enjoy more autonomy than it would have in today's political system, all else being equal. But the schools in a market system might serve a more disparate set of students than the schools in the political system serve and consequently develop school organizations that vary more, not less, than politically controlled schools vary. For example, if a market were to sort kids into schools that range from selective academies for child prodigies to holding pens for juvenile delinquents—a specter often painted by market critics—then the benefits of autonomy might indeed be offset. A politically controlled system, with variable bureaucratic constraints but less variable student bodies, might then provide more equal educational results, from one school to the next, than a market system would provide.

There is no way to know for certain how a public system of school choice would sort children into schools. As we said, sorting is substantially a matter of design. And public authorities can take measures to ensure that student bodies do not vary widely in average ability or behavior. The most important of such measures is guaranteeing that every child has available to him or her the same price of admission. Today, the composition of schools in both the public and the private sectors is strongly influenced by the ability of families to pay—tuition in private schools and housing costs in public schools. Many public schools therefore serve student bodies in which every child lives in poverty, whereas other public schools serve children who are uniformly rich. The same goes for private schools. Although the families in private schools must all come up with some tuition money (unless they are offered complete scholarships), certain private schools charge $10,000 and attract children of economic privilege, whereas others charge $750 and serve children who are decidedly poor.

A look at private schools today, therefore, cannot tell us everything we might need to know about the composition and organization of schools that a public system of choice might produce. On the one hand, today's private schools serve only a fraction of the student population and provide only a limited view of how choice might work. On the other hand, today's private schools may provide a good view of how choice might operate at its "worst"— where parents are charged widely varying tuitions, where ability to pay influences enrollments, and where the admissions process is completely unregulated. In other words, today's private schools may help tell us how schools will differ in quality when their student populations are sharply stratified along class lines but when all schools nevertheless enjoy the organizational benefits of markets and autonomy.

SOCIOECONOMIC STATUS AND SCHOOL PERFORMANCE

We begin our analysis with an overview of the schools in today's public and private school systems. First, we considered the full distribution of schools in each sector. Some of what we found is completely unsurprising. The average private school has students who are higher in socioeconomic status than the average public school has. This is a sizable difference—.865 standard deviations—and surely reflects the fact that parents who make tuition payments, however small, have more income than parents who do not. We also found that private schools post average math and reading scores that exceed public school scores by .753 standard deviations. Given the public-private difference in average school socioeconomic status, this test score difference is likewise unsurprising.

What is surprising, however, is what we found when we shifted our attention from the means of the distributions to the variances. We found, first, that the socioeconomic status of private schools varies considerably more than the socioeconomic status of public schools. The variance of the average socioeconomic status of student populations in the private sector is two thirds greater than the comparable variance in the public sector. Although private school families represent a narrower and more affluent part of the total distribution of socioeconomic status, the schools that they attend vary more than the schools attended by public school families in average socioeconomic status. As we suggested, private schools operate at widely varying costs and charge widely varying tuitions, producing a distribution of schools that varies much more than public schools vary in the class composition of each school. Private schools may then provide a good test of how school quality might vary when schools are socioeconomically stratified but free to operate as they judge best.

What then is the surprise? Despite the greater variation in socioeconomic status across private schools, there is less variation in test scores across private schools than across public schools. From school to school, the private sector is more diverse than the public sector in student background but less diverse in test scores. This is rather remarkable because test scores are well predicted (and influenced) by family socioeconomic status. All things being equal, private schools ought to have a wider distribution of average test scores than public schools do because private schools have a wider distribution of average class backgrounds. It appears, however, that all things are not equal. Test scores and class background do not seem to have the same relationship to each other in the two sectors.

Why might this be? One explanation—the one we proposed—is that private schools are more equal in quality than public schools are. The differences between the best and the worst private schools are not as great as the differences between the best and the worst public schools. Thus, the market-place can organize children into schools that differ on average more than public schools differ in socioeconomic status. But because private schools are more similar in organization and effectiveness than public schools are, children in socioeconomically disparate private schools end up reaching more similar levels of academic achievement than children in less disparate public schools. If this interpretation of these data is correct, the equalizing effect of a market system may indeed be great. Private schools are two thirds more diverse than public schools in average class background but slightly less diverse in average student performance.

There are, however, other possible explanations for these distributions. One is that the socioeconomic variance of private schools is deceptively large, inflated mostly by extraordinarily affluent independent schools. The test score variance of private schools only looks narrow by comparison because these affluent schools cannot post the extraordinary test scores that would be required to match their socioeconomic status. Another possible explanation is that the socioeconomic variance of private schools is deceptive in a different way. Private schools may indeed serve groups of children that vary from unusually poor to unusually rich, but the families at the lower end of the distribution may be unrepresentative of the poor. The poor families in private schools may be unusually interested in or supportive of education, and, more to the point, the children of these families may bring relatively strong achievement levels to private school with them. In other words, economically poor students in private schools may be something of a disadvantaged elite that private schools are fortunate to enroll but that private schools do not especially help to learn.

To evaluate these explanations, we divided schools into two categories— schools with student bodies above the median socioeconomic status of all schools, which we label "rich," and schools with student bodies below the median of all schools, which we label "poor." This division enables us to look separately at schools that serve mostly advantaged children and schools that serve mostly disadvantaged children.

Looking first at rich schools, we found that private ones in this category are more affluent on average than public ones and that the private distribution of schools is wider than the public distribution. When we look at test scores, moreover, we found precisely the same thing. The average test score of private schools is higher than the average test score of public schools, and the distribution of average test scores is wider in the private sector than in the public sector. In rich schools, it appears that the socioeconomic makeup of the students and the achievement of the schools are in much the same relationship in the public and the private sectors. It does not appear that extraordinary affluence in certain private schools is the source of the equalizing relationship found in the sample of all schools.

What about poor schools? Several things are of interest. First, the private schools in this category are indeed poor. Their children average nearly one standard deviation below the median socioeconomic status of all schools, and their children are lower in socioeconomic status than the children of poor public schools. The poor private schools are, however, more socioeconomically diverse than the poor public schools, their respective variances differing nearly two to one. If average test scores were predicted by socioeconomic status, as they are in rich schools, the variances of test scores in poor private and public schools would differ similarly. They do not. The variance of poor private school test scores is less than the variance of poor public school scores—despite the greater socioeconomic diversity of the private sector— and private scores are one third of a standard deviation higher.

Unless students in poor private schools are academically rich in some still undisclosed way, it appears that the public and private systems differ in the distribution of quality schools, with the key difference manifest in schools serving relatively disadvantaged children. In the private sector, poor schools are more disadvantaged and more diverse than poor schools in the public sector, yet test scores in poor private schools are higher and less diverse than scores in their public counterparts. Private schools serving poorer children seem to be doing a better and more equal job of promoting academic achievement than public schools serving comparable children. If this is so, the greater equalizing effect that private schools as a whole seem to have is primarily attributable to the threshold of quality that private schools appear to meet for the education of even the most disadvantaged.

A CLOSER LOOK AT STUDENTS IN POOR SCHOOLS

So far, we have considered only the average socioeconomic status of families as we have tried to understand potential causes of performance in poor schools. But what about other student characteristics? Do public and private school children differ in other ways that might explain their different test scores? We began by considering one leading possibility: family composition. We found that students in poor public and private schools are not very different in this regard. Many of these kids, more than in the general population, come from homes where the mother and father are not both present. Private school children have a slight edge in living with their mother and father together, but private school children are also more likely to live with their mother alone. If living without both parents in the home is a handicap— and research suggests that it is—children in poor public and private schools are equally disadvantaged. There are no statistically significant differences.

Much the same is true of family size. Research suggests that children from larger families fare slightly worse in school than children from smaller families, all else being equal. The reason is not entirely clear but undoubtedly has something to do with sibling rivalry for parent attention. At any rate, children in poor public and private schools come from families that are not significantly different in total size. The story is similar for race. There is not a statistically significant difference in the percentage of white students in poor public and private schools. There is a difference, however, in the percentage of black students, although not in the expected direction. Poor private schools, not public schools, enroll a higher percentage of black students—26.5% in the former, only 18.0% in the latter.

Finally, we considered parent education, a component of socioeconomic status, but probably the best predictor of student achievement among individual measures of family background. Here we found some difference, in the expected direction, between public and private school families. Most noticeably, poor private schools enroll only half as many students with parents lacking a high school degree as poor public schools do. This difference is then mirrored in small private school advantages at some but not all higher levels of education. Overall, however, the differences in parent education are not large enough to be confidently labeled statistically significant. The differences are close enough to accepted significance levels not to be ignored, but they may also be meaningless.

In total, the student populations of poor public and private schools look pretty similar. There are no significant differences between them on the measures of family background that are most strongly associated with student achievement. To be sure, the students still differ in one potentially crucial respect: the families of the private school kids decided to sacrifice and pay for private school, whereas the families of the public school kids decided not to make the same sacrifice. In our analysis, we cannot measure or control directly for this difference. But before we concede too much importance to this analytical hurdle, it is important to bear in mind that we are interested not primarily in whether or why private schools are better on average than public schools. We are concerned with whether and why private schools produce less variable results.

If we assume that every private school child gets an unmeasurable boost from unusually supportive parents, we have reason to expect higher achievement from every child in private school than in public school, all else being equal. But we have no reason to expect the distribution of achievement among those equally advantaged private school children to narrow relative to the distribution of achievement among children in public schools. We would only expect unmeasured parental influences to reduce achievement variation among private schools relative to public schools if we expected parental influences to be stronger in private schools *and* less variable too. Researchers tend to agree that unmeasured parental influences are generally stronger in private schools than in public. But whether such influences are also less variable in private schools is unclear. There is good reason, then, to look beyond families to the schools themselves to understand differences in the distribution of achievement across public and private schools.

THE ORGANIZATION OF
PUBLIC AND PRIVATE SCHOOLS

Schools perform differently, we believe, because they are not all equally well organized for the task. This is true of differences between successful and unsuccessful public schools, private schools, or both. The immediate cause of school performance is not the institutional system; the immediate cause is school organization. Institutions are important primarily because of their influence on school organization. Market institutions, we think, produce school organizations that are more effective and more equal than those that current political institutions produce. We have now seen indirect evidence that this may be true. Private schools have higher and less variable average test scores than public schools do, especially among the less advantaged schools, and these differences are not well explained by the types of students in the schools.

Might these differences be explained by organization? We do not have space for a complete exploration of this possibility, but the evidence suggests that organization is important. We saw this first when we considered several basic measures of school organization, and the scores of rich and poor public and private schools on them. Several important relationships emerged from these indicators. The first is that organizational conditions (in the view of school principals) are much better in poor private schools than in poor public schools. For example, in most poor private schools, principals strongly agree that "teachers encourage students to do their best," and that "teachers do not have negative attitudes toward students." The same is true in only half of the poor public schools. The differences are equally stark on all indicators. Perhaps these differences explain why poor private schools, despite being lower in socioeconomic status than poor public schools, post noticeably higher test scores.

Another interesting relationship concerns variation within sectors. On average, the differences in key organizational conditions between rich and poor schools are of similar magnitude in the public and private sectors. In public and private schools alike, principals in rich schools are about 5% more likely than principals in poor schools to agree strongly that educational conditions in their schools are positive. On some indicators—for example, "teachers do not have negative attitudes toward their students"—the differences between rich and poor schools exceed 10%, whereas on other indicators, rich and poor are similar. And other indicators show the gaps between rich and poor schools to sometimes be greater for public schools and sometimes greater for private. Overall, the sectors display similar amounts of variation from schools serving privileged students to schools serving the disadvantaged. What is interesting about this finding is that private schools serve a wider range of socioeconomic groupings than public schools do and should therefore display more disparate school conditions—if student characteristics overwhelmingly determine school climate. Private and public sectors being equally homogeneous in school organization suggests that the market forces shaping private schools may have a more equalizing influence on school quality than the political and bureaucratic forces molding public schools.

This evidence, moreover, is not the strongest indication that markets may have benefits for educational equity. Most remarkable about the organizational attributes of the schools we examined is not that poor private schools look better than poor public schools or that poor private schools are more similar to their rich counterparts than expected. What is most striking about poor schools in the private sector is that on these indicators of school organization and climate, they look better than *rich* schools in the public sector. On average, principals in poor private schools are more than 20% more likely than principals in rich public schools to agree strongly that key conditions in their schools are positive. For example, although 61% of principals in rich public schools agree strongly that "teachers encourage students to do their best," 90% of principals in poor private schools do the same. The major point about private sector organization, it seems, is not that market pressures encourage private schools to be more alike in quality than public schools— although this seems to happen—it is that market pressures encourage all schools, including especially those serving the disadvantaged, to develop important attributes of effective school organization—teamwork, high expectations, and attention to individual needs.

These conclusions are reinforced by additional indicators of organizational effectiveness that are also examined—extra hours that teachers spend working with students and teacher absenteeism. Here we found the same public and private differences as before. The greatest public-private differences occur in poor schools. There we found 15.7% of public school teachers giving less than 5 hours a week in extra time to students but only 1.6% of private school teachers being so stingy. The modal number of extra hours spent by private school teachers is 10.5 to 14 per week; the mode for public school teachers is 5.5 to 10. Among teachers in poor private schools, only 6.3% are absent more than 2 days in a semester; among teachers in poor public schools, the figure is 37.3%. Teachers in poor private schools exhibit greater devotion to their work than teachers in poor public schools do.

In fact, teachers in poor private schools show greater commitment than teachers in rich public schools. And this is the most important finding for evaluating equity under political and market conditions. Even when private schools serve very disadvantaged students, they manage to develop the attributes of effective organization.

Conclusion

The analysis summarized in this chapter is the beginning, and not the ending, of an investigation that we hope will help clarify fundamental sources of inequality in American education. Our suspicion is that the institutions responsible for running American education bear major responsibility for inequality—not because of ill intent or poor design but as a result of their normal functioning. Driven by political conflict, these institutions have developed a bureaucratic control structure that seems to have institutionalized inequality. Within schools, the structure reinforces a system of student classification and educational specialization that exacerbates differences in achievement among students—differences that often run along class and race. Between schools, the structure imposes the most burdensome constraints on the schools that can least tolerate them—schools serving the disadvantaged—and pushes those schools even further behind schools serving the advantaged. Public education consequently produces results that are not only lackluster but also unnecessarily unequal.

We say unnecessarily because, as we saw in our look at private education, it is plainly possible to do better. Public education is not overtly discriminatory in its dealings with disadvantaged students; indeed, there is some evidence of affirmative action on their behalf. But public education could do much more. It could place children of different abilities together in the same groups and classes more often than it does now, exposing slower students to the curriculum and expectations provided to swifter students. It could provide accelerated programs to a higher percentage of students. It could ensure that children organized into different groups, classes, and tracks are provided programs and teachers equally high in quality. And it could work to provide schools now stymied by urban bureaucracies the type of autonomy that promotes effective organization in urban private schools. If public education took these steps, it would surely raise the achievement of its most disadvantaged students and, without jeopardizing the achievement of its best students, raise the average achievement of the system as a whole.

The problem is, these steps cannot easily be taken. If we are correct, the qualities of organization that breed inequality within and between public schools are rooted in the institutions that govern public schools. Unless these institutions are changed, the organization of public schools is unlikely to change—at least in any substantial way. School reformers, after all, have been criticizing tracking and bureaucracy for years; yet efforts to solve these organizational problems have been generally disappointing. We believe institutional reform is necessary. And we believe the market provides the most promising model for carrying it out.

In *Politics, Markets, and America's Schools,* we made the case for institutional reform, based on markets, primarily on grounds of educational efficiency and effectiveness. Now, we would consider taking the case one step further. Markets appear better suited than institutions of direct democratic control to promoting educational equality. Markets seem to encourage the more equitable treatment of students within schools and the more equal distribution of quality across different schools. With public regulation aimed at further promoting their fair operation, markets appear to provide a more promising foundation on which to rebuild public education than the institutions that now govern them. In any case, if the inequality and ineffectiveness that now plague American education are to be substantially reduced, research and reform must work harder to get to their roots.

Notes

1. For a critical introduction to the literature on ability grouping and tracking, see Oakes (1985).

2. For a brief review of the research literature on grouping and tracking, see Gamoran and DeMare (1989).

3. An important exception to this generalization is research into the egalitarian practices of Catholic schools, especially Bryk, Lee, and Holland (1993), Camarena (1990), Coleman and Hoffer (1987), and Lee and Bryk (1988).

4. A data appendix describing the variables used in this chapter is available from the authors on request. Write John E. Chubb, The Edison Project, 521 Fifth Avenue, New York, NY 10175.

5. Some schools, particularly smaller Catholic schools, offer only one eighth-grade math course. Although not titled algebra, such a singular offering will often include the advanced math necessary to prepare students for college track math in high school.

6. Our estimates are from student self-reports. Information from principal surveys suggests that private school students may sometimes report their track as general when in fact it is academic. Our student data may therefore underestimate private student enrollment in academic programs.

7. We do not model the history and science tests because scores in those subjects can be strongly and legitimately influenced by school-to-school variations in curriculum sequences.

References

Alexander, K., & Cook, M. (1982). Curricula and course work: A surprise ending to a familiar story. *American Sociological Review, 47,* 626-640.

Alexander, K., Cook, M., & McDill, E. (1978). Curriculum tracking and educational stratification: Some further evidence. *American Sociological Review, 43,* 47-66.

Bryk, A., Lee, V., & Holland, P. (1993). *Catholic schools and the common good.* Cambridge, MA: Harvard University Press.

Camarena, M. (1990). Following the right track: A comparison of tracking practices in public and Catholic schools. In R. Page & L. Valli (Eds.), *Curriculum differentiation* (chap. 8). Albany: State University of New York Press.

Chubb, J. E., & Moe, T. M. (1990). *Politics, markets, and America's schools.* Washington, DC: Brookings Institution.

Coleman, J. S., & Hoffer, T. (1987). *Public and private high schools: The impact of community.* New York: Basic Books.

Gamoran, A., & DeMare, R. (1989). Secondary school tracking and educational inequality: Compensation, reinforcement, or neutrality. *American Journal of Sociology, 94,* 1146-1183.

Gutmann, A. (1987). *Democratic education.* Princeton, NJ: Princeton University Press.

Heynes, B. (1974). Social selection and stratification within schools. *American Journal of Sociology, 79,* 1434-1451.

Lee, V., & Bryk, A. (1988, April). Tracking and achievement in public and Catholic schools. *Sociology of Education,* 80-94.

National Center for Education Statistics. (1990, July). *National education longitudinal study: A profile of the American eighth grader* (NELS:88). Washington, DC: U.S. Department of Education.

National Center for Education Statistics. (1992). *National education longitudinal study: First follow-up survey.* Washington, DC: U.S. Department of Education.

Oakes, J. (1985). *Keeping track: How schools structure inequality.* New Haven, CT: Yale University Press.

Persell, C. H. (1977). *Education and inequality.* New York: Free Press.

Slavin, R. E. (1990). *Cooperative learning: Theory, research, and practice.* Boston: Allyn & Bacon.

Mythical Choice and Real Standards

Albert Shanker

During the past 12 years, we have heard a great deal of talk about how the salvation of American education lies in allowing public dollars to follow students to private and parochial schools. So-called private school choice was at the heart of the Reagan and Bush administrations' education agendas. It continues to be the subject of education hearings, bills, and referendum initiatives in many states. It continues to crop up at the local level. And, in Milwaukee, Wisconsin, private school choice exists, that is, in the form of a state-initiated experiment that allows a small portion of the district's low-income students to use state education dollars at the few nonsectarian private schools that have agreed to participate in the program.

Of course, this 12-year period does not represent the first time the public has been asked to subsidize the tuition costs of families who choose, and whose children are chosen by, private schools. Nor is Milwaukee the only place in the nation where public dollars support students in private schools. In fact, private and parochial schools enjoy a considerable amount of public assistance. But what has distinguished this movement for public aid to private education from all others is that this one has been marketed almost exclusively on the basis of education reform and improvement—indeed, as the education reform that would eliminate the need to make any other improvements in our schools.

The pitch goes something like this:

> Students in private schools achieve at much higher levels than do public school students. Private schools, particularly Catholic schools, accept students just like the ones attending public schools and do a far better job of educating them. It should be no surprise private schools do so much better. After all, they don't have bureaucracies, teacher unions, tenure, desegregation orders, affirmative action, bans on school prayer, or due process in student expulsion cases to contend with; they are subject only to the discipline of the market. Therefore, to overcome the crisis in education and for the sake of equity, we should use public funds to help all parents, and especially poor parents, send their children to private schools. And choice will turn around America's poor record of student achievement.

The Value of Choice: Mythical or Real?

Are the claims of private school choice supporters substantiated? Certainly, a number of private schools are doing marvelous things for low-income youngsters they choose to admit. It is equally true that a number of public schools are doing marvelous things for low-income youngsters, although these public schools cannot select their students and, more often than not, have not a handful of low-income students but an entire schoolful.

But the answers to the question of private school choice should not turn on a war of anecdotes; each side has heartwarming cases in its arsenal. And although I doubt that research will settle this debate, it can certainly inform it more than anecdotes. What, then, does the evidence tell us about whether private schools are outperforming public schools and about whether they are working with the same kids but getting far better results?

The most relevant, and largest-scale, evidence comes from the federally funded National Assessment of Educational Progress (NAEP), which has been measuring the achievement of a nationally representative sample of 4th-, 8th-, and 12th-graders (previously, 9-, 13-, and 17-year-olds) in a variety of subjects for more than 20 years. Although some previous NAEPs included private school students, it was not until the 1990 NAEP (1991) in mathematics that comparisons between the achievement of public and private school students were made public. These results show virtually no difference in the performance of public and parochial and other private schools (see Table 8.1). Appallingly, students in both sectors are achieving at disastrously low levels. This evidence means that under so-called private school choice, if half or even all of our public school students were to "choose" and be chosen by private

TABLE 8.1 Average Proficiency and Percentage of Students at or Above Four Anchor Levels on the NAEP Mathematics Scale by Type of School (NAEP's 1990 Assessment)

	Percentage of Students	Average Proficiency	Percentage of Students at or Above			
			Level 200	Level 250	Level 300	Level 350
GRADE 4						
Public schools	88 (1.2)	214 (0.9)	70 (1.3)	10 (0.8)	0 (0.0)	0 (0.0)
Catholic schools	8 (1.1)	224 (2.0)	83 (2.6)	16 (2.2)	0 (0.0)	0 (0.0)
Other private schools	4 (0.8)	231 (2.8)	89 (3.8)	22 (3.4)	0 (0.0)	0 (0.0)
GRADE 8						
Public schools	89 (1.3)	264 (1.2)	97 (0.5)	66 (1.3)	13 (1.3)	0 (0.1)
Catholic schools	7 (1.1)	278 (2.6)	100 (0.2)	84 (2.6)	22 (3.4)	0 (0.2)
Other private schools	4 (0.7)	274 (2.4)	100 (0.5)	80 (3.8)	18 (2.9)	0 (0.0)
GRADE 12						
Public schools	90 (1.3)	295 (1.1)	100 (0.1)	90 (0.7)	45 (1.4)	5 (0.6)
Catholic schools	6 (1.1)	302 (3.0)	100 (0.0)	96 (1.2)	54 (4.5)	4 (1.0)
Other private schools	4 (0.8)	301 (3.1)	100 (0.0)	97 (1.1)	51 (4.8)	4 (1.8)

SOURCE: National Assessment of Educational Progress (1991, Table 2.6 and Executive Summary, pp. 6-7).
NOTES: The standard errors of the estimated percentages and proficiencies appear in parentheses. It can be said with 95% certainty that for each population of interest, the value for the whole population is within plus or minus two standard errors of the estimate for the sample. When the proportion of students is 0%, the standard error is inestimable. Although percentages less than 0.5% are rounded to 0%, a few eighth-grade public school students (0.2%) and Catholic school students (0.1%) reached Level 350.
Description of NAEP Levels:
  Level 200: Simple additive reasoning and problem solving with whole numbers; content typically covered by third grade.
  Level 250: Simple multiplicative reasoning and two-step problem solving; content typically covered by fifth grade.
  Level 300: Reasoning and problem solving involving fractions, decimals, percents, elementary geometry, and simple algebra; content introduced by seventh grade.
  Level 350: Reasoning and problem solving involving geometry, algebra, and beginning statistics and probability; content generally covered in high school math courses in preparation for the study of advanced math.

schools tomorrow, we would still be a nation at risk. We also would be a nation that had abandoned its common school ideals.

What, specifically, do the 1990 NAEP math results in Table 8.1 indicate about public and private school performance? The most logical place to start is with the 12th grade, the end of the elementary-secondary school road, where we can make some judgments about the value added by a public or private school education. The first thing to notice is that there is only a 6- or 7-point difference, on a 500-point scale, in average scores among seniors in public, Catholic, and other private schools. That is not much of a difference, and it is certainly not evidence of the superiority of private over public education.

It is true that slightly more than half of the seniors in private schools achieve at the 300 level, which means they can handle questions involving decimals, fractions, percents, elementary geometry, and simple algebra. This is a few percentage points better than the public school figure, but, again, it is hardly evidence for the excellence of private school education. The relevant fact is that both school sectors performed miserably: Approximately half of the graduating seniors, from both public and private schools, cannot handle math operations they should have mastered before they even entered high school.

For still worse news, let's look at the proportion of graduating seniors who achieved at or above level 350, which NAEP terms an indicator of readiness to tackle college-level math. The proportion is 5% in the public schools and 4% in both the Catholic and other private schools. Five percent is nothing to cheer about, but neither is 4%. It is, of course, possible that this public school figure is higher than the private school figure only because public schools have a higher dropout rate; more of the kids who would have scored poorly are gone. But if you adjust for public school dropout rate, and even if you ignore the private school dropout rate, the result is that 4% of students graduating from public school are prepared to take on college math, as are 4% of students graduating from Catholic and other private schools. And yet about 30% to 35% of American high school graduates go on to 4-year colleges.

These results are even more shocking when compared with the achievement of students in our competitor nations, in which 20% to 35% of students meet standards that are more rigorous than NAEP's 350 level to get into college. Given those international standards, it is not unreasonable to assert that 95% of U.S. public and private high school graduates would not be admitted to college anywhere else in the industrialized world.

"OK, so there's not much difference between the performance of public and private schools in the 12th grade, and their students are in a dead heat at NAEP's highest level," private school choice supporters might say. "But look at the 4th- and 8th-grade average scores. There's a 10 to 17 spread in points there, and a clear case of private school superiority."

Let's say, then, that it makes more sense to concentrate on results one third or two thirds of the way through the education process instead of on the end results. From this perspective, one could just as readily argue that the NAEP results show that the longer students stay in private schools, the worse they do, and the longer students stay in public schools, the better they do; private school children end up scoring like public school children, and public school children end up scoring like private school children. Rather than constituting proof of private school superiority, the evidence suggests that public schools add more value to their students than do private schools!

This conclusion looks less glib—and the small differences between public and private school achievement in all the grades look more shocking—when examining how different public school students are from the youngsters who attend Catholic and other private schools. Because contrary to what private school choice supporters claim, especially about Catholic schools, the students that public and private schools educate are not alike, not even remotely so. In fact, given the dramatic differences in their socioeconomic status and in the courses they take, to name just two, what is surprising is not that private school students, on average, performed slightly better than public school students but that they did not leave public school students behind in the dust.

Private school choice proponents like to talk as if the only barrier to a private school education is tuition, a barrier public dollars could topple (although clearly not at the more expensive private schools, whose tuition is many times the amount even the most generous voucher proposals would offer). Tuition is certainly a barrier, but the other basic difference between public and private schools is that private schools can and do select their students and turn away applicants who do not meet their standards. For example, 71% of Catholic high schools require an entrance exam, as do 43% of other religious schools and 66% of independent schools. Moreover, 71% of Catholic high schools cite student discipline as their chief admissions criterion, and 80% require that entering students have successfully completed their previous year of school (National Center for Education Statistics, 1987). Virtually all private schools require interviews with students and parents to see how they will "fit," and most religious schools either do not admit outside their faith or give preference to students from that faith. In other words, private schools are not obliged to take all comers, as public schools must, and they are free to get rid of students who do not work out, who generally end up in the public schools. Private school choice really means, then, that parents may choose a private school, but it is the private school that ultimately decides whether or not to choose the child.

So who are these students? They turn out to be children who should have given private schools an enormous edge over public schools in achievement. According to the background data in the sample of 12th-grade students tested by NAEP, about 50% more private school youngsters than public school youngsters have college-graduate parents (see Figure 8.1). For the nation as a whole, the difference between public and private school students in level of parent education is even more dramatic, as illustrated in Figure 8.2: 30% of parochial school students' parents and 57% of the parents of students in other private schools had graduated from college, in comparison with 19% of public school students' parents.

If education research tells us anything, it is that higher education translates into higher incomes and that both are strongly associated with higher academic achievement. Even on the basis of family income alone, private school students should have performed dramatically better. According to the national

Figure 8.1. Education Level of Parents for Public and Private School Students: Grade 12
SOURCE: NAEP (1991).

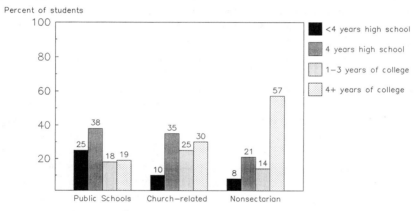

Figure 8.2. Parental Education Levels of Elementary and Secondary Students in Public, Parochial, and Other Private Schools
SOURCE: National Center for Education Statistics (1991, Figure 3-6, p. 47).

figures in Figure 8.3, about three times as many public school students as private and parochial school students had family incomes under $15,000, whereas twice as many parochial school students and more than three times as many other private school students had family incomes of $50,000 and

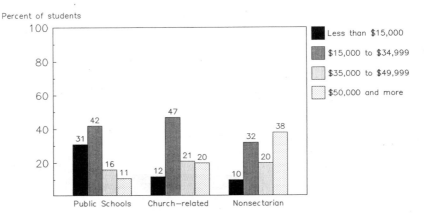

Figure 8.3. Family Income of Elementary and Secondary Students in Public, Parochial, and Other Private Schools

SOURCE: National Center for Education Statistics (1991, Figure 3-5, p. 46).

more. Consider, too, that private schools in the NAEP sample and nationally are dramatically underrepresented in rural and disadvantaged communities, in which the nation's poorest youngsters live, and that poverty is strongly associated with lower academic achievement.

Socioeconomic status makes a big difference in student achievement, but school counts, too. And there are big differences in what public and private school students take in school. For example, 81% of the private school seniors and only 56% of the public school seniors in the NAEP sample were in an academic track. (More on this private school "advantage" later—and on why ending choice of curriculums in public school is a far better strategy for improving education than starting a private school choice system.) So why, given that taking more academic courses, like having better-educated and wealthier parents, is strongly associated with higher scores, did public and private schools have an identical record in the percentage of students they produced who were prepared to handle college-level math? And why were the average scores of private school seniors so close to those of public school seniors?

In fact, these considerable differences between the family and academic backgrounds of public and private school youngsters explain why, when you look only at *average* test scores, private school students do somewhat better— although well below what you would expect, given their advantages. But what happens when you compare the NAEP scores of public and private school

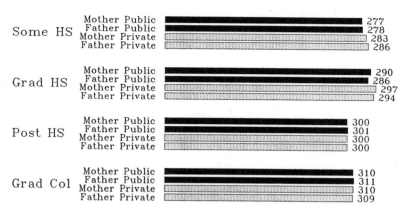

Figure 8.4. Mathematics Achievement at Grade 12 by Level of Parental Education: Public and Private Schools

SOURCE: NAEP (1991).

students who have similar family backgrounds and who have taken similar courses—if you compare apples with apples? The answer is that their achievement is almost identical (see Figure 8.4).

For example, when you compare (in Figure 8.4) the scores of public and private 12th graders whose parents have similar education levels, the sector differences become even narrower. Or look at the results in Figure 8.5 when 8th graders are matched according to the math courses they have taken: Public school students who have had pre-algebra score 274, and private school students score 273. The results are similar for 8th graders who have taken algebra, except that public school kids score four points higher than kids from private schools: 298 as opposed to 294.

It is the same story in Figure 8.6 when you compare the scores of public and private school seniors who have taken similar courses. Among kids who have taken only Algebra I, private school students score slightly better; among kids who have taken more advanced courses, public school students score slightly better. But the point is that for private and public school kids who have done the same course work, there are no big differences in their achievement; there is no private school "advantage." When you consider that these comparisons by courses taken did not factor in the big differences in public and private school students' backgrounds, the proposition that public schools are adding more value to their students than are private schools becomes even more plausible.

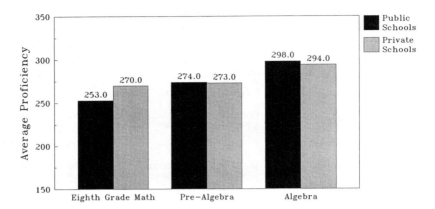

Figure 8.5. Average Overall Mathematics Proficiency by Students Taking Similar
Courses: Grade 8
SOURCE: NAEP (1991).

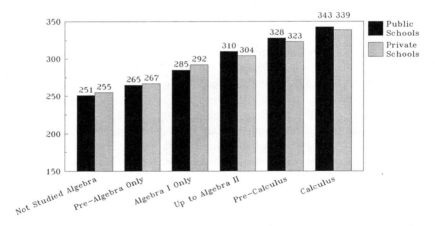

Figure 8.6. Average Overall Mathematics Proficiency by Students Taking Similar
Courses: Grade 12
SOURCE: NAEP (1991).

Now, Chubb and Moe (1991) have contended that the reason public and
private school achievement is so close in the 12th grade is that public high
schools get many private school student transfers. These well-prepared trans-

fers, according to their argument, are the yeast that makes public school achievement rise. The source of data for Chubb and Moe's contention is the National Education Longitudinal Study of 1988, known as NELS:88 (National Center for Education Statistics [NCES], 1990), which tested a large group of students in 8th grade and again in 10th grade and found that the youngsters in private schools had made much greater gains than public school students. Like comparisons of public and private schools using "average" test scores—be they NAEP, the SAT, or any other instrument—this turns out to be half the story, however.

A whopping 37% of students left parochial school for public school after eighth grade. But who were these kids? It turns out that almost half of them came from families whose socioeconomic status fell in the bottom 25%. The transfer of these private school students into public schools almost certainly did not raise public schools' scores; rather, their departure from private schools almost certainly raised parochial school scores. The evidence points in exactly the opposite direction from what Chubb and Moe claim (NCES, 1990).

Chubb and Moe have further suggested that the 1990 national NAEP results in mathematics are an anomaly. Yet that, too, does not withstand scrutiny. First, although this was the first time that NAEP reported out public-private school comparisons, it is not the first time that NAEP collected private school data. In 1988, Chester E. Finn, Jr., who was then an assistant secretary in the U.S. Department of Education, presented unpublished public-private school comparisons from the 1986 NAEP assessments of reading, history, and literature to the annual meeting of the National Association of Independent Schools (see Goldberg, 1988). According to Finn, private school students (including parochial school kids) scored, on average, only about four points higher than public school students on reading and six points higher on history and literature. He also said that the soon-to-be-released 1986 math exams would show a similarly insignificant differential. Finn then pointed out that twice as many private school students as public school students taking the tests had parents who were college graduates, which probably explained the slightly higher average private school score. He suggested that because of the differences in parental education, perhaps there was no school effect. He advised private schools to improve (faster than public schools) if they wanted parents to keep paying high tuition (Goldberg, 1988).

Second, the American Federation of Teachers has conducted preliminary analyses of the national NAEP assessments in science in 1990 (NAEP, 1992) and math in 1992 (NAEP, 1993) similar to those for the 1990 NAEP (1991) in math. All these analyses are consistent with the conclusions I have presented here.

Even Coleman, whose 1981 analysis of public-private school performance is cited as the premier source of scientific evidence of private school superiority, warned that "one should not make a mistake: Our estimates for the size of the private-sector effects show them not to be large" (p. 19). A small army of other researchers have shown that the small private school edge found by Coleman disappeared when differences in students' family background and course taking were examined.

That leaves Chubb and Moe's *Politics, Markets, and America's Schools* (1990). Lots of politicians and op-ed writers have repeated their findings as gospel, and many individuals have become converts to public aid for private education on their academic authority. But as their peer reviewers and even a few statistics-savvy journalists have pointed out, Chubb and Moe's study of public and private high schools also did not find a private school advantage once students' background characteristics and academic courses were taken into account; their "choice" recommendations were not supported by the results of their analysis.

The failure of Chubb and Moe's (1990) analysis to yield them support for their conclusions is not particularly surprising. The evidence they use comes exclusively from the High School and Beyond Study, the same data that failed to yield Coleman sizable private sector effects. Moreover, despite the considerable print they expend on discussing why their handling of these data is an advance over other researchers' methods, Chubb and Moe virtually ignore all that has been learned about how to work responsibly with what is now acknowledged to be this deeply flawed, if not worthless, data set. What they do instead is highly unorthodox. A short list includes throwing in elite private and other private schools along with Catholic schools in a way that automatically conferred a private school advantage in their public-private analysis; constructing a school organization measure of 50 variables, making it almost impossible to single out the effects of any one variable; pioneering the use of a dependent variable that measures achievement change in a way that exaggerates high and low performance differences—and then conceding, in a footnote in the back of their book, that this has no substantive meaning; and reporting results in terms of average differences between schools in the highest quartile of performance (87.5th percentile) and the lowest quartile (12.5th percentile), which makes for extreme comparisons. As Witte (1991b) has decisively pointed out,

> They never directly test the *differential effect of public and private schools on achievement*. . . . Prior studies either ran separate regressions for public and private school students, or analyzed all students together but included a variable indicating whether the student was in a public or private school. They did neither. (p. 21)

Methodological pyrotechnics notwithstanding, Chubb and Moe still fail to prove their hypothesis: *All* of their variables taken together explain only about 5% of the variation in achievement. Even when they ask what would happen if we moved students from a school in the lowest quartile of effective organization to the highest, the answer is they would get less than one more answer correct on a 115-item test (Bryk & Lee, 1992; Rosenberg, 1990-1991; Shanker & Rosenberg, 1991; Witte, 1990, 1991).

Two other pieces of evidence debunking the private school superiority myth come from Milwaukee. The first concerns Catholic schools, and it is a rare find because Catholic and other private schools are not required to report their students' test scores to the public. When Catholic schools do on occasion, it is always in average scores aggregated at the local or national level. But Marie Rohde, the religion reporter for the *Milwaukee Journal,* persisted in asking the Milwaukee archdiocese to provide a finer breakdown, and her request was eventually granted. In her story, Rohde (1991) reported that test results revealed that minority elementary students in Milwaukee's Catholic schools experienced the same achievement gap as their counterparts in public schools. The test was the same one used by the Milwaukee public schools, the Iowa Test of Basic Skills. The scores, Rohde concluded, contradicted the prevalent claim that Catholic schools did a better job of educating students who were disadvantaged. In fact, although the scores of public school minority students have been stable, those of minority children in the Milwaukee Catholic schools have declined.

Rohde also reported that John Norris, superintendent of the Catholic schools, pointed to the disadvantaged backgrounds of the students to explain the gap and argued against comparing Catholic school and public school achievement. But 2 years earlier, it was the archdiocese that made such a comparison, albeit an illegitimate one using scores from a test that was not used in the public schools and without breaking down results by individual school or by race. The lesson of this "comparison" that the archdiocese drew for the public was that Catholic schools were superior to public schools, managing to perform above the national average even while serving disadvantaged minority students. A more appropriate lesson, however, is that averages can obscure as much as they illuminate.

The other piece of evidence from Milwaukee comes from its much vaunted, state-initiated voucher experiment. The product of a coalition between Polly Williams, a Democratic state legislator from Milwaukee and the former chair of Jesse Jackson's presidential campaign efforts in Wisconsin, and Governor Tommy Thompson, a conservative Republican, the Milwaukee voucher program began in September 1990 and was open to a maximum of 1,000 low-income children in a district in which about 60,000 children met the law's definition of poverty. The voucher was worth $2,500, paid out of the public schools' budget. The law excluded religious schools from participating, but 22 private schools were eligible. In the first year of the program, only 7 eligible schools volunteered to participate. By the 1994-1995 school year, 23 schools were eligible and 12 participated (Witte, 1991a; Witte, Thorn, Pritchard, & Claibourn, 1994).

More than 80% of the voucher students were concentrated in only 4 schools. Three of the 12 participating schools in 1994-1995 were somewhat integrated, 4 were almost exclusively African American, with 4 others predominantly so, and 1 school was 93% Hispanic. The fourth-year evaluation report terms this pattern "partly the result of conscious specialization on the part of schools (for example, African American cultural schools and a bilingual school); and partly the result of locations" (Witte et al., 1994, p. 11).

Enrollment in the voucher program has increased slowly but steadily, from 341 students in the first year to 830 presently, but enrollment has never reached the maximum allowed by the law. Applications have exceeded seats by a current low of 64 to a high of 307 in 1993-1994. The private schools determine the number of seats available to voucher-eligible students, as well as who they will admit, and they are not forbidden to use achievement or behavioral information about students in making admissions decisions. Several schools explicitly state in their literature that they cannot handle learning disabled or emotionally disturbed youngsters; public schools are required by federal law to do so (Witte et al., 1994).

Some of the participating schools are not on firm financial footing. The worst case occurred in the first year of the program and involved a financially strapped religious school that had dropped (arguably) its religious orientation to participate in the program and attract new students and money. The school nonetheless went bankrupt, and 150 students, 63 of them voucher students, essentially lost a year's worth of schooling. Evaluators' recommendations that schools participating in this publicly funded voucher program be required to conduct and file an annual financial audit that meets accounting standards for private, nonprofit organizations have not been heeded—nor have their recommendations that participating schools have a formal governance structure and at least some board members without a proprietary interest in the school. The same is true of their recommendation that participating private schools be required to meet state standards for student outcomes, including tests and dropout reporting (Witte, 1991a; Witte, Bailey, & Thorn, 1992, 1993; Witte et al., 1994).

Because the law limits participation to parents who are poor, it is no surprise that the voucher-program families, like low-income Milwaukee public school parents, are poor. There are some notable differences, however, between the voucher parents and comparison groups of parents in the Milwaukee public schools. The voucher parents had fewer children, higher levels of education (particularly among the mothers), higher educational expectations of their children, and greater involvement in their children's school and in their educational activities at home. Thus, the low-income voucher parents are a more "select" group than the low-income public school parents. In prior student achievement, however, the children of the voucher parents were comparable with the low-income public school students. Comparisons of behavior records were not discussed in the evaluation reports, but the evidence is clear that the academic performance of the voucher students had not been good in their prior public schools.

What about the achievement of the voucher students in their new private schools? Because greater academic achievement was the prime justification for the voucher program and the superiority of private over public schools the prime hypothesis of the voucher experiment, this is the most important question. The answer is that there were certainly no dramatic gains in achievement made by the voucher students in private schools, either in absolute terms or relative to the Milwaukee public school (MPS) students. The generally poor prior academic record of the voucher students did not turn around, and the private schools, despite their "advantages," did not outperform the public schools.

In the first year, voucher students' reading scores increased slightly, as did MPS students' scores. In the second year, reading scores of voucher students fell significantly, whereas MPS students' scores increased. In the third and fourth years, voucher students' reading scores remained the same, and MPS students' scores declined insignificantly. Math scores for voucher students were flat in the first 2 years of the experiment, increased significantly in the third year, and declined significantly in 1994. Math scores for the MPS students rose significantly in the first year, were flat in the second year, declined significantly in the third year, and were essentially unchanged in 1994.

According to the fourth-year evaluation report (Witte et al., 1994), more fine-grained regression analyses

controlling for a number of factors and comparing choice students to MPS students show mixed and mostly insignificant results over the four years. *Thus there is no systematic evidence that choice students do either better or worse than MPS students once we have controlled for gender, race, income, grade and prior achievement.* In addition, when we included variables distinguishing the number of years choice students were in private school, the results varied (the signs of the effects changed) and were not statistically significant at conventional levels. (italics added; pp. v, 12-19)

Have there been any benefits from this experiment—any positive results to justify the continued rhetoric about the great gains to be realized from a school voucher system? It seems that the parents of the voucher students—at least those parents who did not leave the program—are happier with the private schools than they had been with their children's prior public schools. Their children are achieving no better, but they are more content. This is pleasing, but it is hardly justification for a radical change in public policy and in our traditions. We do not, moreover, have a crisis of happiness of this nation; we do have a major program with academic achievement. As the Milwaukee results show, vouchers get us nowhere on this problem while creating a host of new and perhaps irremediable problems of their own.

Applying Real Standards

The evidence is fairly overwhelming, then, that all the talk about how private schools are doing a better job than public schools, especially with disadvantaged students, is just talk. This does not mean, however, that private schools have nothing to teach public schools. For instance, public schools could stop giving students a choice of curricula—they choose easier ones—and insist that they take more academically challenging courses, the way they do in Catholic and other private schools. Indeed, in addition to choosing students, the main private school advantage consists of not offering their students much choice. If making public-private school comparisons has taught us anything, it is not that choice will turn around our schools; it is that clear and rigorous standards in education are absolutely essential.

The public school system also could start heeding the message many parents, especially poor minority parents, have been trying to convey when they remove their children to Catholic and other private schools: Teachers can't teach and students can't learn when a handful of violent or disruptive kids are allowed to terrorize the school community. Something needs to be done for those kids, but right now the failure of many school boards to face up to the issue means that public school youngsters who want to achieve, and that is a majority, are held hostage by a small number of destructive kids. Private schools do not tolerate that, and neither should public schools.

Another lesson private schools have to teach policymakers and the public is about children in poverty. As the NAEP results (1991, 1992, 1993) indicate, most of the advantage private schools have in average scores is because of their more advantaged students. In fact, the results of NAEP and other assessments demonstrate that childhood poverty is not only bad for America morally and socially but also a disaster educationally. Of course, many poor children do well in school, and education continues to be a major route out of poverty. But it is also the case that poverty, especially when it is accompanied by family and community disintegration, is associated with lower academic achievement. Overcoming childhood poverty may not solve our crisis in education, but it would take us a good stretch down that road.

Would permitting public dollars to follow children to private and parochial schools turn our education system upside down? Would it destroy neighborhood schools and transform public education into a system for the have-nots? Would it violate the separation between church and state to the detriment of both? Could it lead to public money going to cult schools, radical schools (of the left and the right), and crassly commercial schools thrown together by people out for a quick buck? Would it mean less accountability in education because private and parochial schools, unlike public schools, are not required to publicly report their test results or their finances? Might it sanction a school system stratified by class, religion, ethnicity, and race and thereby undermine our pluralistic democracy?

The risks involved in public aid to private education are substantial, and they are not balanced by any evidence of educational benefit. In fact, the results of NAEP and other national studies show that if we want American children to meet world-class education standards—or even be able to do junior high math by the time they leave high school—then spending tax dollars to send them to private and parochial schools is a bankrupt strategy.

The dismal performance of private schools also means that those who have charged that bureaucracy or teacher unions or desegregation orders or democratic control is chiefly responsible for our crisis in education had better look elsewhere, because private schools are not constrained by any of these. But it further means that public schools cannot blame their dismal performance exclusively on the deterioration of families and communities. Because even if public schools were to get the types of kids private schools have—handpicked and with parents who are relatively well educated and able and/or motivated to spend money on schooling—and even if public schools, like the private schools, were to have smaller schools or class sizes or more flexibility in removing troublemakers, the evidence indicates that student achievement would still be at a level that is far below the best international standards.

That is shocking, but it should not cause us to despair. Rather, it underscores, and in the strongest possible way, the case for restructuring our schools. The majority of our youngsters—even the handpicked, more academically tracked students in private schools—are not achieving at the levels they and this nation need. As surprising, then, as the results of the public-private school comparisons may be, they are not really shocking: Public and private schools by and large have the same textbooks, the same curricula, the same internal organizations—and the same mediocre academic standards. Exceptions exist in both sectors, which, of course, means these are not sectoral differences.

Public and private schools also have students who are subject to the same incentives for working hard in school—that is, few such incentives. College-bound students in both public and private schools know they will be able to find a college that will accept them, no matter how poor their grades are or how little they know, as long as they have a high school diploma and, usually, money—and in the latter case, the private school kids do have an advantage. The one exception is students in either school sector who hope to attend elite universities; they have to work hard indeed.

As for going to work from high school, students in both public and private schools know that employers don't ask to see high school transcripts and don't even offer decent jobs to high school graduates until they are 24 or so, if then. So students who have worked hard at rigorous courses will be competing for the same poor job at the same low pay with students who have filled their schedules with soft courses that they barely passed. And these bad lessons are learned by students in public and private schools alike.

What about parents? Why aren't they making sure youngsters apply themselves? That's easy. Whether kids are in public or private schools, most parents will not be successful at pressuring them to work harder when the kids can tell them, "I've already done what I need to do to get what I want."

As for teachers, they have a hard enough time, under the best of circumstances, persuading kids that history or physics or even regular attendance is "relevant" to their future lives. But when the kids can say, "I don't need that to get into college or to get a job; it doesn't count" or "Taking that course will pull my average down," the battle is lost before it starts.

One solution, although no means the only one, is for American businesses to link getting jobs with high school achievement and for colleges to do the same thing in setting admission standards. Elementary and secondary schools would then have backup for upholding standards. Parents and teachers would have backup when they say, "Unless you turn off the television set and work harder, you're not going to make it." And our students would have evidence that working hard and learning something are essential to getting what they want. At the least, they would see a reason to achieve, and because they are no less able than students in competitor nations, they would.

The poor outcomes of both public and private education also indicate that there is not much to the argument that the competition that school choice would produce would in turn serve as an excellent accountability system. As the argument goes, parents would make school decisions on the basis of educational excellence, so bad schools would go under and good schools would thrive and be replicated. But there are parents who choose private schools and who keep their youngsters there despite, as NAEP tells us, their mediocre performance. This suggests that under a choice system, schools would not necessarily compete, nor parents choose, primarily on the basis of educational quality and outcomes. It is well worth remembering that the majority of American parents believe that their youngsters, and the schools they attend, are performing well.

Conclusions

Choice, then, may be a reasonable incentive if we want schools to work hard to attract customers, but it is a poor incentive for getting them to focus on improving student achievement. The only way to do that is to do so directly, that is, to move to a standards-driven education system and to design school-wide incentives in which there are rewards for improving student achievement and consequences for failure.

The idea of an accountability system for schools that involves rewards and consequences is radical and controversial, and it would need to be tested to see what works, when, and how. But the idea of an accountability system based on private school choice is also radical and controversial, and the evidence tells us it would not work. This much is clear: Even if the public rejects private school choice, it will not stand for the status quo in public education. Either there will be a new accountability system in education that both the public and educators can believe in, or some crazy accountability scheme that would be disastrous both for education and for this nation will be imposed on us.

The private school choice schemes that are pushed across the nation will not help kids find out that they need to work hard in school to get what they want, just as they must on the athletic field and in the world of work. They will not stimulate schools to focus on improving student achievement and to experiment with new ways of doing so. They will not help poor schools get better, nor will they empty them out. They will not produce greater account-ability in education; they undoubtedly will yield less. They certainly will not eradicate the effects of childhood poverty. And they will not solve the crisis in education because that crisis afflicts public and private schools alike.

References

Bryk, A. S., & Lee, V. E. (1992, December). Is politics the problem and markets the answer? An essay review of *Politics, markets, and America's schools. Economics of Education Review, 11*(4), 439-451.

Chubb, J. E., & Moe, T. M. (1990). *Politics, markets, and America's schools.* Washington, DC: Brookings Institution.

Chubb, J. E., & Moe, T. M. (1991, July 26). The private vs. public school debate. *Wall Street Journal,* p. A8.

Coleman, J. S. (1981). Response to Page and Keith. *Educational Researcher, 10,* 18-20.

Goldberg, K. (1988, March 9). "Gravest threat" to private schools is better public ones, Finn warns. *Education Week,* p. 1.

National Assessment of Educational Progress. (1991, June). *The state of mathematics achievement: NAEP's 1990 assessment of the nation and the trial assessment of the states* (Report No. 21-ST-04). Washington, DC: U.S. Department of Education, National Center for Education Statistics, Office of Educational Research and Improvement.

National Assessment of Educational Progress. (1992, March). *The 1990 science report card: NAEP's assessment of fourth, eighth, and twelfth graders* (NCES Report 92-064). Washington, DC: U.S. Department of Education, National Center for Education Statistics, Office of Educational Research and Improvement.

National Assessment of Educational Progress. (1993, April). *NAEP 1992 mathematics report card for the nation and the states: Data from the national and trial state assessments* (Report No. 23-ST02). Washington, DC: U.S. Department of Education, National Center for Education Statistics, Office of Educational Research and Improvement.

National Center for Education Statistics. (1987). *Private schools and private school teachers: Final report of the 1985-86 private school study.* Washington, DC: U.S. Department of Education.

National Center for Education Statistics. (1990, July). *National education longitudinal study of 1988: A profile of the American eighth grader* (NELS:88). Washington, DC: U.S. Department of Education.

National Center for Education Statistics. (1991, February). *Private schools in the United States: A statistical profile, with comparisons to public schools.* Washington, DC: U.S. Department of Education.

Rohde, M. (1991, August 1). Minority test scores at Catholic schools mirror lag in city. *Milwaukee Journal,* p. 1.

Rosenberg, B. (1990, December/1991, January). Not a case for market control. *Educational Leadership, 48*(4), 64-65.

Shanker, A., & Rosenberg, B. (1991, Winter). *Politics, markets and America's schools: The fallacies of private school choice.* Washington, DC: American Federation of Teachers.

Witte, J. F. (1990, August 30-September 3). *Understanding high school achievement: After a decade of research, do we have any confident policy recommendations?* Paper presented at the 1990 annual meeting of the American Political Science Association, San Francisco.

Witte, J. F. (1991a, November). *First-year report: Milwaukee parental choice program.* Madison: University of Wisconsin.

Witte, J. F. (1991b, September). *Public subsidies for private schools.* Madison: University of Wisconsin.

Witte, J. F., Bailey, A. B., & Thorn, C. A. (1992, December). *Second-year report: Milwaukee parental choice program.* Madison: University of Wisconsin.

Witte, J. F., Bailey, A. B., & Thorn, C. A. (1993, December). *Third-year report: Milwaukee parental choice program.* Madison: University of Wisconsin.

Witte, J. F., Thorn, C. A., Pritchard, K. M., & Claibourn, M. (1994, December). *Fourth-year report: Milwaukee parental choice program.* Madison: University of Wisconsin.

PART IV

Two Strategies for Empowering People:
Politics and Markets

Reweaving the Fabric

The Iron Rule and the IAF Strategy for Power and Politics

Ernesto Cortés, Jr.

Introduction

The Industrial Areas Foundation (IAF) is the center of a national network of broad-based, multiethnic, interfaith organizations in primarily poor and moderate-income communities. Created more than 50 years ago by Saul Alinsky and currently directed by Ed Chambers, it now provides the leadership training for more than 30 organizations representing nearly 1,000 institutions and more than 1 million families. The central role of the IAF organizations is to build the competence and confidence of ordinary citizens and taxpayers so that they can reorganize the relationships of power and politics in their communities, allowing them to reshape the physical and cultural face of their neighborhoods. The IAF works with organizations in the New York

AUTHOR'S NOTE: This chapter was previously published as "Reweaving the Fabric: The Iron Rule and the IAF Strategy for Power and Politics" (pp. 294-319), in *Interwoven Destinies,* Henry G. Cisneros, Ed., New York: W. W. Norton & Co., 1993. Copyright © 1993 The American Assembly, Columbia University. Reprinted with permission.

City area, Texas, California, Arizona, Maryland, Tennessee, and the United Kingdom and is assisting the development of about a dozen more in other regions.

Challenges of the 1990s

There is a consensus that the quality of life in our cities has seriously deteriorated during the last 20 years. This thesis runs through a number of popular works, including Robert Reich's (1991) *The Work of Nations,* John Kenneth Galbraith's (1992) *The Culture of Contentment,* William Julius Wilson's (1987) *The Truly Disadvantaged,* and William Schneider's (1992) *Atlantic Monthly* article on the growing suburbanization of American political life. Clearly, what has occurred is Reich's "secession of the successful," that is, the distancing of the wealthy and fortunate from the fate and communities of the less fortunate. As a result, there has been a deterioration in the quality of life of our cities that has profoundly affected the economic, social, and political health of this nation.

There are, in fact, a number of serious crises affecting our society: (a) the decline of our cities, particularly the exodus of meaningful employment and leadership opportunities; (b) the crisis of our educational system; (c) the changing structure of our economy; (d) a pervasive cynicism and withdrawal from public life; and (e) an attenuated moral, cultural, and civic infrastructure. Unfortunately, to the extent that these issues are addressed at all, well-meaning people tend to develop solutions that deal with crises in isolation from one another, thereby limiting understanding of the mutually reinforcing and cumulative impact. This conceptual failing contributes to our political incompetence and lack of political imagination.

There has been widespread agreement heretofore that our politics and our political leaders have been unable to address these problems in any effective, relevant fashion. As a result, most of our adult population believes that politics is largely irrelevant to them. Our public discourse has become impoverished amid a growing disillusionment and stasis inhibiting our ability to act collectively to acknowledge and confront urban decay.

At first glance, the decline in political institutions and public discourse may seem to have little place in a discussion on poverty. Yet clearly, one of the most significant causes of poverty in the United States is the inability of working people to absorb the costs of change in the economic and political institutions of the United States (Mishel & Frankel, 1991). There are always costs to change in a dynamic economy, and invariably those who are the least articulate, least connected, and least well organized bear an inordinate share of the burden of these costs.

Reagan economics, excessive financial deregulation, the acquisition of enormous corporate debt, and the burden of financing that debt have disproportionately affected the poor and working people in the United States. The globalization of economic competition has left U.S. firms facing intense competition from lower-cost producers in other countries. These lower production costs are frequently due to lower wages paid by Third World employers. Additional competition is due to more efficient, higher-quality production methods by producers in industrialized nations such as Germany and Japan that may actually pay higher wages than U.S. firms. U.S. companies are under intense pressure to cut costs, which usually means cutting jobs.

As documented in Frank Levy's (1990) *Dollars and Dreams,* real income in the United States has been declining since 1973, affecting most seriously the incomes of the less well educated. Whereas one job used to be sufficient to keep a family above the poverty line, a similar standard of living now requires two or more such jobs. Families that used to survive on the income of just one adult worker now have to have at least two, and possibly three or four—the third or fourth often children. This development has driven more and more families below the poverty line, leaving even those above poverty without the time or the energy for their children, their families, or their communities.

The potential impact of the North American Free Trade Agreement (NAFTA) is another case in point. Even though in the long run, NAFTA will probably be beneficial to people who live in the United States and Mexico, in the short term there will be tremendous costs on both sides—costs that will once again be borne primarily by the least powerful and least articulate. For example, the immigration that is expected to result from NAFTA, particularly as Mexico phases out corn farming subsidies, will affect most severely the urban poor in the United States and the rural poor in Mexico. The influx of immigrants willing to work long hours for low wages has already depressed wage levels and increased competition for relatively unskilled, low-wage jobs in the Los Angeles area. As Jack Miles (1992) articulated in his disconcerting *Atlantic Monthly* article, the African American underclass in Los Angeles has been largely squeezed out of the unskilled labor market by Latino immigrants, who in turn are forced to compete with even more recently arrived immigrants. By the end of the 1980s, 40% of all Los Angeles residents were first-generation immigrants. Aside from the economic tension this situation has created, the lack of shared values or common history has made the Los Angeles community increasingly vulnerable to fragmentation. The resulting polarization makes it very difficult to identify shared interests.

Despite the obvious political nature of issues such as the costs of change in a dynamic economy and the divisiveness of competition for a limited pool of resources, political and social renewal is rarely discussed as a means of alleviating poverty. Instead, society focuses on the results of the crises rather than the causes, results such as hunger, homelessness, unemployment, violence, and so forth. Although attention to the immediate needs of the poor is an important facet of the resolution of these crises, such a short-term solution will have only limited success without corresponding long-term changes in social and political institutions.

Importance of Political Renewal

The premise of the IAF is that the most important strategy for the alleviation of poverty is one that is embedded in the re-creation of cultural and civic institutions that identify and mentor people capable of exerting the leadership to organize constituencies for the development of stronger, more active and cohesive communities. Such an approach recognizes that the problem of poverty is more than the lack of sufficient income. It is a crushing burden on the soul. Yet because such pressure is so deforming to the human spirit, the impoverished often view themselves as incapable of participating in the life of the civic culture and political community. This makes creating broad-based institutions extraordinarily difficult. Yet there can be no transformation of the human spirit without development of practical wisdom and meaningful action through the practice of collaborative politics.

Politics, properly understood, is about collective action initiated by people who have engaged in public discourse. Politics is about relationships enabling people to disagree, argue, interrupt one another, clarify, confront, and negotiate, and through this process of debate and conversation to forge a compromise and a consensus that enable them to act. Practical wisdom is equivalent to good judgment and what the Greeks called *praxis,* the action that is aimed, calculated, and reflected on. People must be given the opportunity to develop practical wisdom, to develop the kind of judgment that includes understanding and responsibility. In politics, it is not enough to be right, that is, it is not enough to have a position that is logically worked out; one also has to be reasonable, that is, one has to be willing to make concessions and to exercise judgment in forging a deal. Elections understood in this sense are not to discover what people want but to ratify decisions and actions the political community has reached through argumentative deliberations.

Aristotle said that we are political beings: There is a part of us that emerges only to the extent that we participate in public life. Sheldon Wolin (1989), in *Presence of the Past,* describes as our birthright our political identity, which involves our capacity to collaboratively initiate action with other human beings. This action enables us to open schools, change the nature of schools, create job-training problems, and initiate flood control programs, and by so doing, re-create and reorganize the way in which people, networks of relationships, and institutions operate.

Politics is where our moral dimensions emerge. We are social beings. We are defined by relationships to other people. These include family and kin. These also include the less familiar people with whom we engage in the day-to-day business of living our lives in a complicated society. When people do not have the opportunity to connect to meaningful power and participate in public life effectively, they learn to act irresponsibly—a complaint that is frequently voiced about the residents of our inner cities.

Focusing on the least important elements of political action—voting, elections, and turnout—trivializes our citizens by disconnecting them from the real debate and real power of public life. We fail to recognize that voter participation is the wrong measure of the health of our politics. Voter turnout was high in Pinochet's Chile. Voter turnout was never a problem in the totalitarian countries. Becoming mere voters, clients, taxpayers, and plaintiffs, rather than citizens, renders people incompetent, making them passive viewers of an electronic display. If there is to be genuine participatory politics in this country, there must be opportunities for ordinary people to initiate action about matters that are important to their interests.

Power

Understanding politics requires understanding the nature of power. Frequently people shy away from the discussion of power. "Power tends to corrupt," said Lord Acton, and few people want to appear power-hungry and corrupted. What we must realize is that powerlessness also corrupts—perhaps more pervasively than power itself.

It is important to recognize that there are two kinds of power. Unilateral power tends to be coercive and domineering. The use of unilateral power is that in which one party of authority treats the other party as an object to be instructed and directed. Relational power is more complicated. It involves a personal relationship, subject to subject, developing the relational self. The IAF teaches people to develop the kind of power that is embedded in relationships, involving not only the capacity to act but the reciprocal capacity to allow oneself to be acted on. In this context, relational power involves becoming calculatingly vulnerable—understanding that a meaningful exchange involves getting into other people's subject and allowing them to get into yours—in a word, empathy.

There is no power without relationships: Two or more people come together, express and argue their concerns, develop a plan and the intention to exercise that plan, and take some sort of action. The challenge is how to teach them to get enough power to do the things they think are important. This can happen through two routes, organized people or organized money—obviously the poor have more of the former than the latter. Two or even 10 people by themselves may not be able to do much, but if they begin to build coalitions with other people and learn the rules of politics, including relational power and reciprocity, then they begin to learn the process through which they can take advantage of the opportunities presented by economic, social, and political change.

The IAF believes in the importance of expanding the sphere of public participation. In every community throughout the nation, there are literally thousands of people with the potential to participate successfully in public life. Such participation is the crux of the IAF's strategy for resolving the crises of poverty. It is not that the IAF views other strategies as inappropriate policy but rather that they should be connected to broad-based institutions working to develop this human potential.

The Iron Rule

The human potential of ordinary people emerges when they engage diverse human beings in the serious business of the *polis,* particularly the issues of family, property, and education—which have been the central work of the IAF for the last 50 years. IAF organizations have witnessed thousands of ordinary people developing extraordinary capacities to lead their communities into action and interpret those actions into the possibility of development and change—both for themselves and for their communities. The daily work of the IAF's organizers is searching for, identifying, challenging, testing, and developing potential leaders within our organizations. Each of the IAF's victories is the fruit of the personal growth of thousands of leaders—homemakers, clergy, bus drivers, secretaries, nurses, teachers—who have learned from the IAF how to participate and negotiate with the business and political leaders and bureaucrats we normally think of as our society's decision makers. The IAF lives by the Iron Rule: "Never do for others what they can do for themselves." The IAF has won its victories not by speaking for ordinary people but by teaching them how to speak, to act, and to engage in politics for themselves.

This is the centerpiece of the IAF's organizing and educational philosophy. It is the practical consequence of Alfred North Whitehead's warning about the danger of teaching inert ideas—ideas that are merely received without being used, tested, or thrown into fresh combinations. Inert ideas make people the passive receptacles of disconnected information. The Iron Rule recognizes that the most valuable and important aspect of intellectual development is self-development, which is critical to the accountable use of power. The Iron Rule recognizes the preciousness of self-discovery. As John Stuart Mill said, "If a person possesses any tolerable amount of common sense and experience, his own mode of laying out his existence is the best, not because it is the best in itself, but because it is his own mode" (cited in Thompson, 1976).

The Iron Rule is a process that stimulates curiosity, inquiry, judgment, and mastery of new areas of understanding through action and reflection. It recognizes as John Stuart Mill did that people can learn confidence only through competent participation. We learn by doing.

The Iron Rule goes beyond the rejection of paternalism; it is centered in a vision of autonomous yet interdependent persons who respect each other and appreciate the values of reciprocal accountability. In the IAF vision, healthy relationships in public life are developed through the back and forth of conversation, in contrast to the unilateral communication that our modern world directs at people in much of daily life. Just as conversation demands listening as well as speaking, public relationships demand reciprocity. They are a process that demands an openness, a willingness to suspend judgment, to argue and yet be willing to adjust one's own views. Public relationships demand an openness to others. One enters into public relationships not with self-righteousness but with a commitment to the dignity and respect of others. As in a conversation, the exchange of a relationship does not have a foreclosed beginning and ending. It represents rather a moment in a relationship—a relationship that builds long-term trust through collaborative action.

Role of Broad-Based Organizations

The development of such public relationships will be possible only to the extent that there is an institution, a broad-based organization, that teaches ordinary people how to engage others in conversations and arguments, to reflect on their actions, and enable them to make informed political judgments. These must be mentoring institutions that cultivate curiosity, imagination, and a vision of what is possible for citizens and their families. Simply designing isolated programs and making them available to a community will not expand the capability, vision, and political acumen of the community's residents. The development of judgment is critical. In the modern political campaign, electioneering and voting have become our most common "political" encounters. This places an inordinate amount of importance on the measuring of opinions and preferences, which reinforces the learned helplessness that comes from being disconnected and isolated. Such a focus reinforces dependency, rendering citizens incompetent as mere voters, customers, and clients. Too often our citizens have become professional plaintiffs who are unwilling to responsibly engage their fellow citizens and neighbors on any serious collaborative initiation, instead selecting a course of either costly litigation or exit strategies.

People in the United States have been left with litigation and exit as the most common mechanisms for the expression of dissatisfaction. As Albert Hirschman (1990) outlines in *Exit, Voice and Loyalty,* the ideology of exit is very powerful in America. The nation was settled because of it, expanded westward because of it, and views upward social mobility as one of the most valuable expressions of it. "Love it or leave it" is a uniquely American expression, one that is embraced more and more frequently as citizens retreat into the walled security and complacency of the suburbs and enclaves. The theory behind the ideology of exit is that such an expression of dissatisfaction will force "management" to correct the problems that are driving people away. Because the exit mechanism destroys social capital and weakens the mediating institutions of the community, however, it becomes in the self-interest of the "managers" for the vocal "troublemakers" also to exit, allowing the further disintegration of community to occur unimpeded. "Managers" are left with the most inarticulate, vulnerable, and compliant members of the community—those least likely to agitate for change.

The alternative to the exit mechanism is that of voice—designed to bring about change through internal agitation. This is the paradigm that the IAF is trying to teach, that people are citizens and neighbors who have to learn the art of making judgments and taking action. Institutions must be created to allow citizens to develop their alternative of voice, to learn to exercise their political nature, and to reclaim their political birthright. The importance of discourse and debate in the deliberative process exemplifies the need to make judgments in relationship with other people. Anyone can be rendered incompetent by not having access to interpretation or context or by not having a frame of reference or access to other people's reactions and interpretations.

Because the art of making judgments is an interpretive process, one of the most important aspects of a broad-based organization is that it be action oriented. What we mean by "action" is not just displacement of energy, not just reaction to a crisis, but rather *praxis.* In *praxis,* the most important part of the action is the reflection and evaluation afterward. Our organizations plan "actions"—public dramas, where masses of ordinary people collaboratively and collectively move on a particular issue with a particular focus—which sometimes produce a reaction that is unanticipated. This reaction then produces the grist for the real teaching of politics and interpretation—how to appreciate the negotiations, the challenge, the argument, and the political conversation.

An IAF broad-based organization is like a "mini-university." Our organizations have multiple agendas, traditions, and independent dues-based financing structures and include a wide variety of individuals. Universities and broad-based organizations are two types of institutions in which persons can engage in constrained conflict, opening the conflicts of our traditions to the inquiry and reflection of our citizens. Acknowledging and welcoming these tensions allows for the tempering of conflict to a manageable level. Repressing these conflicts can lead to war. Like a good university, a broad-based organization does not just teach people about skills. It does not treat inquiry as a technique. It also teaches people about perspective. In the words of William Galston (1989), there are two types of education: a philosophic education, which is about inquiry and the rules thereof, and also a civic education, which is about character formation, enabling persons to effectively conduct their lives and provide support for building and sustaining their community. Civic education requires institutions, because character depends on culture, values, and perspective. We do not learn those as isolated individuals. We learn those only in relationships with others and in the context of our history and traditions. Institutions, be they familial, religious, cultural, or political, provide the framework within which civic education, character development, and leadership development must be nurtured. The IAF believes that both types of education are important, and indeed within a democratic society, each augments and supplements the other.

The organizations of the IAF are primarily federations of congregations; they are connected to institutions of faith and agitated by their traditions of faith. In this context, the term *faith* does not mean particular religious beliefs but rather a more general affirmation that life has meaning. Congregations are the conveyors of tradition, which connects people and holds them accountable to both their past and their future. They force us to recognize that we are encumbered beings who have a responsibility to deal regularly with the business of transformation, thereby engendering hope. These institutions, churches, synagogues, mosques, and temples are built on networks of family and neighbors. Tragically, they are virtually the only institutions in society that are fundamentally concerned with the nature and well-being of families and communities. In addition, religious institutions have a commitment, albeit somewhat attenuated, to the vitality of the city. They are accountable to the vision of the prophet Jeremiah, who stated clearly, "Seek ye therefore the shalom [welfare] of the city. For there you shall find your own shalom."

Through these institutions, we learn to accept the tension between what we are—our nature and our limits—and what we can be. We have to be able to embrace the dialectic of that tension and not yield either to cynicism or romantic sentimentality. We learn that there are always intended and unintended consequences to actions and that to practice politics, citizens must be prepared to deal with both. Most important, and this is perhaps the crux of the tension, we must accept that the best often gets in the way of the good and that there will never be total justice. This is a precept that is difficult to deal with unless one is situated in a political context. Political beings understand the limits and boundaries of power and action and do not try to make inordinate claims on life. That is why there has to be in the teaching, the mentoring, and the evaluating the constant attempt to grapple with the human condition: what is the self, what is the relationship of the self to its situation and context, and how do we begin to understand the potential for the development of personhood. Our politics have to be connected to that search for meaning, for authenticity, and for identity.

Religious faith, history, and tradition are important because they embody the records of the struggles of those who have gone before their struggles both to understand and to act. Others have made efforts, sometimes succeeding and sometimes not. In this context, one learns not to take one's self too seriously and to recognize that there are limits to what one can accomplish in a lifetime or in a generation. Traditions, to the extent that they are meaningful and useful, enable us to deal with the realities of ambiguity, irony, and tragedy. They convey to us, through symbols, those dimensions of the human experience.

The root of the word *religion—religare*—means to bind together that which is disconnected. There is always an effort to connect. The best of religious traditions try to be inclusive. They respect diversity. To the extent that they are good traditions, they convey a plurality of symbols that incorporate the experiences of diverse peoples. The whole concept of the mixed multitudes in Sinai and Pentecost is central to the Judeo-Christian tradition; there is a constant incorporation of different traditions in the reweaving of the social and political fabric.

Social Capital

The IAF is concerned with the social capital embodied in relationships among adults in a democratic public life. Broadly defined, *social capital* is a term identifying the value of a community's relationships. In contrast to human capital, which is locked up in the skills of an individual, social capital is a measure of how much collaborative time and energy people have for each other: how much time parents have for their children, how much attention neighbors will give to each other's families, what type of relationships people in congregations have with each other, the relationships in organizations such as PTAs and scout troops, and the quality of many other potential webs of relationships in a community. The social capital of a democratic public life comprises relationships among adults who are equal in essential aspects and yet unequal in their virtues. The IAF is concerned with the relationships of people who aspire to learn and to grow—to acquire the virtues of leadership and satisfactions of becoming, in the phrase of Thomas Jefferson, "participators in the affairs of government."

Social capital is not a familiar term in the current debate, but it is as crucial to the resolution of crises and the alleviation of poverty as are the other forms of capital we already understand. For community development (both economic and social) to be successful, there have to be investments in human capital, physical capital, and social capital so that financial capital or entrepreneurial activity can be productive. The 1980s were absorbed by concern with financial capital, and now the United States is paying the price for that narrow focus. Differing types of capital must be mixed with each other to be productive. The items of physical capital such as machinery alone are not enough but require workers with the human capital of skills to operate them. Teams of workers need not only tools and skills but the trusting relationships of social capital to work together. They all need financial capital to facilitate the exchanges and investments central to economic life. Men and women of vision must be able to coordinate these different kinds of capital.

To think of our relationships as "capital" suggests a different way of thinking about other people. To create capital, we must invest labor, energy, and effort in the here and now to create something for later use. We must expend energy now in creating a tool, learning a skill, saving money, or building a relationship to put it to use in the future. Investment requires the ability and discipline to defer gratification, to invest energy not only in the needs or pleasures of the present but also in the potential demands of the future.

Capital also requires maintenance and renewal. Workers find that their tools wear out with use and rust with disuse. Knowledge and skills must be updated and refined. Similarly, the partners in a venture must renew the means of trusting one another. Neighbors in a community or members of a family must maintain their relationships to renew the social capital they represent.

University of Chicago sociologist James Coleman (1989) has examined a particular example of the importance of social capital in the context of education. He identifies the social capital of a school as "attention from responsible adults" that students receive in the various institutions of their daily lives—their schools, families, churches, and neighborhoods.

Coleman studied public, Catholic, and non-Catholic private schools in Chicago and found that Catholic schools had been more successful at educating students than either public or non-Catholic private schools. Even when he took into account the advantages and disadvantages of varying family backgrounds and incomes (i.e., different levels of human and financial capital), students at Catholic schools had slightly higher achievement rates on math and verbal skills and *dramatically* lower dropout rates. In fact, the dropout rates were *one quarter* the level of public schools and *one third* the level of other private schools.

Coleman argues that the strong, informal adult-student relationships of the Catholic school and community were responsible for the significantly lower dropout rates. Even when children had relatively diminished attention from adults at home—as in the case of single-parent families—the Catholic schools were able to keep them in school. He suggests that adults in the Catholic community were attentive to the children's growth and willing to intervene early when they saw trouble. They provided role models and mentored children. By their example and their actions, they taught children how to relate collaboratively with others. They were available to ask for help or guidance.

The concept of social capital places credence as much in the quality of relationships among people as simply their number or availability. Social capital implies a richness and robustness of relationships among people, that the members of a community are willing and eager to invest in one another. Our broad-based organizations are trying to build, expand, and agitate the social capital that is embedded in the networks of human relationships.

The Development of Leadership

IAF leaders begin their development in one-on-one conversations with a skilled organizer. Individual meetings are not interviews. Rather than a communication of information, convictions, or instruction, they represent an exchange of views, judgments, and commitments. The organizers see themselves as teachers, mentors, and agitators who cultivate leadership. Their job is to teach people how to form relationships with other leaders and develop a network, a collective of relationships able to build the power to enable them to act. They begin with small, winnable issues—fixing a streetlight, putting up a stop sign. They move into larger concerns—making a school a safe and civil place for children to learn. Then they move to still larger issues—setting an agenda for a municipal capital improvement budget; strategizing with corporate leaders and members of the city council on economic growth policies; developing new initiatives in job training, health care, and public education. When ordinary people become engaged and begin to play large, public roles, they develop confidence in their own competence.

IAF leaders are women such as Virginia Ramirez of San Antonio's Communities Organized for Public Service (COPS), who was afraid to speak out because she felt she wasn't educated. But she was angry at the injustice done to her neighborhood—at watching a neighbor die because she did not have heat in the winter. COPS taught Mrs. Ramirez to tap that anger and forge it into a tool for the renewal of hope in herself and her community. She learned to speak publicly, to lead actions, to take risks with herself, and to guide others. The IAF process taught her to develop relationships within which she could challenge the indifference and apathy of corporate and government officials. She learned how to negotiate with the holders of power: how to compromise, how to confront when necessary, and how to rebuild collaboration. She gained the confidence to negotiate with the city council and mayor. She went back to school at age 44, earned her general equivalency diploma, and entered college.

Virginia Ramirez is now president of her parish council. She is also a cochair of COPS and represents her community at the negotiating table with the head of the Chamber of Commerce, the mayor, and the bankers of San Antonio. She leads a team of community leaders and clergy engaged in transforming the public hospital system to truly serve the inner city. She guides and mentors young leaders, some of whom are the sons and daughters of founders of COPS from 20 years ago.

Mrs. Ramirez, as a result of being part of COPS, has learned how to exercise power—relational power. She has learned not only how to act but how to be acted on. She has learned how to collaborate. She has learned how to develop a political institution inside the COPS organization. She has learned how to leverage that institution in a relationship with the city government and the corporate community. As a result, San Antonio has one of the most creative community development block grant (CDBG) programs in the country. In addition, a new, innovative housing strategy has been created, including a $10 million Housing Trust Fund. COPS has used public dollars to leverage many more private dollars for construction and purchase of single-family homes. As a result, the organization has literally physically and spiritually revitalized neighborhoods so their residents have the opportunity to generate stability and growth.

Virginia Ramirez and her personal and political growth are extraordinary but not unique. The IAF has developed more than 20 institutions that have transformed the lives of thousands of persons like her, who felt a deep anger at the injustices done to their lives but believed they had no ability or right to speak out to make their communities more just and more fully human. The

IAF organizations have been schools for the development of politics and community.

What Politics Has Brought

One of the 12 Texas IAF organizations is Allied Communities of Tarrant (ACT) in Fort Worth, composed of 14,000 families from 22 congregations of diverse faiths and ethnic backgrounds. ACT is a broad-based institution, involving African American, Anglo, and Hispanic leaders from both Protestant and Catholic congregations. Formed in 1982, ACT has organized its families in a number of efforts to direct public investment to the inner city. Among other accomplishments, it guaranteed the passage of a bond referendum to finance $57 million of new streets, sewers, and other improvements in 1985.

In 1986, ACT leaders began to work closely with the principal of Morning-side Middle School, a predominantly African American school that had all but ceased to function as anything other than a holding place for children and adults. Its students ranked dead last on measures of performance among the district's 20 middle schools. Half of the children were failing at least one subject. Half failed the state writing skills test. The police were called to the school two to three times a day. The school's parent-teacher organization had one or two persons attending meetings.

In collaboration with the principal, ACT leaders developed a plan to rebuild the relationships among the parents, teachers, and students of the school to revitalize the school. The principal took the lead in building a leadership team within the school's staff. ACT built leadership among the parents through a two-pronged strategy.

First, ACT congregations near the school organized periodic "Recognition Days" in which the congregation as a whole would applaud children for progress at school. Each congregation took care to recognize every child for some form of progress, no matter how small. These ceremonies generally formed part of the worship service. Often the homilies were directed toward recognizing and supporting families in their efforts. Nearly 20 local congregations held "Recognition Days" for the children of the school.

Second, ACT leaders organized a series of individual meetings in which they met or attempted to meet with the parents or guardians of every child, regardless of whether they belonged to an ACT congregation or to any congregation at all. The building of relationships in individual meetings is slow, hard work, but there is no shortcut or substitute. It is the means by which people begin to recognize and understand their own interests. It is how they articulate their vision of themselves and their hopes for their families. It is how they build reciprocal relationships with others.

More than 600 meetings were conducted in a year and a half. Although leaders learned about parents' concerns, the more important result was that they began to build relationships to draw them into involvement with the school. Parents attended training sessions on how to support their children's study habits. They began to meet more often with their children's teachers individually.

The most visible sign of change was the school's transformation into a successful institution. The children's performance on standardized tests rose from 20th of the district's 20 middle schools to 3rd. The percentage of students passing the state writing skills test increased from 50% to 89%. The percentage of children failing at least one subject decreased from 50% to 6%. Police calls fell off to virtually none. Now it is not unusual for 200 or more to attend parent assemblies at the school to learn about drug awareness, study habits, or other education-related themes. Parents also staff an after-school enrichment program that ACT and the principal of the school jointly conceived and implemented. Leaders in other churches and schools have begun to duplicate this effort in another middle school and three feeder elementary schools (see Coleman, 1989).

Beyond making the school a more successful institution, parents became successful in ACT, a mediating institution, and developed the capacity to negotiate with other institutions to pursue their interests and the interests of their children. In the second middle school, parents identified the need for substantial physical renovation of the building. They drew up a $1.8 million plan and negotiated it with the school board. The board approved the plan and doubled the capital spending originally allocated to the school.

Such accomplishments are only the outward signs of the organization's real achievement—the development of mediating institutions that shape and support their families in both their private and public lives. Whereas before the children had been failing, the new relationships built among parents strengthened their family lives and enabled them to succeed in school. One ACT leader has commented that the project calls parents to be parents, changing the culture within families. Through their experiences in ACT, parents learned how to organize and how to act. They no longer merely celebrate their values and their hopes as fantasies in the privacy of home or pew but have acquired the power to make them a real part of the public life of Fort Worth.

Communities Organized for Public Service in San Antonio is the oldest and most established of the IAF organizations. For 20 years, one of COPS's focal points has been pioneering a strategy to rebuild the infrastructure of its inner-city community. With its sister organization, the Metro Alliance, COPS has brought more than $750 million of sewers, streets, sidewalks, parks, libraries, clinics, streetlights, and other infrastructure to the poor west, east, and south sides of the inner city. The IAF organizations in San Antonio have helped working families build more than 1,000 units of new housing, rehabilitate 2,600 existing units, and purchase 1,300 more. Beyond these new homes and infrastructure, however, the most important accomplishment of the IAF organizations is the leadership development of people such as Virginia Ramirez.

In the early years of the San Antonio housing efforts, professional organizers worked intensively to identify and mentor individuals who would form a core of leadership, equipping them to reshape city policy. This core group, and the thousands of others whom they led and collaborated with, organized hundreds of house meetings, neighborhood actions, and research visits, which built both the COPS housing agenda and the power to move it forward.

COPS's first major housing initiative came to be known as the Select Housing Target Areas program. Unlike many other cities, in which substandard housing was razed or refurbished without regard to the original low-income residents, COPS was able to develop a strategy in which community improvements did not dislocate residents. Their aim was not to redevelop real estate but to rejuvenate communities. Formulated in cooperation with city officials and the San Antonio Development Agency (SADA), the program has build more than 900 new homes and rehabilitated 2,600 more since its inception in 1984. Ninety-five percent of homeowners have chosen to rebuild their homes in the redeveloped neighborhoods, rather than seek housing in the suburbs.

COPS leaders, when encountering obstacles or gaps in the community redevelopment strategy, have been able to initiate new programs to complement existing ones. One gap identified from the experience of the Target Areas program was the need to help young families purchase their own homes. Working families in San Antonio, like others in the United States, have seen their wages and incomes fall in real terms during the last decade, while the price of housing has risen. In the words of one COPS leader, they saw young families "losing the American dream of owning their own home." Many were able to afford monthly payments, but were unable to raise the lump sum of down payment, closing costs, and prepaid insurance and taxes.

To address this barrier, COPS and Metro Alliance leaders worked with SADA to create the Homeownership Incentive Program (HIP) to help young families finance the lump-sum payments. HIP enables moderate-income families who quality for FHA-insured loans to receive a 30-year, zero-interest second mortgage to use as a down payment. Since 1988, the city has made loans to leverage private mortgage funds to more than 1,300 families. These families have an average annual income of $17,500, and 18% are headed by single mothers.

The central component of the San Antonio IAF organizations' work to redevelop the city's neighborhoods has been the annual community development block grant program, $4 million of which remains the principal funding for the Target Areas and the HIP effort. Designed to replace numerous federal categorical programs with a single, flexible grant to cities, the CDBG program since 1974 has been a steady, though small and diminishing, source of funds for the redevelopment of inner cities across the country. COPS and the Metro Alliance have ensured that the funds are used carefully and effectively, maximizing expenditures for durable capital improvements and minimizing the demands on CDBG for operating expenditures of city and private agencies. In fact, San Antonio's program has been recognized nationwide as a model CDBG project.

COPS leaders drive the annual CDBG process, in which residents of eligible neighborhoods meet in their homes, schools, and churches to draw up their lists of potential projects, the costs of which are always three or four times their neighborhood's CDBG allocation. People begin their bargaining, trimming some projects and delaying others in exchange for mutual support. They proceed from house meetings concerned with one street or drainage issue, to neighborhood meetings proposing a package of projects, to meetings in each city council district to shape a proposal with the council member, and then, in collaboration with the city council member, community leaders finalize the selection of the year's project. COPS leaders have incorporated into the organization's collective culture the expertise to plan projects and the skills of negotiating and facilitating the bargaining among neighborhoods.

The principal constraint on COPS's efforts has been the lack of resources. San Antonio had received roughly $40 million a year in federal aid in the early 1970s in various categorical urban programs. Now that amount has fallen to $14 million through the CDBG program.

COPS and Metro Alliance leaders have sought new sources of funds to complement the limited resources from CDBG. In 1988, leaders from the two organizations developed a plan for the creation of a City Housing Trust Fund. They researched the operation of local trust funds across the country, designed their own proposal, and negotiated with the city council to establish it. The city council was more willing to create the fund than to actually fund it, but a windfall of $22 million from the sale of San Antonio's cable television franchise gave the IAF organizations an opportunity. IAF leaders negotiated with the council and representatives advocating other capital spending priorities to set aside $10 million of the $22 million sale to endow the City Housing Trust Fund, ensuring an annual stream of $500,000 to $1 million in new funding for housing.

San Antonio's City Housing Trust Fund provides an important source of flexible financing to fill gaps left by other sources too restricted or too highly taxed to be accessible to low-income families. So far, the City Housing Trust Fund has financed the planning of several housing projects for older persons and one affordable single-family development—the Brighton Park subdivision.

The Brighton Park story is one that begins not with a government housing program but with the frustrations of neighbors with a trashy vacant lot. House meetings were convened to discuss possible uses for the lot. Each house meeting, where 10 or 15 neighbors would gather for an hour or so of conversation, reported back to the leadership with the same issue: housing for young families. Neighbors became so excited when they imagined the prospect of new, modern, single-family homes as good as the ones in the new subdivisions outside San Antonio's Outer Loop.

The story proceeds through the development of a core of dedicated and competent neighborhood leaders, who for 5 years worked doggedly to secure the participation of the city government, commercial banks, the San Antonio Development Agency, the City Housing Trust Fund, and private builders. In essence, the COPS leaders became developers. The story concludes with young families moving into a new neighborhood of 16 custom-designed homes—the first new subdivision in the south side of San Antonio in more than 20 years.

Time and again, COPS and the Metro Alliance have initiated new ideas for the creative use of local, federal, and state public dollars to help working families rebuild their neighborhoods, both physically and socially. They formulate their goals and strategies from the experiences and dreams of working families. These IAF organizations have institutionalized a culture of politics in which citizens have both the real power to act on their hopes for their communities, as well as the responsibility to put forward not just complaints but constructive plans. They have created a culture of reasoned debate, accountability, negotiations, respect, and compromise within which the powers of a city can collaborate to guide its destiny.

Other situations in which disenfranchised citizens have developed the power to initiate action to improve their communities include the following.

The Nehemiah Homes Project in Brooklyn and Bronx, New York. East Brooklyn Congregations has built more than 3,000 new single-family homes for working families, renewing completely devastated neighborhoods. This was possible because the broad-based church organization, under the auspices of the Industrial Areas Foundation, leveraged land and tax abatements from the city of New York and no-interest construction financing from religious institutions. In addition, each home carries an interest-free second mortgage loan from the city government of $15,000 as a lien repayable whenever the house is sold. A similar Nehemiah program was established in Baltimore by BUILD, also an IAF organization.

Job training in San Antonio. COPS and the Metro Alliance, the business community, the city of San Antonio, the local Private Industry Council (PIC), the governor of Texas, and several other state and local agencies have collaborated to create a $7-million, high-skill job training effort. Employers have committed several hundred high-skill positions—primarily in health care. The governor committed $2.3 million in state funds for development. The city government committed $2 million for income maintenance. The PIC committed $2.6 million for job training. COPS and Metro committed the sweat equity of neighborhood leaders to holding job trainees accountable to the community for a commitment to long-term training.

Commonwealth in Baltimore. The corporate community in Baltimore contributed $20 million in scholarship funds, to be matched by funds from local universities, for high school graduates achieving good grades and attendance. The BUILD organization helps to raise additional resources from government sources and mobilizes the participation of families and local schools. COPS and the Metro Alliance created a similar program called the San Antonio Education Partnership.

Colonias in South Texas. The state of Texas has pledged $250 million in grants and low-interest loans (which is helping to leverage federal and local funds) to build water and sewer systems in the 400-plus unincorporated rural communities along the Texas-Mexico border. *Colonia* is a Spanish word for neighborhood, and along the border in Texas it is a word for communities of people who were deceived by unscrupulous land developers—hard-working people who were promised complete utility services but were left with open sewage ditches, unpaved streets, no running water, and an unfathomable number of public health problems. Valley Interfaith, the Border Organization, and the El Paso Interreligious Sponsoring Organization (EPISO), with support from the entire network of Texas IAF organizations, initiated and promoted the legislation in collaboration with the elected leadership of the state government, the Texas Water Development Board, and local providers.

Moral minimum wage. In 1987, after 9 months of hard dialogue and negotiation with Southern California IAF, the California Industrial Welfare Commission raised the state's minimum wage to $4.25 an hour, then the highest in the nation. This case is one in which the work of the Southern

California IAF made a positive difference in the real income of families, and contrary to the prophecies of the opposition, subsequent studies have demonstrated no adverse effect on levels of employment.

Community policing in Hudson County, New Jersey. The Interfaith Community Organization (ICO) in Jersey City and Hoboken has worked for 3 years with police departments to create a new culture of community policing—an approach to public safety that involves the commitment of a city's resources to the day-to-day work of building relationships between police and neighborhood residents. Although the struggle ran the gamut from replacing the police chief to developing a true public consensus on community policing as a priority, ICO's work has led to a firm commitment of resources and personnel for eight neighborhoods in Hudson County.

Texas Alliance schools. The Texas Education Agency has pledged additional resources to 32 schools that are collaborating with local community organizations to seriously reorganize neighborhood schools. Modeled on the experience of Fort Worth's Morningside Middle School, in which leaders of Allied Communities of Tarrant rewove the fabric of community linking families, teachers, administrators, and community leaders, the Alliance Schools project works to build a constituency and commitment among stakeholders in education to make dramatic improvements in the performances of the schools and develop an effective constituency for education reform.

The Role of the Government

Reinvigorating urban life requires a new vision of civil society appropriate to the challenges of this age. The IAF believes, with Arthur Okun (1975), that the two primary institutions of modern times, the market and the state, have their places in social life but must be kept in their places. Without strong countervailing institutions, the imperialism of the market will dominate and penetrate all relationships, in both public and private spheres, as it did in the 1980s. The healthy functioning of an enterprise-market system depends on balanced relationships among society's major institutions—family, community, and church—and market mechanisms. These institutions teach the values of social intercourse, reciprocity, trust, exchange, and accountability, which are requisite for the effective functioning of the market system.

Americans have already seen contemporary politics—both electioneering and governing—reduced to marketing strategies. Politics no longer mediates the market but is part and parcel of it. The advertising executives and media consultants now shape campaigns centered not on debates of public philosophy or the governance of what Daniel Bell called the "public household" but on negative 30-second television ads. Even worse, the media advisers now attempt to govern, fashioning the rationale of war and peace by opinion polls. The result is an incoherent, inarticulate, and trivial political leadership and a growing, cancerous cynicism and alienation in the community. The failure to center public life on genuine discourse is poisoning the reservoirs of goodwill in social relationships. Trust is unraveling not just in the political sphere but in other public spheres—between doctors and patients, pastors and parishioners, teachers and students.

The tools of a market mechanism—money and prices—are effective signals for what is to be produced, how much, and for whom. The market is also an effective mechanism for the creation of wealth, the coordination of economic activity, and the buffering of citizens from the state. Yet the market has fundamental limits. It accepts grossly unequal distributions of income and power, which distort the very workings of the market process. The market cannot deal with external factors, nor can it calculate intergenerational costs. Market mechanisms often seem oblivious to the many examples of market failures that led to air and water pollution, environmental degradation, and social imbalance—what John Kenneth Galbraith called private affluence in the midst of public squalor.

Government provision of consumer goods, services, transfer payments, or tax credits will provide some relief from the conditions of poverty. To the extent that they allow some people more choices, such policies are useful. Yet these consumables, however benignly bestowed, will not provide a long-term solution to the culture of poverty and despair that exists in communities today. The alleviation of poverty requires not just an increase in income but the development of the capacity to act—to make choices. This means that any strategy to alleviate poverty must also address the question of inequities of power. The role of those who have power in shaping political and economic decisions is critically important. If poor people are to have any real dignity, they must play a meaningful role in making these decisions. Market-oriented strategies are not sufficient. There must also be strategies for developing political entrepreneurship.

Just as the government cannot create entrepreneurial economic activity, neither can it create political entrepreneurship. The government cannot "empower" people, because power is not something that can be bestowed. Government can facilitate, encourage, recognize, and reward grassroots organizing, but it cannot create it. Government cannot create local initiatives, but it can understand the importance of these initiatives having an institutional base rooted in people's imagination, curiosity, values, and search for meaning.

The IAF has developed an innovative proposal that is rooted in our organizational community base. We propose that the federal government structure a matching grant strategy to leverage the commitments of states, local municipalities, and communities. The strategy would be based on the concept of an augmented community development block grant program and a more flexible Job Training Partnership Act. Communities would receive a certain minimum entitlement based on need, as in the current program. The federal government could then increase the amount of the grant to the extent that a results-oriented strategy had been developed that would reward the achievement of certain outcomes. These outcomes could include some combination of the following: increases in meaningful employment, reduction of a percentage of poverty, increased access to health care, improvements in infrastructure and security, facilitation of first-time housing purchases, and so forth. Essentially, the federal government would provide matching grants for local investments of money, resources, and sweat equity. Ideally, these efforts should be developed as part of a larger strategy for state and local governments, corporations, and private sector institutions to make available resources to match the social capital of authentic indigenous local community-based organizations.

Theoretically, the granting of additional monies to cities in which such strategic organizing is taking place should generate interest in other locales, thus facilitating the replication and dissemination of a new institution-building process. At the same time, this strategy recognizes the necessity for macroeconomic initiatives to ensure a growing economy and full employment. In addition, it also recognizes potential labor demand and supply problems. Thus, there is the need to develop job training initiatives strategically, with consideration for the future as well as the current situation in which the local economic structure is embedded.

Conclusion

The task of rebuilding our civic and political institutions is an urgent one. People in modern industrial societies, particularly those living in the cities, are atomized and disconnected from each other. Particularly in the suburbs, far too much of the American search for "fulfillment" is centered on the individual, making his or her relationships utilitarian and narcissistic in nature. This fragmentation leaves people increasingly less capable of forming a common purpose and carrying it out. Vaclav Havel pointed out in his address to the World Economic Forum in February 1992 that global civilization is in danger of destroying itself through inattention to any number of massive threats—the population explosion, the greenhouse effect, AIDS, and so on.

The large paradox at the moment is that [the hu]man—a great collector of information—is well aware of all this, yet is absolutely incapable of dealing with the danger. Traditional science, with its usual coolness, can describe the different ways we might destroy ourselves, but it cannot offer us truly effective and practicable instructions on how to avert them. . . . What is needed is something different, something larger. . . . The way forward is not in the mere construction of universal systemic solutions, to be applied to reality from the outside; it is also in seeking to get to the heart of reality through personal experiences. Such an approach promotes an atmosphere of tolerant solidarity and unity in diversity based on mutual respect, genuine pluralism and parallelism. In a word, human uniqueness, human action, and the human spirit must be rehabilitated.

As Havel indicates, this rehabilitation can be done only through a different kind of politics, that is, a politics that creates authentic democratic political institutions that teach, mentor, and build a constituency of leaders and a network of stakeholders to initiate and support appropriate public policies that can rebuild our cities and reinforce the development of viable communities and mediating institutions.

The work of the IAF is in fact designed to create a different kind of politics. Developing a strategy that deals with the structural inequalities built into our dynamic economy requires an organized constituency with the power and imagination to initiate and support policies for change. If we are to create such a constituency and restore health and integrity to our political process, mitigating the distorting role and influence of organized concentrations of wealth, then we must be vigilant in the development of real democratic institutions. The work of the IAF is to create organized constituencies that are effective in teaching real politics.

References

Coleman, J. (1989, November). Schools and communities. *Chicago Studies,* pp. 232-244.

Galbraith, J. K. (1992). *The culture of contentment.* Boston: Houghton Mifflin.

Galston, W. (1989). Civic education in the liberal state. In N. Rosenblum (Ed.), *Liberalism and the moral life* (pp. 89-101). Cambridge, MA: Harvard University Press.

Havel, V. (1992, Summer). Politics and the world itself. *Kettering Review,* 8-14.

Hirschman, A. (1990). *Exit, voice and loyalty.* Cambridge, MA: Harvard University Press.

Levy, F. (1990). *Dollars and dreams.* New York: Russell Sage.

Miles, J. (1992, October). Blacks vs. browns. *Atlantic Monthly, 270,* pp. 41-68.

Mishel, L., & Frankel, D. (1991). *The state of working America.* Armonk, NY: M. E. Sharpe.

Okun, A. (1975). *Equality and efficiency.* Washington, DC: Brookings Institution.

Reich, R. (1991). *The work of nations.* New York: Knopf.

Schneider, W. (1992, July). The suburban century begins. *Atlantic Monthly, 270*(1), 33-44.

Thompson, D. F. (1976). *John Stuart Mill and representative government.* Princeton, NJ: Princeton University Press.
Wilson, W. J. (1987). *The truly disadvantaged.* Chicago: University of Chicago Press.
Wolin, S. (1989). *Presence of the past.* Baltimore: Johns Hopkins University Press.

A New War on Poverty

The Kemp Program to Empower the Poor

John C. Weicher

The housing initiatives undertaken by Secretary of Housing and Urban Development Jack Kemp—the HOPE program—are the center of what he has described as "a new war on poverty."[1] They are in key respects a dramatic departure from the policies of recent administrations of both parties. They can best be understood as a return to one of the original purposes of low-income housing policy—helping those who are poor become more productive members of society—but at the same time, they also take account of the lessons learned during the past five decades and more. This chapter explains the underlying logic of the Kemp program, describes the major initiatives, most of which are not widely understood, and shows how they fit into an overall strategy.

AUTHOR'S NOTE: Data and other information about housing programs for which a source is not cited are taken from unpublished Department of Housing and Urban Development (HUD) program information at the time that I was Assistant Secretary for Policy Development and Research at HUD (1989-1993).

The Macroeconomic and Demographic Background

Before discussing the Kemp programs, however, it is worth reminding ourselves of the larger context in which the programs operate. The specific antipoverty activities of HUD (and other agencies) always take place against a background of economic and demographic conditions that affect both the nature of the problem of poverty and the effectiveness of specific programs to address it. It should be clear that a strong, growing economy is the essential precondition for any effective antipoverty program. For the last two decades, the poverty rate has risen sharply during recessions and declined more gradually during recoveries, fluctuating in a range of 10% to 15% of the population. During that period, there have been a large number of changes in housing and other low-income benefit programs. Most have expanded the scope of benefits, although some have restricted assistance. The effect of macroeconomic conditions on the poverty rate has dominated the effect of program changes, with the probable exception of Social Security with respect to poverty among older persons.

The cyclical pattern of poverty also holds for most demographic groups. The poverty rate for the population as a whole, for married couples with children, and for families consisting of single women with children have all moved together, as economic conditions have changed.[2] The rates do not always have the same turning points, but the turning points are never more than a year apart, and the changes are highly correlated. Clearly, a rising tide may not lift all boats, but it raises *some,* and if the tide is going out, it is hard to raise any boats at all.

But at the same time, it is clear that different demographic groups show a different responsiveness to economic conditions. The poverty rate among married couples with children has responded more to changes in economic conditions than has the rate for single women and their children.[3] A rising tide lifts some boats more than others.

Partly because their economic situation is less responsive to changes in the overall economy than those of other groups, and partly because they have been a growing share of the population, through time single women and their children have come to compose a greater proportion of families in poverty. In 1975, they accounted for just over 40% of all poor people living in families; by 1991, they accounted for just over 50% (U.S. Department of Commerce, 1992). Therefore, it is not surprising that public discussion of poverty has increasingly focused on their problems; they make up a large share of the "underclass," in most conceptions of that term, for example. Because so many long-term poor persons are single women and their children, and because many of the children grow up to become poor single parents themselves, it is easy to conclude that nothing can be done to ameliorate their poverty, except to change their behavior and their values. In effect, this is a counsel of despair; it consigns the present generation of poor single women to permanent poverty, with a hope that some way can be found to reach their children. How that is to be done is not clearly specified, and indeed it is hard to see any effective means for reaching the children, as a matter of public policy, without at the same time reaching their parents.

HUD has substantial experience in providing housing assistance to low-income families consisting of single women with children. HUD assists about 1 million such households. They constitute about one quarter of all low-income households who live in subsidized housing, and the proportion would be substantially higher were it not that one third of assisted households are elderly. More than half are black; about one eighth are Hispanic (HUD, 1992a). A number of major initiatives were undertaken at HUD under Secretary Kemp and President Bush to address the problem of poverty among those households.

The Rationale and Purpose
of Federal Housing Programs

When the federal government was making the first, fateful decisions on federal housing policy during the 1930s, one of the two basic low-income housing policy rationales was that decent housing generated all sorts of social benefits.[4] It was widely believed by social scientists and social workers that people who lived in decent housing were better citizens. There was much more antisocial behavior in the slums—more crime, more vice, and more "shiftlessness." In addition, people who lived in decent housing were healthier, both mentally and physically. Analysts believed that housing conditions alone were largely responsible for these differences between those who lived in the slums and those who lived in decent housing. Indeed, it is not too much to say that in the 1930s, public housing was seen as a full-fledged war on poverty, all by itself.

This consensus affected many of the basic features of low-income housing policy. The public housing program, for example, included a requirement that one slum housing unit should be torn down for each new unit that was built, and the demolition was considered to be as important as the new construction. Through time, it became clear that this view was not valid. Decent housing by itself proved to have limited value as a vehicle for improving the social and economic position of poor persons. Housing program administrators and housing advocates have expressed their disappointment since at least the 1950s (see, e.g., Seligman, 1958). Indeed, by the early 1960s, Jacobs (1961) was writing of "low-income projects that become worse centers of delinquency, vandalism and general social hopelessness than the slums they were supposed to replace" (p. 4), and although her critique of urban planning was controversial, her opinion of public housing went largely unchallenged.

By the time Jacobs wrote, housing policy was beginning to change, albeit slowly. During the 1960s, new programs were created to fund construction of privately owned, low-income housing developments, culminating in 1968 with Section 236. These programs were still based on the premise that it was necessary to build new housing for poor people, although the original antipoverty rationale was already fading. The programs combined housing assistance with federal insurance of the mortgages used to finance the projects; in the postwar period, there was a general consensus that mortgage insurance "worked" and public housing did not, so the combination of private ownership of subsidized low-income housing and insurance by the Federal Housing Administration (FHA) was an effort to solve the housing (and perhaps social) problems of those who were poor.

These programs typically produced housing that was better than public housing and served a somewhat higher income clientele. They were inequitable in two senses: Assistance was provided to some families, whereas others with significantly lower incomes did not receive help; in addition, the housing of those receiving assistance was often better than the housing occupied by middle-income taxpayers. Moreover, the combination of insurance and subsidy was fatal to any federal effort to maintain the quality of the housing once it was built; the government had no effective recourse against a landlord who did not provide decent housing on a continuing basis, because the landlord could always default on the mortgage and force the government to take title to the property, recognize a loss, manage the property, and attempt to sell it—all expensive actions, in both money and staff resources.

A major reconsideration of low-income housing policy occurred in 1973. Part of the National Housing Policy Review (NHPR) in that year involved revisiting the basic rationales for housing programs. By that time, few defended the view that housing per se was enough to solve the social problems of those in poverty. As a staff member of the NHPR, I can attest that few of the housing professionals working on the study believed that the social benefits of housing were important; nor did many outside experts make this argument. The actual experience with housing programs was matched by a body of social, economic, and medical research indicating that low income was a much more significant contributor to the problems of poor persons than substandard housing (see, e.g., Kasl, 1976; Rothenberg, 1976).

This left open the question of why poor people should be given housing assistance in particular.[5] The issue in 1973 ultimately came down to two rationales, with different policy implications: Housing benefits should be provided to poor people as part of the overall effort to alleviate their poverty (but *not* in the expectation that the housing assistance will help them move permanently out of poverty), or, alternatively, that good housing generates external benefits for the surrounding neighborhood and community. The former explanation suggests a program of cash assistance, or housing assistance not tied to specific housing developments; the latter suggests a block grant.

President Nixon chose the former, which was enacted as the Section 8 program in 1974. Section 8 provided project-based assistance for new construction projects, in the manner of public housing and the privately owned projects, but it also provided rental assistance for families looking for decent housing in the private housing stock—tenant-based assistance, whereby the family can choose to move to another unit and retain its subsidy. Between 1975 and 1983, slightly more than half of all incremental assisted housing units (800,000 out of 1.5 million) took the form of project-based assistance, mainly in the Section 8 new construction program (HUD, 1992b). This program was extremely expensive, however, and was terminated in 1983. The existing housing program has continued and is the basic program for providing incremental housing assistance today.[6] Since 1984, residents of more than 500,000 privately owned units have received tenant-based assistance, whereas about 200,000 new project-based units have been added to the assisted housing stock.[7]

The Changing Housing Conditions of the Poor

Buttressing the original antipoverty concept and also the programmatic changes in the 1970s was the quality of the American housing stock. The earliest systematic information on housing conditions in the United States was collected as part of the 1940 Census of Population and Housing. At that time, nearly half of the occupied housing in the country was classified as substandard. By 1970, less than 10% was. The Census Bureau discontinued the traditional definition of substandard housing after 1970, but data from the American Housing Survey show a continuing decline in inadequate housing.[8] This is true for those who are eligible for housing assistance, as well as for the rest of the population. Since 1983, families and elderly individuals with incomes below 50% of the local median income ("very low income families") have been eligible for housing assistance. In 1974, about 800,000 (11%) of these households lived in "severely inadequate" housing, meaning that their residence probably could not be rehabilitated to provide decent housing. By

1989, the number was down to about 400,000 (4%). (See HUD, 1991b, Tables 5 and 6.)[9] At the same time, the problem of housing affordability has become more serious. In 1974, 1.8 million of these households (25%) paid more than half their income for rent, and another 1.7 million (22%) paid between 30% and 50%. In 1989, these figures had risen to 3.4 million (33%) and 2.0 million (20%).

These data are relevant to housing policy. In 1983, Congress categorized very low income renter families and elderly individuals who live in severely inadequate housing, or who pay half their income in rent, as having "worst case" housing needs and gave them priority for housing assistance.[10] Thus, in 1989, there were 3.6 million households with priority housing problems; 400,000 of them lived in severely inadequate housing (half of these households also spent more than half of their income on rent), and another 300,000 lived in crowded conditions, with more than one person per room, while spending half their income on rent. This leaves 2.9 million households whose only serious housing problem was their rent burden.[11]

Although there were 720,000 families and elderly individuals with priority for housing assistance who were occupying severely inadequate housing units or living in crowded conditions in 1989, there were also 1.6 million vacant units that were affordable to very low income families if they received tenant-based assistance.[12] If all 720,000 were housed in vacant units (receiving vouchers or certificates to be able to afford the decent vacant housing), the overall rental vacancy rate would be reduced from 6.6% to 3.6%—a tight market, to be sure, but not impossibly tight. Put another way, at a vacancy rate of 5% (more or less a "normal" vacancy rate), there would be some 340,000 very low income families and elderly individuals who would still live in severely inadequate or crowded housing.[13] At a vacancy rate of 4%, there would be about 100,000.

These are national figures, and all housing markets are local. The same findings hold for individual housing markets, however, as shown by a separate analysis of 44 large metropolitan areas, which among them contain half the renters in the United States and more than half the households with priority housing problems. In many of these areas—19 of the 44—all very low income families and elderly individuals with priority housing problems would be able to find decent vacant housing, which they could afford if they received tenant-based assistance under current programs, without lowering the local vacancy rate below 5%. A total of 203,000 families and elderly individuals would still live in severely inadequate or crowded housing—more than half of them in New York and Los Angeles.[14]

Thus, a large majority of households who have priority for housing assistance suffer only from a high rent burden. With financial assistance, they could continue to live in their present housing unit. A small number live in housing that probably should be replaced. This is a far cry from the slum conditions that were the focus of housing policy in the 1930s.

For these reasons, the basic policy to help these households under Secretary Kemp and President Bush remained financial assistance—housing vouchers and certificates—to be used in the existing private housing stock. Since the mid-1970s, the "voucher/production debate" has been the major issue in low-income housing policy, and in this respect the Bush administration was a continuation of the Reagan administration. The Bush administration annually proposed an increase in the number of housing vouchers rather than funds to construct new public housing developments. Annually, it was only partly successful, as Congress typically continued to fund public housing construction, but the number of voucher and certificate holders continued to rise from year to year. From 1980 to 1992, the number of assisted households increased from 3.1 to 4.7 million. Total outlays for low-income housing correspondingly increased, from $9 billion in 1980 to $18 billion in 1992 (measured in 1992 dollars; HUD, 1992b).[15]

The New War on Poverty

But although they are a generally efficient and effective way to address the housing problems of poor people, vouchers and certificates are not by themselves an effective antipoverty strategy, any more than public housing has been. Given Secretary Kemp's strong desire to address the full range of problems that keep many poor people from becoming productive members of society, HUD developed a set of initiatives that attempted to address other needs as well as housing, in an integrated way. The goal of these initiatives was to empower recipients of housing assistance so that they could work themselves out of poverty and out of needing assistance. Sometimes these initiatives brought together assistance programs administered by several agencies; sometimes they relied mainly on housing but used resources in new and unusual ways. In addition, because HUD's housing assistance programs are so varied, it was necessary to build different antipoverty initiatives around different housing assistance programs.

These initiatives are the core of Secretary Kemp's HOPE program. This section describes them.

FAMILY SELF-SUFFICIENCY

The Family Self-Sufficiency program combines tenant-based assistance—vouchers and certificates—with human capital formation and related programs.

A package of services is tailored to each individual adult participating in Family Self-Sufficiency. The services that are provided with the housing are most often job training and education, to help individuals become self-sufficient, and also child care and transportation, to enable people to take advantage of the job training and education.

The program is administered through the Public Housing Authority (PHA). The PHA establishes a program coordinating committee, including the PHA itself, the local government, the residents, and agencies administering the service programs, such as public and private education and training institutions. The resources for the program committee have come from the Community Development Block Grant, the Community Services Block Grant, and Section 8 administrative fees, in previous demonstrations.

As of fiscal year 1993 (which started in October 1992), a PHA must offer Family Self-Sufficiency to receive new vouchers, certificates, or public housing, which most PHAs do. The size of the program has to be at least equivalent to the total number of incremental families, but it does not necessarily have to serve the incremental families themselves. The program began in fiscal year 1991 on a voluntary basis; in 1991 and 1992, HUD provided housing vouchers to a total of 26,000 families to participate in Family Self-Sufficiency.

The program is voluntary for the family, but families are given incentives to participate. Normally, the rent is paid partly by the family and partly by HUD, with the family's share set at 30% of its income. In Family Self-Sufficiency, the family's rental payment does not rise with its earned income until its income goes above 50% of the local median income. Instead, HUD continues to pay the same amount, and the additional rent that the family would pay goes into an interest-bearing escrow account. When the family's earned income goes above 50% of the median, the amount of the additional rent going into the escrow account is frozen at the amount that went into the account when the family's income was at 50% of the median. Thus, as the family's income increases above 50%, so too will its rent payment.[16] When the family completes the program, it receives the money in the escrow account. Participants also are given priority for homeownership subsidies (which are discussed later in this chapter).

Once a family chooses to participate in the program, there are incentives to encourage it to continue. The family signs a contract of participation, which allows the PHA to withhold or terminate assistance if the family drops out of the program or if participants fail to seek jobs on completion.

As passed in 1990, the program had other features intended to encourage participation and completion, but some of these were attenuated in 1992 legislation. For example, the original program design provided that if the PHA could not meet its quota for Self-Sufficiency from incremental families and those currently receiving assistance, then families on the waiting list who do not want to participate in Self-Sufficiency would be bypassed in favor of those who do want to. This, however, was eliminated in 1992, before it could become effective; families on the waiting list cannot now be bypassed if they are unwilling to participate in Self-Sufficiency.

There is reason to believe that the Family Self-Sufficiency program can be effective. The program builds on two earlier demonstrations: Project Self-Sufficiency, a demonstration for single-parent families conducted by the HUD Office of Policy Development and Research beginning in 1984; and Project Bootstrap, which Secretary Kemp introduced in Miami in 1989. There were 10,000 participants in 155 sites in Project Self-Sufficiency, 3,000 participants in 61 sites in Project Bootstrap. These have been small demonstrations—averaging 50 to 60 per site. They were not identical to Family Self-Sufficiency. In Project Self-Sufficiency, for example, there was an effort to identify participants with a high probability of success, and the program did not include either an escrow account or sanctions.

HUD has not conducted a formal evaluation of Project Self-Sufficiency, but an interim assessment of program data from 40 communities indicates that it worked reasonably well. PHAs very much wanted to participate, although their only incentive was a small increment of housing certificates. Resources for training, counseling, and other services were available. It was expected that they would come from previously existing programs, especially the Job Training Partnership Act (JTPA) and the Work Incentive (WIN) program, and anecdotal evidence indicates that this was the case to a substantial extent. In most locations, however, new or expanded services were created to serve families in the program, and gifts and donations were provided by local public or private sources. These additional resources amounted to about $1,100 per participant.[17]

Most important, the program helped the participants—99% of them single women with children, 60% of them minority—to begin working their way out of poverty. Some 25% were employed at the time they applied; 2 years later, 48% were employed. Wage rates for employed workers were 20% higher at the later date. The typical employed participant was earning income above the eligibility limit for AFDC and Medicaid, although not for housing assistance. These data are roughly similar to those for JTPA participants. Employment rates for Project Self-Sufficiency were about 90% of those for AFDC recipients participating in JTPA in the same communities. Project Self-Sufficiency wage rates were about 6% higher (in this case, the JTPA data are not limited to AFDC recipients but include all participants). These comparisons are not exact; Project Self-Sufficiency data refer to all participants as of the time of the assessment, whether they had completed the program or not, whereas the

JTPA data are for those who have completed training (for further information, see HUD, 1987, esp. chap. 11). And as noted, Project Self-Sufficiency participants were selected on the basis of likelihood of success.

These findings do not constitute a full evaluation of Project Self-Sufficiency, but they give reason for optimism. HUD began a formal evaluation of Project Bootstrap in 1991 and scheduled an evaluation of the initial experience with Family Self-Sufficiency to begin in 1993. It should be possible to learn from those evaluations whether the program is working and what modifications, if any, may be needed.

The various self-sufficiency programs have a number of similarities with the Job Opportunities and Basic Skills (JOBS) program of welfare reform. They have an independent origin, however. Project Self-Sufficiency began in 1984; JOBS was not enacted until 1988. The experience with Project Self-Sufficiency was not considered in the legislative development of JOBS. The later HUD self-sufficiency programs, however, have been coordinated with it. JOBS does not have an escrow account, but it can be used as the basis for the HUD program, and its administrators are supposed to be members of the coordinating committee.

Although Family Self-Sufficiency has been designed primarily for voucher and certificate recipients, it has also been established on a smaller scale for residents of public housing. (This was a congressional addition to the original HUD proposal, which was limited to voucher and certificate holders.) The major difference is that assistance cannot be withheld or terminated for public housing residents if they fail to meet the program requirements. Some 3,000 public housing families participated in Project Self-Sufficiency in 1991 and 1992.

SHELTER PLUS CARE

The same approach of combining services with housing is taken in a new program to help homeless individuals with serious problems besides lack of housing: homeless persons who are chronically mentally ill, those with addiction problems, and those with AIDS.[18] It is clear from the studies of the homeless population that most do have some such serious nonhousing problem. Supportive services for these individuals are not usually provided by the same agency that provides housing. The Shelter Plus Care program combines them. In Shelter Plus Care, HUD provides housing assistance to a state or local government or, in some cases, a PHA; the latter provides supportive services. The services are often programs of other federal government agencies or state or local governments, although they may be privately provided as well. Several programs of the Department of Health and Human Services and the Department of Veterans Affairs—targeted to persons who are mentally ill or addicted, persons with AIDS, and others with serious physical problems—can be used as part of Shelter Plus Care. It can also be combined with special job training or adult education programs established by the Departments of Labor and Education for homeless persons.

The housing can be provided in several ways: sponsor-based rental assistance, under which the local agency contracts with nonprofit sponsors to lease housing; project-based assistance, under which the agency contracts with private owners of buildings to lease housing; the Single Room Occupancy (SRO) Moderate Rehabilitation program, under which SRO housing is rehabilitated and made available to homeless persons; and tenant-based rental assistance, under which the agency provides housing in a manner similar to the Section 8 existing housing program. The flexible rental assistance component can be used to house a homeless person initially in a specific building that provides housing for homeless persons and then support a move into an apartment building as the person progresses through the service component of the program.[19]

As in the case of Family Self-Sufficiency, the program provides incentives for individuals to continue participating in it. In particular, participants can lose housing assistance if they drop out of the medical or training programs. In effect, "shelter" is conditioned on "care."

Shelter Plus Care builds on a demonstration that HUD has undertaken with the Robert Wood Johnson Foundation in nine cities. In the demonstration, HUD is providing housing assistance in the form of rental certificates. The foundation is providing a grant to design a system of comprehensive support, tied to suitable housing. The grantee may be a local government, a private agency, or an agency bringing together both the public and private sectors. The grantee then designs and implements the system. The foundation may also provide seed money—funds for a city to buy housing, as it is doing in Toledo.

RESIDENT MANAGEMENT

Family Self-Sufficiency can be used in conventional public housing as well as the voucher and certificate program, as has already been mentioned. But there are other ways to empower public housing residents as well. One is resident management.

Resident management in public housing developments has two purposes. The original motivation was providing better housing and better living conditions for the residents. The other is the empowerment objective: The goal and hope are that residents will benefit broadly from taking control of their developments. They will develop a sense of self-esteem and self-worth, starting from the feeling that they have control over their housing, as a first step to having control over their lives. Also, as they develop skills in the process of managing their housing, they will be able to transfer these skills into the labor force and become productive members of society. In this sense, resident management is an effort to help the residents work their way out of poverty and dependency, achieving the original purpose of public housing.

Even with respect to the narrower goal of better housing, resident management may seem a dubious strategy. The management of a large multifamily housing development—public or private—requires skills that public housing residents are not likely to have. Experience shows, however, that resident management can and does work. Some public housing developments are poorly managed by PHAs; some of these developments have been turned into spectacular successes when residents took over the management. Experience with resident management goes back to 1972, at the Bromley-Heath development in Boston. There are still many skeptics; the successful examples are thought to be idiosyncratic. Kimi Gray in Washington's Kenilworth-Parkside development is the most visible and widely known resident manager. Located in the nation's capital, she is a dynamic individual. It is easy to argue that without her, resident management at Kenilworth-Parkside would not have been successful. Kimi Gray herself, however, does not think she is unique— she thinks that people like her are in every development. Certainly HUD has heard from people in literally hundreds of developments who at least want to know more about resident management, and many of them want to try it.

HUD released two evaluations of resident management in January 1993. The first describes the performance of 11 resident management corporations (RMCs) that have been in existence for more than 10 years (ICF Incorporated, 1993a). Most residents of these developments are single women and their children; the overwhelming majority are black and poor. They do not, however, consider themselves to be permanently poor, and they are not apathetic. They have taken the initiative to become the managers of their developments, often in the face of at least initial opposition from their PHAs.

The evaluation compared the developments managed by these RMCs with other similar developments located in the same cities and managed by PHAs and with the overall performance of the PHAs. It differentiated between "full-service" RMCs, which perform most of the management functions in their development and which are located in "troubled" PHAs, and "managing-agent" RMCs, which have a narrower range of responsibilities and which with one exception are not located in troubled PHAs. (Until January 1992, HUD designated PHAs as "troubled" on the basis of seven performance standards. Some 23 PHAs were classified as troubled—a small number, but all were large PHAs located in large cities, and together they managed almost 20% of all public housing units.)

The findings cover both housing management and empowerment. With respect to management, the evaluation concluded that these RMCs generally managed their developments better than the PHAs, probably at lower cost. Maintenance was performed more rapidly, for example, with a smaller staff. Management performance in particular was better for full-service RMCs.

With respect to empowerment, residents felt that the quality of life in RMC-managed developments was significantly better, including such aspects as crime and drug problems. Again, this was especially true for full-service RMCs. A larger share of residents went off welfare in full-service RMC-managed developments, although the absolute numbers—12% compared with 6%—are not large (ICF Incorporated, 1993a).

The evaluation could not eliminate the possibility of selection bias. It did not compare successful RMCs with unsuccessful ones.[20] Thus, it cannot directly address the skeptics' argument that resident management depends on the unique talents of a handful of individuals. But it did provide some information on this issue. It found some basis for concern about the depth of management expertise within RMCs and recommended efforts to expand the management cadre among residents. But it also found that RMCs were often cognizant of the potential problem and were actively working to recruit and train additional residents.

Resident management is a multistage process in any particular development, beginning with resident councils and developing into full-fledged RMCs. In the 5 years prior to 1993, HUD provided assistance to resident groups in more than 300 developments to establish resident management organizations. The second evaluation examines the progress of 80 of these organizations that received funding between 1988 and 1990 (ICF Incorporated, 1993b).[21] In the first 2 years after receiving funds, about one third of these organizations reached the point at which they were performing some of the management functions for their development. Two had already begun full management of their developments. If motivation is the key to successful resident management, the preliminary evidence is that many will be successful. Not all will—the evaluation concludes that perhaps 40% do not have good prospects of becoming successful managers of their developments. But the potential exists for substantial improvements in management and in empowerment of residents at many public housing developments.

HOPE

A further method of empowering the residents of public housing is owner-ship of their development. Resident management is not identical to resident ownership, although homeownership is a perfectly logical outcome of resi-dent management (and is possible after 3 years), and resident ownership in some developments has come about through resident management. Some resident management developments, however, may well choose to stop there; Bromley-Heath is an example.

Secretary Kemp has long been identified with resident ownership of public housing. That is an important part of HOPE. But it is only part: HOPE I. The program also includes HOPE II: homeownership in other government low-income multifamily developments, such as FHA-foreclosed or distressed FHA-insured developments, and HOPE III, for single-family housing that is publicly owned by HUD, Veterans Affairs, the Resolution Trust Corporation, other federal agencies, or state or local governments.[22] In addition, there is a significant homeownership component in HUD's strategy for the inventory of privately owned developments whose owners are becoming eligible to prepay their mortgages and convert to market rate housing. If the owners do not want to maintain the developments as affordable rental housing, they have to provide the residents with a right to make the first offer to purchase the property. HUD can make grants to the residents, through a nonprofit sponsor, for purchase and rehabilitation. This feature was added to the preservation program contained in the National Affordable Housing Act of 1990, at HUD's insistence. HUD has estimated that perhaps 225 developments, containing about 25,000 units, might be converted to homeownership.

As with resident management, the goal of resident ownership is to help the residents become self-sufficient and develop marketable skills. But there is an additional rationale: Homeowners are likely to behave differently *because* they own their own home. This is the traditional public policy argument that homeowners are better citizens—people with a stake in the society. Home-ownership thus empowers the poor in two ways: They are better citizens, and they are also more skilled citizens, more productive members of society. The second way is perhaps implicit in the first but has not been emphasized in discussions of the social value of homeownership, so far as I am aware.

These HOPE programs were enacted in the fall of 1990 but not funded until fiscal year 1992. (The appropriated funds in both fiscal years 1992 and 1993 amounted to $161 million for HOPE I, $95 million for HOPE II, and $95 million for HOPE III.) The discussion in this chapter centers on HOPE I, with some attention to HOPE III as well.[23]

HOPE I

In HOPE I, some 231 planning grants were awarded in fiscal year 1992, providing $1,000 per unit, up to $200,000 per development; 18 implementation grants were made, to achieve actual homeownership, at a cost of $22,000 per unit. In addition, local grant recipients—nonprofit organizations or local governments—must match each dollar of federal money with 25 cents from their own resources.

The cost of resident ownership is the subject of much confusion. About 60% of the funds in the implementation grants were spent for costs that HUD would pay anyway, if the developments remained as rental housing: rehabilitation or modernization of the development (about 40%) and operating subsidies (about 20%). The popular discussion of modernization is especially confused. Much of the public housing stock is old—some 43% was built before 1960—and much of it has not been adequately maintained. Congress annually appropriates some $2 to $3 billion for public housing modernization, and studies indicate a backlog of modernization needs of $10 to $20 billion, with the exact amount depending on the quality standard established as the objective of the modernization.[24]

Modernization of individual public housing developments is often quite expensive, independently of whether the developments are converted to resident ownership. Relevant data on its costs are available from seven public housing homeownership conversions of multifamily developments that occurred prior to HOPE I. Costs varied widely: less than $3,000 per unit in three developments, between $10,000 and $30,000 in three others, and up to $61,000 in Kenilworth-Parkside. The high Kenilworth-Parkside figure is politically significant because of the previously mentioned prominence of this development and its leadership. It is not likely to be typical of the nation as a whole; modernization costs in the District of Columbia have been high in other developments also.[25]

HOPE I also permits subsidies to pay the operating costs of the housing for 5 to 10 years. The subsidy is to be phased out during the period, rather than remaining constant for 5 or 10 years and then terminating abruptly. The subsidy can be as large as the operating subsidies given to the development under the Performance Funding System, which provides funds to cover the difference between the cost of operating a development in a well-managed PHA and 30% of the household's income. (Residents are required to pay 30% of their income toward the cost of ownership if they are receiving operating subsidies.) Thus, the annual subsidy to the resident is no larger than the subsidy HUD pays for the development to be managed as rental housing.

Other costs, mainly for technical assistance, were quite modest in the homeownership conversions that preceded HOPE I, ranging from $600 per unit in two developments to $2,000 in Kenilworth-Parkside. These costs are likely to be higher in HOPE I; as noted, the program allows planning grants of up to $200,000 per development and funds for technical assistance as well.

Finally, HOPE I also includes funds to promote economic development activities in resident-owned developments, up to $250,000 per development. The activities are likely to be small-scale service and retailing enterprises, such as child care centers, convenience stores, and housing management services.

Because HOPE I has the objective of improving the economic skills and circumstances of the residents, it includes plans for partnerships with the Departments of Health and Human Services, Education, and Labor to provide supportive services, education, and job training. These include a Child Care Demonstration, so parents of young children can get jobs or job training. As part of this effort, HUD has supported the extension of Head Start in public housing.

In HOPE I (and also HOPE II), ownership of the development will probably be vested in a nonprofit resident cooperative in most instances. Residents will own shares in the cooperative. Other forms of ownership are possible, however, including condominiums and fee simple ownership of single-family housing.[26] A development may be managed by the residents themselves, or the cooperative or condominium association may choose to hire a management agent.

In HOPE I, the housing must be given to the resident management organization by the PHA at no cost, if HUD approves the proposal for homeownership. This is because the federal government already paid for the development when it was built. Units must be replaced on a one-for-one basis, however; an additional subsidized rental unit must be funded by HUD for every unit sold to residents. Units can be replaced by new public housing units, by certificates or vouchers, or by local programs with comparable provisions and benefits.

The sponsor in turn can sell the units (or shares in the cooperative) to the residents. Sales prices must be affordable, that is, families can pay no more than 30% of their income to purchase their homes. The sales price, however, can be subsidized out of the HOPE grant. Thus, the actual cost to a family may be much less than the sales price. The HOPE grant and the local match can cover either the full cost of converting the development to homeownership (including "hard costs" such as rehabilitation and "soft costs" such as counseling) or only certain costs, with the remaining ones financed through a blanket mortgage to the cooperative. Where real costs of converting to homeownership are passed on to the home buyer, mortgages will be necessary. In addition, even in those cases in which all costs are covered by the HOPE grant and the match, the sponsor or the cooperative may want to require purchasers to take out mortgages and use the mortgage payments to create additional homeownership or economic development opportunities.

HOPE III

In fiscal year 1992, HUD awarded 135 HOPE III planning grants, averaging about $74,000 per grant, and 103 implementation grants, averaging about $825,000 per grant, to local governments and nonprofit organizations. Recipients were required to put up 33 cents of their own resources for each dollar of federal money.

The implementation grants provide funds for about 4,100 homeowners, at a cost of $21,000 per home. Most of this money is spent to acquire and rehabilitate a home. The sponsor then sells the home to an eligible low-income buyer, who pays no more than 30% of his or her income toward the cost of the home. If this is less than the value of the home, the remainder becomes a "soft second" mortgage, on which there is no interest and the buyer does not pay the principal until the house is sold, and then only if the sales proceeds are large enough to cover part or all of it. In addition, the soft second mortgage is forgiven through time as the family lives in the house; it is forgiven on a pro rata basis beginning after 7 years and continuing through 20 years, at which time it is completely forgiven. As with HOPE I, the sponsor can use the money from the sale to expand its homeownership program. The home buyer typically pays less than the value of the home and, in addition, receives counseling and training in an effort to ensure successful homeownership.

HOMEOWNERSHIP VOUCHERS

In 1992, the administration expanded the homeownership opportunities available to low-income households by proposing a homeownership voucher, which was enacted by Congress. Vouchers and certificates can now be used by low-income households to buy single-family homes or condominiums. (Previously, they could be used to support homeownership in cooperatives.) The voucher or certificate works in exactly the same way as the corresponding rental program: The household chooses a unit and uses the assistance, in combination with its own resources, to make mortgage payments and pay operating costs on the home. Families are required to obtain their own mortgage financing, with part of the voucher allocated to the lender to cover the monthly mortgage payment. Families that want to buy homes are required to enroll in a Family Self-Sufficiency program modeled on the program for renters and must also participate in a homeownership counseling program. They are required to reach certain self-sufficiency milestones, including 6 months' continuous employment, before qualifying for the homeownership voucher. They are eligible for an escrow account and can use up to 50% of the account for a down payment. Up to 20% of the down payment can also come from state, local, or nonprofit programs for down payment assistance.

Homeownership vouchers increase the housing choices available to low-income families. Some 11% of the owner-occupied housing in the United States is within their means through the voucher: 10% of the central city stock, 8% of the suburban stock, and 16% of nonmetropolitan owner-occupied housing. About 42% of the available owner-occupied housing is located within the suburbs. More than half the homes are single-family houses (HUD, 1992b).

Both HOPE and the homeownership voucher program build on a previous public housing homeownership demonstration, known as the Section 5(h) demonstration, which began in 1985 (for evaluation, see Rohe & Stegman, 1990).[27] Thirteen PHAs participated in the demonstration, selling a total of 320 units during a period of 4 to 5 years. The demonstration shows that public housing homeownership can work and that low-income families do feel a sense of empowerment when they become homeowners. Most buyers were quite satisfied with their homes and, also (to a somewhat lesser extent), their neighborhoods. A majority (60%) indicated that their chief reason for buying a home was to have an asset.[28] A larger majority (75%) also reported feeling better about themselves and enjoying a higher quality of life. Just more than half had an increased sense of control over their lives. About one third reported that they were more involved with their neighborhood and their local government; virtually none were less involved.

Some findings from the demonstration suggested features of the design of HOPE and the homeownership voucher. Homeownership counseling was clearly desirable and therefore was incorporated in both programs. Also, nearly all buyers in the demonstration were employed. For this reason, the homeownership voucher includes the requirement that a participant be employed for 6 months before using the voucher to buy a home. In addition, the home buyers in the demonstration generally had substantially higher incomes than the typical public housing resident. HOPE I therefore makes operating subsidies available for 5 to 10 years for public housing residents who cannot afford the costs of homeownership without assistance; the homeownership voucher, of course, increases the ability of low-income households to afford their own home.

ENTERPRISE ZONES

The enterprise zone is the other major urban initiative that is identified with Secretary Kemp. It is, of course, not a housing program, and it is not often thought of in the same context as resident ownership of public housing, but it has the same objective and to some extent the same means of achieving that objective. One works through the channel of housing programs and one through the tax code, but both are intended to empower poor people—to enable them to take control of their lives and improve their economic position—and both try to achieve this objective by helping poor people acquire assets. The enterprise zone proposal as was advocated by Secretary Kemp is predicated on the belief that low-income *entrepreneurship* is possible for poor people living in poverty neighborhoods, and it seeks to promote entrepreneurship, not just employment, for poor people.

The most extensive enterprise zone legislation was developed by the Bush administration after the Los Angeles riots in April 1992. Unfortunately, it was not enacted. The proposal provided incentives for employing low-income workers and also incentives to encourage entrepreneurship by zone residents. The most important of these were the following:[29]

1. The tax on capital gains on assets located in a federal enterprise zone would have been eliminated; this applied to new investment, either in existing companies or new enterprises.

2. Alternatively, stock purchases in enterprise zone businesses could have been expensed, up to $50,000 per year per investor, or $250,000 lifetime.

3. Residents in enterprise zones or workers in zone businesses (including entrepreneurs) could have received both of these benefits.

4. Businesses could have received the equivalent of plant and equipment expensing, in the form of a back-loaded depreciation schedule with a present value equal to the cost of the equipment (the Neutral Cost Recovery System advocated by Senator Robert Kasten and Representative Vin Weber). This provision was designed to provide incentives to invest in capital assets that would depreciate through time.

5. Small businesses could have expensed up to $50,000 of plant and equipment expenditures, instead of the present limit of $10,000, under Section 179(k) of the Internal Revenue Code.

6. Banks could lend money to businesses located in enterprise zones without paying federal income taxes on the interest, within the current dollar caps for such "exempt facilities" loans. Tax-exempt financing is now available for a narrow range of businesses; it would have been available to a broad range of businesses within enterprise zones.

7. Enterprise zone workers not eligible for the Earned Income Tax Credit would have been allowed to claim the credit. In practice, this applied mainly to young workers without dependents, who would have at least a modest incentive to enter the labor force; they would have been allowed to claim the credit on the same basis as if they had one dependent child. In fiscal year 1993, this credit would

have amounted to up to $1,435 for workers with incomes up to $12,210, phasing out for workers with total annual wages above $23,070. The credit would have been available to workers in enterprise zone businesses, whether or not the workers themselves lived in the enterprise zone.

The first six of these incentives were designed to promote business development in the enterprise zone; the last to promote employment within the zone. The balance between incentives to capital and to labor was about 50-50 in dollar terms. The focus was on new and small entrepreneurial activities. Although it was not a specific component of the legislation, one goal was to promote minority-owned businesses, which now compose an estimated 7% of the total in the United States, some 800,000 out of 12 million enterprises (HUD, 1991a, p. 32).

These benefits were available only in areas of extremely high poverty, with little economic activity and virtually no local opportunities for the residents. Enterprise zones were defined as urban neighborhoods or rural areas with a poverty rate of at least 45% and containing at least one census tract with a poverty rate of 50%. Under this definition, about 200 city neighborhoods and 100 rural areas, with about 3.5 million residents, would have qualified as enterprise zones. The urban zones would have been located mainly in predominantly minority neighborhoods in the largest cities, particularly in the Northeast and Midwest. Since the mid-1970s, the poverty rate within cities has been rising relative to suburbs and nonmetropolitan areas, and within central cities, poverty is becoming more concentrated in and near areas that already have high concentrations of the poor population. The rural zones would have been concentrated along the Mississippi River in Arkansas, Louisiana, and Mississippi; along the Rio Grande in South Texas; and among the Indian reservations of the West and Southwest.

To be designated as an enterprise zone business and therefore to be eligible for the tax incentives, a business would have had to be located in the zone and conduct much of its activity within the zone. In addition, one third of its employees would have had to be residents of the zone. This was intended to discourage businesses from moving into the zone merely to take advantage of the tax benefits, without generating new economic activity that would benefit residents of the zone.

The enterprise zone proposal was narrowly focused on economic opportunities for residents of the zones and other low-income individuals. Thus, the criteria for designation as an enterprise zone and a zone business were more restrictive than those in many of the 37 states with enterprise zone legislation.

Conclusion

For a decade before he was the secretary of HUD, Jack Kemp forcefully advocated public housing resident ownership and enterprise zones, so it should not be surprising that he attempted to put these concepts into practice at HUD. It is not widely recognized that these two apparently dissimilar policies have the same objective of helping poor people become productive members of society or that they are part of an overall effort that includes other initiatives. The agenda stresses two avenues to empowerment: enabling poor persons to acquire assets, particularly to become homeowners, and helping them to develop the skills that they need to work themselves out of poverty. These approaches have been incorporated into a range of housing programs, as well as homeownership for public housing residents and enterprise zones.

The objective of the broad HOPE program is similar to that of the original public housing program. But there are important differences as well. In the 1930s, it was widely believed that tearing down the slums and building new decent housing for the poor was by itself enough to improve the health of people in poverty and make them better citizens. Today few analysts share that belief. Therefore, housing assistance has been combined with other resources to help those who are poor escape from poverty and dependency.

The objective of the HOPE initiative is also similar to the goals of the original war on poverty. HOPE is a contemporary effort to fight poverty systematically, using the tools that are available to HUD and adding other tools from other sources, including other federal, state, and local agencies and the private sector as well. Ultimately, the success of the HOPE initiative will be judged on whether the participants improve their *lives,* rather than just their *housing.*

Notes

1. The HOPE acronym (for Homeownership and Opportunity for People Everywhere) also is used for other programs in the overall antipoverty initiative. The term "a new war on poverty" is used in *The President's National Urban Policy Report* (HUD, 1991a) to describe the administration's program. See especially pages 1 and 2 of the introduction. The term has also been used in numerous congressional hearings and other public statements.

2. For single women and their children, for example, the poverty rate declined during the economic recovery of the late 1970s, from 44.0% in 1975 to 39.6% in 1979; it rose during the subsequent back-to-back recessions to 47.8% in 1982; it declined to 42.8% by 1989; and it rose to 47.1% in 1991, during the recent recession. For married couples with children, the cycles are similar: a decline from 7.2% to 6.1% in the later 1970s; an increase to 10.1% by 1983; a decline

to 7.2% through 1988; and an increase to 8.3% by 1991. These data are taken from U.S. Department of Commerce (1992).

3. These statements are based on simple regression analyses of the poverty rates (both levels and percentage point changes) for the different groups against the unemployment rate. The regressions are not intended as formal models of poverty—indeed, in my judgment, efforts to model the poverty rate have not been particularly successful—but merely to verify that the basic data support the popular and policy concerns about poverty among female-headed single-parent families.

4. The other rationale was macroeconomic; building low-income housing was expected to stimulate the economy and help end the Great Depression. This countercyclical rationale has essentially been discarded; indeed, President Franklin D. Roosevelt chose other construction activities in preference to public housing, in effect reprogramming funds appropriated for housing. In recent years, there has been little academic or political interest in subsidized housing programs as an instrument of macroeconomic policy.

5. One suggested approach was legal: to declare in statute that decent housing was self-evidently important, and leave it at that. This view is expressed in Semer, Zimmerman, Foard, and Frantz (1976). For most social scientists, obviously, this view is unsatisfactory, but it does illustrate the impatience of "practical" housing professionals with attempts to analyze the rationale for the programs that are the basis of their businesses.

6. In the context of this chapter, the distinctions between certificates and vouchers are not important; the statement in the text refers to both.

7. Incremental project-based assistance has continued even though the Section 8 new construction program was terminated. The incremental units have been produced through the original public housing program, the Section 202 program for elderly persons, rehabilitation programs that are variations on Section 8 new construction, and Section 8 new construction units that were completed after the program was terminated in 1983. (Most housing construction programs have had long "pipelines," so that projects are still being completed and occupied several years after the program has been terminated.)

8. The American Housing Survey is a biennial survey of a sample of households. It started in 1973 as an annual survey; then it was called the Annual Housing Survey. See U.S. Department of Commerce (1973-1983) and U.S. Department of Commerce (1985).

9. The measure of severely inadequate housing used in this intertemporal comparison differs slightly from the measure that is currently preferred by HUD. The preferred measure is higher, but by less than one half of one percentage point. The discussion of current priority housing problems later in this section uses the preferred measure.

10. The same patterns hold for nonelderly individuals, who are not eligible for housing assistance unless they are disabled. The incidence of physical problems declined, whereas rent burdens increased between 1974 and 1989. The percentages with either problem are higher than those for families and elderly individuals, but the relative importance of rent burden and inadequacy are similar. In 1989, 44% of very low income nonelderly individual renters paid more than 50% of their income for rent, and 8% lived in severely inadequate housing (about 3% had both problems). For presentation of the data in more detail, see HUD (1991b).

11. Some 300,000 of these 2.9 million households lived in "moderately inadequate" housing, meaning that their units had some maintenance problems or lacked some equipment, but the deficiencies could probably have been remedied.

12. These units rent at or below the fair market rent (FMR) in their local housing market. The FMR is the maximum amount that HUD will pay toward the rent of a unit subsidized under the tenant-based assistance programs. In the case of certificates, it is the maximum rent for a unit; units with higher rents are ineligible for the program. In the case of vouchers, it is the maximum

that HUD will pay, but the household can choose to occupy a more expensive unit and pay the amount above the FMR from its own resources. Families with incomes of zero receive the full amount of the FMR; for families with some income, HUD pays the difference between the FMR and 30% of the family's income.

13. Crowding is not considered a priority housing problem in the legislation but is unacceptable under HUD program standards. Thus, a family with a high rent burden and with more than one person per room would need to move to a larger unit to receive a voucher or certificate.

14. These data are taken from an unpublished tabulation performed by the Office of Policy Development and Research at HUD. They are similar to a published tabulation for a 4% vacancy rate, reported in HUD (1993, Table 10, p. 31).

15. The same upward trend has occurred for low-income benefits as a whole, contrary to popular impression. Welfare spending has been rising since 1983, in real terms, relative to the low-income population. This continues a long-term trend, although there was a decline during the early 1980s. Federal outlays per poor person on income-conditioned programs fell from $3,000 in 1980 to $2,700 in 1983 but then rose steadily and reached $3,200 in 1990 (all measured in 1992 dollars). In 1975, outlays per poor person were $2,700, as they were 8 years later. The 1990 figure was a record high, as were the figures for each year since 1986, even though the economy was expanding during those years.

16. This is a modification, enacted in 1992, of the program as it was enacted in 1990. Originally, half of the increase in the family's rental payment went into the escrow account, and the other half went to the landlord. HUD's payment therefore declined as the family's income increased but only half as much as it would for a family not participating in Family Self-Sufficiency. In addition, there was a notch; when the family's income went above 50% of median, its rental payment increased by half of the total increase between the new rent that it should pay and its original payment. If the family was originally paying $300 a month and would be paying $500 a month if its income were 50% of the local median, then its rent did not increase above $300 until its income rose to 50% of median; but at that point, its rent became $400 per month.

17. Unfortunately, HUD did not collect information on the services that were provided by previously existing programs without expanding their effort.

18. The Family Self-Sufficiency approach was not extended to programs for homeless persons previously enacted (McKinney Homeless Assistance Act programs), which served individuals and families without medical problems. Fundamentally, it was decided that they would generally be able to participate in the basic housing assistance programs, for which they have priority, and therefore it was not necessary to create a separate program that combined housing and services. The Transitional Housing Program already included services and participants in the program were using those services, and a *requirement* for service participation was redundant. Awards for housing construction or rehabilitation under the Transitional Housing Program program were based in part on the coordination of supportive services with the housing. The program was expected to enable participants to make the transition to independent living (perhaps with a voucher or certificate) in 24 months.

19. The program makes various changes to the SRO Moderate Rehabilitation program to make it fit the Shelter Plus Care goals. The original SRO Moderate Rehabilitation program is not targeted to specific groups of the homeless population and does not have a match requirement.

20. Six RMCs that were established as part of a 1975 demonstration were unsuccessful and are no longer in existence. The recent HUD evaluation did not attempt to compare these RMCs with those that are still operating. The 1975 demonstration was conducted by the Manpower Development Research Corporation with funds from the Ford Foundation and HUD. For an analysis of it, see Manpower Development Research Corporation (1980).

21. Many of the resident organizations were in existence before they received funds. They were not involved in management activities, however. This distinguishes them from the 11 RMCs described in the previous discussion and evaluation.

22. The terminology of the program may be somewhat confusing because (as explained in note 1) the HOPE acronym is used both for specific homeownership programs and for the overall antipoverty initiative, including Family Self-Sufficiency and Shelter Plus Care, for example.

23. HOPE II has developed more slowly than the other two ownership programs. Through the end of fiscal year 1992, HUD had awarded two implementation grants to convert government-owned multifamily developments to resident ownership.

24. HUD's current estimate of unfunded modernization backlog is about $17 billion, measured in 1990 dollars; this number is based on one of several possible quality standards. For a discussion of modernization needs, see HUD (1990).

25. That modernization represents such a large share of the cost of HOPE I raises the question of whether HOPE I diverts modernization funds away from developments in which the residents are not interested in homeownership. This seems unlikely. During the legislative negotiations leading up to the creation of HOPE and the appropriations process in subsequent years, there was no discussion of a trade-off between HOPE I and modernization funding; nor do the annual modernization appropriations levels show any reduction or offset as HOPE I was funded. It is only possible to speculate about what the HUD budget and appropriation would have looked like in the absence of HOPE I; my judgment is that the overall funding level would have been lower, and perhaps a few thousand more households would have received incremental assistance.

26. About 10% of public housing units are single-family homes. Beginning in 1993, these homes could be purchased under HOPE III; in 1992, they could be purchased under HOPE I if they were contiguous, or under HOPE III if they were on scattered sites.

27. The factual statements in this paragraph about the demonstration are taken from Rohe and Stegman (1990). Rohe and Stegman tend to stress, however, what they see as inherent limitations on the potential for homeownership for public housing residents. They emphasize, for example, that four PHAs that originally chose to participate in the demonstration did not in fact sell any units during the period and that only about one quarter as many units were actually sold in the demonstration as were originally planned.

28. The most important reasons given for buying a home were "to have good financial investment" (29%), "to have something to leave children" (17%), and "to have something to call ours" (14%).

29. The administration offered and supported somewhat different versions of the enterprise zone legislation in the House and Senate. The discussion in the text combines the two proposals. It is worth noting, however, that the zero capital gains tax rate was limited in the Senate to small businesses, and the Neutral Cost Recovery System was added to the Senate proposal to provide incentives for larger firms. Also, the rate and earnings limits for the Earned Income Tax Credit extension differed between the House and Senate proposals.

References

ICF Incorporated. (1993a, January). *Evaluation of resident management in public housing.* Fairfax, VA: Author.

ICF Incorporated. (1993b, January). *Report on emerging resident management corporations in public housing.* Fairfax, VA: Author.

Jacobs, J. (1962). *The death and life of great American cities.* New York: Random House.

Kasl, S. V. (1976). Effects of housing on mental and physical health. In National Housing Policy Review (Ed.), *Housing in the seventies: Working papers* (Vol. 1, pp. 286-304). Washington, DC: U.S. Department of Housing and Urban Development.

Manpower Development Research Corporation. (1980). *Final report on the national tenant management demonstration.* New York: Author.

McKinney Homeless Assistance Act, Pub. L. No. 100-77, 101 Stat. 482, 42 U.S.C. § 11301 et seq.

National Affordable Housing Act of 1990, Pub. L. No. 101-625, 42 U.S.C. § 12701 et seq.

Rohe, W. M., & Stegman, M. A. (1990, April). *Public housing homeownership demonstration assessment.* Washington, DC: U.S. Department of Housing and Urban Development.

Rothenberg, J. (1976). A rationale for government intervention in housing: The externalities generated by good housing. In National Housing Policy Review (Ed.), *Housing in the seventies: Working papers* (Vol. 1, pp. 267-285). Washington, DC: U.S. Department of Housing and Urban Development.

Section 8 (1974), Pub. L. No. 93-383, 88 Stat 653, 42 U.S.C. § 1437(f).

Section 236 (1968), Pub. L. No. 90-448, 82 Stat. 498, 12 U.S.C. § 1715(z)(1).

Seligman, D. (1958). The enduring slums. In Editors of Fortune (Eds.), *The exploding metropolis* (pp. 92-114). Garden City, NY: Doubleday.

Semer, M. P., Zimmerman, J. H., Foard, A., & Frantz, J. M. (1976). A review of federal subsidized housing programs. In National Housing Policy Review (Ed.), *Housing in the seventies: Working papers* (Vol. 1, pp. 82-145). Washington, DC: U.S. Department of Housing and Urban Development.

U.S. Department of Commerce, Bureau of the Census. (1940). *Census of Population and Housing.* Washington, DC: Government Printing Office.

U.S. Department of Commerce, Bureau of the Census, and U.S. Department of Housing and Urban Development, Office of Policy Development and Research. (1973-1983). *Annual Housing Survey* (Current Housing Reports, Series H-150). Washington, DC: Government Printing Office.

U.S. Department of Commerce, Bureau of the Census, and U.S. Department of Housing and Urban Development, Office of Policy Development and Research. (1985). *American housing survey for the United States* (Current Housing Reports, H-150). Washington, DC: Government Printing Office.

U.S. Department of Commerce, Bureau of the Census. (1992, August). *Poverty in the United States: 1991* (Current Population Reports, Series P-60, No. 181). Washington, DC: Government Printing Office.

U.S. Department of Housing and Urban Development. (1987, December). *Project self-sufficiency: An interim report on progress and performance.* Washington, DC: Author.

U.S. Department of Housing and Urban Development. (1990, April). *Report to Congress on alternative methods for funding public housing modernization.* Washington, DC: Author.

U.S. Department of Housing and Urban Development, Office of Policy Development and Research. (1991a). *The president's national urban policy report.* Washington, DC: Author.

U.S. Department of Housing and Urban Development. (1991b, June). *Priority housing problems and "worst case" needs in 1989: A report to Congress.* Washington, DC: Author.

U.S. Department of Housing and Urban Development. (1992a, March). *Characteristics of HUD-assisted renters and their housing: 1989.* Washington, DC: Author.

U.S. Department of Housing and Urban Development. (1992b). [Program data and briefing summaries]. Unpublished program data.

U.S. Department of Housing and Urban Development. (1993, January). *The location of worst case needs in the late 1980s.* Washington, DC: Author.

11

What We Can Learn
From Grassroots Leaders

Robert L. Woodson, Sr.

From my experience with hundreds of low-income grassroots people who have worked to transform their communities, I have learned one thing: The foundation of enduring change lies in an internal transformation, not simply in external programs and policies.

Not every leader can inspire that type of transformation. There is no shortcut to it. Only persons who are examples of the values they speak of and who are willing to give long-term commitment and personal investment can reach and change the hearts of others. As someone once said, it took Moses about 2 weeks to get the Israelites out of Egypt but 40 years to get Egypt out of the Israelites.

I was impressed with Spike Lee's (1992) film *Malcolm X*. As Malcolm X underwent a personal transformation, he demonstrated that, although people may not be in control of their environment, they can always be the masters of their *response* to the environment. Malcolm X's life changed not because any external circumstances were altered. White people did not become more fair or less racist. The conditions in his prison did not become better. But Malcolm X took control when he embraced a belief in God and changed his view of the world. This type of change is the foundation of nearly every effective community-based program.

Researchers must acknowledge the limitations of isolated academic discourse about how sanctions or incentives should be developed for the poor. Policy theorists abound, and they span a broad spectrum. Some on the right say that the answer to poverty is to cut all support and to starve poor people into self-sufficiency. And there are those on the left who say that antipoverty programs have failed because they have not been funded adequately (e.g., Center for Urban Affairs and Policy Research, 1991; Community Service Society of New York, 1984). They ignore the fact that 70 cents of every dollar spent on them goes not to those who are poor but to those who make their living serving poor people (*Up From Dependency,* 1986). But the debate that rages among these academics has not served the interests of those who are living with the problem. As an old African proverb states, "When bull elephants fight, the grass always loses."

Recently, there has been a realization that there is a gap in this debate about the problems of America's low-income communities. In response, an effort has been made to bring together representatives of the left and right. But getting ideologues together will not produce workable solutions to the problems of the inner city. The crucial information gap is not between academics on the left and academics on the right. It is between the academic community and those who are experiencing the problems. It is fascinating that scholars can spend hours of discussion and years of research regarding low-income people and what should be done about them yet not once directly involve them in the discussion.

During 1992, the National Center for Neighborhood Enterprise (NCNE) coordinated a series of town meetings throughout the country in which hundreds of community leaders and grassroots activists testified about effective programs they have initiated to deal with the myriad of problems that face their low-income neighborhoods. A constant theme in their testimony was the internal transformation that occurred within the people they served, resulting in enduring behavioral changes.

James Q. Wilson has described the importance of the internal, or cultural, factors that affect social deviancy and are at the core of its solution. A current theory holds that economic factors are the exclusive determinants. This, however, is easily disproved. If researchers and policymakers claim that behavior is driven purely by economic incentives and then change those incentives but do not affect behavior, the theory is not very convincing. In fact, a combination of factors come into play when we look at what is happening in the inner cities, including values, beliefs, and perceptions—in brief, "culture." This is evidenced by nearly every community leader who participated in the NCNE town meetings.

Charles Ballard, who testified at the Detroit town meeting (March, 1992), has instituted a program to work with teen fathers. His effort has reached the lives of more than 2,000 young men, many of whom have now gone through court procedures to claim paternity of their children and many others of whom have chosen to marry and establish families.

The Dallas town meeting (September, 1992) featured Freddie Garcia, a rehabilitated drug addict who launched a rehabilitation program, Victory Outreach, which has now helped more than 13,000 former addicts to break their addiction. Some of Freddie's clients had been on hard drugs for 15 or 20 years. They have now been drug-free for an average of 7 years. He has reached out not only to those in his Hispanic community but also to blacks as well, who compose 25% of his program's enrollment.

These remarkable victories result from the consistent personal commitment of these community leaders and the conversion that they engendered. In his testimony, Freddie told of the failed attempts of traditional social service agencies and professionals who worked with him during his own addiction. "When I went into their care, I had a drug problem. After days of analysis, I was told that I was schizophrenic, suffered from low self-esteem, lacked consistency, and was incorrigible. I came out with more problems than I went in with, and I was still a drug addict!"

It is interesting to see how established government agencies have responded to the story of Freddie Garcia's success. Although his rehabilitative techniques consist of counseling and Bible studies and involve no chemical treatment, the authorities have demanded that his program should be licensed and regulated in the same way that medically based treatment centers are. If Freddie does not comply with this demand, he cannot compete for available funds and even risks being closed down.

Moreover, established professionals refuse to acknowledge, much less embrace, programs such as Charles Ballard's or Freddie Garcia's because their founders have lacked academic degrees and traditional credentials. It is ironic and tragic that in our society, the principles that guide the policies and practices of our market economy are abandoned when we consider the social economy.

Experience in the market economy has shown that most innovation occurs at the smallest commercial unit. IBM and Xerox thrived because they bought and built on inventions of smaller companies. In the business arena, businesspersons do not assume that credentials are needed to validate anyone's invention. If a high school dropout creates something that works, his or her invention will be valued purely on the basis of its effectiveness.

When I was in the service, I worked in the space program. One of my coworkers was Frank Risner, a technician with a high school education. One of the projects my department was working on was the development of a telemetry simulator, a box that is placed inside missiles to transmit information to earth regarding fuel consumption and various functions of the missiles. Seven systems engineers—graduates of MIT and other prestigious universities—worked for 6 months to produce this simulator, but as each was tested, it failed. Frank Risner was not assigned to the project, but he worked with the idea and produced a transistorized version of a telemetry simulator. Now the company did not say, "Risner doesn't have a degree, don't bother testing his simulator." The business sector is concerned primarily with outcomes. Risner's model was tested and it worked. He was promoted to senior engineer in charge of research and development for one shift at Cape Canaveral.

Now, let's go through the looking glass and see how the social economy functions. In the past 25 years, the United States has spent more money in our antipoverty programs than we spent fighting World War II—more money than the capital assets of all the *Fortune* 500 companies. Yet after this effort, conditions have not improved and have, in fact, worsened. Our response? To pour even more money into those same failed programs! Now, one of my favorite maxims is "If you keep doing what you are doing, you'll keep getting what you've got." Service professionals have no incentive to develop solutions because their programs are evaluated not for outcome but for process. They are rewarded for the number of people dependent on their services rather than the number they have boosted to self-sufficiency.

In the current system, because the social service industry, for its own sake, must maintain a portion of the population in a state of dependency, its policies are designed to disempower people and to thwart innovation and self-reliance. Within the realm of the social economy, the rules of the market economy are turned upside down. In the market economy, people are encouraged to accumulate savings. In the social economy, a poor person on welfare who manages to save risks being sent to jail. In the market economy, entrepreneurship and the creation of small businesses are encouraged. In the social economy, entrepreneurship is punished.

For example, not long ago, four low-income women on welfare in Baltimore launched a maintenance business with little more than brooms, dust cloths, and will. They approached the owner of one office building and offered to clean it for a week. If their work was satisfactory, they would ask for the contract. They did a superb job and were contracted to clean both that building and an additional one. As their business expanded, they were able to hire 12 more workers. Tragically, when the welfare department became aware of the women's enterprise, it seized their equipment and deducted their income, dollar for dollar, from their benefits (which it threatened to terminate).

In the market economy, effectiveness and efficiency are rewarded. Not so in the social economy. Regardless of their remarkable success, community leaders such as Charles Ballard or Freddie Garcia are ignored or rebuffed by the system's professionals. Despite their success, they are discounted because they do not have the proper credentials, they lack a high school diploma, or they speak with dangling participles and split infinitives. The Ph.D.s in charge of the system will not listen to their experiences. Their success is presumed to be not the outcome of an effective strategy but the results of some elusive personal charisma. Thirteen thousand rehabilitated drug addicts and 2,000 teens called to responsible parenthood are assumed to be simply under the influence of a charismatic leader.

Now, in the realm of medical science, if a physician found some drug that happened to remove the symptoms of AIDS from nine little laboratory monkeys, he would be on the front page of daily papers throughout the country. Even if the actual cure could not be developed for 20 years, we would say that we have to invest resources in this research.

We do not applaud the success of grassroots activism in this way. Before we will accept the results of a community-based program, we screen its strategy to ensure (a) that it does not offend any major unions such as the National Association of Social Workers and (b) that it does not impinge on the turf of any of those who staff what I call the "poverty pentagon"—the multitude of psychologists, counselors, and social service providers. To receive a hearing, community-based programs must not disturb the interest groups that profit from the existence of poverty. Politicians are sensitive to anything that offends these groups. Possibly the worst offense would be to include the *G* word in any program description. *God* is clearly not in the vocabulary of the social service industry. Although NCNE's town meeting testimony showed that the majority of outstanding, effective programs were faith based and value driven, this type of talk is shunned in professional circles and treated as a form of intellectual heresy. At best, the directors of such programs are treated with condescension and assumed to be unsophisticated. At worst, they are labeled as conservatives.

But the fact is, a grassroots revolution is underway that is reclaiming community after community, and the fuel of this movement is its moral and ethical nature. In the NCNE town meetings, the testimony of hundreds of effective community leaders from a variety of racial and ethnic backgrounds revealed that they had one thing in common: A key factor in the success of their efforts was their faith. The audience was filled with young men and women whose lives these leaders had touched who were evidence of their transforming power. Although the crisis of the inner cities involves economic and social factors, it also involves internal or spiritual factors. The grassroots leaders I have met can, uniquely, reach out and deal in this realm.

Those who are at the front of the battle to save our inner cities are not necessarily in line with the spokespersons that purportedly represent them.

Just as in the early days of the civil rights revolution, those who claimed the beachhead did not always speak with the same voice as those who stood at the podiums. In fact, civil rights leaders were vehemently opposed to a strategy of civil disobedience when those young students took the lead and sat in at the now famous Woolworth's counter in Greensboro, North Carolina. But their action ignited a moral brushfire that swept the nation.

Empowerment starts on an internal level, and it starts at the grass roots. Government cannot initiate it, but neither should it oppose it. The various groups mandated to serve poor people must put aside their own interests and begin to study the solutions that are even now employed by those who live within America's low-income communities.

Traditionally, studies on the problems of the inner city amount to no more than a litany of deficiencies. We spend massive funds on social science research each year, and among reams of statistics and reports, one would be hard-pressed to find even one study that focuses on the capacities, rather than the incapacities, of low-income communities. There is no deficiency in the quantity of data, but there is a definite deficiency in their content. The most important data have never been entered in the researchers' computers.

Let us be clear that we do not learn anything from studying failure but how to create it. In the market economy, if we wanted to learn how to establish a computer software company, we would never go to three people who have failed in the business and ask to study their failures. Yet this is precisely what we do in our poverty studies. Researchers go into low-income neighborhoods with their clipboards and ask questions we wouldn't allow them to ask our own families: "Are you sexually active? Are you on drugs? Have you ever been in prison?" What a waste of the efforts of the best minds in our universities! Instead, researchers should be going into these neighborhoods to find out how some people in these same environments are able to raise kids who are not on drugs, in jail, dropping out of school, or having babies in their teens. We must begin to ask what these successful parents are doing that is different from what their neighbors are doing. We have to take what we can learn from them and bring them to speak at public forums, asking them thoughtful questions, recording their answers, and, as professionals, defining the operating principles that explain their success.

We can enhance their efforts and the efforts of effective community leaders. We can provide the training and technical assistance that can augment their success. We must learn how to be "on tap" rather than on top. Our goal should be to transfer our skills to those who are working in their low-income communities and to promote their independence and self-sufficiency. We must, as professionals, begin to measure success not by how many people need our help but by how many people no longer need our help. One tactic would be to take the funds that we currently spend each year on each household in poverty (which ranges from $8,500 to $15,000; see Ferrara, 1994) and give the entire sum directly to those recipients. At least, we must give them an opportunity to own assets and to create wealth. Our discussion should go beyond how to create jobs for those who are poor and focus instead on how to facilitate their enterprise formation and the attainment of assets.

There is no lack of creativity or will in low-income people, as is evidenced by a resourceful enterprise launched by the residents of Cochran Gardens public housing development in St. Louis, Missouri. When a group of residents, organized as the Tenant Affairs Council, realized that a private company was delivering 240 meals-on-wheels within their neighborhood, they recognized the value of their own cooking skills and competed for—and won—that contract. Although meals from the previous company had often been discarded, half-eaten, the demand for meals cooked by the public housing women soared. As one of the cooks explained, "We understand what kind of food these folks like. We threw out the recipe for such items as lamb patties and created our own menu instead." Their delivery route rose to 2,000 units in one year and could increase to as many as 8,000 as they expand their service area to include day-care centers, prisons, and schools. This enterprise created 43 jobs in the community and is still thriving today, along with other entrepreneurial ventures launched by the tenant board such as day-care centers and a transportation service (Tenant Affairs Council, personal communication; "The Roots of Resident Empowerment," 1991).

We should acknowledge the entrepreneurial capacities of low-income people and equip them with the training and technical assistance that can allow their enterprises to expand. In sum, researchers have a moral responsibility to listen to the people who are experiencing the problems before they begin to propose their solutions for them. Much of what is done today in the name of scholarly research is, in fact, no more than intellectual incest. Academics remain in a closed circle, writing about one another's writings, theorizing on each other's theories, and proclaiming what is best for low-income people.

The experts say that low-income kids would not work for a minimum-wage job. But young people *will* work, and they will receive more from their jobs than a paycheck. Although a minimum-wage job may not be training for a career, it imparts to young people the basics of a work ethic and a sense of responsibility. These are things they can carry through life. We should never use the word *menial* to describe work. All work is noble.

The experts say that low-income people should not be held to high standards of accountability. They have created a myth and a fear of employing social sanctions against low-income blacks who are not responsible. This is condescending and insulting. I was divorced when my two sons, now 27 and 29, were 2 and 4. I knew that I had responsibilities as their father. I visited them regularly. I voluntarily paid child support, and whenever I got an increase in my salary, I raised my child-support payments. If there was trouble at my sons' school, their mother and I would be there together to talk with the teacher. From my own experience, I urge my colleagues not to embrace as friends men who do not take care of the children that they bring into this world. We have to restore the understanding that there is right and wrong and principles that must not be violated.

The experts say that a policy that offers school vouchers is not a good idea. But before they speak on behalf of low-income parents, they should listen to what those parents think of the idea. Before we promote or discount a policy recommendation, we should listen to what the people who will be affected by it are saying. Most of the people who are vehemently opposed to school choice or strongly promote busing children do not have their own children in public schools or on those buses. I call this moral inconsistency.

And listening to low-income people does not mean checking in with a figurehead who supposedly represents them. It means asking those people, directly, what they think. A recent national survey revealed a remarkable divergence between the views of black Americans and those commonly identified as black leaders (specifically, 105 representatives of the NAACP, the National Urban League, Southern Christian Leadership Conference, Operation PUSH, National Conference of Black Mayors, and the Congressional Black Caucus). For example, although 77% of the black leaders favored preferential treatment for blacks in employment and higher education, 77% of all blacks *opposed* these preferences. Similarly, 68% of the leaders supported busing, whereas only 47% of all blacks favored it (Lichter, 1985). There is a disconnection between the people who define themselves as leaders and those they purportedly represent.

If policy scholars wish to produce useful studies, they must be willing to go to the people affected by the policy and take note of how it affects them and how they respond to it. If effective solutions are to be developed to the problems that face our inner cities, the "experts" must be willing to learn from those who have established successful programs in their communities and be willing to offer the tools they have to promote the duplication and expansion of these efforts.

References

Center for Urban Affairs and Policy Research. (1991). [Cook County, Illinois (Chicago) welfare system]. Research conducted at Northwestern University, Evanston, IL.

Community Service Society of New York. (1984). *New York City's poverty budget.* New York: Author.

Ferrara, P. (1994). *Issues '94.* Washington, DC: Heritage Foundation.

Lee, S. (Director). (1992). *Malcolm X* [Film]. Burbank, CA: Warner Brothers.

Lichter, L. S. (1985, August/September). Who speaks for black America? *Public Opinion,* 42-43.

The roots of resident empowerment. (1991). *Agenda Magazine, 1*(3), 2-5.

Up from dependency. (1986, December). Washington, DC: U.S. Domestic Policy Council, Low-Income Opportunity Working Group (under the auspices of the Interagency Low-Income Opportunity Advisory Board).

PART V

Job Training:
From Welfare to Payrolls

Welfare and Poverty
Strategies to Increase Work

Judith M. Gueron

For the last 30 years, there has been widespread agreement that the nation's welfare system should be reformed, but disagreement about the specifics and resistance to providing the funds needed for large-scale change. Critics of welfare—depending on their beliefs—alternatively argued that it encourages dependency and discourages work; undermines families and values; provides insufficient support; is intrusive, dehumanizing, and stigmatizing; and is wasteful of both government resources and human potential. During the 1980s, culminating in the Family Support Act (FSA) of 1988, reform efforts focused on welfare-to-work approaches that simultaneously provided work-directed services and introduced a participation obligation. The evidence to date is that such programs result in positive and cost-effective—but modest—gains but do not lift large numbers of people out of poverty. At the same time, economic forces have led to dramatic reductions in the real resources of low-income families, pushing increasing numbers of children into poverty.

AUTHOR'S NOTE: This chapter is based on my article titled "Welfare and Poverty: The Elements of Reform," published in the *Yale Law & Policy Review,* Vol. 11, No. 1 (1993), pp. 113-125.

These developments have prompted interest in reforms in two areas: fully implementing the opportunities and obligations envisioned in the FSA so that the character of welfare really changes and taking steps to ensure that work is rewarded. This chapter discusses the several approaches that state and federal governments can use to reduce welfare and encourage work. It concludes that a combined strategy—linking welfare-to-work program mandates with increased rewards for low-wage work—offers promise. In an environment of change, the trade-offs and lessons from the past provide guidance on how to translate a vision of reform into a concrete program that will better meet multiple policy objectives and transform established institutions.

Background

The country's struggle to design social welfare policy has reflected an effort to meet two distinct objectives at a reasonable cost: reducing poverty among children and encouraging work and self-support by their parents. Through the years, and for different people, these two goals have assumed more or less importance.

When the Aid to Dependent Children (ADC) program was created as part of the Social Security Act of 1935, the emphasis was on children, and the program represented "a national commitment to the idea that a mother's place is in the home" (Steiner, 1971, p. 54). The architects of the program sought to provide what they then thought would be a relatively small group of poor widows with adequate income to stay home and take care of their children in accordance with prevailing middle-class norms.

However, four developments eroded public support for this vision. First, there was a dramatic increase in the employment of women (including mothers of small children). Only 22% of women with children under 18 and 14% of those with children under 6 were in the labor force in 1950, but this had increased to 60% and 52%, respectively, by 1988. With most women working at least part-time, the case for excusing single mothers on welfare from work became hard to defend, especially because there was no strong evidence that increased work was hurting children (e.g., see Garfinkel & McLanahan, 1986).

Second, the number of families receiving Aid to Families with Dependent Children (AFDC)—as it was renamed—grew to levels that far exceeded the expectations of the 1930s, and the marital status of mothers on welfare changed, so that they are now overwhelmingly never married, separated, or divorced.

Third, there was a striking increase in the number of single-parent families and a fear that welfare was contributing to this. (Fully 21.6% of all children lived with single mothers in 1990, compared with 7% in 1960.) More alarmingly, today more than half of the nation's children will spend some time in a mother-only family and half of such families will be poor. Finally, although most people stay on welfare for a relatively short time, approximately one quarter of those ever on AFDC will stay for 10 years or more. For them, welfare can become a way of life, with high costs for children and taxpayers (see, e.g., Ellwood, 1986).

These changes undermined the idea that welfare should provide an alternative to paid work. Reformers have been stymied, however, in their efforts to meet the antipoverty and self-sufficiency goals in a way that satisfies prevailing values, partly because reduced poverty and increased self-sufficiency do not always go together. One reason is the heavy reliance on means-tested programs such as AFDC. Inherently, such programs discourage work because benefits are reduced as income grows. Further, the more seriously we take the antipoverty goal and make the programs more generous, the more we risk undermining self-reliance and decreasing the incentive for welfare recipients to take low-paying jobs. Yet in view of an increasing interest in universal programs, it is important to remember why we have relied on means-tested programs so heavily in the past: They reflect an effort to contain costs, target scarce resources toward the most disadvantaged, and get the most antipoverty payoff for the money spent.

In this country, people are particularly concerned—compared to other nations, one might almost say obsessed—with the behavioral effects of government programs, especially with the extent to which generous cash transfers reduce work effort. Because of this, although the trade-off between antipoverty and self-sufficiency program goals has been evident for years, we appear paralyzed by the choices. As a result, we fail to combat poverty *or* to increase self-sufficiency, and we continue to seek reforms—both incremental and fundamental—that can improve performance in one area without sacrificing too much in the other, thereby bringing the system more nearly in balance with underlying public values.

This trade-off is vividly illustrated by the story of a young woman in a current, 16-site national demonstration program called New Chance, which is being managed and evaluated by the Manpower Demonstration Research Corporation (MDRC) (see Quint, Fink, & Rowser, 1991). New Chance offers a comprehensive program of education, training, and personal development services intended to lead to self-sufficiency for young mothers on welfare and improved developmental outcomes for their children. Recently, an MDRC staff member visiting a site in a state with relatively low welfare grants was asked by the program director how her staff should respond to the dilemma facing a young woman who had just completed the program. Through New

Chance, she had gotten a GED (high school equivalency certificate); acquired subsidized work experience and vocational skills; improved her decision making, problem solving, and other life management skills; and gotten child care in place. She was ready to take the big step toward employment and self-sufficiency.

But the economics did not work. The jobs she had been offered—with low wages, limited hours, and no health benefits—would make her less well off than she would be by staying home and continuing to receive AFDC and related benefits, especially when work expenses were factored in. The irony for the director of the program was that she knew the program had succeeded when the young woman was able to calculate the complicated benefit-cost equation that work versus welfare represented and felt a responsibility to ask how she could put her family at risk by going to work.

MDRC's studies of state welfare-to-work programs have shown that many women leave welfare for low-paying jobs, and in so doing trade "leisure" for no noticeable gain in income. Economics obviously is only one factor in the equation; the stigma of welfare and the broader promises of a job represent other strong forces, and people respond. But clearly the deck is often stacked against work. In pushing poor people to work, we are often asking them to make the very decisions that economic theory suggests a rational person should reject.

What can state and federal governments do to alter the equation and encourage welfare recipients to work? How would these different approaches affect attainment of the other societal goal: reducing poverty at an affordable cost? This chapter address these questions for single mothers receiving AFDC benefits.

Potential Policy Responses to Make Work Pay

Strategy #1: Make Welfare Less Attractive

One strategy to encourage work is to make welfare less attractive. This is the strategy most states followed by default over the last 20 years. Between 1972 and 1991, AFDC benefits eroded by a dramatic 41% in real terms. In 1970, AFDC benefits amounted to 71% of the poverty threshold for a family of three; by 1991, they were only 40%. Even if offsetting increases in food stamps are taken into account, combined real benefits fell by 26% during this period. As a result, despite the addition of a new Food Stamp Program, average combined real benefits in 1991 were at the same level as AFDC benefits alone in 1960, before the creation of the Food Stamp Program (see U.S. House of Representatives, 1992).[1] In the face of rising caseloads and unprecedented budget demands, cutting benefits is a strategy that some states are now proposing more consciously.[2] Clearly, this approach will increase work incentives, but in the short run at least, it will clearly also increase poverty.

Strategy #2: Make Welfare a Reciprocal Obligation

A second strategy is to redefine the social contract that is the AFDC program to make it less an entitlement and more a set of reciprocal obligations focused on self-sufficiency. This approach—the approach of mandatory welfare-to-work programs—says, in effect: "You can receive welfare on the condition that you do something while receiving it that can lead to self-sufficiency." In its most common form, this strategy requires welfare recipients to take a job or participate in employment-directed activities—such as job training, job search, and education—or risk losing some welfare benefits. At the same time, it requires government to provide not only a cash grant but also services and supports designed to help the recipient obtain employment.

This reformulation of welfare began with the Work Incentive (WIN) Program in the 1960s. It was expanded and refined by state initiatives and was reaffirmed in the Job Opportunities and Basic Skills Training provisions (JOBS) of the Family Support Act. In 1992, President-Elect Clinton and some members of Congress proposed tightening the mandate further, for example, by setting a time limit on the "opportunity" side of the reciprocal obligation, after which people would be required to work, either in the private sector or at a community service position (or have their AFDC grant reduced or terminated).[3]

In their 1980s version, welfare-to-work programs saved money and increased employment somewhat but did little to reduce poverty (for summary of the lessons from research on these programs, see Gueron, 1987, 1990; Gueron & Pauly, 1991). These programs required participation in low- to moderate-cost services stressing immediate job placement, sometimes followed by short-term, mandatory assignments to unpaid work in public or nonprofit agencies. The long-term effect of the JOBS emphasis on getting people better jobs through education and training and on targeting long-term recipients is not yet known.[4]

Strategy #3: Make Work Pay

A third approach is to make welfare less attractive by making work more appealing—that is, by "making work pay" (for a discussion of the importance of this approach, see, e.g., Ellwood, 1988). The argument for this strategy arises from developments in the low-wage labor market. In 1970, when the minimum wage was $1.60 an hour, a full-time job would provide approximately $3,200 in pretax income, which was above the poverty threshold of $3,099 for a three-person family (the size of the typical AFDC case). In 1990, in contrast, a minimum-wage job provided $7,600 in pretax income, fully 27% below the poverty line of $10,419 (adjusted for inflation since 1970). Thus, AFDC mothers who enter the job market at the bottom, earning the minimum wage, no longer earn their way out of poverty. In a related development that may discourage marriage among single mothers, the earnings of less-skilled men have been falling since 1973—precipitously in the last 10 years (see Blackburn, Bloom, & Freeman, 1990).[5] It is trends such as these that, between 1979 and 1989, led to a more than 50% increase in the proportion of Americans who were working full-time, year-round but who were being paid wages too low to lift a family of four out of poverty. (In 1991, nearly one in five Americans earned wages this low (see U.S. Department of Commerce, 1992).

Under the "make work pay" strategy, work incentives may be increased by changing the welfare system—for example, by reducing the extent to which the AFDC grant or other benefits tied to welfare, such as child care and Medicaid, are cut when people go to work. Other changes might be accomplished outside the welfare system, for example, by directly augmenting wages or by providing complementary cash or in-kind benefits to the working poor. Such actions are likely to be substantially more expensive than the other two strategies and may produce uncertain effects on the amount of work people do, but they are more certain to reduce child poverty.

The argument for changes within the welfare system comes in part from Congressional action in 1981 that sharply reduced the extent to which the AFDC program provided support to families who left the rolls to go to work but remained poor (Omnibus Budget Reconciliation Act of 1981). Although the implicit tax rate in AFDC has always been high, under the current structure, 4 months after they go to work, welfare recipients lose one dollar in benefits for every dollar they earn, an effective tax rate of 100%. Added expenses (e.g., for clothing and transportation, which may exceed the allowance provided) and decreased noncash benefits (e.g., transitional child care and medical benefits, which end a year after someone leaves welfare) mean that people can easily be worse off working than on welfare. Several states (e.g., Michigan, New Jersey, Utah, and Wisconsin) have sought federal waivers to increase the amount of earnings that is disregarded (i.e., not counted) in reducing welfare grants when someone goes to work.[6] A number are also seeking waivers to extend the period during which someone who leaves AFDC to take a job can receive subsidized child care, case management, or Medicaid (for a discussion of these waiver provisions, see Greenberg, 1992).

Outside the welfare system, potential measures to make work pay include increasing child support enforcement[7] and having the federal government guarantee child support if fathers do not pay (the child support assurance concept); instituting a refundable tax credit for families with children; further increasing the Earned Income Tax Credit (EITC); providing health insurance and child care subsidies to the working poor; and increasing the minimum wage or indexing it to inflation.

In the welfare reform context, advocates of efforts to make work pay argue that it is unreasonable to expect people to leave welfare for work if that will make them worse off, that poor women will not be able to work their way out of poverty (even after participating in JOBS education and training programs), and that reducing child poverty should receive priority. Advocates of universal, "nonwelfare" approaches assert that the country should assist the increasing number of working-poor families and move away from categorical policies toward programs that reward equally the working and welfare poor. They argue that targeted programs will never have the public support and generosity of universal ones and that income from multiple sources will be needed if people are to earn their way out of poverty.

During the past 20 years, state and federal policymakers have used all three of these approaches to encourage work: AFDC grants have been cut; states have more or less mandated participation in activities focused on immediate employment; and some payments to the working poor (e.g., the EITC) have been expanded, although at a time when other changes acted to undercut this (i.e., work incentives within the AFDC program were reduced, and real wages for those at the bottom of the income distribution stagnated or declined). The result in 1991, compared with the situation in the early 1970s, is roughly constant real AFDC outlays, higher rates of child poverty (reaching 22% in 1991), and perverse work incentives. The strategies of the 1980s *have* succeeded in discouraging welfare—caseloads have not grown as fast as the demographics would suggest, except for the increase during the current recession—but they have failed to provide security for children.[8]

WIN and JOBS: What Is and Is Not Known?

Although all three approaches may encourage work, there is little direct evidence as to the effectiveness of the first and third in this regard. It is with respect to the second strategy—welfare-to-work programs—that we have very reliable (if still incomplete) data on what can and cannot be achieved.

Before reviewing the results, it is important to note that these programs—
WIN and now JOBS—mean very different things to different people. This
reflects divergent views of the basic goals and thus the appropriate tools of
reform. Some state and local administrators emphasize raising earnings and
reducing poverty; others, reducing dependency and welfare costs. These
different emphases get translated into program designs that place more or less
priority on the service and obligation sides of the reciprocal responsibilities
of welfare recipients and government. Those who argue that welfare recipients
want to work but lack the education and skills needed to obtain jobs that ensure
a decent standard of living tend to advocate programs that offer choices, serve
volunteers first, provide education and training, and do not require people to
take low-wage jobs. Those who assert that jobs are available and believe that
welfare recipients are either unwilling to work or too discouraged to try tend
to favor programs that set clear expectations, require participation for those
not already employed, provide low-cost job placement assistance rather than
expensive training, and mandate community service work ("workfare") for
those who remain on the rolls.[9] Finally, and more typically, those who share
elements of both positions advocate programs that mix opportunities and
obligations.

The 1980s began with great skepticism about the feasibility and value of
large-scale welfare-to-work programs. Because of the commitment of states
and counties during the past 10 years, both to new initiatives and to rigorous
evaluation—and the availability of Ford Foundation, federal, and other funding to study those programs—there is now overwhelming evidence from a
substantial number of unusually reliable studies that employment-directed
services and mandates for single mothers on AFDC can be implemented
effectively and can be successful in encouraging work and self-support.[10]

This threshold question has been tested and answered. The evidence comes
not only from small-scale demonstration programs but also from full-scale
programs run by regular staff working within ongoing welfare systems.
Furthermore, the programs that were studied operated in a wide variety of
settings and under stronger and weaker economic conditions. Studies involving 100,000 people in 21 states—mostly of WIN programs, but with early
results in from California's JOBS program—show unequivocally that states
and counties can implement effective, large-scale programs and that different
approaches can be double winners: producing increases in employment and
reductions in welfare receipt. Some proved to be highly cost-effective—that
is, they were an investment with a clear and rapid payoff, returning to
taxpayers close to $3 per $1 invested and reducing welfare costs for the
mandated group by as much as 19% (for more detail on the results of these
studies, see Gueron, 1987, 1990; Gueron & Pauly, 1991).[11]

TABLE 12.1 Key Findings From Studies of Different 1980s Welfare-to-Work Programs

Short-term, low-cost job search and work experience programs, with varied levels of sanctioning
- Feasible to operate on a large scale with substantial participation
- Modest earnings impacts
- Modest welfare savings
- Impacts sustained during a 3-year follow-up
- Rapid payoff—relatively large welfare savings per dollar spent

But:
- More people got jobs, not "better" jobs
- Modest increase in total income; many remained in poverty and on welfare
- No consistent earnings impacts among more disadvantaged persons

Baltimore "Options": somewhat more intensive and expensive; job search, work experience, and education and training; choice of services; little or no sanctioning
- Somewhat larger earnings impacts
- Earnings impacts increased over time
- Some evidence that people got better jobs
- But no welfare savings—a caution

San Diego "SWIM": somewhat more intensive and expensive; sequence of job search and work experience followed by education and training; relatively high levels of sanctioning
- Among highest impacts on employment, earnings, and welfare payments
- Large earnings impacts and welfare savings for more disadvantaged
- Effective for men (AFDC-Us)

Overall, the results, though modest—and certainly no panacea—demonstrate that cost-effective welfare reform is achievable. Moreover, there is no reliable evidence that another welfare reform approach could produce comparable increases in employment, let alone doing so while saving taxpayers money and without further increasing poverty.

Table 12.1 summarizes the highlights from the 1980s studies, which included evaluations of structured job search and unpaid work experience programs in Arkansas, Chicago, West Virginia, Virginia, and San Diego, and of somewhat more intensive programs (including some education and training) in Baltimore and again in San Diego (the Saturation Work Initiative Model [SWIM]).

The findings on welfare-to-work programs are particularly striking in the current environment, when states are searching for new ideas to reduce welfare by modifying personal behavior. All of the available evidence suggests that this will be extremely difficult to do. There may be many important reasons to try, but we already have strong evidence that an approach requiring participation in a welfare-to-work program or employment itself can succeed in increasing employment and reducing the welfare rolls. If policymakers want to reshape welfare to reach these goals, they should cull from the state welfare-to-work programs the most successful efforts, and seek to put these best practices in place in large-scale JOBS programs across the country.

It is important to remember these reliable and consistent findings because of the apparently unshakable skepticism that government can ever deliver and because the current pressure on state budgets has left 40% of the federal funds for state JOBS programs unspent (see U.S. House of Representatives, 1992, p. 621).

However, there are other critical findings suggesting that, even with these programs, many people remained on welfare[12] and that most of those who went to work got relatively low-paying jobs, which triggered reductions in their welfare grants that often substantially offset their earnings gains, resulting in little increase in their combined income from earnings and welfare. Also, by themselves, the programs did not increase the self-sufficiency of long-term welfare recipients—the people on whom the most is spent. (See Table 12.1.) These clear limitations provided the rationale for the education and training emphases in the Family Support Act (FSA). The hope was that these more intensive services would succeed with the more disadvantaged, get people markedly better jobs, and result in more substantial increases in family income.

Early findings are encouraging from the first large-scale evaluation of a JOBS program that emphasizes education—California's JOBS program, which is called the Greater Avenues for Independence (GAIN) Program. MDRC is studying it for the state's Department of Social Services. The study (Riccio and Friedlander, 1992) points to three key results (see Table 12.2):

1. First, during the study and through a variety of strategies, the six counties in the study (representing 50% of the state's AFDC caseload) succeeded in getting large portions of their targeted mandatory caseloads to participate in GAIN and were successful in providing them with education, training, and other services. Because of this, there was a clear change in the welfare environment, with real obligations and real opportunities.

2. Second, in the first year, despite GAIN's focus on investing in education and skills training—a marked departure from the job search/work requirement approach studied earlier—the results were as encouraging as those from prior studies, with first-year earnings increases of 17% and welfare savings of 5%. There was also evidence that the second year would probably look substantially better.

3. Third, there was notable variation in the results across counties, variation that the study will track through time. In the first year, there were strong results in several counties, weak results in others, and large impacts in Riverside County, where

TABLE 12.2 Lessons From GAIN: First-Year Findings

GAIN
- The nation's largest JOBS program
- Similar to other JOBS approaches in its emphasis on basic education and the priority of serving (potential) long-term recipients
- Different in its greater specificity of service sequences and California's relatively high grants

Study
- 33,000 people randomly assigned, about half enrolled prior to July 1989
- Single parents (mostly women with school-age children) and two-parent heads of households (mostly men)
- Six counties with diverse conditions and GAIN approaches: Alameda, Butte, Los Angeles, Riverside, San Diego, and Tulare

First-Year Findings for AFDC Single Parents
- Increases in employment and earnings: for the six counties (weighted equally), average earnings gains of $271 (17%)
- Reductions in welfare grants: for the six counties (weighted equally), average grant reductions of $281 (5%)
- Varied effects by county: largest impacts in Riverside, with average earnings gains of $969 (65%) and average welfare reductions of $686 (12%); no impacts in Tulare

First-Year Findings for AFDC-UP Two-Parent Cases
- Increases in employment and earnings: for the five counties (weighted equally), average earnings gains of $375 (15%)
- Reductions in welfare grants: for the five counties (weighted equally), average grant reductions of $420 (6%)
- Varied effects by county: largest impacts in Riverside, with average earnings gains of $765 (26%) and welfare reductions of $975 (17%); no impacts in Tulare

Context for Findings
- Notable to find impacts so quickly because large proportion of clients in education and training programs (instead of job search), and many of those active at end of first year
- First-year earnings results comparable to prior studies; welfare findings more favorable
- Prior studies showed impacts typically increased from first to second year of follow-up

Open Questions (Overall and by County)
- Other impacts (educational attainment, income, wages) and longer-term effects
- Benefits compared to costs

---

earnings of single mothers went up an average of $1,000, or 65%, and welfare decreased by $700 on average, or 12%. Riverside also achieved strong impacts for long-term recipients.

If impacts of this magnitude—which are averages for every person in the program, those who did not get jobs as well as those who did—could be replicated

TABLE 12.3 Ten Key Open Questions for Welfare Employment Programs

1. Is it feasible to operate more intensive programs at scale?*
2. What are the impacts of more intensive programs providing education and training to welfare recipients—both single parents (usually mothers) and heads of two-parent households (usually fathers)? Who among each group benefits the most and least?*
3. What are the benefits compared to the costs of more intensive programs?*
4. Are some JOBS approaches more effective than others? Specifically, what are the relative impacts and cost effectiveness of programs emphasizing human capital development versus those emphasizing immediate job search?*
5. What are the impacts and cost effectiveness of welfare employment programs targeted to single parents with preschool children and teen parents?*
6. What are the nature and duration of the economic and non-economic impacts of intensive programs on welfare recipients?*
7. What are the impacts of mandatory programs on the children of welfare recipients?*
8. What is the most effective way to order the sequence of services and manage the services?*
9. Are mandatory or voluntary programs more effective?
10. What are the impacts and cost effectiveness of providing transitional child care and Medicaid?

NOTE: *The national JOBS Evaluation is being designed to address these questions.

elsewhere, JOBS programs could have a substantial effect on work effort and AFDC costs.

During the next year, the GAIN evaluation will provide further information about the payoff to California's investment in JOBS and the relative effectiveness of the different counties' approaches. This study—plus state-, foundation-, and U.S. Department of Health and Human Services-sponsored evaluations in Florida, Georgia, Michigan, Ohio, Oklahoma, and other states—should determine whether the JOBS program delivers on its promise and more effectively meets the two goals of promoting work and reducing child poverty. (See Table 12.3 for a list of the major open questions being addressed in these ongoing evaluations.)

Although this initial report card on GAIN and JOBS is promising, a sobering note is derived from the reality states faced in 1992, a year in which fiscal imperatives shortened the cost-effectiveness time frame. Unless there is a major change in the financing of JOBS, there is no evidence that adequate resources will be available for it to change the AFDC system and to achieve its demonstrated potential for real reform (see, e.g., Hagen & Lurie, 1992). Although the program will provide some services, it is not likely to achieve what most people favor: an effective marriage of opportunities and real participation obligations that will change the basic character of welfare.

The Next Stage of Reform:
Welfare-to-Work Mandates and Rewards for Work

In conclusion, the debate continues about how to restructure social welfare policy to deal with the increasing number of poor children, long-term welfare dependency, and nonwork; the fact that recent reforms (including the Family Support Act [FSA]) have not yet changed the fundamental nature of welfare; and the growing number of people who work full-time but earn below-poverty wages. In recent years, efforts have focused on increasing work and self-sufficiency and on linking the AFDC entitlement to an obligation to participate in an employment-directed program. Welfare-to-work programs have been the primary policy response and the critical building block of most state waiver proposals. This is not surprising because such programs are the major vehicle for getting people off welfare and for meeting the public's interest in placing work-related demands on recipients. But although JOBS's new emphasis on education and training may increase the impacts of these programs, the limited earnings capacity of most women on welfare, combined with stagnating or falling wages for low-skilled workers, constrains success. Even if they work full-time, the majority of women receiving AFDC are not likely to earn much more than they receive on welfare, particularly in states that provide relatively high welfare grants. Some people leaving welfare for work earn more than $10,000 a year, but many earn far less.[13]

The transitional child care and Medicaid provisions of the FSA and the recent increase in the Earned Income Tax Credit are significant, but even with these changes, many mothers on welfare face the dilemma of the New Chance participant described earlier; they have little economic incentive to choose work over welfare. That they continue to do so in fairly large numbers, even when the short-term economic calculus works against it, is a striking statement about how strongly people want to get off welfare.

The evidence that welfare-to-work programs increase work but do not seem to reduce poverty is not surprising, given economic developments in this country during the last 20 years. In order for single mothers to earn their way out of poverty, they must work full-time and have access to jobs paying above-poverty wages. As noted earlier, minimum-wage jobs no longer provide this.

The structural transformation in the economy, reflected in the recent slow productivity growth and stagnant or declining wages for low-skilled persons, puts a brake on the potential achievements of welfare-to-work programs. Unless the education component in JOBS really makes a much greater difference in earnings than we have seen to date from some early and limited evidence, these programs may continue to increase work effort, but not be the answer to reducing poverty. This suggests that children will need access to the income of both parents (e.g., through stepped-up child support collections)[14] and that there will need to be further measures to make work pay.

The lesson from these economic trends and evaluation results is the need for more than one policy response. If as a nation we care about both of the goals mentioned at the beginning of this chapter—increasing self-sufficiency and reducing poverty among children—it will be important to ensure that the JOBS program is fully implemented and to make other changes that tilt the economic balance in favor of work. On their own, JOBS and other mandates are not likely to achieve dramatic success on both fronts; nor are economic incentives likely to be generous enough to carry the full burden. But if implemented in combination, reforms outside the welfare system may make the work programs within it more effective in reducing dependency by creating incentives that support, rather than pull against, our strongest values. In doing this, the expanded welfare-to-work programs and universal incentives may also reduce public anger at a welfare system that seems to provide people with a long-term alternative to work, whereas those not on the rolls work full time and remain poor.

The experience of the last 20 years suggests that changing the nature of welfare is feasible and can have positive results. It also cautions against overpromising about either the speed of institutional change or the likely effect of reform on the welfare rolls and costs.

Notes

1. As a result of these benefit cuts, by 1992, the maximum combined assistance available through AFDC and food stamps puts family income below 80% of the poverty level in all but 14 states and below 60% of poverty in 8 states.

2. For example, California reduced AFDC grants by 4.4% in 1991 and 5.8% in 1992. Furthermore, although promoted primarily as mechanisms to discourage childbearing and migration, a number of federally approved demonstrations are also efforts to reduce grant levels: New Jersey and Wisconsin (for teens, and only in some cases) specify that grants not be increased to cover children born on welfare; Wisconsin ties new state residents' grants to AFDC benefit levels in the states from which they moved (see Ferreira, 1992, p. 76).

3. One Republican proposal would have limited receipt of welfare to 4 years, mandated JOBS and/or work experience for 10 hours per week during that period, and allowed the states to fund subsidized employment in lieu of food stamps. Then Governor Clinton suggested a 2-year limit on educational services, followed by a work requirement, combined with measures to supplement earnings from low-wage jobs.

4. This chapter focuses on efforts to increase work, but in a related development, states have also initiated changes in the social contract intended to promote responsible behavior in other areas (e.g., marriage, fertility, mobility, health care, and attendance in school), changes that have collectively been called the "new paternalism." The effect of such measures is very uncertain,

although there will be results soon from Ohio's Learning, Earning, and Parenting (LEAP) program, which mandates school attendance for teenage parents on welfare.

5. Freeman and Holzer (1991) note the "historically unprecedented" and massive decline in the real earnings of 25- to 34-year-old men with less than a high school education.

6. Under Section 1115 of the Social Security Act of 1935 (Title XI, Chapter 531, as amended), states can waive provisions of the act for an experimental or demonstration program. Since the 1970s, this provision has been applied broadly to allow states to experiment with far-reaching reforms of the AFDC program.

7. Recognizing the importance of providing children with support from both parents, the Family Support Act also included a number of new child support enforcement provisions: mandatory wage withholding, uniform guidelines for the establishment of support orders, an emphasis on establishing paternity for all children, and periodic review and modification of support orders.

8. Reality is thus at odds with the prevailing view of an AFDC program in crisis, or at least suggests that the crisis is as much for the children receiving AFDC as for the taxpayers. Although Medicaid costs (primarily for people not on AFDC) have increased very rapidly during the past 15 years, AFDC outlays have not. Total AFDC costs, at \$22.9 billion in 1991, are relatively small, accounting for less than 1% of the federal budget and 3.4% of the average state budget. See U.S. House of Representatives (1992, pp. 654, 1795); see also National Association of State Budget Officers (1991, p. 37).

9. See, for example, Mead (1992) for the argument that addressing recipients' inability or unwillingness to work should be a prime focus of welfare reform.

10. For a discussion of the major findings, the importance of random assignment field experiments to the credibility of the results, and the role of this research in the passage of the Family Support Act, see Wiseman (1991).

11. These are the findings for single parents (usually women). Studies of programs for two-parent welfare families have been fewer and have produced less positive results. One reason is that men who enrolled in these programs did much better on their own (as shown by the behavior of a control group) than did the women; thus, welfare-to-work programs for men had a harder time "beating" the control group. The women, in contrast, did relatively poorly on their own, and the programs proved to have a real impact.

12. At best, welfare receipt declined by 7 percentage points among people targeted by the program (Gueron & Pauly, 1991, pp. 142-143).

13. For example, a study of one pre-JOBS program in San Diego found that about one quarter of welfare applicants who were employed 16 to 27 months after applying for welfare earned \$10,000 or more during that 12-month period; among those who were already on the rolls when the study began (a harder-to-employ group), only 16% did. See Hamilton and Friedlander (1989).

14. According to the April Child Support Supplement to the Current Population Survey in 1989, 25% of AFDC families reported receiving some child support during the year. This was about half the rate of non-AFDC single-parent families.

References

Blackburn, M. L., Bloom, D. E., & Freeman, R. B. (1990). The declining economic position of less skilled American men. In G. Burtless (Ed.), *A future of lousy jobs?* (pp. 31, 33-79). Washington, DC: Brookings Institution.

Ellwood, D. T. (1986). *Targeting "would-be" long-term recipients of AFDC.* Princeton, NJ: Mathematica Policy Research.

Ellwood, D. T. (1988). *Poor support: Poverty in the American family.* New York: Basic Books.

Family Support Act of 1988, Pub. L. No. 100-485 § 201-204, 102 Stat. 2356-2381.

Freeman, R. B., & Holzer, H. (1991). *The deterioration of employment and earnings opportunities for less educated young Americans: A review of evidence.* Unpublished paper.

Garfinkel, I., & McLanahan, S. (1986). *Single mothers and their children: A new American dilemma.* Washington, DC: Urban Institute.

Greenberg, M. (1992, September). Welfare waivers and the working poor. *Labor Notes, No. 76,* 1-9. Washington, DC: National Governors' Association.

Gueron, J. M. (1987). *Reforming welfare with work.* New York: Ford Foundation.

Gueron, J. M. (1990). Work and welfare: Lessons on employment programs. *Journal of Economic Perspectives, 4*(1), 79-98.

Gueron, J. M., & Pauly, E. (1991). *From welfare to work.* New York: Russell Sage.

Hagen, J. L., & Lurie, I. (1992). *Implementing JOBS: Initial state choices.* Albany: State University of New York, Nelson A. Rockefeller College of Public Affairs and Policy, Professional Development Program.

Hamilton, G., & Friedlander, D. (1989). *Final report on the Saturation Work Initiative Model.* New York: Manpower Demonstration Research Corporation.

Mead, L. M. (1992). *The new politics of poverty: The nonworking poor in America.* New York: Basic Books.

National Association of State Budget Officers. (1991). *State expenditure report.* Washington, DC: Author.

Omnibus Budget Reconciliation Act of 1981, Pub. L. No. 97-35 § 2301-2304, 95 Stat. 843-845.

Quint, J. C., Fink, B. L., & Rowser, S. L. (1991). *New Chance: Implementing a comprehensive program for disadvantaged young mothers and their children.* New York: Manpower Demonstration Research Corporation.

Riccio, J., & Friedlander, D. (1992). *GAIN: Program strategies, participation patterns, and first-year impacts in six counties.* New York: Manpower Demonstration Research Corporation.

Social Security Act of 1935, 42 U.S.C. § 1315 (1988).

Steiner, G. Y. (1971). *The state of welfare.* Washington, DC: Brookings Institution.

U.S. Department of Commerce, Bureau of the Census. (1992). *Workers with low earnings: 1964 to 1990* (Current Population Reports, Series P-60, No. 178). Washington, DC: Government Printing Office.

U.S. House of Representatives, Committee on Ways and Means. (1992). *1992 green book: Overview of entitlement programs.* 102d Cong., 2d sess., 1992, 1190. Washington, DC: Government Printing Office.

Wiseman, M. (Ed.). (1991). Research and policy: A symposium on the Family Support Act of 1988. *Journal of Policy Analysis and Management, 10,* No. 4, 588-589.

13

Raising Work Levels Among the Poor

Lawrence M. Mead

This chapter attempts, with a broad brush, to describe the problem of low work levels among people who are poor, assess the usual explanations for it, and suggest the best approach to solving it, which I believe lies in work requirements within the welfare system. Few poor adults work regularly, which is the main reason they are poor, and it is difficult to trace the problem to limitations of opportunity, such as low wages or lack of jobs. Efforts to raise wages for low-skilled persons or to raise skills through voluntary training programs can be worthwhile but have little effect on poverty.

The much greater need is simply to cause poor adults to put in more hours at the jobs they can already get. Voluntary programs or other opportunity measures do not achieve this. To raise work levels, an effort to *enforce* work is unavoidable. Work requirements show promise. This approach is also more realistic than radical-sounding proposals to end or transform welfare, such as those that surfaced during the last presidential campaign. The effort to enforce work as well as other civilities in the city, however, is deeply controversial. Dispute over what can be expected of poor people, not lack of

AUTHOR'S NOTE: I gratefully acknowledge comments from Margaret C. Simms, Director of Research Programs for the Joint Center for Political and Economic Studies, who was the discussant at the UCLA Conference on Reducing Poverty in America.

opportunity, is the main reason why chronic poverty persists in America today.[1]

Poor persons are highly diverse, as are the causes of poverty. I will not discuss children or older people who are poor, although their problems are important. My analysis applies mainly to working-age adults, who are the most controversial of the poor population and the key to any solution to poverty. I also concentrate mainly on long-term poor adults, meaning those who are poor for more than 2 years at a stretch, because they are the hardest to help and the most important politically. This is the group that most exercises the public and is most debated among experts. In the urban setting, these poor people primarily mean long-term welfare mothers and low-skilled single men, who are often the absent fathers of welfare families. These long-term, employable, poor adults are not a large group—perhaps 5% of the population (Sawhill, 1989, pp. 4-6)—but this group is at the core of the social problem.

I know little specifically about Los Angeles, the site of riots in 1992. From what I have read, its problems do not appear dissimilar to those of other large cities. In Los Angeles as elsewhere, the poor population is characterized above all by lack of steady employment. The great question is how this can occur when all around the ghetto most adults, including immigrants, are regularly employed.

The Employment Problem

Overwhelmingly, today's working-age poor are needy, at least in the first instance, because the adults in these families do not work normal hours. American society assumes that families will be supported mainly by parents' earnings. Table 13.1 shows that more than three quarters of the heads of American families were employed in 1991, and more than half worked full-year and full-time. Even among single mothers, who have child-rearing responsibilities, the work level was nearly two thirds. For heads of households generally, work levels have fallen slightly since 1959, but among female heads they have risen, reflecting the movement of women into the labor force. Other data show that families with children have increased their work effort since 1970 (Congressional Budget Office, 1988, Table A-15), in their oft-noted struggle to keep up with inflation.

But as Table 13.2 shows, work levels among poor people are dramatically lower and have fallen much more sharply. Only half of poor family heads reported any work at all in 1991, down from two thirds in 1959, whereas the share working full-year and full-time dropped by half to only 16%. For the moment, I say nothing about causes. There may have been an upturn in

TABLE 13.1 Work Experience of All Heads of Families, 1959-1991

	1959	1970	1975	1985	1991
Percentage of all heads who					
Worked at any time	85	84	80	76	77
Full-year and full-time	63	63	58	57	56
Did not work	—	14	19	23	23
Percentage of female heads who					
Worked at any time	—	61	58	63	64
Full-year and full-time	28	32	31	37	38
Did not work	—	39	42	37	36
Percentage of married-couple heads who					
Worked at any time	—	87	83	79	80
Full-year and full-time	67	67	63	61	60
Did not work	—	11	15	20	20

SOURCE: Data are from U.S. Department of Commerce, Bureau of the Census, *Current Population Reports* (Selected years), Series P-60, No. 35, Tables 3 and 13, and No. 68, Table 8 (for 1959); No. 81, Table 20 (for 1970); No. 106, Table 27 (for 1975); No. 158, Table 21 (for 1985); and No. 181, Table 19 (for 1991).
NOTE: Full-year means at least 50 weeks a year, full-time at least 35 hours a week. *Married-couple heads* means male heads in 1959 through 1975, heads other than single mothers in 1985, and the husbands of married-couple families in 1991. Some figures do not add to total because of rounding or the omission of workers in the armed forces.

TABLE 13.2 Work Experience of Poor Heads of Families: 1959-1991

	1959	1970	1975	1985	1991
Percentage of all heads who					
Worked at any time	68	55	50	50	50
Full-year and full-time	31	20	16	16	16
Did not work	31	44	49	49	50
Percentage of female heads who					
Worked at any time	43	43	37	40	42
Full-year and full-time	11	8	6	7	10
Did not work	57	57	63	60	58
Percentage of married-couple heads who					
Worked at any time	75	62	61	60	59
Full-year and full-time	38	28	24	25	24
Did not work	23	37	38	38	41

SOURCE: Data are from U.S. Department of Commerce, Bureau of the Census, *Current Population Reports* (Selected years), Series P-60, No. 152, Table 4 (for 1959-1975); No. 158, Table 21 (for 1985); and No. 181, Table 19 (for 1991).
NOTE: Full-year means at least 50 weeks a year, full-time at least 35 hours a week. *Married-couple heads* means male heads in 1959 through 1975, heads other than single mothers in 1985, and husbands of married-couple families in 1991. Some figures do not add to total because of rounding or the omission of workers in the armed forces.

poverty work levels in recent years, but statistically there has been no clear change since 1978 (U.S. Department of Commerce, 1992a, pp. xiv-xv); most of the decline was before then. Work levels among poor welfare recipients are also low, with only 7% of welfare mothers reporting employment in a given month, even part-time (U.S. House of Representatives, 1992, p. 670).

There is some evidence that poor adults work more than they report. Poor families appear to spend more income than they say they receive. Half or more of welfare recipients may work over time, often without reporting the income to avoid reductions in their grants. Some conclude from this that most of the apparently nonworking poor really are employed. They simply do not acknowledge it to keep welfare support or because their jobs are in the underground economy. In this view, the cause of poverty is not low work levels but low wages that do not allow mothers to live on earnings alone, and welfare rules do not allow them to combine work and welfare legally because earnings are largely deducted from their grants (Edin & Jencks, 1992; Harris, 1992). Such conclusions go too far. Welfare mothers are needy mainly because of low working hours, not low wages or grants. Unreported work is seldom sustained and is uncommon among long-term dependent persons.[2] Work levels among single mothers on welfare are clearly much lower than among single mothers not on welfare, among whom the work rate is about 85% (Moffitt, 1988, p. 16).

Much of the decline in work levels, it is true, reflects the decline in the poverty level since 1959. As real wages rose, most working poor people earned their way out of poverty. It is now difficult to work normal hours and remain poor, so almost by definition the remaining poor are mostly people without jobs. But there clearly is a work decline even allowing for this. If poverty were defined relative to average incomes, rather than in absolute terms as it is by the government's poverty measure, then the poverty line would rise with economic growth, and there would be more working poor. Let us define the poor as the bottom fifth of the family income distribution. There now is no clear work decline after 1970 for families in general, but there still is for families with children, whose poverty is the most critical. These low-income families worked less, just when better-off families were working more (Congressional Budget Office, 1988, Table A-15).

The decline is not because of a fall in the share of poor persons who are of working age. It is often thought that needy people are increasingly made up of children or older persons. Actually, the proportion of poor who are working-aged (ages 18 to 64) rose from 42% to 49% between 1959 and 1991 (U.S. Department of Commerce, 1992a, Table 3). The reasons for this include a decline in the number of children per family and the drop in poverty among retired persons because of rising social security payments. Rather, the decline

TABLE 13.3 Employment Status of Persons 16 and Over and Family Heads By Income Level, in Percent: 1991

	Persons	All Heads	With Children Under 18	
			All Heads	Female Heads
All income levels				
Worked at any time	69	77	88	68
Full-year and full-time	42	56	65	39
Did not work	31	23	12	32
Income below poverty				
Worked at any time	41	50	55	44
Full-year and full-time	9	16	17	10
Did not work	59	50	45	56

SOURCE: U.S. Department of Commerce, Bureau of the Census, 1992a, Tables 14 and 19.
NOTE: Full-year means at least 50 weeks a year, full-time at least 35 hours a week.

is linked to the growth in female-headed families, mostly at the lowest income levels. Poor female heads themselves are not working less—as Table 13.2 shows, their work level has always been low. But now more such families are among the poor, and this reduces the work level for the poverty population as a whole.

Female-headed families do not necessarily produce a work decline, as many suppose, because work effort by female heads in general is rising. Poor female heads, however, work less than others, and poor adults seem to be working less whether or not they are married. Among blacks, who compose most of the long-term poor population, two thirds of poor female-headed families were needy before the breakup of the parents as well as after, equally because of nonwork (Bane, 1986). As Table 13.2 shows, even among the heads of poor married-couple families, a sizable work decline has occurred. Some of this reflects greater retirement among older persons and persons who are disabled. But even if one defines the employable stringently, excluding persons who are older and disabled, students, and parents with children under 6, since 1967 the share of poor family heads who could work has risen while the share actually working has fallen (Danziger & Gottschalk, 1986).

Table 13.3 compares work levels among the general population and the poor population for individuals and for several groupings of family heads in 1991. In all categories, the difference is enormous. Employment is 20 or 30 percentage points higher for the general population than among poor people. Most significant, the multiple for full-year, full-time work, is four or five times. It is lack of steady work, not lack of all employment, that mostly separates poor adults from nonpoor adults. If one compares poor persons with nonpoor persons, rather than with the overall population, as in Table 13.4, the contrasts are even greater.

TABLE 13.4 Employment Status: Contrasting Poor and Nonpoor, 1991

	Poor	Nonpoor
Percentage of individuals 15 and over who		
Worked at any time	39.8	72.0
Full-year and full-time	9.0	45.0
Percentage of family heads who		
Worked at any time	50.4	80.5
Full-year and full-time	15.8	61.1
Percentage of female family heads who		
Worked at any time	42.4	76.1
Full-year and full-time	9.5	54.5
Percentage of families with two or more workers	16.8	62.6

SOURCE: U.S. Department of Commerce, Bureau of the Census, 1992a, pp. xiv-xv.

TABLE 13.5 Poverty Rates by Employment Status of Persons 16 and Over and Family Heads, in Percent: 1991

	Persons	All Heads	With Children Under 18	
			All Heads	Female Heads
Overall	11.8	11.6	17.9	47.1
Worked at any time	6.9	7.6	11.2	30.4
Full-year and full-time	2.6	3.3	4.8	11.9
Did not work	22.8	25.0	67.2	82.4

SOURCE: U.S. Department of Commerce, Bureau of the Census, 1992a, Tables 14 and 19.
NOTE: Full-year means at least 50 weeks a year, full-time at least 35 hours a week.

These differences directly account for most of today's poverty. Table 13.5 shows how poverty rates vary with work level for the same demographic groups as in Table 13.3. The effect of employment is tremendous. Nonworkers suffer poverty at two and three quarters to six times the rate occurring among workers. More than 80% of female family heads with children are poor if they do not work; only 12%—below the average for the population—are poor if they work full-year and full-time. Work has the same potent effect on dependency. Two thirds of female family heads are on welfare among those who do not work, whereas only 7% are on welfare among those who work full-year and full-time (Ellwood, 1986, pp. 3-5).

Of course, other factors than work effort determine whether people are poor. Nonworkers more often have to care for children than workers do, and they would average lower earnings than those currently employed if they took a job. If they worked steadily, more would remain poor even with employment than is true of existing workers. If one allowed for these factors, poverty levels would not vary so extremely with work level as in Table 13.5. Nevertheless, the effect of nonwork is so great that overcoming it is strategic for reducing poverty. And, as discussed below, if work levels among poor people were to recover to former levels, providing aid to poor people would also be more popular.

Nonwork is costly for poor families in other than income terms. It contributes to the problems of lifestyle that, as much as low income, conspire to keep people needy today. It is often said that the problems of poor people are rooted in the family, particularly the absence of fathers. But the greatest reason why poor adults fail as parents is inability to function as breadwinners. Fathers leave families mainly because they do not work steadily. One of the reasons poor children often fail in school and later on the job is that they have not had the example of parents working consistently outside the home.

The Search for Barriers

The work problem is so important that in large part, the debate about poverty is a debate about employment. The great question is why poor adults work so much less consistently than better-off adults. The tradition among experts has been to seek impediments outside poor people themselves. Perhaps low wages leave people poor even if they work or discourage them from working. Perhaps poor people are barred from employment by sheer lack of jobs or child care, racial bias, or the disincentives set up by the welfare system, which reduces a family's grant in proportion to earnings. Perhaps they simply cannot work because of the burdens of child rearing or a lack of marketable skills.

All these theories have drawn intense research attention. In my opinion, that effort has not come up with much. Each of the theories appears to be a little bit true, but none of them—singly or in combination—appears to explain more than a small part of the work problem.[3]

The trouble with the wage theory is that if most poor adults are not even employed, low wages cannot cause their poverty. If "working poverty" were more prevalent, this theory would be more persuasive. It is true that 58% of poor families report earnings by some family member during a year, but poor families with year-round, full-time workers are vastly outnumbered by those with no workers—1.4 million to 3.2 million in 1991 (U.S. Department of Commerce, 1992a, Table 19). It is commonly said that work does not pay low-skilled individuals enough to be worthwhile. But it clearly pays them enough to avoid poverty and welfare in most cases, provided the adults in families work the hours typical of society. That means full-year and full-time for the family head, with at least some work by the spouse or another family member.

Poverty is often blamed on the minimum wage because it is assumed that when poor adults go to work, this is what they earn. It is easy to show that working even full-year and full-time at the minimum wage cannot support a family above poverty. But such calculations mean little, because the vast majority of poor workers actually earn above the minimum wage; they are poor mainly because of low working hours. Few minimum-wage workers have to try to support a family alone. Most are secondary workers, usually spouses or teenage children, in families in which the head is working for more than the minimum wage. For these reasons, the minimum wage actually has little connection to poverty. In 1985, only 19% of minimum-wage workers were poor, whereas only 26% of poor workers earned at or below the minimum wage (Congressional Budget Office, 1986, pp. 15-16, 18-19). The increase in the minimum wage in 1990 to 1991 to $4.25 has reduced the link between it and poverty still further. Poverty also has little connection to low wages in general. As Table 13.5 suggests, few steady workers at any wage are poor. Even low-wage workers today are seldom poor, and they are even more seldom heads of poor families (Burkhauser & Finegan, 1989, pp. 59-60). Again, low working hours are a more important cause of poverty than low wages. One might suppose that low wages barred work for single mothers, who might stay on welfare because they cannot support their families and pay for child care on one income. Most welfare spells are short, however, and most of them end through employment (Harris, 1992, Table 1),[4] so wages must usually be adequate to work off the rolls. By one estimate, if one allows for child support and child care costs as well as wages, half or more of welfare mothers could escape dependency if they worked full-time (Michalopoulos & Garfinkel, 1989). The great majority of single mothers who avoid poverty do work full-time or have working family members (U.S. House of Representatives, 1992, p. 1283). It is valid to say that mothers cannot work off welfare without higher wages only if we accept their current low hours as given.

To contend that low wages or benefits are central to poverty, one would have to show that they were a cause of low working hours as well as low returns per hour. Perhaps low wages and benefits discourage low-skilled people from working, whereas higher returns would cause them to put in more hours. Research has not shown, however, that work effort among the poor responds much to this sort of incentive. The labor supply of low-income workers is remarkably unresponsive to payoff levels (Burtless, n.d.). Employment by welfare mothers is little affected by welfare benefit levels or by the wages the mothers are able to earn (Moffitt, 1983, p. 1033; 1986). It is work effort by the middle class that has responded to stagnant wages in recent decades—and by rising, not falling.

Other theories of nonwork also have small support. There is some evidence that employers discriminate against minorities in favor of whites, if one controls for all factors except race (Turner, 1991). But all factors usually are not equal. Urban businesses typically have found unskilled black workers, especially men, to be unreliable employees. It is mainly this, rather than bias aimed at skin color, that now makes many employers—including blacks—reluctant to hire from the inner city. The opposition is based on experience and does not, like traditional bias, hold nonwhite groups to be inferior in general. There may be some "statistical" discrimination, in that some individuals who would be good employees are not hired because their racial group has a bad reputation. But the extent is probably limited because employers use a number of indicators—class and job history as well as race—to pick among job applicants (Kirschenman & Neckerman, 1991).

Research suggests that welfare disincentives to work are surprisingly weak because work levels on welfare are low across the nation regardless of the level of welfare benefits (Moffitt, 1988, p. 22). A related theory is that welfare recipients are deterred from working by fear of losing health coverage. They get Medicaid while on welfare, whereas many low-wage jobs lack health insurance. In fact, this effect seems confined to the families with the worst health problems and is not a major cause of dependency or nonwork (Blank, 1989; Moffitt & Wolfe, 1990).

The presence of preschool children does not appear to deter welfare mothers from working; numbers of children do deter, but the importance of this has fallen with the size of welfare families, which today mostly include only one or two children. Child care seldom appears to be a serious barrier to employment because it is much cheaper and more available than advocates assert. In 1987, only 9% of child care arrangements relied on institutional facilities such as child care centers, and most mothers paid nothing at all for care. The situation is similar among welfare mothers (Brush, 1987; U.S. Department of Commerce, 1990, Tables 1 and 7).

The most widely discussed barrier to opportunity for those who are poor is an alleged lack of all employment in inner-city areas. This theory was dramatized by claims following the Los Angeles riots that work, especially for minority youth, was simply unavailable in the ghetto. Research has shown, however, that jobless poor people seldom face a situation like the Depression. Groups with high unemployment, such as minorities, women, and youth, are characterized more by rapid job turnover than long-term joblessness.[5] Such individuals usually say they can find jobs, but they also leave them quickly.

The reasons include children at home, conflict with superiors and coworkers, and the low-paid, unattractive character of available jobs.

Of course, jobs are less available during a recession, but people who keep looking for work usually find it. The problem in the ghetto is more that many people are out of the labor force entirely. Even when the urban labor market is hot enough to lower unemployment sharply, this does not significantly increase the proportion of disadvantaged persons who seek to work (Freeman, 1991; Murray, 1990). At present, jobs sufficient to avoid poverty and welfare, if not to be affluent, appear to be widely available in cities, at least to those seeking them at a given time. Possibly, the number would be insufficient if all the nonworkers sought them at once, but a literal job shortage is not now a major cause of poverty.

Economic Trends

The theory that jobs are lacking rests heavily on the notion that the economy today offers much less opportunity to poor persons than it once did. In the last two decades, the decline of manufacturing has idled many workers, real wages have grown little, and inequality among incomes has risen. Less educated workers, especially among younger men, have suffered actual losses in earnings. All this, it is said, is the major cause of today's nonwork and poverty. It seems obvious that the destruction of millions of manufacturing jobs in American cities since the 1970s must have radically reduced the opportunities available to today's low-skilled job seekers (Wilson, 1987).

Popular accounts of the trends, however, typically do not allow for the vast expansion of employment in service industries in the 1970s and 1980s or for the recent drop in the number of new entrants to the labor force because of the baby bust. These trends gradually tightened the labor market in the last decade, despite the decline of factory jobs. Job creation was particularly potent in California at that time. As a result, immigrants from all over the world continued to come to Los Angeles or New York and find work, without hurting opportunities for native-born job seekers (Borjas, 1986).

The theory that deindustrialization is responsible for the disorders of the ghetto has limited support. Although manufacturing jobs clearly are fleeing the inner city, this may be the result and not the cause of social disorders there.[6] And because population is leaving the older cities faster than jobs, the labor market may actually be tightening in urban centers. Although more jobs are available in the suburbs than the cities, openings apparently remain accessible to most people seeking them, wherever they live. Studies that attempt to tie the employment of urban dwellers to the proximity of jobs report weak findings at best. The idea of a spatial mismatch may be partially valid in the most depressed cities of the East and Midwest but probably not in the more prosperous South or West.[7] Some analysts talk instead of a skills mismatch, with the poor lacking the talent to get work in an increasingly high-tech economy because of weak education. Most jobs, however, still demand only low or moderate skills. Urban employers complain mostly about employees' lack of basic work discipline—inability to show up for work and take orders—rather than a lack of advanced skills.

Nonwork is a cause of growing inequality in that the decline of work habits of those at poverty levels is one reason wages and earnings for the low-skilled have fallen. But it is hard to argue the other way, that economic trends explain why few of poor people work regularly. Certainly, economic change has caused hardships, but the impact has been mainly on factory workers with a steady employment history, few of whom are needy. Few poor or homeless men held good jobs before falling into destitution (Rossi, 1989, p. 137). Unquestionably, manufacturing workers face a struggle to preserve their livelihoods, but that battle is going on largely over the heads of the poor population.

The last two recessions, it is true, were especially severe, and this has unnerved the public. The downturn of the early 1980s abruptly cut well-paid blue-collar employment. Since the recession of 1990-1991, many other industries have been downsizing, producing unprecedented unemployment among white-collar workers. Job losses have been especially severe in California. This has led some to fear that the bonanza of job creation is over and that long-term unemployment is due to rise. Concern over jobs was a major factor in President Clinton's election.

But the same fears were expressed a decade ago. Most of those displaced workers found other jobs quickly. Current white-collar jobless persons are likely to do so more easily. Fears that economic change would obsolete any large part of the workforce have never proved valid in the past and are unlikely to in the future. Since growth resumed in 1991, job creation has again picked up, and although many of the new jobs are low paying, the restructuring of the economy is likely to lead in time to larger gains in productivity and higher real wages (Nasar, 1993; "No Need for a Boost," 1993). In the late 1980s, the proportion of the adult population employed reached 63%, the highest figure ever. The recession cut that to all of 62% (U.S. Department of Commerce, 1992b, p. 383). A serious employment problem remains highly improbable.

In any event, the work attachment of long-term poor persons is too limited today for their predicament to have much connection to the vicissitudes of the economy. The problems of the ghetto, including nonwork, are much the same in good times and bad. There are still some working poor people, so the overall levels of poverty and the welfare rolls do rise and fall with economic growth.

But we should not conclude that the bulk of poverty or dependency has economic causes. Since 1980, the poverty rate has varied only between 13% and 15% across two sharp recessions and the longest boom in American history. Although a return to prosperity would no doubt help many poor people in Los Angeles and other cities, the gains would be marginal as long as work levels remain low.

I do not mean that the barriers are unimportant. My judgment is that about a third of the work problem among the seriously poor might be attributable to limits to opportunity in all forms, the extent varying around the country. Differences in opportunity have a great deal to do with who gets ahead in America. Differences in education, especially, heavily determine who gets a good job and who gets a lesser one. Although bias unrelated to conduct appears to be a minor problem for poor persons, it is probably a larger problem for employed minorities, who face white resistance to their assuming positions of authority in government and the private sector. In general, social structure appears to have more influence on employed persons than on jobless poor persons. That is, it has a lot to do with *inequality among workers.* But it has little to do with *failure to work at all,* which is the greater problem for today's needy.

More important than any economic factor as a cause of poverty, I believe, is what used to be called the culture of poverty. Surveys and ethnographic studies suggest that poor adults want to work and observe other mainstream values. Many, however, resist taking the low-paid jobs that are most available to them. A greater number are simply defeated about work or unable to organize their personal lives to hold jobs consistently. These feelings are rooted, in turn, in the historic lack of opportunity that minority groups—who compose most of the poor—knew in this country and in their countries of origin. Of course, most members of these groups are employed and not poor. But some remain unconvinced that it is worth striving in America, despite the equal opportunity reforms of recent decades. This element has given rise to the underclass.

Equally important is that values such as work (on which everyone agrees) are no longer well enforced in ghetto areas. The middle class, which upheld these mores, has largely moved out, and public institutions have failed to fill the gap. In large measure, nonwork results simply because welfare and other public programs do not yet require many adult recipients to work as a condition of support. Similarly, crime results from weak law enforcement, and illiteracy results from the decline of standards in the schools. The loss of authority by these institutions has more to do with poverty than any recent changes in the economy or society (Mead, 1992b, chap. 7).

Voluntary Measures

In light of this analysis, I do not believe that further efforts to improve opportunities for the poor population can overcome poverty, although such efforts can make some contribution.[8] The current vogue is to try to "make work pay." The Clinton administration has already taken steps to raise the returns of low-skilled jobs. But if poverty is mostly because of low working hours rather than low wages, then improving the rewards of work can have only a marginal effect.

Congress last raised the minimum wage in 1989. It might raise it again, but most of the benefit would go to nonpoor persons, simply because most minimum-wage workers are already above poverty. Without more poor people working at or near the minimum, raising the floor is no longer an effective antipoverty strategy (Burkhauser & Finegan, 1989). One could also increase the Earned Income Tax Credit (EITC), a subsidy for low-income workers with children. Because the EITC directly targets poor workers, it is the most efficient means of helping them. Congress in 1990 and 1993 raised the EITC substantially. As of 1996, the credit will pay a low-income worker 34% of the first $6,160 in earnings ($2,094) if the family has one child and 40% of the first $8,900 ($3,560) if there are two or more children (U.S. House of Representatives, 1994). Even if the EITC is generous, however, it cannot reach most poor families simply because few poor adults are employed.

Neither measure is likely to raise working hours. In fact, increases may depress hours. A higher minimum wage probably reduces work levels because it eliminates some jobs, and this causes some youths to withdraw from the labor force. A higher minimum wage and a higher EITC also reduce work effort because low-wage workers who qualify can now make the same income with fewer working hours. This motivation is apparently stronger than the incentive to work more hours that is generated by raising the returns per hour; in the terms economists use, the income effect dominates the substitution effect. Although these reductions are probably small (Brown, Gilroy, & Kohen, 1982; Burtless, 1989), they do suggest that "making work pay" can be counterproductive as long as work levels remain low.

Another approach is to try to weaken the disincentives in welfare that many believe deter the dependent from working. Liberals try to do this by raising work incentives, that is, by limiting the reductions in welfare benefits when welfare recipients have earnings. Conservatives prefer to do it simply by reducing the number of employed or employable people who can get on welfare in the first place. The trouble is that neither strategy has shown much effect on work levels. The work incentives that existed in AFDC between 1967 and 1981 did not palpably raise work effort among recipients, and the Reagan cuts in these incentives and in welfare eligibility in 1981 did not reduce effort.[9]

None of this is to say that higher wages, benefits, or work incentives are not warranted on other grounds. Government may decide that it should ensure workers a living wage or health care or other advantages as an act of justice. Society is entitled to define and redefine the package of rewards and obligations that specify concretely what it means to be an American (Mead, 1986, chap. 11). My point is only that improving the package connected to work can do little to overcome poverty as long as few of the poor are steady workers.

The other popular approach to raising earnings has been voluntary education and training programs. For 30 years, Washington has financed a succession of "compensatory" programs designed to improve the skills of poor persons so that they could get "better" jobs. The evaluations of these programs show that typically they are efficient rather than effective. They raise the earnings of their clients by enough to justify their costs, but the gains are small, not enough to solve the work or poverty problem. The largest increases have been for women, not for men, and most of them have come from causing the clients to work more steadily in jobs they could already get, not from getting them better jobs. It is not surprising that disadvantaged clients find it difficult to learn greater skills because they have usually done poorly in school and are often dropouts.[10]

A more controversial strategy, currently back in vogue, is public employment. If one believes that jobs, or "good" jobs, are lacking for poor persons, government ought to create them. But this strategy was tried in the 1970s, a troubled decade in which jobs were much more plausibly lacking than they are today. Under the Comprehensive Employment and Training Act (CETA), Washington funded up to 750,000 positions a year in local government and nonprofit agencies. The program was costly, gains in earnings were marginal at best, and after CETA most clients did not go on to employment in the private sector. Even liberals abandoned the program, and it was abolished by Reagan. If it were revived, it would hardly change the conviction many poor people have in cities such as Los Angeles that work is impossible for them.

Voluntary approaches tend to assume a solution to the work problem rather than providing it. They all presume that the poor are primed to work and only require a better chance to get ahead. They seek to guarantee, in Ellwood's phrase, that "If you work you shouldn't be poor" (U.S. House of Representatives, 1988, p. 11). But satisfying that *if* turns out to be most of the problem. For if poor persons worked regularly, they would usually not be poor for long in the first place. Voluntary programs tend to reach mainly the transiently poor, the families that already have a work history or working members. They tend not to reach the more disadvantaged welfare recipients and single men, who are much more central to entrenched poverty.

Voluntary programs can play a role in a solution. I do not oppose them out of hand, although costs must be considered. But we must recognize that they do not reach to the core of the work problem, which is the reluctance of poor adults to take and hold the low-skilled jobs they can already get. To "make it," these Americans have to display something more like the tenacity in seeking work that immigrants to this country often do. Without that change in behavior, endless additional training and service programs can be tried and "succeed" without seriously denting the social problem.

Work Enforcement

The nature of the work problem and the policy history point clearly toward the conclusion that work must be enforced. Rather than just promoting employment through benefits or through changes in the surrounding society, government must seek to *require* poor adults to work more than they do. It must *enforce* employment much in the way it collects taxes or upholds the law.

The limitations of voluntary strategies have driven federal social policy in this direction. Since 1967, Washington has tried to use the welfare system to enforce work by requiring employable recipients to seek work or enter training as a condition of support. *Welfare* here means mainly Aid to Families with Dependent Children (AFDC), the cash assistance program for families, although other income programs have also added work provisions. *Employable* has included the few men on welfare plus welfare mothers if their youngest child was over a minimum age, currently 3.

Those policies became more demanding during the 1980s and 1990s, although no locality yet seriously requires work of more than a small share of its caseload. The main point of the Family Support Act of 1988 (FSA) was to strengthen work programs by making states take them more seriously. States are required to involve 20% of their employable recipients in work or training on a monthly basis by 1995 or face cuts in their federal welfare funding. States in turn can require the clients to enter these programs on pain of cuts in their grants. The act also funded more child and health care to help mothers work.

Evaluations of mandatory work programs from the 1980s showed them to be highly promising. Some of these programs recorded substantial impacts on the employment and earnings of clients—still limited but larger than achieved by most voluntary programs. Although most of the programs did not reduce the welfare rolls by much, they did save money for government, as the reductions in grants as clients went to work more than paid for the costs. The common idea that work programs involve spending new money on welfare fails to allow for these savings. The programs have also been notably untroubled by the various barriers that many suppose prevent the poor from working. Lack of jobs or child care has not been a major impediment in most localities.[11]

More important, in my view, the programs raised the work effort of the participants sharply. Recipients participated in employment, job placement, or training at twice the rate or more of recipients not subject to the requirements. Enforcement achieved more change in the *actual work behavior* of those who are poor than any other means. The policy has not yet reduced dependency very much, but it has begun to make the welfare lifestyle less passive, and that is more important (Mead, 1992b, pp. 166-171).

In my view, the key to success in work programs is achieving high levels of participation. It is the obligation to participate in a program that primarily motivates clients to organize their private lives for work and then to move into employment, although support services are also necessary. Provided participation is high, it is less crucial what activity the participants join. Programs offering education can achieve results comparable to those stressing immediate job search, provided remediation does not deter clients from going to work (Mead, 1988). It is also clear that mandatory work programs achieve the highest participation, because only mandatory programs reach the more reluctant recipients, those with the most to gain. Voluntary programs usually involve only the most motivated third of the caseload, who most often would go to work without the program (Mead, 1990).

Enforcement should not be seen as a coercive or punitive policy. Recipients are not forced to do something they oppose. The great majority endorse the work requirement and accept their assignments. If society merely wanted to get tough with the poor, it could achieve this simply by abolishing welfare. Rather, workfare is a paternalist policy. It joins benefits that poor persons need with requirements that they function in improving ways. The combination of supports with demands achieves higher work effort than either could do alone. Other social institutions, such as homeless shelters and inner-city schools, have also moved toward a directive posture. Experience has shown that just giving people benefits without structure seldom changes lives. The current programs leave the extent of enforcement somewhat unclear, and that is politic. The demand that recipients do something mollifies conservatives. At the same time, the current work programs, which usually include some remediation, are easier for liberals to support than more draconic policies because the work programs leave it ambiguous how directly recipients are required to work. Training is offered to participants as well as job search. The insistence is more on joining the program than immediately going to work. Once involved in the program, participants themselves choose to take a job more often than they are "forced" to by government.

The potential of work enforcement was shown by the Saturation Work Initiative Model (SWIM), an experimental program run in San Diego with extra federal funding during 1985 through 1987. Through intense monitoring and follow-up of clients, SWIM achieved monthly participation rates of around half and yearly rates of three quarters, the highest ever recorded. Participation could include part-time work or training activities undertaken by the client as well as activities arranged by the program. Figure 13.1, which records monthly participation levels in SWIM, suggests how the mandate to participate in program activities motivated the majority of clients to go to work or enter other training on their own (Hamilton, 1988).[12] No voluntary policy has shown anything like this effect on lifestyle.

Although SWIM realized unusually large impacts on the earnings and employment of clients, including men, its most notable achievement was to change the nature of welfare. Under SWIM, welfare did more than pay benefits; it seriously required that the dependent persons improve themselves as a condition of support. To achieve such a change nationwide is, in my view, the most constructive meaning that welfare reform can have. Going on welfare would become like going into the army. Those who qualify would receive undoubted financial support and other benefits, but in return they would have to function in clear-cut ways. It is sometimes said that everything in antipoverty policy has been tried and that nothing works. But serious work enforcement such as SWIM has seldom been tried. Public authority is the unexploited resource in antipoverty policy.

The Job Opportunities and Basic Skills Training program (JOBS), the new workfare structure under FSA, is now far and away the most important enterprise in federal social policy. The implementation of JOBS, which began in 1989-1990, has been somewhat checkered. Because of the recession, lack of local funding, and the new services required, most states have found that they could not implement the program fully, and some federal funding has not been claimed. The program is far distant from doing for the national caseload what SWIM did in San Diego. To date, however, most states have met the new requirements, and the initial evaluations of JOBS programs show positive effects—in some cases, quite large ones (Freedman & Friedlander, 1995; Riccio, Friedlander, & Freedman, 1994; U.S. General Accounting Office, 1992). The participation mandates in FSA have already forced big-city welfare programs to start building employment into their routines as never before. Participation clearly is a lever that, if pressed, can force real change in the welfare regime.

It is vital that the participation targets in FSA be achieved, then raised for the years beyond 1995. Some states have had difficulty in meeting the thresholds, in part because of regulations written by the Bush administration that demand that clients, to be counted as participants, be assigned to activities

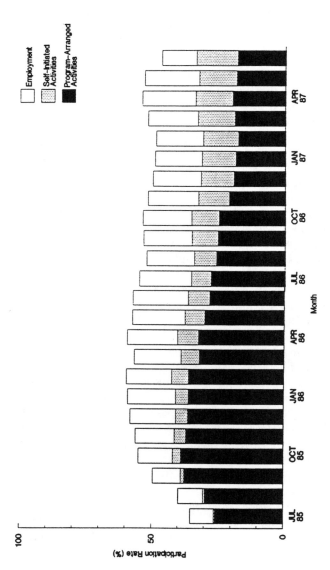

Figure 13.1. SWIM: Percentage of Individuals Eligible for SWIM During Each Month Who Participated in Program-Arranged Activities, Self-Initiated Activities, or Employment, by Type of Activity

SOURCES: G. Hamilton, *Interim Report on the Saturation Work Initiative Model in San Diego* (p. xix), August 1988, New York: Manpower Demonstration Research Corporation. Copyright © 1988 by the Manpower Demonstration Research Corporation; and J. M. Gueron and E. Pauly, with C. M. Loughy, *From Welfare to Work* (New York: Russell Sage Foundation), p. 135. Reproduced by permission of MDRC.

lasting at least 20 hours a week. Some Democrats would like an easier standard. I would rather see the 20-hour rule kept and the participation target raised to 50% or more, to be achieved during several more years with more federal funding. All the welfare reform plans currently under discussion in Washington promise to achieve 50% participation, although they define it in different ways.[13] JOBS should also deemphasize education and training in favor of job search in the private sector. The program currently gives too little emphasis to actual work, and evaluations make clear that work-oriented programs perform best (Freedman & Friedlander, 1995; Riccio et al., 1994; U.S. General Accounting Office, 1995).

If half or more of the employable recipients were participating half-time or more, the welfare experience would be transformed. It is true that a half-time standard would mean that many mothers would not be able to earn their way entirely off welfare. They would require some supplementation from welfare, but politically this would be acceptable provided the mothers really worked. Earnings and welfare together would lift the family above need. The effect would be to regularize and legitimize the subsidy that some mothers now get informally when they work "off the books" without telling welfare. The chief difference between this solution to dependency and "making work pay" is that it does not rely on incentives alone to promote work. Obligation and enforcement are critical to ensuring that more welfare mothers actually take jobs.

Nonwork among men is, perhaps, even more important than among women. Welfare mothers can be required to work in return for receiving welfare benefits. Relatively few men are on welfare, so they are harder to obligate by this route. The best substitute is probably the child support system. Child support collection has been toughened alongside work requirements, although this mandate, too, is a long way from effective enforcement. Fathers who owe child support payments but lack jobs could be made to work in government jobs to pay their judgments. Some states are trying to do this. Otherwise, a work policy for men must rely mainly on law enforcement to shut down alternatives to legal work such as the drug trade, and on educational reform so that more youth will leave school with the skills and attitudes necessary to work steadily. Work policies are just one part of the general effort to rebuild the authority of public institutions in the inner city.

Radical Solutions

Work enforcement sounds extreme alongside voluntary measures, but it is more practical than some other approaches to the poverty problem that may seem more straightforward. Some conservative experts say that federal welfare programs should simply be abolished. Without public support for female-headed families, this argument goes, poor adults could not get away with producing children without supporting them—the central cause of poverty. They would have to marry and go to work, and the disorders of the ghetto would recede. Giving aid sounds humane but inevitably promotes dysfunctional behavior. Denying aid sounds severe but promotes self-reliance and, thus, is the only true way to help poor people (Murray, 1984). A more moderate version of the same idea is to limit the time that recipients may spend on the rolls to 2 or 3 years.

The elections of 1992 and 1994 gave these ideas a serious hearing in Washington for the first time. Both President Clinton and the new Republican majority in Congress have proposed to time-limit welfare. The GOP would also devolve control over most aspects of welfare to the states. House Republicans, in addition, would deny coverage to unmarried teen mothers and to children born on the rolls. But with a Democrat in the White House and most urban states concerned about protecting poor children, it is still unlikely that the principle of aid to the needy will be fundamentally threatened.

I also believe that abandoning dependent persons to the marketplace would do more to increase hardship than raise work levels. The behavior of seriously poor people seems to respond more strongly to direction from public authority than it does to economic incentives. Nevertheless, the idea of abolishing assistance deserves consideration. It may well be that paternalist policies such as workfare are beyond the capacities of American government. The governing class may lack the will to enforce work or other civilities, or the administrative problems of work programs may prove insuperable. In that event, to abolish welfare would be the next best policy.

At the other extreme are traditional liberal proposals to overcome poverty without solving the work problem, simply by transferring income to the poor. In the 1960s and 1970s, liberals proposed to do this by liberalizing the welfare system to cover parts of the low-income population besides female-headed families. A more recent proposal is to pay families a $1,000 refundable tax credit for each child under 18. This would be less controversial than welfare, the argument runs, because the benefit would be universal, akin to Social Security, and would not go just to those who are poor (National Commission on Children, 1991, pp. 94-95). A similar idea is to expand the child support system to provide more income to fatherless families, again for the entire population. If the father did not pay support, an assured benefit would be paid to the mother. It is also claimed that the assured benefit would raise work effort among welfare mothers because it would not be reduced if they worked, as welfare is (Garfinkel, 1992).

These proposals are no more politic than abolishing welfare. Currently, they are probably unaffordable, given the federal budget deficit. More fundamental, the public has made clear that it will not countenance giving more money to poor families until the parents do more to help themselves. Past liberal welfare reform proposals were defeated in Congress mainly because they did not contain serious work requirements (Mead, 1986, chap. 5), and this would likely be the fate of the recent proposals if any president espoused them. The idea that these are universal benefits is unpersuasive unless those who are poor, like other beneficiaries, earn them through employment, and the plans do little to raise work levels. The child tax credit is not, like the EITC, conditioned on employment.[14]

Child support is supposedly earned by the father. But because poor fathers usually do not work enough to pay their judgments, their families would have to be supported by the assured benefit, which is welfare under another name. The work incentives implicit in the scheme would not cause many mothers to work.[15] On the contrary, the main effect of the scheme might be to free the mothers from the work requirements that are now tightening in AFDC. They could shift from welfare to assured child support and escape any serious pressure to work.

Lately, some liberals have tried to combine increased aid with more serious work requirements by proposing to time-limit cash welfare and follow it with government jobs. Adult recipients could draw aid without work for only 2 or 3 years, after which they would have to take a private job or accept one provided by government (Ellwood, 1988; Ford Foundation Project on Social Welfare, 1989; Task Force on Poverty and Welfare, 1986). During his campaign, President Clinton said he would "end welfare as we know it" along these lines.[16] The Clinton welfare reform plan would limit families to 2 years of aid unless the adults went to work. House Republicans would limit aid to 5 years whether or not the adults worked. Rather than seek to enforce work through welfare, this approach counts on the end of benefits to motivate people to take jobs. The situation would be much as in unemployment insurance, under which the time limit on benefits, usually 6 months, is the main device that forces beneficiaries to get serious about returning to work. To time-limit aid, however, would be intensely resisted by most Democrats, even if government jobs were promised to those failing to find work on their own (DeParle, 1992b). It is thus hard to imagine President Clinton signing a reform bill such as this.

A more extreme liberal position is to abolish cash assistance entirely and offer the poor only government jobs, which would presumably drive most to work in the private sector. To hand out jobs instead of cash sounds like the simple, direct solution to the work problem, because it ensures that anyone assisted is working for his or her benefits (Kaus, 1992, chaps. 7-9). In principle, I support this idea, but it is impractical. Government jobs cost much more than simply paying people aid and would be strongly opposed by civil service unions. Simply to guarantee work to all recipients still on the rolls after 2 years of aid might require 1.5 million positions and cost $40 billion a year (DeParle, 1993; Kramer, 1993). It was largely to avoid this cost that the Clinton planners decided to impose their 2-year limit only on welfare mothers born in 1972 or later.

It is true that a serious work policy must ultimately be willing to create jobs, if necessary to employ the recipients. But to date, most work programs have been able to place the great majority of clients in the private sector and have needed only a small pool of public positions as a backup for the hard-to-employ. To be practicable, the Clinton plan also would have to stress private, not government, jobs for most clients, and this would reduce the contrast with current policy—because to seek private placements would require promoting job search by recipients who were still on welfare. This is what JOBS programs are already trying to do. Thus, to execute the Clinton plan would entail much the same struggle to expand work programs that is already going on under FSA.

The moral is that the only true welfare reform is bureaucratic change that reliably moves more clients toward work. Relabeling welfare as a work program does not achieve that if in practice one must exempt most of the clients. Raising participation in work programs does achieve it, albeit slowly, because more of the clients become active in improving themselves. Only if FSA were fully realized—indeed, only if participation in work programs reached 50% or more—would enough recipients be going to work routinely to contemplate a time limit on cash benefits, or any other fundamental change. "Ending welfare as we know it" presumes the full implementation of FSA and is not a substitute for it.

The Limits of Opportunity

Policies to expand opportunity for the disadvantaged on a voluntary basis can make only a limited contribution to overcoming poverty. This is because such policies presume that the cause of nonwork lies in some impersonal constraint. Today's long-term poverty, however, is seldom visited on people by nameless social forces. It is rarely the result of steady workers being shut out of jobs or paid starvation wages. Poverty of this structural type was much more prevalent before 1960 than since. Rather, need usually results in the first instance from self-defeating actions by poor people themselves, particularly nonwork, unwed childbearing, and crime.

The tradition has been to assume that this behavioral poverty, like the structural type, would respond to enhancements of opportunity. Give those who are poor a better chance to make it, and they will behave more constructively. Greater opportunity, through a combination of the private sector and government largess, certainly has been at the heart of the American dream for most people. Liberals want to offer the same chances to poor people by inventing new social programs. Conservatives want to do it through greater reliance on the private sector. Both sides assume that some change in social arrangements can liberate those who are needy to get ahead.

Both approaches, however, make what I call the competence assumption. They presume that the individuals to be helped have the capacity at least to advance their own self-interest, if not society's. Particularly, people will seize the chance to get ahead economically by getting an education and then working hard in the best job they can get. That is the presumption that has proved invalid for many of today's poor people. Too often, they do not get through school or work consistently. Dysfunction has defeated the preferred opportunity approaches of both left and right. Big government during the Great Society era achieved some good things, as did smaller government under Reagan and Bush. But neither approach could eradicate entrenched poverty, in both cases mainly because of the work problem. Neither more government nor less can overcome need as long as poor adults do not reliably take jobs.

My sense is that behavior has remarkably little connection to the opportunity structure. Social arrangements affect how people are rewarded if they function but not whether they function. Rather, the ability to cope stems largely from one's family and upbringing. Children are formed in the family, and once they leave it there is remarkably little government can do to change them or to enhance their capacities. At best, it can restrain the behavior of people who cope poorly, who otherwise would injure themselves and their children, in hopes that the children will function better.

Poverty would be easy to solve if only resources, and not governance, were required. Both left and right naturally search for some way to "invest" that would overcome the social problem without addressing conduct. For liberals, that means spending more on poor families through welfare or intensive service programs (Edelman, 1987). For conservatives, it might mean special education programs to build up skills, job placement programs, or job creation in the private sector. But the effect of even the best such efforts is limited and long-term. It would be better to invest in high-quality social administration because bureaucracy—unpopular though it is—increasingly must manage the lives of those who are seriously poor. In California, fortunately, administrative quality is already high. What made SWIM possible was San Diego's superb corps of skilled and committed employment administrators.

Functioning ability does connect to opportunity, but chiefly well back in time. The root of most of today's serious poverty probably is in the historic denials of opportunity for blacks and other minority groups, who today make up a majority of those who are poor. Black society was actually more coherent under Jim Crow than it is today. But the lack of a fair chance for black men to "make it" in the decades after emancipation took its toll. The majority of blacks kept faith, prepared themselves, and when civil rights came, were ready to advance into the working and middle classes. The others lost faith in America and themselves. The disillusionment of poor blacks and, later, Hispanics caused the ghettoes to crumble just when the doors of opportunity opened (Lane, 1992).[17]

These memories now prevent opportunity solving the social problem. Today's seriously poor people typically do not believe that they will ever have a chance to make it, although black success is now commonplace and discrimination in the old sense is rare. And because their problems are perpetuated by weak families, no further reforms by government are likely to convince them otherwise. They project their hopelessness onto the environment, but it really arises in the first instance from weak or abusive parenting. No improvement in the setting can make them hopeful, because none can undo those early experiences. Their despair has become immune to social change.

The solution lies in rebuilding the family, not society. Most children acquire a sense of possibility not because society is fair to them but because adults near to them are. By identifying with parents and teachers, they internalize values. By meeting their expectations, they also derive a sense of mastery that makes them approach life hopefully, without defeating themselves. The wider world has no comparable influence. If parents are effective, children will be well formed even if the surrounding society is unfair. Exemplary black figures such as Martin Luther King and Marian Wright Edelman were the products of an unjust society, but strong families upheld demanding standards for them (Tomkins, 1989). Conversely today, a family breakdown has undercut functioning even though society has become much more fair. The main task of social policy is no longer to reform society but to restore the authority of parents and other mentors who shape citizens.

Government has no easy way to do that, but the best single thing it can do is to restore order in the inner city. Above all, it can require that poor parents work, because employment failures are the greatest cause of family failures. If parents do not work, no program to help the children is likely to achieve much. To a child, to have functioning parents is worth 25 Head Start programs. Only if parents work and fulfill other civilities, such as obeying the law, can they have the self-respect needed to command the respect of their children. Those who would be free, and bequeath freedom to their children, must first be bound. The source of freedom for today's seriously poor is no longer opportunity but order. For them, the way forward is no longer freedom but obligation.

The Political Problem

The main reason we still lack such a policy is not resistance among the poor, most of whom want order restored. Nor is it resistance among the middle-class. The popular attitude on poverty is receptive to enforcement. The voters typically want to help the needy, but they also oppose the "abuses" that are associated with welfare. The trouble with the standard welfare proposals of the right and left is that they violate one or the other side of this public mind. Abolishing or time-limiting welfare threatens the principle of aiding those who are needy, whereas merely increasing transfers does nothing about the abuses. Work requirements within welfare, although difficult to implement, have the hope of doing both—of helping the vulnerable *and* moving the employable toward work.

At a mass level, the political problem posed by welfare was never dependency as such but the abuses, of which the most important is nonwork. As is often remarked, a great many unemployed and retired people live off the government without controversy, and myriad economic interests receive subsidies from Washington. This "middle-class welfare" differs from AFDC mainly because the beneficiaries have done something to earn their benefits. They can claim an economic function. Equally, if welfare recipients were earning their benefits through some effort on their own behalf, welfare would become more respectable, more like the social insurance programs. Other aid to needy persons and their families would also become more popular.

In the public mind, that the recipients contribute to society in some way is much more important than where their support comes from. For most people in America, helping oneself and getting help from government are not in opposition but go together. Those who work steadily *also* get the most aid from government, and those who do not get little. The middle class justifies its social insurance benefits on the argument that they are earned. The poor get only the scraps from the government's table, primarily because they are unearned. If poor adults worked at higher levels, they would qualify for more support from *both* the private and public sectors than they do now (Mead, 1992b, pp. 57-61).

In the last 2 years, a number of welfare proposals have appeared outside Washington that dramatize these feelings even more than work requirements. A number of states have proposed using various suasions to require recipients to remarry, have fewer children, and keep their children in school. These family policies are likely to be less effective than work programs, but they show a useful concentration on moral concerns, not economics. Although some of the plans also cut welfare benefits, most do not. Some measures would reward the recipients with extra money for behaving well. The focus is much more on altering the lifestyle of the recipients than on changing how much is done for them (Mead, 1992a). Just as in work policy, the watchwords are reciprocity and social contract, on matching benefits with obligations.

The political resistance to enforcement, rather, comes from elites. They interpret the poverty problem much more ideologically than the public. Especially at the national level, the political debate has traditionally been about federal spending and economic interventions, not enforcement of mores such as work. The usual battle between Democrats and Republicans is over the *scale* of government, with one side wishing to do "more" for people through public programs, the other "less." But authoritative social policies primarily involve changing the *nature* of government. A more authoritative welfare state may not change the benefits given to dependent persons much at all. Rather, it demands that they do more to help themselves.

That is not an option that our leadership readily credits. In Washington, helping those who are poor is typically seen as an alternative to their helping themselves, not as a complement. Social policy analysts, most of whom are liberal economists, assume that people who fail in the private sector deserve the most help from government. Conversely, if one demands that those who are poor work, one is taken to mean that government should do nothing for them.

Another difficulty is the rights-oriented nature of the political culture, especially among elites. *Both* left and right naturally seek to address social problems through some version of extending freedom. Liberals want government to give people new opportunities. Conservatives want less government so that the economy can grow faster. Traditionally, neither focused on the behavioral problems that lead to poverty. They both made the competence assumption. The idea that government—certainly the federal government—might have to restore order to society was utterly alien. Authoritative measures may get results, but they sound like tyranny. It is more attractive to continue looking for barriers to getting ahead that more or less government can remove, even if such policies achieve little (Mead, 1986, chaps. 8-9).

In the last decade, first one party and then the other has favored a policy of enforcement, but never both together. During the 1980s, most Republicans wanted to use federal rules to require work in welfare, strengthen local law enforcement, and raise standards in the schools. Most Democrats resisted, fearful of burdening the poor with added stigma and failure. During debates on the Family Support Act, it was Republicans who pressed for tougher work requirements, to which Democrats agreed only reluctantly (Mead, 1992b, chap. 9). Since 1992, however, Republicans have gone back to an antigovernment approach to reform based largely on cutting coverage and devolving control of welfare to the states. It is now Democrats, led by the Clinton administration, who most favor work requirements within welfare, in part as a way of staving off more drastic change.

On these enforcement issues, the public is hard-line. It wants order restored in cities, even if it is divided on family issues such as divorce or abortion. In electoral politics, this social order agenda strongly favors conservatives, just as economic issues of economic opportunity and equality favor liberals. Republican charges that Democrats were "soft" on crime or welfare were a major reason why the GOP controlled the White House most of the time between 1968 and 1992. Carter in 1976 and Clinton in 1992 were able to break the Republican grip partly because economic concerns dominated those elections but also because they took more conservative stances on crime and welfare than their own parties (Brown, 1991; Edsall & Edsall, 1991; Mead, 1992b).

This sentiment, however, does not yet control national welfare policy. Despite President Clinton's rhetoric about "ending welfare as we know it," his welfare reform plan would not in fact require the bulk of welfare adults to work. Congressional Republicans are more interested in cutting spending and devolving responsibility for welfare to the states than in using the welfare system, as the public wishes, to enforce mainstream values. Most Congressional Democrats still oppose any such attempt, and most social policy experts prefer to "make work pay" rather than require it. So disputes about enforcement go on, both inside the Beltway and between Washington and the society.

These arguments are often not what they seem. It is sometimes said that the issue is "values," with conservatives trumpeting the work ethic or law-abidingness and liberals resisting. But liberals also regret nonwork and crime. The real division is over the *enforcement* of values through public authority. Conservatives would have government *tell* the poor how to live, whereas liberals want to offer them the *chance* to get ahead. On the surface, too, the debate can seem to be about barriers, with conservatives arguing that opportunity is available and liberals denying it. But the underlying issue is not society so much as the moral responsibility of the poor. Conservatives want to hold the downtrodden accountable for their personal behavior, whereas liberals will not allow this until society is yet further reformed.

Ultimately, the question comes down to the competence one is willing to attribute to poor persons themselves. One side thinks that the needy can cope with life with less aid if only they are expected to; the other side denies it.

Both sides project their interpretations onto the environment. Conservatives tend to see opportunity in the society because they think people who act rationally in their own interests can overcome any obstacle. Liberals deny opportunity is sufficient, whatever steps are taken to improve it, because to them those who are poor will always be victims. In short, conservatives still believe in the competence assumption, whereas most liberals have tacitly given it up. That difference dominates whatever the facts say about barriers.

Enforcement policies may seem to be hard-line, but they actually take a moderate view of these questions. The paternalists are not as hostile to poor persons, or as optimistic about their self-reliance, as antigovernment conservatives who want to abolish welfare. Nor are they as condescending and pessimistic about those who are needy as liberals who want only to build up antipoverty spending. Paternalism divides the responsibility for overcoming poverty between the government and those who are poor, giving both a role. The former will give benefits and support services provided the latter take steps to help themselves. Enforcement also assumes that benefit recipients have the capacity to satisfy the most basic public expectations, such as working, if not to live fully independent lives. To realize a regime in which the dependent reliably do that is the best that antipoverty policy can achieve.

Above all else, a solution to the inner city requires a political class willing to commit itself to this moderate position. The views that poor people are totally undeserving or that they are victims of whom nothing can be expected must be exiled to the political fringes. Black politicians, who have a power to veto any antipoverty strategy, must join with whites in raising expectations for poor members of their group, in the name of integration. Dependency cannot be abolished in the short run, but it can be made less passive. Sufficiency can come to those who are poor the way it has already come to better-off Americans—through a combination of personal effort and government benefits. For that to happen, poor adults must above all work much more regularly than they do now.

Notes

1. Much of the following is based on L. M. Mead (1992b), *The New Politics of Poverty: The Nonworking Poor in America.* Additional citations not given in this chapter are given there.

2. Edin and Jencks (1992) found that most of welfare mothers' unreported income is not from employment, and Harris (1992) found that only a minority of mothers have earnings during more than half their time on the rolls. The underground or illegal economy is smaller than many analysts presume, and little of it involves the poor; see Mead, 1992b, pp. 52-53.

3. The following is based on Mead (1992b), chaps. 4-6.

4. This study uses monthly Panel Study of Income Dynamics (PSID) data. Studies using annual data find a lower proportion of spells ending through employment.

5. Unemployment as officially measured, however, is mostly because of the long-term cases. See Clark and Summers (1979).

6. Correlations may be found between economic change and inner-city joblessness, but this does not establish which way the causation runs. For an example, see Johnson and Oliver (1992, chap. 4).

7. For a study questioning the mismatch theory for Los Angeles, see Leonard (1986). For a recent review of the mismatch literature, see Holzer and Vroman (1992, chap. 3).

8. The following summarizes Mead (1992b, pp. 159-166).

9. The cuts reduced the proportion of recipients with earnings but only because most of the working recipients were no longer eligible. Incentives may also reduce work levels among low-income workers not on welfare, because they can now more easily qualify for assistance. See Levy (1979).

10. To maximize its effect, remediation must be aimed at concrete skills needed for particular jobs rather than education for its own sake. See Burghardt, Rangarajan, Gordon, and Kisker (1992).

A variant is programs that intervene in families intensively, to try to overcome health, education, and child abuse problems as well as promote employment. Such programs also tend to show useful but limited impacts. See Schorr (1988). There is a limit on how much even the best programs can do for children as long as their parents remain dysfunctional.

11. These conclusions rest on evaluations done by the Manpower Demonstration Research Corporation; for details, see Gueron and Pauly (1991). See also U.S. General Accounting Office (1987).

12. Participation was defined, however, less stringently than under FSA.

13. The Republican plans, however, emphasize block-granting welfare to the states and eliminate specific funding for JOBS, so it is questionable whether they could actually achieve these higher participation levels.

14. The National Commission on Children (1991) gave limited attention to the work problem; see pp. 104-109.

15. According to a simulation reported in Garfinkel, Robins, Wong, and Meyer (1990), the assured benefit would raise working hours among welfare recipients only slightly and might depress them among other workers. It would have little effect on dependency.

In a recent experiment in New York, welfare mothers were offered a child support benefit, somewhat lower than AFDC, in return for much stronger work incentives. This meant they could raise their incomes substantially above AFDC but only if they worked. Only 10% of those eligible took up the offer. See Hamilton, Burstein, Hargreaves, Moss, and Walker (1993).

16. Then Governor Clinton made this pledge in a speech at Georgetown University on October 23, 1991, according to DeParle (1994). See also DeParle, 1992a.

17. This is the most convincing interpretation of black history that I have read.

References

Bane, M. J. (1986). Household composition and poverty. In S. H. Danziger & D. H. Weinberg (Eds.), *Fighting poverty: What works and what doesn't* (pp. 22-31). Cambridge, MA: Harvard University Press.

Blank, R. M. (1989). The effect of medical need and medicaid on AFDC participation. *Journal of Human Resources, 24*(1), 54-87.

Borjas, G. J. (1986). The demographic determinants of the demand for black labor. In R. B. Freeman & H. J. Holzer (Eds.), *The black youth employment crisis* (pp. 191-232). Chicago: University of Chicago Press.

Brown, C., Gilroy, C., & Kohen, A. (1982). The effect of the minimum wage on employment and unemployment. *Journal of Economic Literature, 20*(2), 497-499, 505-508.

Brown, P. (1991). *Minority party: Why Democrats face defeat in 1992 and beyond.* Washington, DC: Regnery Gateway.

Brush, L. R. (1987, October 15). *Child care used by working women in the AFDC population: An analysis of the SIPP data base.* Paper prepared for the U.S. Department of Health and Human Services, Analysis, Research and Training, McLean, VA.

Burghardt, J., Rangarajan, A., Gordon, A., & Kisker, E. (1992, October). *Evaluation of the minority female single parent demonstration: Vol. 1. Summary report.* New York: Rockefeller Foundation.

Burkhauser, R. V., & Finegan, T. A. (1989). The minimum wage and the poor: The end of a relationship. *Journal of Policy Analysis and Management, 8*(1), 53-71.

Burtless, G. (1989). The effect of reform on employment, earnings, and income. In P. H. Cottingham & D. T. Ellwood (Eds.), *Welfare policy for the 1990s* (pp. 103-145). Cambridge, MA: Harvard University Press.

Burtless, G. (n.d.). The work response to a guaranteed income: A survey of experimental evidence. In A. H. Munnel (Ed.), *Lessons from the income maintenance experiments: Proceedings of a conference held in September 1986* (pp. 22-52). Boston: Federal Reserve Bank of Boston.

Clark, K. B., & Summers, L. H. (1979). Labor market dynamics and unemployment: A reconsideration. *Brookings Papers on Economic Activity, 1,* 13-72.

Congressional Budget Office. (1986). *The minimum wage: Its relationship to incomes and poverty.* Washington, DC: Author.

Congressional Budget Office. (1988). *Trends in family income: 1970-1986.* Washington, DC: Government Printing Office.

Danziger, S. H., & Gottschalk, P. (1986). Work, poverty, and the working poor: A multifaceted problem. *Monthly Labor Review, 109*(9), 17-18.

DeParle, J. (1992a, March 14). Arkansas pushes plan to break welfare cycle. *New York Times,* p. 10.

DeParle, J. (1992b, December 20). Clinton social policy camps: Bill's vs. Hillary's. *New York Times,* pp. 1, 24.

DeParle, J. (1993, February 3). Caution on welfare. *New York Times,* p. A16.

DeParle, J. (1994, July 15). The Clinton welfare bill begins trek to Congress. *New York Times,* p. A10.

Edelman, M. W. (1987). *Families in peril: An agenda for social change.* Cambridge, MA: Harvard University Press.

Edin, K., & Jencks, C. (1992). Reforming welfare. In C. Jencks (Ed.), *Rethinking social policy: Race, poverty, and the underclass* (pp. 204-235). Cambridge, MA: Harvard University Press.

Edsall, T. B., & Edsall, M. D. (1991). *Chain reaction: The impact of race, rights, and taxes on American politics.* New York: Norton.

Ellwood, D. T. (1986, March). *Working off of welfare: Prospects and policies for self-sufficiency of women heading families.* Madison: University of Wisconsin, Institute for Research on Poverty.

Ellwood, D. T. (1988). *Poor support: Poverty in the American family.* New York: Basic Books.

Ford Foundation Project on Social Welfare. (1989, May). *The common good: Social welfare and the American future.* New York: Ford Foundation.

Freedman, S., & Friedlander, D. (1995, July). *The JOBS evaluation: Early findings on program impacts in three sites.* New York: Manpower Demonstration Research Corporation.

Freeman, R. B. (1991). Employment and earnings of disadvantaged young men in a labor shortage economy. In C. Jencks & P. E. Peterson (Eds.), *The urban underclass* (pp. 103-121). Washington, DC: Brookings Institution.

Garfinkel, I. (1992). *Assuring child support: An extension of social security.* New York: Russell Sage.

Garfinkel, I., Robins, P. K., Wong, P., & Meyer, D. R. (1990). The Wisconsin child support assurance system: Estimated effects on poverty, labor supply, caseloads, and cost. *Journal of Human Resources, 25*(1), 16-19.

Gueron, J. M., & Pauly, E. (1991). *From welfare to work.* New York: Russell Sage.

Hamilton, G. (1988, August). *Interim report on the Saturation Work Initiative Model in San Diego.* New York: Manpower Demonstration Research Corporation.

Hamilton, W. L., Burstein, N. R., Hargreaves, M., Moss, D. A., & Walker, M. (1993, July). *The New York State child assistance program: Program impacts, costs, and benefits.* Cambridge, MA: Abt.

Harris, K. M. (1992, November). *Work and welfare among single mothers in poverty.* Chapel Hill: University of North Carolina, Department of Sociology.

Holzer, H. J., & Vroman, W. (1992). Mismatches and the urban labor market. In G. E. Peterson & W. Vroman (Eds.), *Urban labor markets and job opportunity* (pp. 81-112). Washington, DC: Urban Institute.

Johnson, J. H., Jr., & Oliver, M. L. (1992). Structural changes in the U.S. economy and black male joblessness: A reassessment. In G. E. Peterson & W. Vroman (Eds.), *Urban labor markets and job opportunity* (pp. 113-147). Washington, DC: Urban Institute.

Kaus, M. (1992). *The end of equality.* New York: Basic Books.

Kirschenman, J., & Neckerman, K. M. (1991). "We'd love to hire them, but . . .": The meaning of race for employers. In C. Jencks & P. E. Peterson (Eds.), *The urban underclass* (pp. 203-232). Washington, DC: Brookings Institution.

Kramer, M. (1993, February 1). Still waiting for Bill's call. *Time,* 37.

Lane, R. (1992, Summer). Black Philadelphia, then and now. *The Public Interest, 108,* 35-52.

Leonard, J. S. (1986, September). Space, time and unemployment: Los Angeles 1990. Berkeley: University of California, School of Business Administration.

Levy, F. (1979). The labor supply of female household heads, or AFDC work incentives don't work too well. *Journal of Human Resources, 14*(1), 76-97.

Mead, L. M. (1986). *Beyond entitlement: The social obligations of citizenship.* New York: Free Press.

Mead, L. M. (1988). The potential for work enforcement: A study of WIN. *Journal of Policy Analysis and Management, 7*(2), 264-288.

Mead, L. M. (1990). Should workfare be mandatory? What research says. *Journal of Policy Analysis and Management, 9*(3), 400-404.

Mead, L. M. (1992a). The new paternalism: How should Congress respond? *Public Welfare, 50*(2), 14-17.

Mead, L. M. (1992b). *The new politics of poverty: The nonworking poor in America.* New York: Basic Books.

Michalopoulos, C., & Garfinkel, I. (1989). *Reducing the welfare dependence and poverty of single mothers by means of earnings and child support: Wishful thinking and realistic possibility.* Madison: University of Wisconsin, Institute for Research on Poverty.

Moffitt, R. (1983). An economic model of welfare stigma. *American Economic Review, 73,* 1023-1035.

Moffitt, R. (1986). Work incentives in transfer programs (revisited): A study of the AFDC program. In R. G. Ehrenberg (Ed.), *Research in labor economics* (Vol. 8, Pt. B, pp. 389-439). Greenwich, CT: JAI.

Moffitt, R. (1988). *Work and the U.S. welfare system: A review*. Madison: University of Wisconsin, Institute for Research on Poverty.

Moffitt, R., & Wolfe, B. (1990, January). The effect of the medicaid program on welfare participation and labor supply. Madison: University of Wisconsin, Institute for Research on Poverty.

Murray, C. (1984). *Losing ground: American social policy 1950-1980*. New York: Basic Books.

Murray, C. (1990, March 8). Here's the bad news on the underclass. *Wall Street Journal*, p. A14.

Nasar, S. (1993, February 17). 90's may be a decade of growth. *New York Times*.

National Commission on Children. (1991). *Beyond rhetoric: A new American agenda for children and families*. Washington, DC: Government Printing Office.

No need for a boost. (1993, February 13). *The Economist*, 15-16.

Riccio, J., Friedlander, D., & Freedman, S. (1994, September). *GAIN: Benefits, costs, and three-year impacts of a welfare-to-work program*. New York: Manpower Demonstration Research Corporation.

Rossi, P. H. (1989). *Down and out in America: The origins of homelessness*. Chicago: University of Chicago Press.

Sawhill, I. V. (1989, Summer). The underclass: An overview. *The Public Interest, 96*, 3-15.

Schorr, L. B. (with D. Schorr). (1988). *Within our reach: Breaking the cycle of disadvantage*. New York: Doubleday.

Task Force on Poverty and Welfare. (1986, December). *A new social contract: Rethinking the nature and purpose of public assistance*. Albany: State of New York.

Tomkins, C. (1989, March 27). A sense of urgency. *New Yorker*, pp. 48-74.

Turner, M. A. (1991, May). Opportunities denied, opportunities diminished: Discrimination in hiring. Washington, DC: Urban Institute.

U.S. Department of Commerce, Bureau of the Census. (Selected years). *Current Population Reports* (Series P-60, Nos. 35, 68, 81, 106, 152, 158, 181). Washington, DC: Government Printing Office.

U.S. Department of Commerce, Bureau of the Census. (1990, July). *Who's minding the kids? Child care arrangements: Winter 1986-87* (Series P-70, No. 20). Washington, DC: Government Printing Office.

U.S. Department of Commerce, Bureau of the Census. (1992a). *Poverty in the United States: 1991*. (Current Population Reports, Series P-60, No. 181). Washington, DC: Government Printing Office.

U.S. Department of Commerce, Bureau of the Census. (1992b). *Statistical abstract of the United States: 1992*. Washington, DC: Government Printing Office.

U.S. General Accounting Office. (1987, January). *Work and welfare: Current AFDC work programs and implications for federal policy*. Washington, DC: Government Printing Office.

U.S. General Accounting Office. (1992, November). *Welfare to work: States serve least job-ready while meeting JOBS participation rates*. Washington, DC: Author.

U.S. General Accounting Office. (1995, May). *Welfare to work: Most AFDC training programs not emphasizing job placement*. Washington, DC: Author.

U.S. House of Representatives, Committee on Ways and Means. (1992). *Overview of entitlement programs: 1992 green book*. Washington, DC: Government Printing Office.

U.S. House of Representatives, Committee on Ways and Means. (1994). *Overview of entitlement programs: 1994 green book*. Washington, DC: Government Printing Office.

U.S. House of Representatives, Select Committee on Children, Youth, and Families. (1988, September 22). *A domestic priority: Overcoming family poverty in America: Hearings before the Select Committee on Children, Youth, and Families*, 100th Cong., 2d Sess.

Wilson, W. J. (1987). *The truly disadvantaged: The inner city, the underclass, and public policy*. Chicago: University of Chicago Press.

14

Training, Work, and Poverty

Margaret C. Simms

It is tempting to equate the employment problems and training needs of urban communities with the welfare-dependent population. That is too narrow a view, although it is one taken by a number of policy analysts. As Besharov points out in Chapter 2, nearly one half of those in poverty are not on welfare. Some 20% work full-time, year-round, and another 25% or so are engaged in market work or other productive activity or are supported by individuals or resources other than welfare.

Moreover, if we focus only on the welfare population, we will not solve the problems of family formation that Murray alludes to in Chapter 5. We cannot do that without, as Mead notes in Chapter 13, directly addressing the problems of men, particularly those of young black and Latino men who have problems making transitions from school or nonactivity to work. This means examining education and school-to-work transitions much more carefully. I do not think that solving the problems of the education system is just a matter of enabling parental choice; it is about what is done in whatever schools our children attend.

Little attention has been given to the role of the business community in reducing poverty in this country. People talk about individual responsibility and governmental roles, but what is business's responsibility? Whether it is President Clinton describing a "new covenant" or others who argue that we need a new social contract, the focus has been on individuals and government, with few addressing the issue of business responsibility. My views on this subject may have been shaped by two visits to Germany and Denmark, where discussion of education invariably leads to the roles and responsibilities of the three "social partners"—government, labor, and business.

The whole welfare reform debate is often set up as one of stark contrasts. This does not do real justice to the issues at hand. To talk about the ways in which these contrasts are really not representative of where, at least, the academics and the policy analysts are in this debate, I refer to Klein's (1993) commentary in *Newsweek*. At the beginning of his article, he puts forth the scenario of an exchange that took place at the Economic Summit in December 1992 between Marian Wright Edelman, president of the Children's Defense Fund, and President-Elect Clinton. In this scenario, the two are discussing the underlying causes of poverty. Klein goes on to portray liberals as those who put all responsibility for reducing poverty on government. In this interpretation, liberals say that the poor are victims of injustice, discrimination, and so forth, and conservatives are portrayed as seeing poverty solely as a cultural or behavioral problem. Klein indicates that a synthesis of these two concepts seems to be an aberration. In fact, that is not so. I argue that many people in the debate now are really in that synthesis mode. More than 6 years ago, for example, the Committee on Policy for Racial Justice (1987), a group of 28 prominent black scholars and activists (including Marian Wright Edelman) associated with the Joint Center for Political and Economic Studies,[1] issued a statement on "Black Initiative and Governmental Responsibility." This document acknowledges that each side has a responsibility for creating a productive society and a comfortable environment for raising children.

Now I will focus more directly on the objectives discussed in Chapters 12 and 13 in this volume. I will then introduce a few solutions, with the same caveat those authors made, which is essentially this: One size does not fit all, and one policy solution does not fit all.

In Chapter 12, Gueron identifies the three objectives of welfare reform: (a) to reduce dependency either partially or completely, (b) to reduce the public cost associated with welfare and dependency, and (c) to reduce poverty. She concludes that welfare reform and training initiatives do some of each but do not do them as well as we might like. Programs can be effective in reducing dependency, but they rarely move people off welfare completely. They do reduce some of the direct costs of the welfare system, but modestly. These programs probably are least effective in reducing poverty, in part because of the regulations governing means-tested transfers and in part because of the types of jobs that people leaving these training programs are able to obtain.

I want to emphasize Gueron's point that the gains depend on the characteristics of the individuals involved. For some, job search is sufficient to move them into the workplace, but perhaps that is not the best use of our money. With more treatment, we get larger gains, and the biggest gains, especially for those who are the most disadvantaged, are associated with intensive training and access to better jobs. This is not an inexpensive proposition, and it certainly is not one that we can accommodate in the short run.

If we wanted to extend the discussion to looking at job training programs beyond the welfare population, to look at some of the experiences from the Comprehensive Employment and Training Act (CETA) and other programs, I say they mirror some of these conclusions. We can make modest gains, but we make them principally through increasing the number of hours employed and not through increasing access to better jobs or jobs with higher wages. This shows up, for example, in CETA programs for men, for which evaluations indicate that although programs were effective for women because they increased their hours of employment, they really did little to change men's characteristics. When they finished the program, men looked a whole lot like they did before they entered. Before training, they had been employed but at chronically low wages. There was little about the light training that changed their characteristics within the job market (for further information on the limited effectiveness of CETA programs, see Simms, 1989).

Gueron's Table 12.3 enumerates a set of open questions for welfare employment programs that raises some questions whether we can take our present experiences and extend them to a larger group of people who are not volunteers but are more likely to be mandatory participants in intensive training. Can we expect the same rates of return? These are important and vital questions if we are to move forward along these lines.

The issues in Mead's Chapter 13 revolve around five basic questions: Are jobs available? For whom are they available? At what wages? For how many hours? And with what possibilities for upward mobility? Mead sets out from the basic premise, with which I basically agree, that one of the main reasons for poverty is not having stable work full-time, or at least for more hours than are currently available.

Chapter 13 spends a lot of time refuting most of the arguments about nonwork among those who are poor: the deindustrialization hypothesis, a scarcity of jobs, discrimination, and the question about minimum wage. A few caveats must be noted concerning Mead's argument. He assumes that if we moved nonworkers into the work category, their experiences would be just like those who are currently working. For example, when he talks about the minimum wage, he suggests that because most minimum-wage workers are not heads of households, we should not look at that as a major deterrent or explanation for why full-time work would keep people in poverty. The argument assumes that if we put these nonworkers into the workforce, they would earn nonminimum wages, which is Mead's assertion; that is, if they were full-time workers like current full-time workers, they would receive more than the minimum wage. Therefore, their incomes would be larger than we are led to believe by others. I argue that this probably is not true: As we change the mix of people in the workforce, we would probably not see the same outcome, either in wage rates or in total income. In other words, don't generalize from who's already there to who's not there.

The second assumption that Mead makes is that job training is not an issue, but at the same time, he contradicts himself by saying that employers do not want to employ some of these people because they lack certain characteristics, such as work ethic, familiarity with work responsibilities and work hours, and so forth. He discusses job availability and argues that there is not a scarcity of jobs because jobs are available—there has been growth in the number of service jobs, and so forth and so on. Certainly, if poverty were not an issue, then we would not have to be concerned about the characteristics of the jobs that are available, because we could focus on employing people without worrying about paying them enough to lift them out of poverty. That is only a partial answer to the question of poverty, which he acknowledges. So, although I do not totally disagree with him, there are two problems with his argument.

But two other issues are actually involved here. One is that you cannot make a national statement or a nationwide city statement about job availability because cities differ. And, in fact, the work done at the Joint Center for Political and Economic Studies looking at changes in poverty conditions for black children through time shows marked differences between the Northeast and Midwest versus the South in working poverty versus dependent poverty (Rexroat, 1994). Through time, there have been large increases in dependent poverty in the Northeast and Midwest. Those are associated with declining employment opportunities for black men and differences in job growth for women. Women in the South tended to have higher work effort than in those in the North and Midwest, but at relatively low wages, leading to a larger proportion of working poor as opposed to dependent poor.

A second issue is that if you look, for example, at some of the findings from the Urban Institute study on discrimination, you do find that young men who come into the market with similar characteristics differing only by race or ethnicity are treated differently in ways that suggest discrimination (Turner, Fix, & Struyk, 1991). Employers, knowing nothing more about their differences, would rather hire a white than a black or a Hispanic, even if they have the same paper credentials. Now one of two explanations is possible: Either it is out-and-out discrimination, or the employers are engaging in what an economist would call statistical discrimination—that is, employers look at the two job candidates and say, "Aha! This black person or this Latino went to an inferior high school, and therefore . . ." or "I know that on average a black person goes to a high school that is inferior to the average high school that the white person goes to, and therefore he is likely to be less qualified for the job." Those are the only two explanations I could come up with for this differential. These are people with no work experience, so prior experience is not an issue.

Let me return to three basic issues with which we need to cope. One is the role of overall economic growth. It has been both alluded to as a solution to all our problems—a rising tide lifts all boats, which assumes, of course, that you have a boat—and on the other hand, it does not make any difference. Well, I think that overall economic growth has to be there; it is a necessary but not a sufficient condition. For example, we can look at what happened during 1992. Although the recession ended in early 1991, according to the National Bureau of Economic Research (Berry, 1992), unemployment rates increased between 1991 and 1992. That's because the labor force grew. Unless jobs grow faster than the labor force, you are going to have an increase in unemployment, even if you have some growth. During 1992, the rate of job growth was about half the rate of labor force growth, resulting in an increase in unemployment (see *Employment and Earnings,* 1993). So we do have a question of overall economic growth, whether it is at the national level or in a particular area. But we also know from experiences of the last 15 to 20 years that a rising tide does not help many, that cyclical changes have made little difference in employment or poverty for certain groups, and that therefore we have to turn to targeted programs to improve the economic condition of those untouched by economic growth.

The second issue is the role of the education and training system. Given limited resources, how much are we going to put into training and employment for the adult population about which we are concerned—the adult poverty population? Are we going to commit sufficient resources so that they can earn their way out of poverty? Or is it sufficient merely to instill greater commitment or connection to the workforce and hope that although that will not affect poor adults directly, it will have an effect on their children and their children's view toward work and toward obtaining education and training. I know other chapters address issues concerning young children. But in this volume, as in other discussions, we seem to skip over those in the next immediate generation. If we do not do something about them, we are going to have a lot more people in the younger generation who are going to be at risk. So the question is, how much are we going to put into moving young men and women from school into work?

The third issue is the role of business. Is business just going to sit there and wait for the people to show up at the door? Do businesspersons have a commitment to training? And if so, what is the nature of that commitment?

From what we know from the experiences of the past 10 years, I think we have to develop either new programs, new mechanisms, and/or a new attitude on the part of businesses. In Chapter 13, Mead says that employers do not want to be bothered with youth who do not have the right work ethic and that this is not confined to white entrepreneurs but probably extends across-the-board. Certainly, small-business owners do not have the time or resources to engage in a lot of training activities. But what is their role?

If we look at some of the youth experiments, we find that employers are reluctant to take up youth who are participating in programs, including stay-in-school programs. Even with a 100% wage subsidy, they seem reluctant to provide jobs. This reluctance shows up, also, in some vocational education programs in selected cities in which the Joint Center has interviewed both educators and business owners about job placement for the students who are in career education. The Joint Center found business managers who say, "Oh, you can't hire those people, they won't work, they don't know about work, they receive poor training." The individuals making those statements do not know the programs and have not participated in their development. Many of the school administrators have said that sometimes businesses adopt a school, show up to announce the fact, and then are not heard from again.

So we have to think about ways in which business can become more actively engaged in the school-to-work transition. It is insufficient to make a verbal commitment about making schools better or commit resources toward passing bond issues—"OK, voters. Get out there and vote for more money for our schools." What resources will businesses put directly into training—into participating in the training process, ensuring that young people who come out of school are qualified for the jobs that they have, and being willing, therefore, to hire them?

Note

1. Prior to 1990, the name of the Joint Center for Political and Economic Studies was Joint Center for Political Studies; cites prior to that date use the latter name.

References

Berry, J. M. (1992, December 23). Recession is officially over, panel declares. *Washington Post,* p. E1.

Committee on Policy for Racial Justice. (1987). *Black initiative and governmental responsibility.* Washington, DC: Joint Center for Political Studies.

Comprehensive Employment and Training Act of 1973 (Pub. L. No. 93-203).

Employment and earnings. (1993, January). Washington, DC: Bureau of Labor Statistics.

Klein, J. (1993, January 18). A poor excuse for poverty solutions. *Newsweek,* p. 27.

Rexroat, C. (1994). *The declining economic status of black children.* Washington, DC: Joint Center for Political and Economic Studies.

Simms, M. D. (1989). The effectiveness of government training programs. In Commission on Workforce Quality and Labor Market Efficiency (Ed.), *Investing in people: A strategy to address America's workforce crisis* (pp. 565-603). Washington, DC: U.S. Department of Labor.

Turner, M. A., Fix, M., & Struyk, R. J. (1991). *Opportunities denied, opportunities diminished: Racial discrimination in hiring.* Washington, DC: Urban Institute.

PART VI

Reducing Poverty
Through Social Intervention

Reducing Poverty

Will the New "Services Strategy" Do Better Than the Old?

Leslie Lenkowsky

More than three decades have now elapsed since Abraham Ribicoff, then secretary of what was then the Department of Health, Education, and Welfare (HEW), presented to Congress a welfare reform program that he said

> will pay dividends on each dollar invested. It can move some persons off the assistance rolls entirely, enable others to attain a higher degree of self-confidence and independence, encourage children to grow strong in mind and body, train welfare workers in the skills which will help make these achievements possible, and simplify and improve welfare administration. (quoted in Steiner, 1966, p. 39)

He was referring to what became the Public Welfare Amendments of 1962, a set of measures to provide a wide range of social services for recipients of Aid to Families With Dependent Children (AFDC). With the strong endorsement of social work experts, the program sought to do no less than reshape the

AUTHOR'S NOTE: Kathleen M. Lenkowsky and Deborah Jones assisted with the research for this chapter.

nation's approach to helping poverty-stricken families. No longer would public officials be content merely to give financial assistance; they would now also try to help the families become self-supporting. "The byword of our new program," Secretary Ribicoff said, "is prevention—and where it is too late—rehabilitation, a fresh start" (quoted in Steiner, 1966, p. 41).

Within a few years, however, policymakers were looking for a fresh start. Even some who had championed the new approach were having second thoughts about its likely effectiveness. Despite suggestions to the contrary, the contribution social services could make to reducing poverty and welfare dependency seemed elusive at best. Thus, one of the program's administrators (Winifred Bell) gave the following testimony in 1967 about a review of grants made under the 1962 act:

> The search was for methods of intervention that worked to cure poverty or to mitigate its consequences, a subject I presumed to be one of the priorities in decision-making in this program. In my judgment, my review revealed that unpromising projects continued to be funded year after year, most studies were inconsequential, hard facts were difficult to locate and when located were rarely useful due to poor original conceptualization, inadequate methodology, failure to include or control sufficient variables, or inability to write clearly and concisely. (quoted in Steiner, 1971, p. 40)

Although social services continued to be part of welfare policy, other ways of dealing with those who were poor and AFDC recipients increasingly engaged the attention of lawmakers and the experts.

Perhaps inevitably, because ideas about how to help poor people seem to repeat themselves, the "services strategy" is now coming back into favor. Experts in areas such as child development and job training are again advocating extensive services as the key to health, wealth, and wisdom. Business leaders are calling for "investments" in social services for the young to ultimately produce a workforce able to compete with the Japanese. At the state and local levels of government, public officials have strained to find clever acronyms for new programs to counsel, teach, employ, and otherwise try to manage those who are poor. And from Washington, the 1988 Family Support Act added another $1 billion annually—plus money for child and health care—for jobs to help welfare mothers obtain jobs. Indeed, so numerous and complex have social service programs for poor people become that some experts and local officials are calling for them to be combined and simplified.

Yet more than just size and complexity distinguish the new services strategy from the old. Today's version tends to be more comprehensive in the types of services provided. Programs often deal with a wide range of problems participants face, from medical and educational to parental and job-related. Eligibility is usually broader as well; mothers with infants and even fathers may be included. Most significantly, welfare recipients are increasingly required to obtain social services to get their welfare checks; failing to take part in a program could result in a loss of assistance. In this way, the new services strategy reflects the philosophy that being poor should not only entitle a person to certain benefits but also entail certain obligations in return, not the least of which is to become less poor or less dependent.

Even so, the question of whether the new services strategy will prove more effective than the old one remains to be answered. Because of its newness, evidence is limited, and what exists raises as many doubts as it settles. Nonetheless, as this chapter will show, the likelihood that the new services strategy will have a large impact on the problems of welfare dependency and poverty seems remote. By looking again at what social services can—and cannot—accomplish, however, identifying at least some ways of improving their effectiveness in reducing poverty becomes possible.

From Services to Income—and Back

The idea that poor people were not incorrigible but could be turned by social programs into productive citizens is an old one, dating at least to the end of the 18th century. In 1798, Jeremy Bentham proposed a scheme for "pauper management" that makes today's plans for intensive social services look lax. Bentham would have had all poor people moved into privately run "industry-houses," where they would have been fed, clothed, trained, and supervised to become gainfully employed. As Himmelfarb (1984) notes, however, no one paid much attention to this notion for turning dross into sterling, which, in effect, sought to combine rehabilitation with the stigmatization of the workhouse.

Not until the latter part of the 19th century did the services strategy really begin to flourish. In the name of "scientific charity," groups such as the Charity Organization Society (COS) sprang up throughout the United States. They rejected the idea of giving money to the poor—except, under some circumstances, through voluntary donations—in favor of addressing the personal or familial causes of poverty, such as alcoholism, illness, and marital discord. Their principal agents were known as "friendly visitors," who went to the homes of poor people, in the words of COS leader Josephine Shaw Lowell, "not to carry alms, but sympathy, hope, courage, in short brains and character" (quoted in Coll, 1969, p. 55). Although this approach remained influential in some cities for decades and contributed to the emergence of social work as a profession, it seems to have had little overall impact, except perhaps to give its practitioners the reputation of being more scientific than charitable—or friendly.

Nonetheless, through settlement houses and other types of associations, a wide range of services continued to be offered to those who were poor. In addition, the expansion of public education, efforts to reform housing codes and labor practices, the public health movement, and other turn-of-the-century social policies usually provided additional forms of "prevention" and "rehabilitation." Indeed, if understood broadly as any program that could help poor persons take advantage of the promise of American life, the services strategy has clearly been the preferred approach to reducing poverty in the United States, once it was admitted that economic growth alone might not suffice.

That began to change with the coming of the New Deal. Although American social policy had always contained measures to provide financial aid to segments of the poor population, including several that had grown into substantial undertakings, the Social Security Act of 1935 not only established a major new set of federal income support programs but, even more important, gave them a coherent rationale aimed at encouraging self-sufficiency.

The key was to tie the receipt of assistance not simply to financial need but to a history of work (and, in the case of those unemployed, a willingness to resume work). Purely need-based help was meant to be only an interim measure, chiefly for those who had not yet worked enough to qualify for the other programs or for nonworking mothers with children (and no husband), for whom the program now known as AFDC was created. (Even this was expected to "wither away," as women became eligible for benefits as widows of workingmen.) Although the New Deal by no means abandoned the idea of providing services to poor people, its most distinctive contribution was to devise an acceptable way of giving money as well—in other words, an "income strategy."

A quarter century later, the seeming failure of this strategy gave rise to the Public Welfare Amendments of 1962. Although much of the American population was now covered under the Social Security Act's work-related programs, large numbers of people continued to rely on its need-based provisions. Indeed, far from decreasing, the number of families on AFDC was growing rapidly and included an increasing proportion in which the father's work history was irrelevant because he had not died but had simply left. Instead of promoting self-sufficiency, the income strategy, and AFDC in particular, seemed—like earlier public assistance programs—to be encouraging greater dependency and poverty.

The 1962 amendments were part of a broader revival of policymaker enthusiasm for the services strategy. Key elements of the War on Poverty, such as Head Start, the Jobs Corps, and the Community Action Program, were based on the view that changing how poor people behaved was essential to reducing poverty. Likewise, the Elementary and Secondary Education Act of 1965 contemplated a variety of efforts to improve educational services for the children of the poor. Proposals to expand access to health care and family planning, as well as to new homes and neighborhoods, reflected a similar outlook.

Partly for reasons of cost and partly because of growing doubts that many of the programs would succeed, however, the ardor for the services strategy died as quickly as it had flared up (for a fuller discussion, see, e.g., Lenkowsky, 1986). (Symbolically, as he was leaving office, Wilbur Cohen, who had succeeded Ribicoff as HEW secretary, signed an executive order distancing service providers from income maintenance workers in AFDC offices.) Although spending on social services continued to grow, the income strategy acquired new advocates, who argued, in effect, that the New Deal's idea for helping poor people was right but that its design was wrong. By restructuring AFDC to create stronger incentives for work and family stability, they claimed, a more efficient and effective way of reducing poverty and encouraging self-sufficiency could be created.

For more than a decade, from the end of the 1960s through the beginning of the 1980s, the question of whether this was likely to be so commanded the attention of both policymakers and experts. The administrations of three presidents prepared plans embodying the income strategy, Congress considered it on several occasions, and a massive series of social experiments was conducted to test its key premises. The result was a stalemate. Spending on income support programs rose, especially those that helped older persons or provided money in-kind, such as food stamps. But proponents of a broader program that would have encompassed low-income families headed by employable men or women were never able to make a sufficiently persuasive case that it would work.

The final blow to the idea was dealt by Murray (1984). In his widely discussed book, *Losing Ground,* Murray argued that since the mid-1960s, federal efforts to help poor persons had actually done them more harm than good. Although he was referring not just to income support measures, his book was generally seen as a critique more of liberalized public assistance programs than of Head Start. And although his numerous critics found fault with both his evidence and his explanations, nonetheless, few disputed his basic conclusion that poor persons were worse off than they had been 20 years before or were ready to assert that adopting an income strategy was likely to improve matters.

What was evolving, both among policymakers and experts, was a so-called new consensus on welfare and poverty (see, e.g., Novak et al., 1987). It held that "the poor" actually consisted of two groups of people: one composed of those temporarily down on their luck and the other, so far removed from the mainstream of American life that they were likely to remain poverty-stricken for a considerable time. The first group was numerically larger by far, but the second was often more visible as gang members, school dropouts, drug addicts, and other figures in the landscape of urban decay. Although an income strategy could be helpful to the first, neither a growing economy nor conventional social policies were likely to do much good for the latter. For these members of this "underclass," a mixture of heroic measures to foster good behavior and sanctions to penalize the bad seemed in order. Out of this new consensus has emerged the new services strategy.

The New Services Strategy

Like the old, the new services strategy has two major thrusts: prevention and rehabilitation. The aim of the former is to intervene with sufficient help at critical points in the life of someone "at risk" to keep the person from becoming poor. Most of these programs are directed at children or young people. By contrast, the rehabilitative measures tend to be directed at adults. They seek to assist those who are poor (or dependent on welfare) to change their behavior in ways likely to result in self-sufficiency. Often they are accompanied by penalties, such as a partial loss of welfare benefits, for failing to accept the services offered.

Of the preventive programs, the best known is Head Start. Since 1965, it has provided a mixture of educational, medical, and social services to 3-, 4-, and 5-year-olds, most of whom come from families in poverty. By compensating for the disadvantages they experience at home, Head Start aims to prepare the children to do well in school and thus to avoid the pitfalls (such as failing to finish high school) likely to keep them poor. Although it still enrolls less than one third of the eligible preschoolers, Head Start not only has grown rapidly since the mid-1980s (from 450,000 to more than 600,000 participants) but also enjoys widespread public support (U.S. House of Representatives, 1992, Table 39).

Among many professionals, however, Head Start is coming to be regarded as just the beginning. In recent years, new programs have been developed that provide more intensive services for a longer time to more members of the child's family than Head Start does. For example, the Comprehensive Child Development Act program, authorized by Congress in 1988, enlists families with children less than a year old and works with them until the children enter school. During this time, a variety of agencies provide a wide range of services—medical, educational, nutritional, job counseling, and more—to both the younger generation and their parents.

Several similar programs, including one operated by Head Start (Family Service Centers), are also getting underway. Although sometimes differing in the services they emphasize, all share the view that preventing poverty requires addressing the multiple problems facing the family as a whole. Simply dealing with the needs of the preschool child is not enough.

Nor are the first few years of life the only period in which preventive measures are being tried. Other parts of the services strategy aim at problems of older youth that often lead to poverty, such as teenage pregnancy or dropping out of high school. Like the preschool programs, however, these too are becoming more comprehensive and intense, moving from the three Cs— classes, counseling, and contraceptives—to highly structured groups involving numerous mentors and concerned with the full range of medical, social, and educational difficulties that may face young persons at risk. In some of these programs, the failure of a child to participate may cost the family a portion of its welfare benefits.

Sanctions such as this more often accompany efforts at rehabilitation than prevention. California's GAIN program, for example, requires a portion of the state's welfare recipients to participate in job search and training activities. If they drop out before they are employed, their benefits could be reduced. Particularly since the enactment of the Family Support Act of 1988, other states have followed suit, although many also have programs in which participation is voluntary.

Whether required to do so or not, because the aim is to enhance their employability, those who enroll in these programs usually encounter a similar menu of services. These range from counseling and skill development efforts to job placement and actual work experience. In addition, help with child care, transportation, and medical needs is often provided. Despite these common elements, however, programs frequently differ in the emphasis they give to one or another.

Preparing welfare recipients for the labor force is not the only goal of the new rehabilitative services. An increasing number of programs are also seeking to help families—particularly single-parent ones—become more stable and nurturing, so that presumably as a result, they are less likely to remain poor (or have their children put into foster care). This usually entails activities such as assisting parents to resolve family crises, teaching parenting and housekeeping skills, and maintaining "friendly visitor"-like contact with the family. Not least important, a handful of these programs are even trying to make the fathers of children on welfare more responsible for them.

In effect, these family-oriented programs are simply extensions and intensifications of long-established child welfare services. Other programs to deal chiefly with problems such as child neglect and abuse and drug use have also been expanding lately; these usually have antipoverty objectives also. Likewise, a significant part of the rationale for reforming education and health care has to do with providing better services for those who are poor. All in all, the new services strategy goes far beyond those programs that have traditionally aimed at reducing poverty or welfare dependency.

Indeed, many of those charged with administering these programs are now calling for greater authority to combine and adjust them, the better to provide the various services a family might require. Some also urge pooling and concentrating resources locally, perhaps even reviving the settlement house, the original multiservice agency that at the turn of the century was a venue for offering comprehensive educational and social services to poverty-stricken neighborhoods. According to legend, places such as Hull House or the Henry Street Settlement were important gateways for poor people into the middle class. If properly organized, would today's services strategy do as well?

The Effectiveness of Social Services

The simplest answer to this question is that we do not really know. The new services strategy is so new that for most of its programs, no reliable information is yet available. Indeed, many of the measures are meant to be experimental and thus ought not to be expected to show dramatic results immediately. Not least important, the new services strategy started in earnest toward the end of the 1980s, just as the nation's sagging economy made reducing poverty and welfare dependency more difficult.

Even so, some preliminary conclusions are possible. In part, they stem from evaluations of several programs, especially those that are longer running. Assessing how well suited social services are for addressing the critical problems facing those in poverty sheds additional light. From either angle, the prognosis for the effectiveness of the new services strategy is by no means dismal, but neither is it especially encouraging.

The evaluative research is perhaps the most familiar and authoritative. For Head Start, the most closely examined of the services programs, a consensus now exists that it can markedly improve the school readiness of the children who take part in it. The differences between them and similar youngsters who did not experience Head Start seem to disappear rapidly, however; within a few years of entering school, in fact, distinguishing the two groups is difficult. That is one reason proponents of early childhood education have advocated a more comprehensive approach. But apart from the oft-cited Perry Preschool program and a handful of other experimental efforts, evidence about the effectiveness of these non-Head Start programs is scarce. And even in the Perry program, although participants did better than a control group, they continued to have high rates of teenage pregnancy, arrest, and welfare dependency (Schweinhart, 1986, p. 14, Table 4).

Measures to prevent teenage pregnancy have also been studied extensively but with much the same result. Although school-based programs combining sex education with clinical examinations and assistance have been able to reduce pregnancy, they do not seem likely to make a decisive difference. According to one review, the best had success rates ranging from 26% to 50%, significant but hardly the whole answer, especially because those who took advantage of the programs were often not from high-risk groups (Foster, 1986, pp. 64-65). Teenagers who already had had at least one child were the focus of another major effort, Project Redirection, which also combined educational, health, family planning, and other services. Although the participants were likely to have higher earnings and less welfare dependency than a control group, the program did nothing to increase their educational attainment, and the rate of repeat pregnancies remained high (Gueron & Pauly, 1991, Tables 3.4 and 5.5).

The rehabilitative programs that have been evaluated fare about as well. According to Gueron and Pauly's (1991) comprehensive review, efforts to help welfare recipients find jobs can lead to increased employment and earnings and lower welfare payments. But the participants often remain on public assistance or in poverty. The evaluation of the initial year of California's GAIN program paints a similar picture, albeit with some important differences among the counties involved in the study (Riccio & Friedlander, 1992).

Likewise, although programs such as Homebuilders, which seeks to help troubled families, can claim some successes, they are generally too small or too new to permit much confidence about their effectiveness (Rossi, 1992). In any event, the services they offer usually aim more at avoiding problems such as child abuse and neglect than at reducing poverty or welfare dependency. One exception is Iowa's Family Development and Self-Sufficiency Program, which explicitly links building stronger family relationships to enhancing economic self-sufficiency. But a recent report on the program cautions that this is a long-term goal, and of the eight cases it describes, only two appeared to have left welfare, neither "securely" (Bruner & Berryhill, 1992, p. 41).

Perhaps the most challenging of the rehabilitative programs is one tested by Public/Private Ventures at six sites throughout the United States. It intends to see whether or not a variety of educational, employment, legal, and social services can help the unwed fathers of children on welfare take responsibility for their families, including working to support them. Although the final results are not yet in, an interim report suggests that recruitment has been slow and hard and retention difficult. Only half of the young men who obtained jobs during the first 12 months of the program were still in them at the end of the year (Watson, 1992, p. 44). Nonetheless, that a group in which nearly 80% were unemployed, almost two thirds had an arrest record, more than 40% were high school dropouts, and 30% had sold drugs took part in the program at all offers at least mild encouragement.

That is about the most one could say for other types of services. Although the past decade has witnessed numerous efforts to reform American education, particularly for those who are poor, little more than a modest increase in basic skills seems to have resulted. To the extent drug use has diminished among those in poverty, stricter law enforcement measures and social pressures more than rehabilitative services are probably responsible.

Even health services have not been unambiguously helpful to those in poverty. To be sure, thanks to Medicaid and several smaller programs, poor persons now have greater access to medical and nutritional services; by most commonly used measures, the results have been good. Nevertheless, as several studies have suggested, the eligibility requirements for these programs—being on welfare or having a low income—may also tug participants toward continued dependency.

Of course, research just beginning on the newer parts of the services strategy could change this assessment of its effectiveness. Although that cannot be ruled out, the chances seem to be slim. The reason is that even state-of-the-art social services may not be well suited to making significant reductions in poverty.

In part, this is because a majority of the poor population may have less need of services than generally thought. Recent surveys suggest that although families in poverty are more troubled and disadvantaged than those not, the differences are relatively small. For example, after adjusting for parental education, family structure, ethnicity, and similar factors, data from the 1988 National Health Interview Survey on Child Health revealed that about one quarter of the children of poor people have serious health and developmental problems. So did one fifth of the children in families that were not poor, however (Zill, Moore, Smith, Stief, & Coiro, 1991, Table 2).

Larger differences appear in findings on the quality of children's home environments from the 1986 National Longitudinal Survey of Labor Market Experience of Youth. Three times as many youngsters in poor families lived in "deficient" environments as those who did not grow up in poverty. Even so, only one quarter of those who are poor faced this problem, and on some measures of the quality of home life (such as its safety), the gap between poor and nonpoor families was much smaller (Zill et al., 1991, Tables 7 to 10).

These results do not imply that social services are unhelpful. To the contrary, they could be interpreted to mean that those with severe family problems, whether they are poor or not, could benefit from participating in good programs. But what these data also say is that the types of problems the services strategy seeks to address may not be a significant barrier for more than a small portion of those who are poor.

Indirect confirmation of this comes from a variety of efforts to determine whether providing child care helps to reduce welfare dependency. Although several studies suggest it does, others—particularly those relying on the self-reports of participants—indicate that it is not a major factor (see review of studies in Cottingham & Ellwood, 1989). Both conclusions may be true; for some mothers to become employed, child care programs will be essential, but for others, they will not. For that reason, a services strategy that invests heavily in such programs is bound to have limited returns.

Compared with other social services, child care at least has the advantage that those who need it would probably make use of it. Efforts to prevent teen pregnancy, induce welfare recipients to become employed, and stabilize unruly homes face the challenge of persuading those who most need help to obtain it. This creates another limit on the effectiveness of the services strategy.

The job-focused programs reveal the nature of the problem. Until recently, participation was largely voluntary, presumably to ensure that those taking part would be more motivated than the average welfare recipient. As a result, only a small portion of the dependent population were involved. Since the passage of the Family Support Act in 1988, programs requiring more extensive participation—and penalizing those who fail to enroll—have proliferated. The jury is still out on whether the requirements are enforced, let alone how well they are working. (Some initial evidence indicates that a tougher-minded approach could be more productive.[1]) But as currently written, in most cases the program's regulations still leave the decision to participate up to the welfare recipients themselves.

Even when enforced, requirements can sometimes backfire. In the Public/Private Ventures Unwed Fathers Project, for example, the men taking part in its job training program were also expected to establish paternity and begin providing support for their children. This requirement apparently hampered the recruitment of participants. Although the sites with the best retention rates also had the highest proportions of fathers who established paternity, this may simply reflect that their participants were the most motivated to begin with (Watson, 1992, p. 18, Tables 13 and 15).

In any case, not all social services programs can devise a reason for compelling those in need to take part. Instead, they must rely on what one program calls "creative and persistent outreach" (Bruner & Berryhill, 1992, p. 50). Although this was perhaps effective in recruiting troubled families, persons not wanting to take part could usually avoid doing so.

If the services strategy aided only those who desired help, it would hardly be a wasted effort. But by the same token, unless more "demand" for the services could somehow be generated, it would hardly have a widespread effect on reducing poverty or dependency.

Yet if these programs ever did manage to enlist those who need to be served, they would require a considerable infusion of resources. For example, providing comprehensive assistance to seriously disadvantaged children or their families is expensive. The Comprehensive Child Development Program, for example, spends approximately $8,000 annually per child, more than twice what Head Start costs. Expanding it to cover all 3- to 5-year-olds in poverty would require more than $17 billion annually, eight times the total spent on Head Start (Besharov, 1992, p. 531; U.S. House of Representatives, 1992, Table 39).[2] Depending on the activities sponsored, job training programs for welfare recipients could consume several hundred to several thousand dollars per participant. Youth corps, which engage teenagers in full-time community service and conservation activities, cost $15,000 to $20,000 per person (Commission on National and Community Service, 1993, p. 77).

Much of this is for staff. The new services programs generally employ many more professionals than traditional ones did and make greater demands on them. In the Homebuilders program, in fact, caseworkers may deal with only two or three families at a time, 18 to 20 per year, and are supposed to be available around the clock (Forsythe, 1992, p. 44).

In short, implementing the new services strategy on a scale (and over the time) necessary to have a significant effect on poverty would be extremely expensive. Without a sizable increase in appropriately trained professionals, it probably could not be done at all. Although the problems of poverty also impose substantial costs on American society, the idea of making the type of commitment necessary—even if the evidence on the effectiveness of these services were more convincing—does not fit well into an era of tight budgets and preoccupation with government deficits.

This is not to say that *some* increased investment in the services strategy would not be worthwhile. Rather, it is to suggest the need for modesty in expectations of what will be accomplished. The old services strategy was quickly discredited partly because its proponents promised more than it could have conceivably delivered. The advocates of the new one should avoid making the same mistake. They should also look harder for innovative ways to improve the effectiveness of social services.

The Future of the Services Strategy

Three decades ago, the famous "Coleman Report," *Equality of Educational Opportunity* (Coleman et al., 1966), stunned American educators by arguing that almost everything they intended to try to improve schooling for minorities was not likely to do much good. After the shock had worn off, some of the educators, as James Q. Wilson (1990) has told the story, began to search for places in which progress was being made. Finding these "effective" schools, they next tried to identify what each had in common and, in time, developed a relatively coherent strategy for improving education. Although American schools still have a long way to go, most reformers are drawing on the insights gained in this effort as they press for change.

Social services programs are now about where American education was three decades ago. More is known about what will not work—or will not have much of an impact—than what will. If the new services strategy is to be more successful than the old, a process not unlike that which the educators undertook ought to commence.

The evaluative research already underway offers some possible lines of approach. For example, differences among programs offered at more than one site may provide clues to critical variables. In the first year of the GAIN evaluation, Riverside did much better moving welfare recipients into the workforce than the other five California counties under study did (see Riccio & Friedlander, 1992). This probably reflected that the Riverside program was more focused on job placement, whereas the others were more concerned about developing skills and job readiness. As with effective schools, effective welfare agencies may well be those that develop a culture conducive to reducing dependency. If so, identifying and finding ways to encourage the spread of that culture should enhance the effect of services programs.

Making better use of information about people in poverty might also help. Although Iowa's Family Development and Self-Sufficiency Program seeks to focus its efforts on families at risk of long-term dependency, the indicators of this danger identified by Bane and Ellwood (1983; Ellwood, 1986) influenced the selection of participants only weakly, at best (Bruner & Berryhill, 1992). Most other programs take even less care in sorting out participants or even considering how to target their resources most effectively.

How the services strategy interacts with other ways of assisting those who are poor could stand more attention as well. Even when they are dealing with the same young people, the extent of coordination between schools and social services is often limited, although some of the newer programs are seeking to change that. Although overall economic conditions seem to have relatively little bearing on the effectiveness of the services strategy, local circumstances, such as the organization of the labor markets, the availability of transportation, and targeted development programs, may make a difference. Not least important, the relationship between income support measures and social services programs needs to be examined, lest as Gueron and Pauly (1991) have noted, those programs that lift earnings continue to fail to reduce dependency and those that reduce welfare spending continue to fail to produce higher incomes for the people who had been receiving welfare.

Older models for delivering services are also worth a second look. For example, the public health movement of the 19th century demonstrated that at least some problems originally thought to be personal or social in nature could be contained—and even eliminated—by medical or antiseptic methods. Is it possible that the recent introduction of a new contraceptive, Norplant, offers an analogous approach to dealing with teenage pregnancy? Injected under a woman's skin, Norplant prevents pregnancy from occurring for up to 5 years; it can be removed at any time and supposedly has no effects on childbearing afterwards. If it works as advertised, proponents of the services strategy might do better looking for ways of persuading teenage girls to use it (such as, perhaps, by offering a financial reward), instead of continuing to rely on counseling and instruction aimed at changing sexual behavior.

Likewise, the arguments against institutional care of children deserve to be reconsidered. Indeed, in a sense, they already have been. Although stopping short of removing youngsters from their homes, proposals to expand Head Start and similar programs to the first year of life amount to efforts to foster alternative child-raising arrangements. Some social services experts have gone even farther and called for a return to "orphanages" for children from severely disorganized homes. Although establishing such institutions would undoubtedly entail numerous problems, including those that their predecessors suffered from, anything less comprehensive may be unable to provide the round-the-clock help many children must have to break out of the cycle of poverty and dependency.

Finally, efforts to remoralize the social services ought to be undertaken. In moving from the friendly visitors of the 19th century to today's case managers, the services strategy has generally abandoned the idea that it ought to instill hope and develop character in those it serves. Yet evidence such as the importance of church attendance among teenagers who avoid unemployment and the successes of inner-city parochial schools points to the power of such approaches to personal renewal. The ability of today's social services programs to embrace the older objectives—or even rely more on organizations with strong moral cultures, such as church-sponsored groups—might make a significant difference in their effectiveness. To enable this, public funds for the services strategy might have to be provided through vouchers to the recipients (which are likely to be constitutionally acceptable for use at religious agencies) rather than as direct grants to the service providers (which are not).

Even if all these ways of improving the services strategy prove fruitful, the role that social intervention could play in reducing poverty will still be modest. Regardless of the quality of help provided, the questions of how much those who are poor need social services and will participate in them, as well as whether sufficient resources are available to sustain the intensive casework that would be necessary, will remain. But as long as we do not expect the services strategy to do everything, there is no reason it cannot do something.

Epilogue

. . . An America where we end welfare as we know it. We will say to those on welfare: You will have and you deserve the opportunity through training and education, through child care and medical coverage, to liberate yourself. But then when you can, you must work, because welfare should be a second chance, not a way of life.

Bill Clinton
Democratic National Convention, July, 1992

Notes

1. Of the six counties participating in the evaluation of California's GAIN program, Riverside was the most successful in increasing the earnings of long-term welfare recipients. It also used penalties for failure to participate more than the other counties. See Riccio and Friedlander (1992).

2. These estimates are based on 1991 costs for Head Start. As suggested earlier, not all children in poverty should be assumed to need such comprehensive services.

References

Bane, M. J., & Ellwood, D. T. (1983, June). *The dynamics of dependence: The routes to self-sufficiency.* Paper prepared for the U.S. Department of Health and Human Services, assistant secretary for planning and evaluation, Washington, DC.

Besharov, D. J. (1992, January). New directions for Head Start. *The World & I,* pp. 515-531.

Bruner, C., & Berryhill, M. (with Lambert, M.). (1992). *Making welfare work: A family approach.* Des Moines, IA: Child and Family Policy Center.

Clinton, B. (1992, July). [Speech]. Address presented at the Democratic National Convention, New York.

Coleman, J. S., Campbell, E. Q., Hobson, C. J., McPartland, J., Mood, A. M., Weinfeld, F. D., & York, R. L. (1966). *Equality of educational opportunity.* Washington, DC: U.S. Department of Health, Education, and Welfare.

Coll, B. D. (1969). *Perspectives in public welfare: A history.* Washington, DC: Government Printing Office.

Commission on National and Community Service. (1993, January). *Report: What you can do for your country.* Washington, DC: Author.

Comprehensive Child Development Act, Pub. L. No. 100-297, 102 Stat. 130, 42 U.S.C. § 9881 et seq. (1988).

Cottingham, P. H., & Ellwood, D. T. (Eds.). (1989). *Welfare policy for the 1990's.* Cambridge, MA: Harvard University Press.

Elementary and Secondary Education Act of 1965, Pub. L. No. 89-10, 79 Stat. 27 (1965).

Ellwood, D. T. (1986). *Targeting "would-be" long-term recipients of AFDC.* Paper prepared for the U.S. Department of Health and Human Services, Washington, DC.

Family Support Act of 1988, Pub. L. No. 100-485, 102 Stat. 2343 (1988).

Forsythe, P. (1992). Homebuilders and family preservation. *Children and Youth Services Review, 14*(1/2), 33-47.

Foster, S. E. (1986). *Preventing teenage pregnancy: A public policy guide.* Washington, DC: Council of State Policy and Planning Agencies.

Gueron, J. M., & Pauly, E. (1991). *From welfare to work.* New York: Russell Sage.

Himmelfarb, G. (1984). *The idea of poverty: England in the early industrial age.* New York: Knopf.

Lenkowsky, L. (1986). *Politics, economics and welfare reform.* Washington, DC: American Enterprise Institute.

Murray, C. (1984). *Losing ground: American social policy 1950-1980.* New York: Basic Books.

Novak, M., Cogan, J., Bernstein, B., Besharov, D. J., Blum, B., Carlson, A., Horowitz, M., Kondratas, S. A., Lenkowsky, L., Loury, G. C., Mead, L., Moran, D., Murray, C., Nathan, R. P., Neuhaus, R. J., Raines, F. D., Reischauer, R. D., Rivlin, A. M., Ross, S., & Stern, M. (1987). *A community of self-reliance: The new consensus on family and welfare.* Washington, DC: American Enterprise Institute.

Public Welfare Amendments of 1962, Pub. L. No. 87-543, 76 Stat. 172 (1962).

Riccio, J., & Friedlander, D. (1992). *GAIN: Program strategies, participation, patterns, and first-year impacts in six counties.* New York: Manpower Demonstration Research Corporation.

Rossi, P. H. (1992). Assessing family preservation programs. *Children and Youth Services Review, 14*(1/2), 77-97.

Schweinhart, L. (1986). *The preschool challenge.* Ypsilanti, MI: High-Scope Education Research Foundation.

Social Security Act of 1935, Pub. L. No. 74-271, 49 Stat. 620, 42 U.S.C. § 301 et seq. (1988).

Steiner, G. Y. (1966). *Social insecurity: The politics of welfare.* Chicago: Rand McNally.

Steiner, G. Y. (1971). *The state of welfare.* Washington, DC: Brookings Institution.

U.S. House of Representatives, Committee on Ways and Means. (1992). *Overview of entitlement programs: 1992 green book.* Washington, DC: Government Printing Office.

Watson, B. H. (1992). *Young unwed fathers pilot project: Initial implementation report.* Philadelphia: Public/Private Ventures.

Wilson, J. Q. (1990, October 8). Multiple choice test [Review of *Politics, markets, and America's schools* by J. E. Chubb and T. M. Moe]. *New Republic,* pp. 39-42.

Zill, N. A., Moore, K. A., Smith, E. W., Stief, T., & Coiro, M. J. (1991). *The life circumstances and development of children in welfare families: A profile based on national survey data.* Washington, DC: Child Trends.

16

Reshaping Early Childhood Intervention to Be a More Effective Weapon Against Poverty

Edward Zigler
Sally J. Styfco

Nearly 30 years ago, the United States declared an all-out war against poverty, but it is a war we did not win. Through the years, the enemy has become stronger, its victims more numerous, and its consequences more devastating. In 1987, approximately 32.5 million Americans were poor, 40% of them under the age of 18. Among children under 6, nearly one in every four lives in poverty (National Center for Children in Poverty, 1990). Compared with the 1960s, the environments in which poor children are raised today include more homelessness, street violence, illegal drugs, and single-parent families; affordable health and child care services have become less accessible; and many schools in poor districts have become war zones rather than centers of learning. The AIDS crisis—nonexistent three decades ago—and the soaring incidence of prenatal drug exposure have jeopardized the futures of tens of thousands of poor children even before their births.

A less quantifiable sign of defeat in the War on Poverty is the loss of spirit and hope among poor people—the hope that through education and self-help,

310

they could pull themselves up the socioeconomic ladder. The median earnings of young families have plummeted since the 1960s, making them the first generation of Americans who cannot look forward to a better standard of living than their parents attained.

Although the face of poverty has grown uglier, most of the programmatic weapons of the War on Poverty have been either blunted or dismantled. An exception is Project Head Start, still standing on a foundation of hope that poor children can learn to succeed and that their parents can be empowered to improve their own life chances. Through the years, the program has been successful in promoting these goals among participants. Millions of preschool graduates have entered school healthier and better prepared to learn; their parents have acquired better child-rearing skills and become involved in their children's education; many have gained job skills and employment through Head Start. These accomplishments have earned Head Start a broad base of grassroots support and, recently, zealous endorsement by policymakers. A widespread hope is that if the program is made available to all poor preschoolers, they will not grow up to be poor.

But Head Start did not end poverty in the 1960s, nor can it conquer the crueler circumstances of poverty that have taken hold in the 1990s. No single program, no matter how good, can overcome the need for decent housing, jobs that provide a living wage, safe neighborhoods, and positive role models. Head Start did show that it is possible to enhance the educational outcomes of poor children and to boost some aspects of their families' functioning, but these are small pieces of a solution to a multidimensional problem. Yet because it is a viable solution to one of the intertwined causes of poverty, its expansion is justified. Updated and improved, Head Start has the potential to become a more successful weapon in the antipoverty arsenal.

Lessons From Head Start

Head Start has many good features that can facilitate its modernization and help it to better serve the needs of today's economically disadvantaged population. First, the basic concept, methodology, and goals are sound. When young children receive comprehensive services (including health, nutrition, and a developmentally appropriate educational program), when their parents are involved in their activities, and when their families receive needed services and support, they do become more competent socially and academically. Second, since Head Start began, the fields of early intervention, preschool education, and family support have blossomed and produced a wealth of research and theories to inform the direction for change. Much of this work was inspired by Head Start itself, which has always been committed to experimentation and evaluation. Finally, Head Start is flexible by design, a trait required in a program that is tailored to meet local needs.

Experience is another asset that should help Head Start adapt to the times. The original planners and administrators, myself (Zigler) included, made some serious errors that still haunt the program, but at least we can learn from past mistakes.

QUALITY PROBLEMS

When the planning committee began to design a program for poor preschoolers in 1964, it was entering virtually unchartered territory. With the exception of a few experimental projects, there was little research on identifying, much less trying to meet, the special needs of economically disadvantaged children. This lack of precedent was both an asset and a liability to the planners. On the one hand, we were free to entertain any and all ideas because nothing had been proved or disproved. But because of this lack of proof, we had no way of knowing if we were on the right track. The social scientists on the committee would thus have preferred to begin with a small pilot project to allow us to determine not just program effectiveness but the best way to proceed with implementation. Science and politics are not always harmonious endeavors, however, and when Head Start opened its doors just a few months later, more than one-half million children were enrolled.

This large-scale, abrupt beginning to the Head Start program was actually necessary at the time. This was a war, after all, one mounted to eradicate poverty as quickly as possible. The money was there; indeed, one reason that the Johnson administration's chief strategist in the War on Poverty, Sargent Shriver, pursued the notion of a program for preschoolers is that much of the War's Community Action Program funds were unspent (see Zigler & Muenchow, 1992). The administration wanted a large national program and did not give the committee much of a say on program size, which escalated fivefold in enrollment and budget between the planners' first meeting and opening day. Our fears were somewhat allayed by the belief that the proposed services would at least do no harm. Providing children with health and dental care and nutritious meals in particular would certainly do some good, making it difficult to justify restrictions on the size of enrollment.

Although necessary, the unfortunate consequence of starting off so big and so fast was a lack of quality control. In a matter of 3 months, a system had to be developed for processing thousands of applications, awarding grants, and distributing funds—which left little time to ensure that all potential grantees could deliver the program in the manner intended. I (Zigler) remember asking Jule

Sugarman, then associate director of Head Start, if he was concerned about the quality of the program applications. He said that he was, but he assured me that once Head Start was implemented, any programs that were found to be poor would be closed and the funds shifted to better programs. But a few years later, I found that it is not so easy for administrators to stop the flow of federal funds to a program once it has started. One of the first questions I asked after assuming the responsibility for overseeing Head Start in 1970 was how many of the original programs had been shut. I was told that one had *almost* been closed but that none had actually been defunded. To date, only a few programs have had their grants withdrawn, and then only for the most blatant disregard of essential service components. Although Head Start now has national performance standards and other safeguards, quality remains inconsistent. Some Head Start centers are excellent, others are mediocre, and some are simply terrible.

The gravity of the quality problem cannot be overemphasized. The early intervention literature makes clear that only high-quality programs can deliver meaningful benefits. Not long ago, I (Zigler) warned in testimony before the U.S. Senate (1990) that "Head Start is effective only when quality is high. . . . Below a certain threshold of quality, the program is useless, a waste of money" (p. 49). Thankfully, recent moves to expand the program have brought the quality issue to the forefront, and many thoughtful recommendations for improvement have been issued (e.g., Chafel, 1992; National Head Start Association, 1990; Zigler, Styfco, & Gilman, 1993). Lawmakers have responded by mandating that funds be set aside for quality improvements. The Human Services Reauthorization Act of 1990 requires that 25% of Head Start budget increases (after inflation) be set aside to enhance quality, including better salaries and benefits, training, technical assistance, and facility improvements. In our opinion, these efforts are just as important to Head Start at this time as is the capacity to serve every poor child.

SOCIOECONOMIC SEGREGATION

Another aspect of Head Start's planning that has grown problematic is the lack of socioeconomic integration. Of course, Head Start was initiated as a War on Poverty program, so its constituency was necessarily limited to poor children and their families. Yet the planners realized that just as it was wrong to segregate children by race, it would be wrong to separate them by socioeconomic status. They therefore recommended that centers open 10% of their slots to families above the poverty line. This limited percentage would be nothing more than a token gesture if followed; the guideline was issued only as a signal for the future evolution of the program. Yet because centers must give priority to low-income applicants, and because there have never been enough funds to serve all of those eligible, even the 10% above-income enrollment has never been achieved. The inevitable result has been that poor children attend Head Start and wealthier children attend other settings.

This lack of integration cannot prepare children from either income level for the real world, and it denies them the opportunity to learn from interactions with one another. Recognizing the fault with exposing children to segregation at an early age, two major advisory groups convened on Head Start's 15th and 25th anniversaries recommended that models for serving socioeconomically mixed groups be developed (National Head Start Association, 1990; U.S. Department of Health and Human Services, 1980). With the current push to enroll all *poor* preschoolers, however, limited space and funds have pushed this goal even further out of reach.

Designing Head Start as a program for poor children—or more accurately, for those children whose family incomes fall below the official poverty line—has also had the deleterious effect of stereotyping. Families who are below poverty are grouped as having homogeneous needs that can be addressed by Head Start, whereas those above the line are viewed as not needing such services. Yet many poor families function quite adequately despite limited financial resources; others who are slightly or even well above the official index are beset with many problems that hinder parenting and other life activities. Individual differences in family needs certainly existed in 1965, and they are perhaps even more conspicuous today.

The official poverty index, based on food consumption standards in the 1950s adjusted for inflation, is terribly outdated (National Head Start Association, 1991; Urban Institute, 1990). Forty years ago, being poor did mean not having enough food to put on the table, but today it can also mean not having a home in which to put the table. The index also does not take into consideration differences in the cost of living in different geographic areas. In 1990, for example, the poverty line for a family of three was $10,419. In New Haven, Connecticut, where one-bedroom apartments start at $600 per month without utilities, a single person would be unable to survive on that amount. The federal food stamp, Medicaid, and Women, Infants, and Children (WIC) programs have raised income guidelines to serve families in genuine need. Yet Head Start, cast in the mold of an official poverty program, is unable to serve these overincome individuals.

LIMITED HOURS

Another problem that has lingered since Head Start's hasty beginnings is the half-day, school-year program model. Some grantees do offer summer programs, and a small percentage have extended daily hours to accommodate children whose parents work. But in general, Head Start does not provide full-day, yearlong services. We have heard many stories of parents who quit their jobs so their children could attend Head Start. At the other extreme are children eligible for Head Start who are enrolled instead in poor-quality child care because their parents cannot leave work in the middle of the day to shuffle them between preschool and day care and certainly cannot take the summer off. With the implementation of the Family Support Act of 1988 (FSA) and its JOBS program, which requires welfare recipients with preschool-age children to work or receive training, many more children who could benefit from Head Start services may be denied them because of conflicts between working hours and preschool hours.

The irony here is that Head Start was begun in the hope that it could prevent poor children from repeating the cycle of welfare. The purpose of the FSA is to help their parents get off of welfare, but without quality child care, the goal of both programs is thwarted. In a national survey, the Children's Defense Fund (1992) found that the amount many states pay for child care under the FSA is far below market rates, mothers are given little guidance in making child care arrangements, and payment policies typically provide reimbursement for paid expenses rather than money to pay tuition when it is due. Mothers who do secure jobs are entitled to child care assistance for an additional year, but 35 states do not tell them that these subsidies are available. In 16 states, transitional child care was paid to 5% or less of eligible families, and nationwide less than half the funds allocated for this part of the JOBS program were spent.

Although statistics are not available, the result of this lack of attention to child care needs is not hard to guess. Few welfare mothers will be able to enter or remain in JOBS, and fewer will be able to attain self-sufficiency when their training ends. Their children are placed in informal, mostly unregulated child care that is generally the least stable type of arrangement. Some will receive care that is so poor their optimal development will be compromised. Their mothers may be enabled to leave welfare while the children are raised to be the next generation of welfare recipients.

Head Start has always been a two-generation program, providing services for children as well as their parents. About half of Head Start families receive welfare, and if they are forced to participate in JOBS, both generations may be denied the Head Start opportunity. The time has come for Head Start to expand its commitment to parents by offering full-day services to those who need them. The Department of Health and Human Services administers both Head Start and FSA and should act to link the programs, a union now being tried in a handful of areas.

DEVELOPMENTAL CONTINUITY

A final problem we will discuss is the brevity of the Head Start intervention. The project was conceived during a naive and optimistic era of American social history. A belief shared by respected theorists and laypersons alike was that the "right" environment, supplied at the "right" time, could permanently alter the course of human development. When Head Start began as a summer program, it was heralded as just such a timely intervention that would inoculate children against the ill effects of continuing poverty in their lives. These high hopes are echoed in the rhetoric surrounding current expansion efforts. The belief seems to be that if we can deliver a dose of Head Start to all poor 4-year-olds, they will be immune to future failure.

Fortunately, the early planners did not accept the idiocy of the inoculation model. They knew that 6 or 8 weeks of Head Start would not do much for a child. Even after the program was extended to a school-year schedule, they knew that poor children would still be poor after the experience and would have a difficult time keeping up with more advantaged classmates in school. It is surprising that so many were surprised that preschool graduates, who began school with the skills they needed to be ready to learn, soon fell behind in grade school. Some observers argued that the program came too late, that by the time a child was 3 or 4 years old, development was already marred by socioeconomic deprivation. Others believed that because Head Start was meant to help poor children succeed in school, the intervention could more appropriately be delivered during the school-age years. Experimentation within Head Start quickly proved both sides to be right.

Because the planners never believed that they had found the best solution to the learning problems of poor children, they recommended that Head Start continue to experiment with program development. These research efforts were not limited by the age constraints of the preschool program model. In fact, the biggest portion of Head Start's experimental agenda has been to develop ways to serve very young children.

Just 2 years after Head Start began, 33 Parent and Child Centers (PCCs) were opened to provide supportive services and parent education to families and children from birth to age 3. Other efforts to reach younger children include the Parent and Child Development Centers, the highly successful but discontinued Child and Family Resource Program, and the new Comprehensive Child Development Centers (CCDCs)—all designed to provide comprehensive health care and developmentally appropriate learning activities to children from the time of birth and to offer family support and opportunities for participation to their parents. More specifically targeted initiatives are the Head Start family day care and the Indian and Migrant Head Start programs. These efforts all tend to be preventive rather than remedial, aiming to reach disadvantaged families of very young children before developmental damage occurs.

Head Start also inspired several programs to meet the needs of children beyond the preschool years. Just 2 years after the project began, Follow Through was launched to continue services through the early years of school. The plan was for Follow Through to become a national service delivery program of the same scope as Head Start, but the expected funding was never delivered. The program was allowed to continue as an experiment in planned curriculum variation, and it still exists in this form. The original concept was never abandoned, however. In 1974, Project Developmental Continuity was created to coordinate the educational and developmental approaches of Head Start and the public schools and to provide continuous health and social services for preschool graduates and their families. The new Head Start Transition Project (discussed below) is the most recent attempt to extend comprehensive services into the primary grades.

The many efforts to develop interventions for infants, toddlers, preschoolers, and school-age children were not all successful. Many were not given the time or resources to accomplish their goals. Evaluations—crucial to ascertaining whether the ideas were working—were not always well planned or completed. The net result of all of these projects, however, was to establish a new field of early intervention that embraces the consecutive stages of child development. We have now come to realize that a year or two of preschool cannot turn children into geniuses or forever free them from poverty. Instead, we hope to optimize development so that all children grow to become all that they can be. Quality preschool services are one part of the process to facilitate this goal, but we must not neglect other formative stages. The years between birth and age 3 are a period of rapid growth that lay the physical and socioemotional foundations for all later development, including the capacity to benefit from preschool. And the advantages derived from preschool can be quickly lost without a smooth transition to a school environment that builds on previous gains.

These insights form the cumulative contribution of the Head Start experiment. We now know what quality components are necessary to build successful interventions. We know that with very high-risk groups in particular, services must be delivered for a long enough time to impart meaningful benefits. The time has come to put this wisdom to use.

Making Head Start Better

The first of the national education goals is that by the year 2000, all children will enter school ready to learn. Preschool education is the obvious strategy, and Head Start is the nation's tried-and-proven model for achieving school readiness. The program has been preparing preschoolers for elementary school for more than 25 years, and the evidence is convincing that those who attend high-quality Head Start centers are ready for school when they get there. To continue its success, however, Head Start must be modernized. The previous discussion highlights some of the areas in need of improvement. Quality must be upgraded, the issue of socioeconomic integration must be dealt with, full-day child care services must be offered, and the program must last longer if long-term benefits are to be expected.

Policymakers appear to envision a different future for Head Start. They are committed to program expansion, vowing to deliver full funding so that all eligible children are given the opportunity to attend. This is an admirable goal but one that must be better defined. At this time, the term *full enrollment* means different things to different people, and none of them can say how much it will cost. Because it would undoubtedly mean a tremendous number of children and a huge bill for the deficit-ridden treasury, the Bush administration attempted to hone the limits of *full* to mean a single year of a half-day Head Start program for poor 4-year-olds. In light of what we know about the importance of developmental continuity, this plan goes against the wisdom of the field and shortchanges the participants. A proposal that is closer to our thinking about full enrollment was the School Readiness Act of 1991, which would have made Head Start a 2-year, universal program and steadily increased services for children from birth to age 3. Without a method of funding, however, the "entitlement bill" remains more a vision than a plan of action.

Further complicating the controversy over what full enrollment means are the rational pleas to make children from near-poor families eligible for Head Start. It is undeniable that many children of working poor families could benefit from Head Start, but the program has not been allowed to raise its income criteria as other social welfare programs have done. The large size of the near-poor population makes this primarily an issue of cost. If Head Start were to adopt Medicaid guidelines of 133% of the poverty line, for example, an additional half-million children would become eligible (National Head Start Association, 1991). When only one third of currently eligible children are served by Head Start, it appears that it will be some time before slots can be created for others in need of the program. Full socioeconomic integration is an even more distant dream.

Our advice to policymakers is to stop playing this numbers game. Head Start is a sound program that delivers many benefits to poor children and families. It should be expanded eventually to serve all those who can be helped by this type of program, including those whose poverty status is not official. It should be offered for 1 to 2 years, full- or part-day, depending on individual need. This expansion goal will not be reached overnight, but it can be attained if we steadily commit the resources required to make meaningful progress each year. Already, however, expansion monies have fallen far below those authorized in the 1990 Human Services Reauthorization Act. In fiscal year 1993, $2.8 billion was appropriated, less than half of the $5.9 billion authorized. If our intention is to fully fund Head Start, we must begin to do so and not just talk about how nice it will be.

QUALITY IMPROVEMENTS

Head Start expansion is occurring simultaneously with improvement efforts. The National Head Start Association (1990) Silver Ribbon Panel, convened in 1989 to make recommendations for the program's future, flatly warned that "program expansion should *never* occur at the expense of quality" (p. 35). Both efforts can proceed without conflict only if the funds allowed by the reauthorization act reach the intended levels and are used for the intended purposes.

The act mandates that one quarter of Head Start's budget increases after inflation be set aside to enhance quality. Half of the set-aside is to be used for improved salaries and benefits—necessary means to enable programs to recruit and retain qualified staff. Training and technical assistance must be expanded. Soon all classrooms must have at least one teacher with a Child Development Associate credential. Facilities must be modernized and transportation must be better arranged. These are all necessary improvements, but they are by no means the only ones needed.

The Silver Ribbon Panel and others (e.g., Chafel, 1992; Zigler et al., 1993) discuss several areas that demand attention. The basic components that form the core of Head Start services have deteriorated through the years because of lack of funding and changes in the population served. For example, social services and parental involvement are elements that need to be strengthened throughout Head Start, which is now serving a high proportion of dysfunctional families with myriad needs. At the national level, changes in agency responsibility for health care have left a void in leadership for this vital program component. Research, evaluation, and dissemination have long guided Head Start's evolution and must be given a higher priority to direct the days of change ahead. Finally, at a time when the large majority of mothers work outside the home and when legislation requires welfare mothers to work, we repeat that Head Start must offer full-day care.

These changes are all consistent with the original concept of Head Start and with current performance standards. In fact, they promote closer adherence to the standards that, along with better monitoring, should enable all Head Start centers to deliver the quality services that children deserve and that are necessary for positive developmental outcomes. Such services must be provided regardless of how many children are enrolled because they are the raison d'être of Head Start.

A PRESCHOOL PROGRAM MODEL

Head Start's success has sparked a national preschool movement, spurring growth not only in the federal program but also in public school prekindergartens nationwide. According to a 1989 survey by Mitchell, Seligson, and Marx, 27 states funded 33 preschool programs and 12 contributed to Head Start. Both types of effort typically serve 4-year-olds and, like Head Start, two thirds of the state programs are for children deemed at risk of having problems in public school. On the surface, the combined federal and state preschool developments suggest that universal enrollment will soon be a reality and that the goal of having all children ready for school will indeed be achieved. The push to move and move quickly, however, may result in programs that are not carefully planned and do not provide the quality that is absolutely necessary to produce benefits.

The early intervention literature makes clear what elements are required for programs to be successful. Essential practices include health care, family support, an appropriate curriculum, and parent involvement—practices that define Head Start and that have been refined through continuing years of program operation. But instead of building on this experience, many state prekindergartens have been designed in the mold of the typical elementary school program. In Texas, for example, teacher to child ratios in public preschools are greater than 1:20, more than twice the 1:10 ratio recommended for Head Start and for early childhood programs seeking accreditation by the National Association for the Education of Young Children. Mitchell et al. (1989) report that only half of public preschools are required to provide services that go beyond education; few do so, and none approaches the level of services in Head Start. Even Head Start's educational component generally surpasses the state preschools in that it is more appropriate to the developmental needs of children at the ages served. Early childhood professionals fear that there will be a downward extension of the academic program from public grade schools to their preschools (see Kagan & Zigler, 1987). We agree with Farran, Silveri, and Culp's (1991) view that "without attention to the developmental nature of the programs offered, we do not believe they will work" (p. 71). Finally, parental involvement is a concept often preached by public school educators but not as often practiced.

Programs that lack the services poor children need to become ready for school will not attain their goal. Although they may do no harm to children, they have created some problems for local Head Start centers that are better designed to promote school readiness. As states continue to initiate prekindergartens in the public schools and redirect education funds for school-age children to preschoolers, there is increased competition with Head Start for children, staff, funds, and other resources. Mitchell et al.'s (1989) analysis provides some telling examples. In Texas, school districts with at least 15 children who are 4 years old and poor, or with limited proficiency in English, must provide them with prekindergarten. As a result, Head Start has lost its space in some school buildings as well as some teachers. Because public systems generally pay more than the federal programs, their introduction of a preschool can drain the area of available teachers. For Head Start, this can result in high turnover and leave less qualified personnel in charge. Instead of teaming up to coordinate programs, the new competition between Head Start and the public schools may only exacerbate historically poor relations between them.

The duplication of effort and lack of attention to quality components are not the ways to achieve the national education goals. States, which to some extent depend on the federal government for educational assistance, should be given assistance in their preschool efforts by the federal Head Start program. At the least, more must be done to disseminate the lessons of this great educational experiment. For example, the National Governors' Association, a partner in forming the education goals for the year 2000, would undoubtedly be receptive to presentations by Head Start and other early intervention specialists about proven practices. Unproductive competition could be eliminated by a joint federal-state preschool initiative. Head Start and the public preschools might combine teacher training sessions, share staff who provide or make referrals for health care and family support, and perhaps focus on different segments of the populations that each is best equipped to serve.

Whether independent or working cooperatively with Head Start, public preschools can be designed to avoid some of the delivery problems inherent in the federal model. As the preschool trend intensifies, it seems likely that in the near future, all states will offer prekindergarten not just for poor children but as part of the free public education system. These programs would thus provide universal access and be more socioeconomically integrated than is Head Start. The state preschools might also find it easier to institute full-day child care, a service already appearing in increasing numbers of public schools. Child care would not only enable them to better meet the needs of children and families but also provide another means to promote integration.

Families of all economic classes need quality child care, and a sliding fee scale on the basis of family income would open the service to everyone residing in the district. The notion of a Head Start-like public preschool-child care program is already appearing in many states and localities as part of the School of the 21st Century movement (Zigler, 1989; Zigler & Lang, 1991).

Head Start must maintain a leadership role in the design of public prekindergartens and in the delivery of preschool services for poor children. But in light of what we now know about the importance of developmental continuity, we must never again be so naive as to believe that a preschool education will guarantee all children a successful school career. Child development does not begin and end at the age of 4. To promote optimal development, and indeed for our preschool programs to be maximally effective, we must attend to prior and succeeding years. Head Start, the nation's laboratory for designing interventions for younger and older children, must provide leadership in these efforts as well. Head Start can become "a model of quality, a catalyst for change and a source of innovation" for the entire system of early childhood services (National Head Start Association, 1990, p. v). In the next two sections, we will discuss how to apply the lessons of Head Start to programs for very young children and for children in the early elementary grades.

Very Early Intervention

In recent years, much has been written about the crucial importance of the first years of life. It goes without saying that children need good nutrition and health care from the moment of conception. They need predictable caregiving, ample stimulation, love, and guidance to develop the intellectual and emotional tools they will need to succeed in school and in life. When one or more of these environmental nutrients is absent, a situation more likely to occur when a child is born into poverty, developmental delay or damage can ensue and wreak lifelong consequences. Preventive interventions begun early in life are thus the most effective means of ensuring that a child has a chance for a normal course of development.

Given the overwhelming evidence, there is no need to provide a rationale for offering early childhood services to at-risk groups. Required at this time is a plan to define and deliver these services to the population in need of them. A wealth of professional expertise has been devoted to this undertaking. Theorists and researchers from many disciplines have mounted and evaluated a variety of zero-to-three programs, including several within Head Start itself. Some of the nation's most respected professional organizations, advocacy groups, and private foundations have sponsored countless panels and reports on the need for a federal effort on behalf of young children and have put forth inspiring plans to achieve one. With this momentum, and with the knowledge and dedication represented by this cadre of experts, the country today has the human resources necessary to mount a national intervention program for disadvantaged infants and toddlers. This opportunity poses the most promising chance we have had since 1965 to attempt new ways to address the ills of poverty and the causes of school failure.

Our long experience with Head Start is another invaluable resource. The experiment taught us not only about effective methods of intervention but about how to implement a national service delivery program. As a member of Head Start's original planning committee, I (Zigler) feel obligated to share some advice with those who will design a very early Head Start project. First, we will underscore the assets and point out the pitfalls to the process that were discovered in those deliberations nearly three decades ago, and then we will not resist the temptation to plead for certain features that we see as essential to the new effort. (Early Head Start became reality in 1995.)

DESIGNING A FEDERAL ZERO-TO-THREE PROGRAM

The idea and plans for Head Start were developed by a committee of 14 scholars drawn from a variety of disciplines. This format worked well, and a similar committee should be called to design a national program for very young disadvantaged children. The committee should also be charged with naming the new effort. Unlike the time of Head Start's planning, when interdisciplinary early childhood intervention was virtually untried, there are many experimental projects and much intellectual talent that can be used to inform the direction of the program. As just some examples, members of the American Academy of Pediatrics, the Child Care Action Campaign, the Children's Defense Fund, the National Association for the Education of Young Children, and Zero to Three: National Center for Clinical Infant Programs have expertise in this area. We strongly recommend that the committee represent a variety of professions, a configuration that gave Head Start the comprehensiveness that is its strength. To chair the committee, precedent suggests the First Lady is an ideal choice. Lady Bird Johnson served as the honorary chair of the Head Start committee, and her efforts and support were important in putting the program into place. Hillary Clinton's background in child and family issues and her desire to be the national spokesperson for children's concerns are qualities perfectly matched to the requirements of designing this new effort.

Although we want to repeat the successful elements involved in Head Start's planning, we also want to avoid the mistakes. The harshest lesson we learned is that it is unwise to begin too quickly and on a national scale. The new program must be more carefully developed and should be tried out as a pilot project before large-scale implementation is considered. Keeping the program to a manageable size will make it easier to study what does and does not work and to correct any problems with implementation quickly before they become ingrained. Then we can expand gradually, continuing evaluation and remaining watchful. This pace may seem unbearably slow to those eager to get on with the program, but it will give the final project a better chance for success. An idea that can facilitate the pilot phase is to use the PCCs and CCDCs as demonstration sites: They have the facilities, personnel, and community contacts necessary to launch the project, and their location in all states will provide a nationally representative sample of participants and providers.

The Children's Defense Fund (personal communication, December 10, 1992) suggests that 5% of Head Start expansion funds be used to increase services for very young children. In its proposal, which accelerates the rate of expansion, this would amount to $50 million the first year, increasing to $172.5 million in the fifth year. This amount, combined with the sums Head Start already spends on services for very young children, would fund a reasonably sized demonstration phase and provide for well-paced expansion.

REQUIRED PROGRAM COMPONENTS

The exact details of the zero-to-three intervention will be the responsibility of the planning committee. We warn them to clearly specify their goals at the outset, because a confusion about Head Start's mission in the early years led many to misjudge the program's effectiveness. The general structure of the new program must include all the components that experience has proved to be necessary for good developmental outcomes: health care and nutrition, parent involvement, family support, age-appropriate educational and social experiences, and developmental continuity. The content of these services must of course be adjusted to the special needs of infants and toddlers. Health care and good nutrition, for example, must begin prenatally and must focus on the mother throughout pregnancy and nursing. Parents are the child's first and primary teachers, so other aspects of the intervention must center on them as well. As the planners think about how to structure the basic service components for families and very young children, they must also consider the relative emphasis that each component must be accorded. Today, the demographics of the impoverished population make certain services more crucial than they have ever been.

Rising rates of divorce and out-of-wedlock births have created soaring numbers of single-parent families. The vast majority of these are headed by women, whose earnings potential is generally lower than that of men. Although births among teenage mothers have not escalated as rapidly, many more of them are likely to be outside of marriage: 90% of black teenage mothers are single, as are 40% of their white peers (National Commission on Children, 1991).

Young and/or single parents can be helped to be better caregivers if they receive emotional and practical support from their communities (see, e.g., a review by Seitz, 1990). Although services may be available to help families meet needs such as housing, food, and child care, they may require assistance in accessing these programs. In the new intervention program, this help might come from a family services coordinator, a position created in Head Start centers that serve disabled children and now mandated for programs serving disabled infants and toddlers under the Education for All Handicapped Children Act of 1975. Parenting education is generally less available than other social services, so it must become a strong component of the intervention effort. With young parents in particular, knowledge about child care and the developmental process can relieve anxieties and lead to better parenting. Both home visitor and classroom approaches have proved to be effective ways to enhance parenting skills, and there are dozens of promising models that can be studied for adaptation to a national zero-to-three program.

Another demographic change that must be addressed in the early intervention program is the rise in the number of working mothers. Today more than half of mothers with infants under 1 year old work outside the home. Mothers who receive welfare do not have to work or enter job training until their children are 3, but the Family Support Act of 1988 allows states to require mothers of younger children to attend school if they are teenagers or have not completed high school. Quality child care services must be available to these at-risk infants. The intervention program must make available a day care setting tailored to the needs of infants and toddlers. This could be a center or a network of family day care providers who receive training and practical assistance from program personnel. The Head Start Family Day Care Initiative is one effort of this type that is in the demonstration phase and, depending on results, may become a suitable prototype.

Quality services in the child care component must be ensured by performance standards similar to those mandated for preschool Head Start but adapted to the needs of younger children. There must be trained personnel, good caregiver to child ratios, small group sizes, and programs that provide educational and social experiences to promote sound development. Because growth patterns are erratic during the early years of life, the program must be individualized to the unique needs of each child. These quality elements are absolutely necessary for at-risk children to have a chance at proper development. Today, too many young children are in child care settings that are horrific, devoid of so many environmental nutrients that their optimal development may be impaired. For children whose futures are already threatened by poverty, such child care only places them in a rut in the road leading to their own socioeconomic failure.

An early intervention program that includes a child care component has the potential for socioeconomic integration. Parents of all economic classes are finding good infant care unavailable, unaffordable, or both. If the care was offered on a sliding fee scale on the basis of family income, it is highly likely that wealthier parents would enroll. This would create a degree of socioeconomic heterogeneity not currently found in publicly funded child care settings. Another benefit is that the existence of federal quality standards would set an example for the private sector to enhance the quality of care delivered to millions of nonpoor children.

Dovetailed Programming for the Early School Years

Just as the knowledge gained from Head Start can be applied to intervention with children well before they reach preschool age, it can be, and in fact already has been, generalized to programs for children in early elementary school. By way of background, in the early years of Head Start, studies were nearly unanimous in showing that preschool graduates began school with better academic skills than poor children who did not attend. This initial advantage was soon found to fade away, however, leaving critics to argue whether Head Start or the public school system was to blame. Later research showed that Head Start and similar programs do have lasting benefits in the areas of social and academic adjustment (e.g., Consortium for Longitudinal Studies, 1983), but sustained improvement in academic performance is better achieved when preschool services are followed by coordinated programming in elementary school (see below). A continuation of comprehensive services and developmentally appropriate curricula and efforts to involve parents in the educational system appear to give children the footing they needed to continue to succeed in school.

The logic of this approach was apparent long before this evidence was in. Just a year after Head Start opened, plans were discussed to begin successive school-age programming for preschool graduates. The result was Project Follow Through, which still exists but because of political and financial reasons has assumed different goals. The original concept was never abandoned and is now the foundation of the new Head Start Transition Project. This program, currently in the demonstration phase, begins at the transition from the preschool to the school environment and lasts through the third grade.

The Transition Project clearly is based on the knowledge accumulated in the early intervention field: It contains all the elements known to characterize successful programs. Comprehensive services will be continued for 4 years beyond Head Start, giving children more protection against common health and social problems that can interfere with learning. Also to be continued through the transition years are Head Start's individualized and developmentally appropriate program. Preschool and school educators will be required to coordinate their curricula and pedagogies, making the two school experiences less fragmented for young learners. Parental involvement is ensured, because as in Head Start, each transition grantee must have a plan for including parents in the design, management, and operation of the program.

Each grantee also must have a supportive services team that includes state and local agencies that serve the same population and must appoint family services coordinators to serve as liaisons between the team and each child's family. That these services will be available for 4 years of transition offers hope that families will receive support long enough to overcome some major problems.

A small but convincing body of evidence indicates that the Transition Project should be a success. We (Zigler & Styfco, 1993) discuss reports of longitudinal studies of children who attended both early childhood and dovetailed school-age programs in the Abecedarian Project, the Chicago Child-Parent Centers, New Haven Follow Through, the Deutsch's early enrichment program, and Success for All. The combined results strongly support the premise of the Transition Project that continuous intervention for an adequate length of time can help poor children succeed. Once the demonstration program overcomes the trials of implementation, it will be compelling to move the project into the educational mainstream where its potential can be realized nationwide.

Unlike starting a federal zero-to-three program, which must be thought through, designed, and piloted, plans for a school-age Head Start have already been operationalized. Expansion of the Transition Project to serve all Head Start graduates is the next logical step toward the goal of providing developmentally continuous services to the nation's disadvantaged children. This will take money, however—money that we believe should come from redirecting the massive Chapter 1 education program (see Zigler & Styfco, 1993). Chapter 1 receives well over $6 billion annually—more than twice as much as Head Start—but has not had any significant impact on the achievement levels of poor children (see Arroyo & Zigler, 1993). The program must be reshaped if it is to accomplish its goals and make wiser use of substantial tax dollars. We propose that Chapter 1 adopt the model of the Transition Project and become the school-age version of Head Start.

PROBLEMS WITH CHAPTER 1

Chapter 1 began the same year as Head Start under Title I of the Elementary and Secondary Education Act of 1965. The act deployed federal funds to impoverished school districts to help them improve educational services for economically or educationally deprived children. As the program evolved, it became a source of funding for local schools rather than a coherent effort with specific methods and meaningful goals. Even today, the program contains none of the elements that we now know are necessary for successful intervention: It is remedial rather than preventive, services are academic rather than comprehensive, and parent involvement and developmental continuity are minimal. Until recently, evaluation was voluntary and thus not very helpful.

The failure of Chapter 1 has recently been pointed out by a national commission, which has recommended sweeping changes in the program's operation (Commission on Chapter 1, 1992). Although we agree with many of their suggestions, we do not believe they build strong enough components for comprehensive services, parent involvement, or developmental continuity. If Chapter 1 instead becomes a national Head Start Transition Program, a change not inconsistent with the commission's proposals, it would more likely be successful.

Some of Chapter 1's problems result from poor targeting. Although its budget is huge, the money is apportioned to most schools in America to serve students from preschool through high school. Today, about 80% of program funds are spent on children in preschool through grade 6; more than half of them are "educationally deprived" but not poor (Arroyo & Zigler, 1993; Slavin, 1991). Eliminating Chapter 1 grants to nonpoor school districts would enable providers to concentrate resources on those who are both economically *and* educationally impoverished. The Chapter 1 commission did recommend eliminating the criterion of "educationally deprived," and Congress earlier took the initial step of reserving some funds for concentration grants to districts serving predominantly low-income children.

By further reducing the target population to children in the early primary grades, Chapter 1 could turn around its history of lackluster results. We already know that it is easier to affect the developmental trajectory of the child early in life rather than waiting for latent problems to grow. It also makes sense that early school experiences prime the skills and attitudes that carry throughout the years of school. Concentrating intervention efforts on children as they begin school is thus a logical course, one already followed to some extent by many Chapter 1 grantees. If the program were to focus exclusively on at-risk students in kindergarten through third grade, an effective prevention program could be built that would reduce the need for remedial services at later ages. This program should be built around Transition Project plans.

A CHAPTER 1 TRANSITION PROJECT

As Head Start expands to eventually serve all eligible children, Chapter 1 can continue intervention in grammar school. Coordinated curricula and continued parent involvement and comprehensive services will then be firmly placed in schools that serve populations below the poverty level. Students above the income standards can also be expected to benefit because Chapter 1 no longer will be basically a pull-out program but will involve teachers in all classrooms that have former Head Start students. Ineligible students could perhaps obtain the noneducational services of the program such as health and child care for a fee, a notion spelled out in the popular but ill-fated Comprehensive Child Development Act of 1971. This would help integrate the federal educational intervention program to a degree not currently possible.

There are many benefits that will accrue to Chapter 1 itself by assuming the model of the Transition Project. It will finally earn an identity as a true national program with distinguishable procedures and goals. Currently, Chapter 1 consists of a heterogeneous array of educational services that differ in type, delivery, and quality among schools across the country. The adoption of consistent program components such as comprehensive services and parental involvement will give Chapter 1 services a common core. As with Head Start, delivery of these components can be expected to vary according to local needs, resources, and desires. Each Chapter 1 site may develop its own curriculum, for example, and health services may be delegated to the community in areas that have adequate medical resources or delivered through the program in areas in which supply is short. Instead of thousands of individual programs, Chapter 1 sites will have a common structure and theme but vary in detail—a design that has served Head Start well through the years.

Making changes "that research has demonstrated to be most likely to bring about meaningful improvements in student achievement and in the processes of schooling" is consistent with the way Congress and the U.S. Department of Education are addressing Chapter 1 improvement requirements (Stringfield, Billig, & Davis, 1991, p. 605). Becoming the national school-age Head Start would be just such an informed change. It would also supply one of the three sections of a national intervention system to serve disadvantaged children from birth through grade 3, optimizing their opportunity to succeed later in school.

Conclusion: Toward a National
Early Childhood Policy for Children in Poverty

The three-stage intervention system we have described in this chapter would constitute a meaningful effort to enable children and families to overcome the hindrance of poverty. A parent-child program would begin prenatally and continue through the age of 3. Quality preschool services would then be provided, overlapping with the start of elementary school to ensure a smooth transition between the preschool and school environments. To keep the momentum toward success going in the long process of public education, dovetailed services would continue from kindergarten through grade 3. Each phase of the intervention would provide health care and nutrition, developmentally appropriate social and educational experiences, and quality child care if needed. Parents would be involved in the program and would receive parenting education and family support to promote healthy family functioning.

The idea for an extended intervention system for economically disadvantaged families and children from birth to age 8 is not new. It has already been tested and proved in the Child and Family Resource Program (CFRP). Begun in 1973, the CFRPs provided parents and children from birth to age 8 with a variety of support services (e.g., health care, child care, preschool, housing assistance, and job training) from which families could choose those they needed. The multifaceted nature and long-term commitment of the CFRPs was heralded by developmental theorists and social scientists and even earned the praise of the U.S. General Accounting Office, whose usual activity is to find problems with the way programs spend federal funds. The CFRPs were terminated by the Reagan administration in 1983, but not before they had demonstrated the value of supporting families in their roles.

The basic concept of the CFRPs has survived in somewhat diluted form in the Parent and Child Centers (PCCs), serving children ages 0 to 3, and the Comprehensive Child Development Centers (CCDCs) for ages 0 to 5. Recent legislation to expand both programs indicates that policymakers have accepted the need for and wisdom of providing comprehensive services for young disadvantaged children and their families. In addition to the PCCs and CCDCs, they have instituted many federal programs with this goal. These efforts are not all carefully defined, however, and a lack of coordination between them has resulted in duplication as well as service voids.

To give some examples, the Administration for Children and Families has been remiss in regulating the activities of the PCCs. The centers, of course, must have flexibility if they are to fill local needs, but without some standards they do not form a coherent program that can be articulated or evaluated. The CCDCs are as yet too new to determine their operations or effectiveness, but it is clear that they serve the same population as the PCCs but for 2 additional years. Another example of overlap is Chapter 1's Even Start, which is supposed to offer a range of services to parents and children ages 1 to 7. The effort is becoming a literacy program for poor parents, a function recently mandated for Head Start's array of infant and preschool programs. Policymakers appear eager to do something for very young children, but they are in obvious need of a sense of direction.

The situation for older children is not any clearer. Head Start and Chapter 1 are both authorized to serve preschoolers. Disadvantaged school-age children are eligible for the Transition Project, Follow Through, and Chapter 1. These programs all have compatible goals and serve similar if not the same populations, yet they are authorized by different acts, subsections, and amendments and compete with one another for shares of the federal budget. John Ralph (1989), a researcher at the Department of Education, wrote that the entangled policies show that "supporters have exhausted any notion of whom they mean to help . . . or simply how" (p. 396). On another level, this overlap suggests that time, effort, and money are wasted.

Beginning with the assumption that we do not need so many separate programs but instead desire a coherent effort that puts their best elements together, we need the guidance of a concise federal policy for early childhood intervention. Nearly 30 years of experimentation in this area makes clear what this policy should be: There is no quick fix or single antidote for poverty, so we must commit to a comprehensive services program for children and their families for a long enough time to have a true impact. This policy can be implemented through the three-stage intervention system presented in this chapter. We must design a zero-to-three program, continue to expand and improve the preschool Head Start program, and turn Chapter 1 into a Head Start-like program for children in kindergarten through grade 3.

We already have the knowledge and many of the human resources that will be needed to build a national early intervention system for children and families in poverty. By making better use of current federal expenditures in this area, we can also supply some of the financial resources that will be required. Instead of having many different infant-parent programs, for example, we should put their budgets together to create a unified effort that is both stronger and larger than the independent projects. The Children's Defense Fund's proposal that 5% of Head Start expansion funds be contributed to this effort is sensible in that Head Start already attempts to serve this age group. Chapter 1's sizable grant and Follow Through and Transition Project funds can be applied to the K-3 component.

Of course, to give access to all disadvantaged children in need of intervention services, further outlays from tax coffers will be needed. At a time of deficit crisis, these added expenditures may seem out of the question. Yet if we think of them as an investment in human capital, they are not difficult to justify. Preventive services are less costly than remedial ones. Children who begin life healthy and acquire the skills and motivation to learn have a good chance of learning. As they grow to become contributing members of the society, the small investment made in their early years will have compounded to reap a handsome dividend.

References

Arroyo, C. G., & Zigler, E. (1993). America's Title I/Chapter 1 programs: Why the promise has not been met. In E. Zigler & S. J. Styfco (Eds.), *Head Start and beyond: A national plan for extended childhood intervention* (pp. 73-95). New Haven, CT: Yale University Press.

Chafel, J. A. (1992). Funding Head Start: What are the issues? *American Journal of Orthopsychiatry, 62,* 9-21.

Children's Defense Fund. (1992). *Child care under the Family Support Act: Early lessons from the states.* Washington, DC: Author.

Commission on Chapter 1. (1992). *Making schools work for children in poverty.* Washington, DC: U.S. Department of Education.

Comprehensive Child Development Act of 1971, H.R. 6748, 92d Cong., 1st Sess. (1971).

Consortium for Longitudinal Studies (Ed.). (1983). *As the twig is bent: Lasting effects of preschool programs.* Hillsdale, NJ: Lawrence Erlbaum.

Education for All Handicapped Children Act of 1975, Pub. L. No. 94-142, 20 U.S.C. § 1401 et seq.

Elementary and Secondary Education Act of 1965, Pub. L. No. 89-10, 79 Stat. 27 (1965).

Family Support Act of 1988, Pub. L. No. 100-485, 102 Stat. 2343 (1988).

Farran, D. C., Silveri, B., & Culp, A. (1991). Public school preschools and the disadvantaged. *New Directions for Child Development, 53,* 65-73.

Human Services Reauthorization Act of 1990, Pub. L. No. 101-501, 42 U.S.C. § 640.

Kagan, S. L., & Zigler, E. (Eds.). (1987). *Early schooling. The national debate.* New Haven, CT: Yale University Press.

Mitchell, A., Seligson, M., & Marx, F. (1989). *Early childhood programs and the public schools.* Dover, MA: Auburn House.

National Center for Children in Poverty. (1990). *Five million children: A statistical profile of our poorest young citizens.* New York: Columbia University School of Public Health.

National Commission on Children. (1991). *Beyond rhetoric: A new American agenda for children and families.* Washington, DC: U.S. Government Printing Office.

National Head Start Association. (1990). *Head Start: The nation's pride, a nation's challenge* [Report of the Silver Ribbon Panel]. Alexandria, VA: Author.

National Head Start Association. (1991, December 2). *Outdated guidelines deny Head Start services to many poor children* [Press advisory]. Alexandria, VA: Author.

Ralph, J. (1989). Improving education for the disadvantaged: Do we know whom to help? *Phi Delta Kappan, 70,* 395-401.

School Readiness Act, S. 911, 102d Cong., 1st Sess. (1991).

Seitz, V. (1990). Intervention programs for impoverished children: A comparison of educational and family support models. *Annals of Child Development, 7,* 73-103.

Slavin, R. E. (1991). Chapter 1: A vision for the next quarter century. *Phi Delta Kappan, 72,* 586-592.

Stringfield, S., Billig, S. H., & Davis, A. (1991). Implementing a research-based model of Chapter 1 program improvement. *Phi Delta Kappan, 72,* 600-606.

U.S. Department of Health and Human Services. (1980). *Head Start in the 1980's: Review and recommendations.* Washington, DC: Author.

U.S. Senate. (1990, August 3). *Human Services Reauthorization Act of 1990: Report to Accompany H.R. 4151* (S. Rep. No. 101-421).

Urban Institute. (1990). Redrawing the poverty line: Implications for public policy. *Urban Institute/Policy and Research Report, 20*(2), 4-6.

Zigler, E. (1989). Addressing the nation's child care crisis: The school of the twenty-first century. *American Journal of Orthopsychiatry, 59,* 484-491.

Zigler, E., & Lang, M. E. (1991). *Child care choices: Balancing the needs of children, families, and society.* New York: Free Press.

Zigler, E., & Muenchow, S. (1992). *Head Start: The inside story of America's most successful educational experiment.* New York: Basic Books.

Zigler, E., & Styfco, S. J. (1993). Strength in unity: Consolidating federal education programs for young children. In E. Zigler & S. J. Styfco (Eds.), *Head Start and beyond: A national plan for extended childhood intervention* (pp. 110-145). New Haven, CT: Yale University Press.

Zigler, E., Styfco, S. J., & Gilman, E. (1993). The national Head Start program for disadvantaged preschoolers. In E. Zigler & S. J. Styfco (Eds.), *Head Start and beyond: A national plan for extended childhood intervention* (pp. 1-41). New Haven, CT: Yale University Press.

PART VII

Reducing Poverty in America

17

The Real Issues for Reducing Poverty

James H. Johnson, Jr.

I have been asked to summarize the major themes and to discuss the salient outcomes of this volume. Toward this end, this chapter is organized as follows: First, I comment briefly on the goal, structure, and organization of this volume. Second, I discuss, in considerable detail, a set of central issues in the poverty-underclass debate that were not addressed previously in this volume. Third, building on the discussion of these unaddressed or neglected issues, I present a heuristic model that captures the range of contemporary theories about poverty and the underclass in America. I argue that only through the rigorous empirical testing of the competing hypotheses inherent in models of this type are we likely to develop effective policies to reduce poverty in America. Fourth, I discuss a topic to which little attention was devoted in the other chapters: how the nation's top business schools and the business community can contribute to the amelioration of the poverty problem in America. Finally, I conclude by outlining a near-term strategic plan for alleviating persistent poverty in America.

Goal, Structure, and Organization of the Volume

The primary goal of this volume is to identify ways to reduce poverty in America. Toward this end, the chapters were commissioned dealing with a

REDUCING POVERTY IN AMERICA

number of the currently debated antipoverty strategies, including welfare reform, school reform, and community empowerment, as well as other social interventions. The goal was to create a critical dialogue on these antipoverty strategies by selecting authors who are perceived to have diverse perspectives on the causes and consequences of poverty in America.

In my opinion, however, the volume does not adequately reflect the diverse perspectives that exist on the poverty-underclass problem in America. Almost no attention is devoted, for example, to the work of the noted sociologist William Julius Wilson. After nearly 20 years of scholarly inattention by liberal and progressive scholars and policy analysts, his seminal book, *The Truly Disadvantaged* (1987), is largely responsible for the reemergence of poverty as a critical research and policy issue in the late 1980s. Furthermore, Wilson's ideas on the contemporary poverty-underclass problem have spawned a number of other scholarly and policy-relevant publications, including *The Urban Underclass* (Jencks & Peterson, 1991) and *The Ghetto Underclass* (Wilson, 1989), which also received only scant attention in the other chapters.

I dissent from what I believe is an incomplete picture of the nature and extent, as well as the causes and consequences, of contemporary poverty in America. The prevailing view in many of the other chapters is that the growth of welfare benefits, and liberal government programs more generally, are largely responsible for the lack of progress in reducing poverty in America during the past quarter century. Such programs, several of the authors argued, have created a cycle of dependency among the poor and contributed to the erosion not only of traditional family values but also of individual morality and spirituality.

Flowing from these narrow and circumscribed assessments of the causes of the contemporary poverty problem is a set of paternalistic policy prescriptions that are aimed not at *reducing poverty* per se but rather at *reducing dependency* on the social welfare system. Moreover, in concentrating on liberal welfare policy as the primary cause of poverty in America, the other chapters are devoid of any consideration, discussion, and analysis of the role that conservative policies, implemented during the past 12 years at both the federal and state levels of government, have played in exacerbating poverty and inequality in America (Johnson, Jones, Farrell, & Oliver, 1992; Johnson & Oliver, 1992).

Conservative Policies and the Poverty Problem

Elsewhere, my colleagues and I (Johnson et al., 1992) have identified four areas in which conservative policies have been implemented to the detriment of poor people in America. The laissez-faire business climate, the dismantling of the social safety net, criminal justice policies, and educational policies are discussed in the following sections.

LAISSEZ-FAIRE BUSINESS CLIMATE

There is strong evidence that the federal government's effort to create a laissez-faire business climate to facilitate the competitiveness of U.S. firms in the global marketplace has drastically altered the structure of economic opportunity in American society. During the past two decades, changes made in antitrust laws and their enforcement have resulted in a growing concentration of large, vertically and horizontally integrated firms in key sectors of the U.S. economy. These large conglomerates, because of their economic power and control of markets, have been able to move capital quickly and efficiently to various regions of the country as well as to international locations. This has been done in large measure to take advantage of cheap labor. There is growing evidence that the federal government, especially during the Bush administration, may very well have used taxpayers' dollars to provide incentives for U.S. firms to relocate abroad, especially to Central American and European countries (Hinds, 1992).

Furthermore, to facilitate the competitiveness of firms remaining in the United States, the federal government, especially during the Reagan years, relaxed environmental regulations and substantially cut the budgets and/or reduced the staffs of governmental agencies charged with the enforcement of laws governing workplace health, safety, and compensation, as well as hiring, retention, and promotion practices (Palmer & Sawhill, 1984).

This shift toward a laissez-faire business climate is partially responsible for the wholesale exodus of manufacturing employment from central city communities on the one hand, and the emergence of new industrial spaces in the suburbs, exurbs, and nonmetropolitan areas in this country, as well as the movement of manufacturing activities to Third World countries, on the other (Johnson & Oliver, 1992). Research indicates that the new industrial spaces emerging in the United States are usually in places with few blacks in the local labor market and few blacks within reasonable commuting distance (Cole & Deskins, 1988).

The effects of these business policy developments are evident on the Los Angeles landscape, where the worst civil unrest of this century occurred in the spring of 1992 (Johnson, Farrell, & Oliver, 1993). Between 1978 and 1989, approximately 200,000 "good-paying" manufacturing jobs disappeared from the Los Angeles economy. As my colleagues and I have shown elsewhere (Johnson

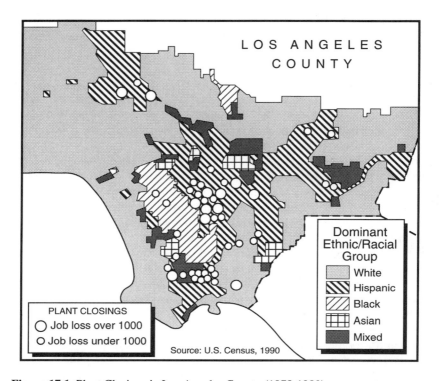

Figure 17.1. Plant Closings in Los Angeles County (1978-1982)

SOURCE: *Plant Shutdown Directory* (1978-1982); U.S. Department of Commerce (1991).

et al., 1992), the South-Central Los Angeles community—the traditional industrial core of the city—bore the brunt of this deindustrialization (Figure 17.1).

The marked expansion of job growth beyond the boundaries of the traditional industrial core has also adversely affected the socioeconomic well-being of the residents of South-Central Los Angeles. Although the well-paying and stable manufacturing jobs were disappearing from this area, local employers were seeking alternative sites for their production activities. These seemingly routine decisions stimulated the emergence of new employment growth nodes or "technopoles" in the San Fernando Valley, in the San Gabriel Valley, and in El Segundo near the airport in Los Angeles County, as well as in nearby Orange County (Scott, 1988; see Figure 17.2). These communities have small or nonexistent black populations and are geographically inaccessible to a majority of the residents of South-Central Los Angeles.

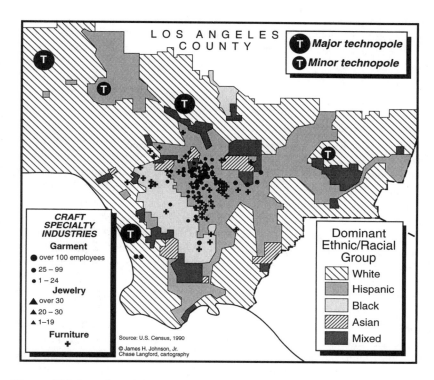

Figure 17.2. Location of Craft Specialty Industries and Job Growth Technopoles in Los Angeles County (1990)

SOURCE: Blum, Carlson, Morales, Nussbaum, and Wilson (1992).

At the same time, a number of Los Angeles-based employers were establishing production facilities in the Mexican border towns of Tijuana, Ensenada, and Tecate. Between 1978 and 1989, at least 215 Los Angeles-based firms, including Hughes Aircraft, Northrop, and Rockwell, as well as a host of smaller firms, participated in this deconcentration process (Soja, Morales, & Wolff, 1983). Such capital flight, in conjunction with the plant closings, has essentially closed off access to what were formerly well-paying, unionized jobs to the residents of South-Central Los Angeles (Bluestone & Harrison, 1982; Squires, 1982).

Although new industrial spaces have been established elsewhere in Los Angeles County (and in nearby Orange County as well as along the U.S.-Mexican border), new employment opportunities have emerged within or near the traditional industrial core in South-Central Los Angeles. But unlike the manufacturing jobs that disappeared from this area, the new jobs are in the competitive sector of the economy, which includes the hospitality services industry (i.e., hotels, motels, restaurants, and entertainment) and such craft specialty industries as clothing, jewelry, and furniture manufacturing (Johnson et al., 1992; see Figure 17.2).

Competitive sector employers survive only to the extent that their prices remain competitive vis-à-vis national and international firms. To remain competitive, they often structure their workforces in illegal ways, have unattractive working conditions, and pay, at best, the minimum wage. Research indicates that the newly arriving Latino immigrants have been preferred over blacks in the competitive sector firms because of their undocumented status (Johnson & Oliver, 1989; Muller & Espenshade, 1984). Lax enforcement of federally mandated hiring policies and workplace health and safety laws, as I noted previously, has allowed competitive sector employers free reign to engage in these illegal and discriminatory practices.

In part as a consequence of these developments, and partly as a function of employers' increasingly negative attitudes toward black workers (Kirschenman & Neckerman, 1991), when the police brutality verdict was handed down on April 29, 1992, South-Central Los Angeles communities were characterized by high concentrations of two disadvantaged populations: the *working poor,* who are predominantly Latino, and the *jobless poor,* who are predominantly black (Figure 17.3). At the time, the black male jobless rate in some of the residential areas of South-Central Los Angeles hovered around 50% (Johnson et al., 1992).

In addition to the adverse impacts of a laissez-faire business policy on the structure of employment opportunities in America, the failure of local governments to devise and implement plans to redevelop and revitalize disadvantaged communities has further exacerbated the economic plight of those who are poor. Instead, local officials typically have pursued a policy of downtown redevelopment in an effort to lure international capital to their cities (Holcomb & Beauregard, 1983).

Evidence from Los Angeles suggests that the "power of the pocketbook" appears to be driving this redevelopment strategy. Data compiled by Clifford, Connell, Braun, and Ford (1992) indicate that

> since 1983, Los Angeles city officeholders and candidates have received $223 million in political contributions, mostly from the Westside, the San Fernando Valley, and Downtown businesses. . . . Critics say the contributions make elected officials more attuned to corporate interests and the suburbs than to the city's poorer areas. (p. A1; see Figure 17.4)

The transformation of the skylines of the Los Angeles downtown and the so-called Wilshire corridor—that 20-mile stretch extending along Wilshire

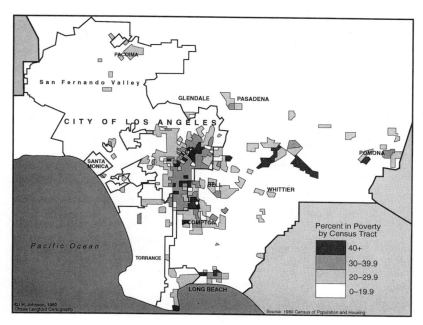

Figure 17.3. Poverty Areas in the Los Angeles Area
SOURCE: U.S. Department of Commerce (1981).

Boulevard from downtown to the Pacific Ocean—is evidence of the success
of this redevelopment strategy. A symbol of Los Angeles's emerging trans-
actional economy, this area now houses the headquarters of a number of
multinational corporations and other advanced services sector employers.

This redevelopment has done little to improve the quality of life of the
disadvantaged residents of the city, especially poor blacks residing in South-
Central Los Angeles, the region most heavily damaged during the recent civil
unrest. Jobs in the revitalized downtown area and along the Wilshire corridor
typically require high levels of education and technical training—the ability
to do "head work" as opposed to handwork—that most of the disadvantaged
residents of South-Central Los Angeles do not possess. The only low-skilled
employment opportunities that exist in this area are low-level service and
custodial jobs, which typically are filled by newly arriving Latino immigrants.

Several of the other chapters in this volume underscore the importance of
welfare-to-work programs in reducing poverty in America. Given the changing
structure of employment opportunities in the American economy, and especially the polarization of the labor market into high-wage and low-wage

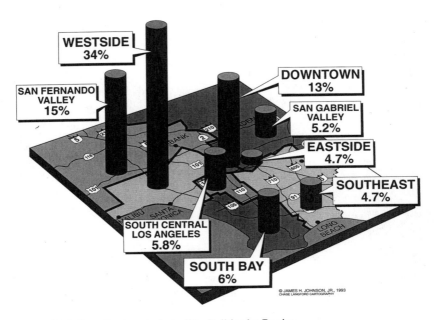

Figure 17.4. Contributions to L.A. City Politics by Region
SOURCE: Grant and Johnson (1995, p. 149). Copyright © 1995 JAI Press. Reprinted by permission.

sectors, such programs may not generate the desired outcome. It is, I believe, unrealistic to think that job training programs will provide welfare-dependent mothers with access to jobs in the economic sectors that pay livable wages. High-wage sector jobs require advanced levels of education and technical skills that most poor women will not possess even after they complete job training programs. At best, welfare-to-work transition programs are likely to channel these women into jobs in the low-wage sectors of the economy that tend to be part-time or temporary and carry no benefits. Thus, although they may reduce *dependency,* it is unlikely that welfare-to-work transition programs will substantially reduce the incidence of *poverty* in America. Welfare-to-work transition programs will have to be supplemented by substantial wage subsidies to move poor women with children out of poverty.

DISMANTLING OF THE SOCIAL SAFETY NET

The federal government's dismantling of the social safety net in poor urban communities through massive cuts in federal aid to cities has also exacerbated the problems of poverty and the underclass. As Niblack and Stan (1992) have shown in the city of Los Angeles, "The decline in federal aid is striking: in 1977 the city received federal aid worth $370 million; by 1990 these grants had dropped to $60 million—or from almost 18 percent of the city's operating budget to less than 2 percent" (p. 267).

Perhaps most devastating for poor communities such as those in South-Central Los Angeles has been the defunding of community-based organizations (CBOs) as a consequence of this massive loss of federal assistance (Johnson & Oliver, 1992). Historically, CBOs were part of that collectivity of social resources in the urban environment that encouraged inner-city disadvantaged persons, especially disadvantaged youths, to pursue mainstream avenues of social and economic mobility and to avoid dysfunctional or antisocial behavior. In academic lingo, CBOs were effective *mediating institutions* in the inner city (Oliver, 1988).

In 1981, when President Reagan took office, CBOs received an estimated 48% of their funding from the federal government (Salamon, 1984). As a consequence of the Reagan administration's elimination of the revenue sharing program, Los Angeles and other cities have been forced to substantially reduce grant support for community-based programs that traditionally have benefited the most disadvantaged people in the community. In South-Central Los Angeles and other inner-city communities, teenagers have been most negatively affected by this defunding of CBO initiatives and other safety net programs.

CRIMINAL JUSTICE POLICIES

The poor and the underclass populations have been disproportionately affected by the implementation of conservative anticrime policies at both the federal and the state levels of government (Mauer, 1992). Paralleling the dismantling of social programs that discouraged disadvantaged youths from engaging in dysfunctional behavior and that rehabilitated those who did, states, with the encouragement and support of the federal government, have pursued for nearly three decades a policy of resolving the problems of the inner city through the criminal justice system (Mauer, 1992).

This policy shift is most apparent in the federal crackdown on drug offenses (Ellis, 1992). Rather than allocate ample resources for drug treatment and rehabilitation, the federal government has engaged in often suspicionless, dragnet sweeps of inner-city neighborhoods (sanctioned by the U.S. Supreme Court) and has implemented a range of other, racially discriminatory laws. Under current federal law, for example, there is a *minimum* 5-year mandatory sentence without the possibility of parole for the personal use of 5 grams of crack cocaine, the drug most often used in the inner city and by poor minorities. By contrast, the possession of the same amount of powder cocaine, which is more widely used by whites and outside of the central city, is a misdemeanor punishable by a *maximum* sentence of 1 year. In addition, there are enormous racial disparities in pretrial detentions and in prison sentences for drug offenses, especially for first-time offenders. Blacks and Latinos are far more likely than whites to be both detained and sent to prison (Ellis, 1992).

Once a leader in the rehabilitation of criminals, the state of California epitomizes this shift in crime policy (Petersilia, 1992). In 1977, the California Legislature enacted the Determinant Sentence Law (Petersilia, 1992), "which embraced punishment (and, explicitly, not rehabilitation) as the purpose of prison, required mandatory prison sentences for many offenses formerly eligible for probation, and dramatically increased the rate at which probation and parole violators were returned to prison" (p. 176). As a consequence of the promulgation of this law, the California prison population skyrocketed between 1980 and 1992, increasing from 22,500 to 106,000, or by 371% (Petersilia, 1992).

To accommodate this increase, California expanded the capacity at 7 of its existing prison facilities and built 13 new ones to bring the current total to 25. Six additional correctional facilities are currently under construction or in the planning phase. During a recent 5-year period, spending on the criminal justice system increased by 70%, roughly four times greater than total state spending. By comparison, state spending on education increased by only 10% during this same time (Petersilia, 1992).

Minorities and those who are poor have been disproportionately affected by California's get tough on crime policy (see Davis, 1990). Two thirds of the prison population are black or Hispanic. Blacks constitute 35% of the total (Petersilia, 1992). How have the minority residents of South-Central Los Angeles fared under the currently policy?

Reliable statistics to answer this question are difficult to assemble, but the number of people arrested during the recent civil unrest who already had a criminal record is probably a fairly accurate barometer. Approximately 40% of arrestees had a prior brush with the law (Lieberman, 1992). What are the prospects of landing a job if you have criminal record? As I have noted elsewhere, "incarceration breeds despair and in the employment arena, it is the scarlet letter of unemployability" (Johnson & Oliver, 1992, p. 144).

EDUCATIONAL POLICIES

Poor youths have been adversely affected by educational initiatives, enacted at the state level during the late 1970s and the early 1980s, which were designed to address the so-called crisis in American education (Orfield, 1988). As is noted elsewhere in this volume, research shows that policies such as tracking by ability group, grade retention, and the increasing reliance on standardized tests as the ultimate arbiter of educational success have in fact disenfranchised large numbers of black and brown youths. In urban school systems, they are disproportionately placed in special education classes and are more likely than their white counterparts to be subjected to extreme disciplinary sanctions (Orfield, 1988; Orfield & Ashkanize, 1991).

The effects of these policies in the Los Angeles Unified School District (LAUSD) are evident in the data on school-leaving behavior (California Basic Educational Data System [CBEDS], 1989). In the LAUSD as a whole, 39.3% of all students in the class of 1988 dropped out at some point during their high school years. For high schools in South-Central Los Angeles, however, the dropout rates were substantially higher, between 63% and 79% (Figure 17.5). The dropout problem is not limited to the high school population. According to data compiled by LAUSD (1989), approximately 24% of the students in some of the junior high schools in South-Central Los Angeles also dropped out during the 1987-1988 academic year (Figure 17.6).

Twenty years ago, it was possible to drop out of high school before graduation and find a good-paying job in heavy manufacturing in South-Central Los Angeles. Today, such employment opportunities are no longer available because of the wholesale loss of manufacturing jobs. With the juxtaposition of the adverse effects of deindustrialization and the discriminatory aspects of educational reforms, what emerges is a rather substantial pool of inner-city black men who are neither at work nor in school.

These individuals are, in effect, *idle*; previous research indicates that this population is most likely to be involved in gang activity, drug trafficking, and a range of other criminal behaviors (Freeman, 1991, 1992; Viscusi, 1986). Moreover, studies show that this population of idle black men experiences the most difficulty in maintaining stable families, which accounts, at least in part, for the high percentage of female-headed families with incomes below the poverty level in South-Central Los Angeles and other ghetto poor communities in U.S. cities (Wilson, 1987).

Giving those who are poor greater choice in deciding what schools their children will attend was advocated at the conference as the way to end the savage inequalities that characterize the U.S. public school system. The encouragement of educational choice among public and private schools—using public dollars—needs to be carefully monitored. Although school choice is promoted as the solution to the crisis in public education, poor parents are at risk of being losers in a system in which choice is unchecked.

The much heralded Wisconsin Parental Choice Plan has achieved a modicum of success because this public-private initiative was carefully designed

348

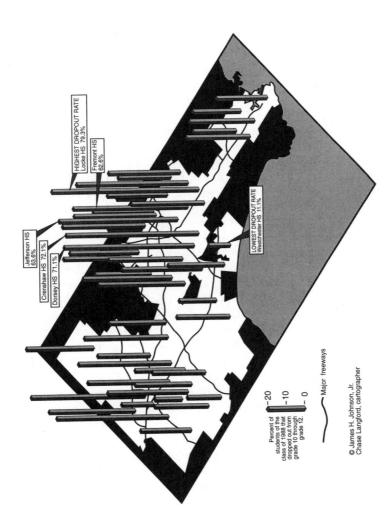

Figure 17.5. Dropout Rates in Los Angeles Unified School District Senior High Schools for the Class of 1988
SOURCE: California Basic Educational Data System (1989).

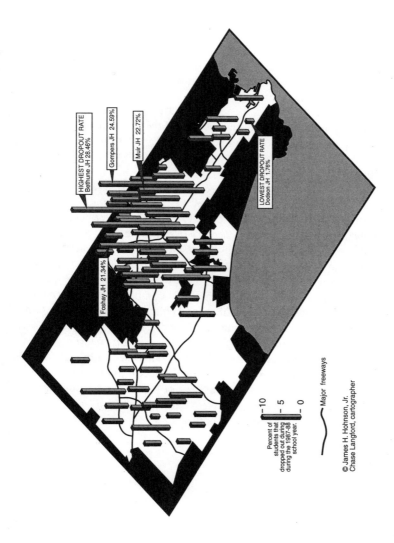

Figure 17.6. Dropout Rates in Los Angeles Unified School District Junior High Schools, 1987-1988
SOURCE: Los Angeles Unified School District (1989).

349

to meet the educational needs of children who are poor (Farrell & Mathews, 1990). The legislature structured it to mandate that private educational providers develop their recruitment strategies and curricular offerings specifically to accommodate poor students (George & Farrell, 1990). Because nonpoor children have their interests served in our educational system, school choice should be driven by the needs of those who are poor to revitalize public education.

A Heuristic Model of Competing Perspectives on Poverty

In contrast to the view that the growth of welfare benefits is primarily responsible for the incidence of poverty in America, a growing number of scholars argue that nonattachment or weak attachment to the labor force is the principal causal agent (Johnson & Oliver, 1992; Kasarda, 1989; Wilson, 1987). Furthermore, these researchers contend that the ability to find and maintain a well-paying job in the restructured American economy has been made more difficult for minorities and poor persons by the discriminatory education and crime policies highlighted previously (Johnson & Oliver, 1992; Orfield, 1988; Orfield & Ashkanize, 1991).

My colleagues and I (see Johnson & Oliver, 1990) have developed a heuristic model that delineates how most of the macro- and microlevel causal agents discussed in the contemporary poverty-underclass literature, individually and collectively, influence the structure of opportunity, especially access to jobs, in American society. I highlight the model here to illustrate that the debates about the poverty-underclass problem in America are much more complex than the other authors of this volume would have us believe.

The heuristic model, as Figure 17.7 shows, is composed of five *exogenous* variables (labor market context, neighborhood context, school context, family context, and individual human capital attributes) and five *endogenous* variables (social resources, cultural capital attributes, group-specific employer attitudes, job search behavior, and employment outcomes). Embedded in the structure of the model are a number of the competing perspectives on the poverty-underclass problem in America. Four of them are presented here: the Wilson Hypothesis, the Kirschenman-Neckerman Hypothesis, the Mead Hypothesis, and the Social Resources Hypothesis.

THE WILSON HYPOTHESIS

Wilson's (1987) theory of the underclass attributes the high rates of joblessness in urban America to the decline in high-wage, highly unionized manufacturing

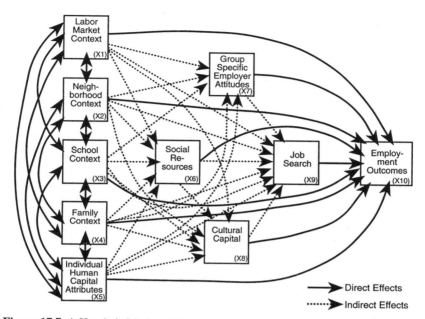

Figure 17.7. A Heuristic Model of Employment Outcomes

SOURCE: Johnson, Oliver, and Bobo (1994, p. 83). Copyright © 1994, V. H. Winston & Son. Reprinted with permission.

employment (i.e., deindustrialization) and to the increasing social (and spatial) isolation of inner-city neighborhoods from mainstream economic opportunities. In the heuristic model, as Figure 17.8A shows, Wilson's thesis reduces to five specific testable hypotheses, which can be summarized as follows:

Hypothesis 1. Employment outcomes are directly influenced by local labor market conditions. Individuals who find themselves in local labor markets that have experienced deindustrialization are more likely to be unemployed or outside of the normal workings of the labor market than their counterparts in local labor markets experiencing rapid job growth in the economic sectors that match local skill requirements.

Hypothesis 2. Employment outcomes are directly influenced by the individual's neighborhood environment. Residents of poor inner-city neighborhoods (i.e., concentrated poverty communities) that are isolated, socially and geographically, from mainstream employment opportunities are less likely to find jobs than residents of more affluent and geographically accessible neighborhoods.

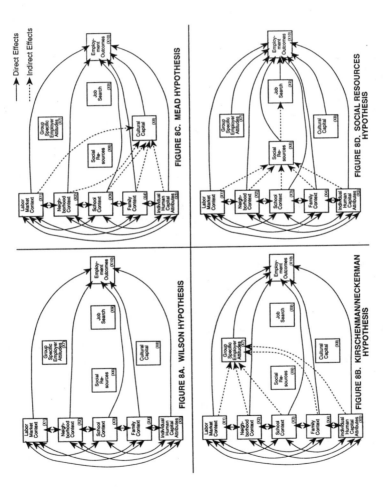

Figure 17.8. Competing Research Hypotheses

SOURCE: Johnson, Oliver, and Bobo (1994, p. 84). Copyright © 1994, V. H. Winston & Son. Reprinted with permission.

Hypothesis 3. Employment outcomes are directly influenced by the type of school an individual attends. Individuals attending inner-city schools are less likely than their counterparts attending suburban schools to have the requisite skills to compete for jobs in the restructured economy.

Hypothesis 4. Employment outcomes are directly influenced by the individual's family context. Individuals who have grown up in higher-status, well-educated, and traditionally structured families are more likely to be employed than individuals who have grown up in low-status, less well educated, and alternatively structured households.

Hypothesis 5. Employment outcomes are directly influenced by an individual's human capital attributes. Young individuals who are high school dropouts and have criminal records are less likely to find jobs than their counterparts who have finished high school and have not had a brush with the law.

THE KIRSCHENMAN-NECKERMAN HYPOTHESIS

The employer surveys conducted by Kirschenman and Neckerman (1991) in Chicago suggest that employment outcomes are directly influenced by employer attitudes and stereotypes of the work ethic and by the *perceived* reliability and dependability of prospective job applicants and jobholders. Their work, along with the recent surveys by Moss and Tilly (1991) in Detroit and Los Angeles, suggests that employer attitudes and stereotypes vary along racial or ethnic and gender lines and that they are often applied categorically. For Kirschenman and Neckerman, then, employment outcomes are not a direct function of the exogenous forces in the heuristic model, as postulated by Wilson. Rather, as Figure 17.8B shows, they argue that the exogenous forces in the model influence employment outcomes indirectly through employer attitudes. Individuals who are members of groups about whom employers have negative attitudes and stereotypes (e.g., black men) are more likely to have experienced discrimination in the labor market and less likely to be employed than individuals who are members of groups about whom employers have positive attitudes and stereotypes (e.g., Latino men and white, black, and Latino women). On the basis of Freeman's (1991) work, employer attitudes are likely to exert the strongest influence on employment outcomes in labor surplus environments and a much weaker influence in tight labor markets.

THE MEAD HYPOTHESIS

Mead argues, both in Chapter 13 of this volume and in his recent book (1992), that the high rates of joblessness and poverty in urban America are due neither to structural constraints in the labor market, as posited by Wilson, nor to employer discrimination, as postulated by Kirschenman and Neckerman. Rather, Mead contends that the existence of these problems reflects character deficiencies and deviant values of inner-city residents. Mead argues that inner-city residents actually choose not to work regularly and that this unwillingness to work is embedded in the nature and culture of the inner city. Negative attitudes toward work, he asserts, are rooted in "ghetto life" (the breakdown of authority and lack of disapproval of antisocial behavior); ethnicity (the lack of value placed on getting ahead by some ethnic groups); black culture (a history of slavery and dependence on whites created a worldview among blacks that makes them uniquely prone to antiwork attitudes); and the Third World origins of immigrants (less industrious work attitudes shaped by African and Latin rather than European origins of today's poor population).

For Mead, then, employment outcomes are directly influenced by the individual's collective of cultural capital attributes. Individuals who do not possess the appropriate attitude toward work (i.e., willingness to work at any job even if it is part-time or temporary, pays poverty-level wages, and does not provide benefits) and other cultural capital attributes valued in the workplace (e.g., adherence to appropriate norms of work attire, punctuality, etc.) are less likely to be employed than their counterparts who do possess the appropriate cultural capital package. See Figure 17.8C for conceptualization of Mead's hypothesis.

THE SOCIAL RESOURCES HYPOTHESIS

In contrast to Wilson, Kirschenman and Neckerman, and Mead, who emphasized the role of structural changes in the economy, employer discrimination, and individual attitudes and values, respectively, an emerging school of thought posits the centrality of access to social resources as a key determinant of employment outcomes (Johnson & Oliver, 1990). Social resources have been broadly defined as contacts through which individuals maintain their social identity and receive emotional supports, material aid and services, information, and new social contacts (Putnam, 1993; see also Coleman, 1988; Granovetter, 1985). Such support can be obtained from individuals (e.g., immediate and extended family members, friends, co-ethnics, etc.), institutions (e.g., churches, CBOs, schools, etc.), or both.

The ability to find and maintain a job, some studies suggest, depends on access to these types of social resources. Studies by Granovetter (1983, 1985) and others (Coleman, 1988; Putnam, 1993) indicate, for example, that a majority of employed persons found their jobs not through employment agencies, newspaper ads, and the like but rather through an acquaintance, friend, or relative. But access to valuable social resources varies by the individual's race, ethnicity, gender, neighborhood contacts, and human capital attributes. Thus, as Figure 17.8D shows, access to valuable social resources is a critical mediating variable in determining employment outcomes.

The real challenge, as I noted earlier, is to rigorously test these alternative hypotheses to assess their relative weight in explaining the incidence of joblessness and other so-called underclass behaviors in America. My colleagues and I are in the process of collecting data in four U.S. cities that will enable us to assess the validity and reliability of these competing perspectives.

Reducing Poverty:
The Role of Business Schools and Corporate America

Except for the discussion of enterprise zones, little direct attention has been devoted to the role of the business community, including the nation's top business schools, in alleviating poverty in America. Enterprise zones are touted as a key economic revitalization and job creation tool, especially for poor urban communities. It is assumed that businesses will locate in poor urban and rural communities if the capital gains tax is eliminated and other levies are reduced or eliminated. There is no history, however, of success of such strategies in poor communities. Research indicates that the major priorities for businesses when making locational decisions are access to markets, access to a quality labor force (code words for no blacks), infrastructure, and crime rates. These business factors are considered to be much more important in site selection than tax rates (Osborne, 1989; Pierce, 1989). Where enterprise zones have been successful, employers have brought their workforce with them rather than employing community residents, or they have used these enterprise locations as warehouse points that need few workers.

In view of these problems with the enterprise zone concept, some policy analysts advocate the promotion of entrepreneurship and microbusiness development among the residents of poor communities as a more viable revitalization and job creation strategy (see Lopez, 1992). Data from the most recent survey of minority-owned business enterprises (MBEs) suggest that this is a potentially more realistic policy option to pursue.

Between 1982 and 1987, MBEs grew by more than four times the rate for all businesses (64% vs. 14%). In 1987, minorities owned about 9% of all U.S. firms, up from 6% in 1982 (O'Hare, 1992). Moreover, these gains have occurred not in the traditional areas of minority business development (i.e., retail and personal services, with secondary concentrations in "other services" and construction); rather, they have occurred in the so-called emerging areas of minority entrepreneurship: business services; finance, insurance, and real estate; transportation and communications; and wholesale trade. According to Bates and Dunham (1992),

> The emerging area firms are most commonly started by better educated owners, many of whom have attended four or more years of college. Financial capital investments are higher than in traditional lines of business. Consequently, emerging firms tend to be larger scale, have lower failure rates, and generate more jobs relative to their traditional cohorts. (p. 244)

Bates and Dunham note further that the growth of these emerging firms has been facilitated by "opportunities offered by government minority business preferential procurement and set-aside programs" (p. 244).

Despite the recent rapid growth in economically more viable minority business establishments, major obstacles remain for minority business development. This is especially the case for blacks who aspire to pursue entrepreneurship in central city communities. In fact, recent reports suggest that many of the minority entrepreneurship gains made during the 1980s may have been reversed as a result of the Supreme Court decision in *City of Richmond v. J. A. Croson Co.* in January 1989 (Hinds, 1991).

The *Croson* decision imposed strict limits on programs aimed at encouraging government to do business with minority concerns. Thirty-two states and 200 cities and counties had minority set-asides prior to the *Croson* decision. By 1991, according to Hinds (1991), many of the states, including New York, New Jersey, and California, and at least two dozen of the cities had suspended their set-aside programs. In most of the other jurisdictions, Hinds notes that the programs were either challenged in court or were under administrative review.

In addition to the deleterious effect of the *Croson* decision, there are also other institutional and procedural barriers to the formation, survival, growth, and continued diversification of actual and potential minority business enterprises in central city communities (Bates, 1991). The institutional barriers include the inadequate flow of capital for minority business development, growth, and diversification from commercial banks, savings and loans, and other financial institutions (Lee, 1992); the hesitancy or outright refusal of commercial insurance companies to grant coverage to business enterprises in poor central city areas (Peterson, 1992); and inadequate attention to management and technical training by governmental agencies that have been established to support and encourage minority business development (Bates, 1991; Vartabedian, 1991).

The procedural impediments include the failure of counselors in schools to advise prospective graduates of career and business opportunities in the skilled trades; the operation of the old boy network in all phases of the government procurement process, including certification, notification, and contract letting; and the refusal of federal procurement officials to downsize government contracts to facilitate the participation of small minority businesses (Bates, 1991).

These institutional and procedural constraints are likely to be especially problematic for poor central city residents who aspire to pursue entrepreneurship and microbusiness development as an avenue of upward mobility and financial security. These individuals are least likely to have the requisite education and training, business skills, knowledge of the banking system, and access to the social capital resources (i.e., family, friends, and role models with expertise in these areas) to form and maintain a successful business.

If entrepreneurship and microbusiness development are to be successful economic development and job creation policy tools, then programs are needed to provide managerial and technical assistance to existing and aspiring minority entrepreneurs. To fill this void in central city communities, a colleague and I (Johnson & Kasarda, 1993) have proposed the establishment of an Urban Enterprise Corps. The program is modeled after the highly successful MBA Enterprise Corps, which recruits and trains talented graduates of a consortium of leading graduate business schools to provide on-site technical and managerial assistance to small and large companies in the emerging market economies of Eastern Europe.

The individuals selected for participation in the Urban Enterprise Corps would assist nascent and struggling businesses to (a) overcome the institutional, procedural, and personal impediments that currently thwart their development, growth, and expansion and (b) establish the fundamentals of good business practice. More specifically, Urban Enterprise Corps members would assist would-be entrepreneurs and existing minority enterprises to

1. deal with the commercial banking system;
2. identify alternative sources of financing for business start-ups, growth, and expansion;
3. comply with ever changing environmental rules and regulations governing business ownership and expansion;

4. recruit and train a quality workforce;
5. identify untapped markets, including potential markets outside the central city;
6. establish a sound fiscal management and accounting system;
7. develop strategic and long-range business plans;
8. identify locations for business expansion; and
9. develop a network of social capital resources to facilitate business success.

Corps members would also assist emerging and long-standing community-based economic development organizations to better serve the needs of nascent and struggling minority business enterprises. Several types of community-based institutions would be targeted for program participation, including community development banks, for-profit subsidiaries of churches, peer support-microlending programs, and minority-owned banks, savings and loans, and credit unions.

A competitive compensation package is a must to attract talented MBAs, who already have forgone at least 2 years of employment and salary, to the Urban Enterprise Corps. Such a package could take the form of a direct payment of a competitive salary (including benefits), estimated to be in the range of $40,000 to $45,000 per corps member for a 12-month assignment, or some combination of the following: salary and benefits, loan forgiveness, credit toward an advanced degree, and/or corporate sponsorship that guarantees employment on completion of the corps assignment. Thus, the business community can support this initiative in two ways: (a) by loaning new MBA hires to the Urban Enterprise Corps and (b) by donating funds directly to the program, which, in turn, will be used, in conjunction with foundation and private donor support, to assemble competitive compensation packages for corps members.

The Urban Enterprise Corps is consistent with President Clinton's vision of what needs to be done to revitalize the economic base of central cities and to create jobs for the residents of these communities (Johnson, 1993). The intention in proposing the establishment of the Urban Enterprise Corps is not to create a cycle of dependency for community-based economic development institutions and small businesses in the central city. Rather, supplying a steady stream of young, committed, enthusiastic, and well-trained MBA talent would *empower* these entities to control their own destinies and become self-sufficient, thereby shaping the nature and trajectory of change in their communities.

This type of empowerment, I contend, is likely to be far more successful than programs such as former secretary of HUD Jack Kemp's Project HOPE, which is designed to empower the poor by making them homeowners. Project HOPE is based on the theory that individuals will have a stronger commitment to maintaining that which they own and to joining in other efforts to enhance their general neighborhood environment. As I have argued elsewhere (Johnson et al., 1992), programs such as Project HOPE will lock poor people into communities that are isolated from mainstream employment and educational opportunities. They would do nothing to expand the housing stock. Project HOPE is analogous to the reservation status provided to Native Americans in the government's efforts to empower them. Partly as a result of their isolation through time, Native Americans currently experience some of the highest rates of unemployment, alcoholism, and domestic abuse of any American ethnic and racial group.

Conclusion

The central theme of this volume is that we can bring those who are poor into the mainstream of American society by enhancing their acceptance of personal responsibility and improving their personal values. But a change in personal values alone will not substitute for job training, job creation, and the removal of racial stereotypes and discrimination. The spatial concentration of poverty presents significant challenges to policymakers and human service providers alike. Although numerous programs and initiatives have been instituted to combat these problems, they suffer from major weaknesses. Three are highlighted here.

First, there is a lack of coordination among programs aimed at improving the life chances in poor communities. Second, only a few of the existing efforts have been systematically evaluated to ensure that the programs are effectively targeting the "hardest to serve," adults with low skills and limited work history and youths who are teen parents or school dropouts. Third, there is no comprehensive strategy for planning future resources allocations as needs change and as these communities expand in size.

A recent study of training and employment programs under the Job Training and Partnership Act revealed that little has been done to address the remedial education needs of high school dropouts and that those with the greatest need for training and employment services are not targeted (Fitzgerald & Patton, 1994). Overcoming these and other program weaknesses, however, is not sufficient to solve these complex problems. A strategic plan is needed to alleviate the social ills associated with concentrated poverty.

Needed is a comprehensive inventory of agencies and institutions that provide services to populations in poverty areas. We also need to assess and evaluate the service providers' performance in an attempt to identify strengths, weaknesses, and missing links in their service delivery systems. On the basis of these findings, a strategy should be devised for a more effective and coordinated use of existing resources and for generating new resources to address unmet needs. Finally, we need to propose a plan of action to encourage the development of the new types of program networks that will be required in the 1990s and beyond—those that link together the various initiatives.

Most important, representatives of the affected ethnic and racial groups must be in key decision-making roles if these efforts are to achieve success. Citizens of color, individually and through their community, civic, and religious institutions, bear a responsibility to promote positive values and lifestyles in their communities and to socialize their youths into the mainstream (Wilson, 1992; Woodson, 1992). But they cannot do this alone.

They cannot be held accountable for the massive plant closings, disinvestments, and exportation of jobs from urban centers to Third World countries. To resolve the poverty problem, there must be an equality in status in responsibility and authority across race and class lines. Government, in bipartisan fashion, must direct its resources to those programs determined to be successful with those who are poor; poor people must be permitted to participate in the design of programs for their benefit; and society at all levels must embrace personal responsibility and a commitment to race and gender equity. Nothing short of such a comprehensive effort is likely to reduce poverty in America.

References

Bates, T. (1991). *The major studies of minority business: A bibliography review.* Washington, DC: Joint Center for Political and Economic Studies.

Bates, T., & Dunham, C. R. (1992). Facilitating upward mobility through small business ownership. In G. E. Peterson & W. Vroman (Eds.), *Urban labor markets and job opportunity* (pp. 239-281). Washington, DC: Urban Institute.

Bluestone, B., & Harrison, B. (1982). *The deindustrialization of America.* New York: Basic Books.

Blum, M., Carlson, K., Morales, E. J., Nussbaum, R., & Wilson, P. J. (1992, May). *Black male joblessness, spatial mismatch, and employer preferences: A case study of Los Angeles.* Unpublished paper prepared for the University of California at Los Angeles, Center for the Study of Urban Poverty.

California Basic Educational Data System. (1989). *Three year summary: Number of dropouts in California public high school instruction.* Sacramento, CA: Author.

City of Richmond v. J. A. Croson Co. (1989), 488 U.S. 469 (1989).

Clifford, F., Connell, R., Braun, S., & Ford, A. (1992, August 30). Leaders lose feel for city. *Los Angeles Times,* p. A1.

Cole, R., & Deskins, D. (1988). Racial factors in site location and employment patterns of Japanese auto firms in America. *California Management Review, 31,* 9-22.

Coleman, J. S. (1988). Social capital in the creation of human capital. *American Journal of Sociology, 96*(Suppl.), 95-121.

Davis, M. (1990). *City of quartz: Excavating the future in Los Angeles.* New York: Vintage.

Ellis, A. (1992, May 14). A glaring contrast: Criminal justice in black and white. *Wall Street Journal,* p. A13.

Farrell, W. C., Jr., & Mathews, J. E. (1990). School choice and the educational opportunities of African American children. *Journal of Negro Education, 59,* 526-537.

Fitzgerald, J., & Patton, W. (1994). Race, job training, and economic development: Barriers to racial equity in program planning. *Review of Black Political Economy, 23,* 93-112.

Freeman, R. B. (1991). Employment and earnings of disadvantaged youths in a labor shortage economy. In C. Jencks & P. E. Peterson (Eds.), *The urban underclass* (pp. 103-121). Washington, DC: Brookings Institution.

Freeman, R. B. (1992). Crime and the employment of disadvantaged youths. In G. E. Peterson & W. Vroman (Eds.), *Urban labor markets and job opportunity* (pp. 201-237). Washington, DC: Urban Institute.

George, G., & Farrell, W. C., Jr. (1990). School choice and African American students: A legislative view. *Journal of Negro Education, 59,* 521-525.

Granovetter, M. (1983). The strength of weak ties: A network theory revisited. In R. Collins (Ed.), *Sociological theory* (pp. 201-233). San Francisco: Jossey-Bass.

Granovetter, M. (1985). Economic actors and social structure: The problem of embeddedness. *American Journal of Sociology, 93,* 481-510.

Grant, D. H., & Johnson, J. H., Jr. (1995). Conservative policymaking and growing urban inequality in the 1980s. *Research in Politics and Society, 5,* 127-159.

Hinds, M. (1991, December 23). Minority business set back sharply by court's ruling. *New York Times,* p. A1.

Hinds, M. (1992, November 11). Survey cited to assail Bush on overseas jobs. *New York Times,* p. A20.

Holcomb, B., & Beauregard, R. (1983). *Revitalizing cities.* Washington, DC: Association of American Geographers.

Jencks, C., & Peterson, P. E. (Eds.). (1991). *The urban underclass.* Washington, DC: Brookings Institution.

Johnson, J. H., Jr. (1993). The Clinton presidency and the future of U.S. cities [Special postelection issue]. *Kenan-Flagler Business School Magazine, 5*(8).

Johnson, J. H., Jr., Farrell, W. C., Jr., & Oliver, M. L. (1993). Seeds of the Los Angeles Rebellion of 1992. *International Journal of Urban and Regional Research, 17,* 115-119.

Johnson, J. H., Jr., Jones, C., Farrell, W. C., Jr., & Oliver, M. L. (1992). The Los Angeles Rebellion of 1992: A retrospective view. *Economic Development Quarterly, 6,* 356-372.

Johnson, J. H., Jr., & Kasarda, J. D. (1993). *A proposal to establish an urban enterprise corps.* Chapel Hill, NC: Kenan Institute of Private Enterprise.

Johnson, J. H., Jr., & Oliver, M. L. (1989). Interethnic minority conflict in urban America: The effects of economic and social dislocations. *Urban Geography, 10,* 449-463.

Johnson, J. H., Jr., & Oliver, M. L. (1990). *Modeling urban underclass behaviors: Theoretical considerations* (CSUP Occasional Working Paper Series, Vol. 1, No. 2). Los Angeles: UCLA Center for the Study of Urban Poverty.

Johnson, J. H., Jr., & Oliver, M. L. (1992). Structural changes in the U.S. economy and black male joblessness: A reassessment. In G. E. Peterson & W. Vroman (Eds.), *Urban labor markets and job opportunity* (pp. 113-147). Washington, DC: Urban Institute.

Johnson, J. H., Jr., Oliver, M. L., & Bobo, L. D. (1994). Understanding the contours of deepening urban inequality. *Urban Geography, 15,* 77-89.

Kasarda, J. D. (1989). Urban industrial transition and the underclass. *Annals of the American Academy of Political and Social Science, 501,* 26-47.

Kirschenman, J., & Neckerman, K. (1991). We'd love to hire them, but . . .: The meaning of race for employers. In C. Jencks & P. E. Peterson (Eds.), *The urban underclass* (pp. 203-232). Washington, DC: Brookings Institution.

Lee, P. (1992, March 29). Recession strikes minority business with extra fury. *Los Angeles Times,* p. A1.

Lieberman, P. (1992, May 19). 40% of riots suspects have criminal records. *Los Angeles Times,* p. B1.

Lopez, R. (1992, September 20). "Micro" means business. *City Times* (Los Angeles Times Weekly), pp. 8-21.

Los Angeles Unified School District, Research Development Department. (1989). *Dropout rates in LAUSD junior high schools, 1987-88.* Los Angeles: Author.

Mauer, M. (1992, Winter). Americans behind bars. *Criminal Justice,* 12-18, 38.

Mead, L. (1992). *The new politics of poverty.* New York: Basic Books.

Moss, P., & Tilly, C. (1991, October). *Raised hurdles for black men: Evidence from employer interviews.* Paper presented at the meeting of the Association for Public Policy Analysis and Management, Bethesda, MD.

Muller, T., & Espenshade, T. (1984). *The fourth wave: California's newest immigrants.* Washington, DC: Urban Institute.

Niblack, P., & Stan, P. (1992). Financing public services in Los Angeles. In J. Steinberg, D. Lyon, & M. Vaiana (Eds.), *Urban America: Policy choices for Los Angeles and the nation* (pp. 255-280). Santa Monica, CA: RAND.

O'Hare, W. (1992, January). Reaching for the dream. *American Demographics, 14,* 32-36.

Oliver, M. L. (1988). The urban black community as network: Towards a social network perspective. *Sociological Quarterly, 29,* 623-645.

Orfield, G. (1988). Exclusion of the majority: Shrinking college access and public policy in metropolitan Los Angeles. *Urban Review, 20,* 147-163.

Orfield, G., & Ashkanize, C. (1991). *The closing door: Conservative policy and black Atlanta.* Chicago: University of Chicago Press.

Osborne, D. (1989, April 3). The Kemp cure-all. *New Republic,* 21-25.

Palmer, J., & Sawhill, I. (1984). *The Reagan record.* Washington, DC: Urban Institute.

Petersilia, J. (1992). Crime and punishment in California: Full cells, empty pockets, and questionable benefits. In J. Steinberg, D. Lyon, & M. Vaiana (Eds.), *Urban America: Policy choices for Los Angeles and the nation* (pp. 175-206). Santa Monica, CA: RAND.

Peterson, J. (1992, June 8). Private sector is crucial to the rejuvenation effort. *Los Angeles Times,* pp. D1, D4.

Pierce, N. (1989, June 5). Kemp's enterprise zones: Breakthrough or chimera? *Nation's Cities Weekly,* p. 4.

Plant shutdown directory. (1978-1982). Oakland, CA: Data Center.

Putnam, R. (1993). The prosperous community: Social capital and public life. *American Prospect, 13,* 37.

Salamon, L. (1984). Nonprofit organizations: The lost opportunity. In J. Palmer & I. Sawhill (Eds.), *The Reagan record* (pp. 261-285). Washington, DC: Urban Institute.

Scott, A. J. (1988). Flexible production systems and regional development: The rise of new industrial spaces in North America and Western Europe. *International Journal of Urban and Regional Research, 12,* 171-186.

Soja, E., Morales, R., & Wolff, G. (1983). Urban restructuring: An analysis of social and spatial change in Los Angeles. *Economic Geography, 58,* 221-235.

Squires, G. D. (1982). Run-away plants, capital mobility, and black economic rights. In J. C. Raines, L. E. Berson, & D. M. Gracie (Eds.), *Community and capital in conflict: Plant closings and job loss* (pp. 62-97). Philadelphia: Temple University Press.

U.S. Department of Commerce, Bureau of the Census. (1981). *1980 census of population and housing* (Census tracts). Washington, DC: Government Printing Office.

U.S. Department of Commerce, Bureau of the Census. (1991). *1990 census of population.* Washington, DC: Government Printing Office.

Vartabedian, R. (1991, July 7). U.S. program to help minority firms plagued by failures. *Los Angeles Times,* pp. D1, D7, D8.

Viscusi, W. K. (1986). Market incentives for criminal behavior. In R. B. Freeman & H. Holzer (Eds.), *The black youth employment crisis* (pp. 301-351). Chicago: University of Chicago Press.

Wilson, J. Q. (1992, June 1). How to teach better values in the inner cities. *Wall Street Journal,* p. A12.

Wilson, W. J. (1987). *The truly disadvantaged.* Chicago: University of Chicago Press.

Wilson, W. J. (Guest ed.). (1989). The ghetto underclass [Special issue]. *Annals of the American Academy of Political and Social Science, 501.*

Woodson, R. (1992, June 1). Transform inner cities from the grassroots up. *Wall Street Journal,* p. A12.

☐18

No More Something for Nothing

Ben Wattenberg

Before reflecting on the state of knowledge on reducing poverty in America as considered in this volume, let me start with a couple of little stories to which I will return. We frequently can learn something from the state of political humor, so I want to remind you of the biggest George Bush joke of 1992. This was a standard one that all of us pundits went around the country with: "How is George Bush unlike Mafia mobster John Gotti?" The answer is "Gotti has one conviction." George Bush and the last other one-term failed president, Jimmy Carter, were convicted on the charge of no convictions. They each ran what you might call a Chinese menu presidency—one from Group A, one from Group B, one from Group C, which translates in the popular press as a presidency with "no vision," a charge that we heard about George Bush. In the media age, let me assure you, having no vision is very bad politics. I don't think George Bush was such a bad president. I would give him a B or B+, but he came across as a no-vision president. In large measure, I think that is why he lost.

Now for my second story. Bill Clinton ran on a vision. He called it the "new covenant." Of course, it turned out that the new covenant had only eight commandments when we finally learned about it. But it was a central theme, and when Clinton got into political trouble, in the last week or 10 days of the campaign, he went back to his new covenant theme. The commercials he put on the air in the last week were not about the economy. In the close states, he didn't go around saying, "It's the economy, stupid;" he ran commercials about welfare and crime. He was saying in effect, "Voters, it is not the economy, stupid. I am a different Democrat because I care about domestic social issues, like welfare and crime." I think, and I think Bill Clinton thinks, that is why he got elected. Those are my two little stories, his commercials and no convictions, to which I will come back.

I may be a card-carrying, bellowing, roaring American optimist, but I am troubled that when people write about a problem, they tend to concentrate on the problem and not about the progress that has been going on in this country. But if that progress forms a lot of the context in which the problem operates, then it is misleading if you forget about the progress. Let me mention just a few things in that context. My colleague Besharov did a wonderful job in Chapter 2 of laying out the case. Unfortunately, he laid out, in my judgment, a too simple model about the nature of the economy in the last 20 years: We haven't made any progress since 1973. This view is based on a couple of Bureau of Labor Statistics (BLS) series. It is in direct opposition to what the Census Bureau says on family income, per capita income, and household income.

In point of fact, even if you buy the BLS series, it is V-shaped. We suffered a great inflation in the 1970s. We lost ground from point A to point B and have come back in the 1980s. In the last decade, we created 19 million new jobs, most of which were not hamburger-flipping jobs at McDonald's. Many of them were in the service industry. We have not actually lost manufacturing jobs in this country, although we have become more productive.

It is appropriate and proper that we dwell on the troubled condition of blacks in the inner city, but we should not dwell on that without understanding that in these last 20 years or so, there has been a remarkable amount of socioeconomic progress among the mainstream black community in this country. Blacks have just about reached a parity at the level of high school graduation with whites. There have been massive increases in the rates of blacks living in suburban communities and sharp upgrading in the occupational rankings. For a lot of black people in this country, many of whom 20 years ago were in the inner city, there are ways out for millions, for tens of millions. We have already seen it happen.

The same thing is true, I think, perhaps in an even sharper way among the Latino community. The figures presented in Chapter 3 by Hayes-Bautista, as I understand them, have been validated recently by a fascinating survey sponsored by the Ford Foundation and the Rockefeller Foundation. There has been substantial socioeconomic progress among Latinos in the United States, particularly if you disaggregate that population and look at the difference between people who have been here 10 years or longer, or were born here, and compare them with the new surging immigrant population. We know from a mountain of literature that it takes immigrants a while to adjust in America. So, if there is a massive inflow of new immigrants, which I think is a healthy thing for this society, the aggregated data will not show a whole lot of progress. But the socioeconomic data for Latinos who have been here 10 years or longer or who were born in this country will show that they have already achieved the American averages in income, occupation, and language proficiency.

Divisiveness in this country is, of course, a problem. I have been recently studying exogamy (intermarriage) in the United States. My own sense is that we can talk all we want about divisiveness in this country, but young people are doing something very interesting about it: They're marrying each other. There are remarkable, sensational rates of intermarriage in this country. This is a replaying of an old theme. Israel Zangwill wrote about intermarriages in the early part of this century in his play *The Melting Pot*. Later on Broadway, we had *Abie's Irish Rose*. That is happening with Asians, with Latinos, and with blacks.

When I was growing up, if an Irish Catholic married an Italian Catholic, that was a big scandal. Today, Ethel Kennedy and Mario Cuomo's kids got married, and everybody thought it was a wonderful thing. The Jewish intermarriage rate in this country has gone in a generation and a half from 5% to 50%. We are creating a new American folk here at precisely the moment everybody is saying that we are splitting apart.

I see the 1980s in the context of what has always been called the American way of life: upward mobility, markets, and all those good things. I think that context is important as we think about the problem of poverty. We searched here for a diagnosis for disease, and most of the authors diagnose the disease underlying poverty as eroding values or a lack of personal responsibility. One of Bill Clinton's key phrases, which he repeated hundreds of times on the campaign trail, was "no more something for nothing." What would we have said if Ronald Reagan ran on that? He would have been pilloried as a hopeless conservative, racist, nuthatch, and right-winger. Yet that is what Bill Clinton ran on: No more something for nothing. It is not a bad test. I urge that we test proposed solutions against that idea.

19

Cultural Aspects of Poverty

James Q. Wilson

Much of this volume is organized around three issues that I'd like to explore. The first issue is, "What is the problem?" Is it to reduce poverty, or is it to reduce the underclass? The two are not the same thing. If we wish to reduce only poverty, we can do so through income maintenance programs ranging from a negative income tax to an expanded earned income tax credit—but at a price. The price is creating further dependency among some people and encouraging a certain amount of family breakup. If we wish to reduce the underclass, we will want to increase self-reliance and self-discipline and become tough on crime and drugs, but we do so at a price. The price is to make some people, at least in the near term, poorer. The second issue is, "What causes the problems we are concerned about?" Two answers were given. The first is incentives or objective factors: jobs, incomes, opportunities. The second is culture: single-parent families, out-of-wedlock births, and a decaying work ethic. The third question is, "Whatever the problem is and whatever the causes are, what will produce an improvement in the problem?" My colleagues write about large-scale, government-driven programs and also about personal, spiritual redemption.

I want to reassert the evidence showing that in addition to an incentive and opportunity problem, there is a culture problem. I emphasize this and not the other because the other has received such ample documentation in the rest of this volume. But recall that there has been a dramatic increase in AFDC participation rates during the last 30 years, independent of changes in the economic conditions. Until about the mid-1960s, the AFDC rolls moved in harmony with the unemployment rate. Then they split apart; they have moved independently ever since. Recall that ethnic groups—blacks, Asians, and Latinos—differ substantially in their rate of single-parent families and AFDC participation. Hayes-Bautista makes this point clearly in Chapter 3. Recall that the rise in out-of-wedlock births, which has affected both whites and blacks, but blacks more dramatically than whites, cannot be adequately explained by changes in welfare benefits, economic conditions, or job availability, although each of those factors played some role. Recall that we cannot explain the changes in crime rates that have been occurring since the early 1960s (e.g., the more than 300% increase in the rate of violent crime)[1] by any combination of economic factors, the changing age structure of the population, or the probability of punishment. Those all played a role, but taken together they leave a great deal of unexplained variance.

There is a tendency to think that if the problem is poverty, the solution is incentives and the appropriate strategies are large-scale government programs. There is a tendency to think that if the problem is the underclass, it is caused by cultural factors, and the only solutions are personal programs that involve either shaping children when they are very young or adult spiritual redemption, or both. That is not necessarily the case. We can imagine changing culture by changing incentives, and we can imagine changing the value of incentives by changing the culture.

Let me explore some of the implications of the incentives explanation. To the extent that the problems that we face, whether poverty or the underclass, are the result of objective or structural changes in our society, we must be aware of what those changes are if we hope to correct them. There were at least three changes that gave rise to what we now call the inner-city problem, meaning some combination of poverty and the underclass. First, there was a massive out-migration not only of jobs but also of people and of social structure. The jobs left, but so did the PTAs and the other means of social control staffed by the middle class. The residential separation of black social classes is far greater today than it was when I was first studying it on the south side of Chicago in the late 1950s. The second massive change was the development of a pervasive intergenerational pattern of crime and the accompanying ever present fear that is found in many inner-city neighborhoods. The third change was the bureaucratization of many inner-city institutions. Public housing projects became more bureaucratic. The school system, always bureaucratic, became far more bureaucratic. The workplace became more bureaucratic as the number of permits, requirements, taxes, insurance forms, and eligibility requirements was multiplied. And welfare became more bureaucratic such that only academic specialists or welfare recipients can understand it. Now if these are the forces that shaped the problem, we must remember how massive they were. The out-migration of people and jobs, the bureaucratization of inner-city institutions, and the development of a pervasive concern for crime did not occur overnight. They are the result of profound, long-term changes in our national life.

Now if the forces were this massive, we are not likely to find more than marginal benefits coming from most of the programs discussed in this volume. If we make changes in welfare rules and if we find a way of institutionalizing in local welfare offices a culture that leads to the good-faith implementation of these rules, then we can expect some benefits, but not large ones. If we change the pattern of arrest and convictions so that the probability of arrest and conviction gets higher, we can cause some reduction in the crime rate, but not a large one. If we have job creation programs on the retail basis that Rebuild L.A. is trying to produce, we can expect some gains, but the gains will be modest. If we have site-based school management, we will have some gains in some schools. In those schools in which a dedicated principal can actually exercise the authority that the Los Angeles Unified School District claims it will give to him or her, we may have some isolated changes. But they will not be systemwide changes because every system of governmental decentralization with which I am familiar, whether in the military, the police, or the schools, tends to reverse itself after one generation. It was politics that produced centralized bureaucratization; politics will not go away.

I am suggesting that to make major changes in the powerful, long-running forces that have created these problems, we have to think big. "Dream no small dreams." We have to think about wholesale changes. The difficulty is that we really don't know what wholesale changes will work. We can have enterprise zones, turbocharged or not, and this may make a difference. But we do not have much evidence yet as to what a massive enterprise zone would produce. We might produce major change if we create property rights in public housing, but we do not yet know how big those gains will be. We might try parental choice in the school system (as I believe we should), but we do not yet know what gains this will produce. We might try large-scale housing vouchers linked to efforts to move inner-city residents out to the periphery of the city, but we do not yet know what difference this will make. We might try debureaucratizing the rules governing small enterprises to avoid turning the economy of inner-city Los Angeles into something that resembles that of Lima, Peru, but we do not know what will happen.

To the extent the problem is culture, we have to ask in what sense has it changed and why has it changed before we can ask what can be done about it. It is difficult to talk clearly about broad cultural changes. To avoid vagueness, let me make the meaning of culture clear and personal. What is the culture as seen through the eyes of young men? That I can answer. I grew up in Southern California, not far from Watts, in the 1930s and 1940s. I think the cultural rules were about as follows. Boys were sexually active; girls were sexually active. (Neither were as active as they are today.) If a girl got pregnant, one of three things happened. One, she took an unexplained absence from school and went home to her aunt and uncle in Iowa, had the baby, and then put it up for adoption. Two, she stayed home, and the boy married her. Three, the boy said he wasn't going to marry her, and so her brothers came around and beat him up. If you were not in school and you were a young boy, you were expected to either have a job or join the Navy. Hanging around on street corners was an invitation for a store owner to call the police and have you arrested on vagrancy charges. If you were of the wrong color and entered the neighborhood where I lived, you were chased out, often violently. If you tried to move in and you were the wrong color, you were chased out, often violently. If you tried drugs, you were ridiculed because, as the phrase went, "Only Mexicans do that." If your parents had a family outing and you wanted to go out with your friends instead, you went with your family. Family came first whether you liked it or not. If you acted up in school, you were thrown out. Many boys that I knew dropped out of school, but it was invariably either to join the Navy or to get a job as a stucco plasterer building bungalows in Lakewood.

I think all of that has changed, partly for the better, partly for the worse. We are now more enlightened; as a consequence, we are less likely to chase people of the "wrong" color out of our neighborhoods. People do not label drug use as the peculiar problem of a particular ethnic group. Those are some of the gains. But we have also paid a price. Now if a girl gets pregnant, she stays in school. The boy doesn't marry her because in the boy's eyes, it's her problem. Boys want action, girls want commitment; if the boys can get action without commitment, they will take it.

Now I was a white boy growing up in an all-white neighborhood. Life for black or Latino boys my age was probably different. But I suspect it was not radically different, because when I was growing up, only 22% of all of the black children in the United States were born out of wedlock. Now, 66% are born out of wedlock (see, e.g., Chapter 2). What has happened? I summarize the cultural change this way. We have celebrated personal freedom and individual self-expression in a way that has materially reduced the social stigma once attached to unwed pregnancies, drug use, and male idleness.

I am not sure that one can change this. We have experienced a worldwide cultural revolution, not only in this country but in every industrialized nation with the possible exception of Japan. Wherever you look in the West, crime and drug abuse rates have been going up. School dropout rates have increased. The rate of burglary and auto theft is about as high in Germany as it is in the United States. The rate of auto theft is about the same in England as it is in the United States. What happened to modern culture and how, if at all, can we rebuild it? It seems to me that the prudent strategy is to combine an emphasis on incentives with a reaffirmation of cultural principles, but we don't. Few writers on public policy mention spiritual redemption as do Woodson and Loury (see Chapters 11 and 6 in this volume). We cannot put into law an obligation for personal redemption. Given the Supreme Court's preoccupation with maintaining a wall of separation between church and state, we often have great difficulty allowing churches to run social service programs (although they are among the few institutions in society that are good at it).

Liberals and conservatives alike prefer incentives, although they disagree about what direction the incentives should take. Liberals would like to improve welfare benefits; conservatives, to slash them. Liberals would like to shorten prison terms; conservatives, to lengthen them. Depending on which group is in power in Washington or Sacramento, one side or the other gets the upper hand temporarily. But neither side wants to step out of that mold. When we do step out, we tend to embroil ourselves in a culture war. One side says that emphasizing culture is "judgmental." (Indeed it is.) Culture reflects a "male Eurocentric view." (I doubt that.) The common theme in these remarks is that it is wrong to blame people for acting badly, that we should blame only people who fail to "understand" or "cure" bad behavior. That is a mischievous view.

I am under no illusion that the culture war can be won. So let us try to do three things. First, do those things that have been shown, in careful evaluations, to produce modest gains. Gueron, Mead, and Zigler and Styfco have named some of these things and explained why the gains are likely to be modest. Second, we should experiment with big dreams. We should try an enterprise zone on a big scale; eliminate all the taxes, eliminate most of the permits. Try real parental choice in some school system, somewhere. Try in many places public housing ownership. But we should try all of these things experimentally, confident in advance that we do not know the answers and that we cannot learn the answers by arguing about it here. Third, we should be clear about what we are trying to achieve. We are trying to produce right behavior. We don't simply want to reduce poverty. As I said, we could do that overnight, although it would cost a lot of money and would produce a lot of bad behavior. We want to be able to say that there are some things we all know are right and some things we all know are wrong, and we wish to design public programs not that have rightness or wrongness as the goal but that are conspicuously informed by our willingness to make judgments about what is right and wrong.

Note

1. The violent crime rate, as reported to the FBI, more than tripled between 1962 and 1982 (U.S. Department of Commerce, 1975, Table H-953; U.S. Department of Commerce, 1993, Table 300).

References

U.S. Department of Commerce, Bureau of the Census. (1975). *Historical statistics of the United States: Colonial times to 1970* (Vol. 1). Washington, DC: Government Printing Office.

U.S. Department of Commerce, Bureau of the Census. (1993). *Statistical abstract of the United States: 1993*. Washington, DC: Government Printing Office.

Index

About the Authors

Douglas J. Besharov is a Resident Scholar at the American Enterprise Institute for Public Policy Research in Washington, D.C. and teaches law and policy at Georgetown University Law Center. He was the first Director of the U.S. National Center on Child Abuse and Neglect and served as Administrator of the AEI/White House Working Seminar on Integrated Services for Children and Families. He has written or edited 14 books and more than 120 articles on various social welfare topics. His most recent book is *Recognizing Child Abuse: A Guide for the Concerned.* His current research interests include the relationships between child care, child support enforcement, child abuse and neglect, welfare reform, and family breakdown and family poverty.

John E. Chubb is Director of Curriculum and Founding Partner of The Edison Project, as well as a Nonresident Senior Fellow with the Government Studies program at The Brookings Institution. From 1984 to 1992, he was a Resident Senior Fellow at Brookings. He is the author of numerous books and articles on education policy and politics, including *Politics, Markets, and America's Schools* and *A Lesson in School Reform From Great Britain,* both coauthored with Terry M. Moe.

Ernesto Cortés, Jr., is the Southwest Regional Director of the Industrial Areas Foundation (IAF), a nonprofit organization founded in Chicago by the late Saul Alinsky. He has played a key role during the past 20 years in developing the IAF's successful approach to institution-based community organizing. In 1974, he established the San Antonio, Texas, organization known as COPS (Communities Organized for Public Service), which has become a model for organizing efforts around the country. He also established similar organizations in Los Angeles, Houston, and other cities in the Southwest. He has received widespread recognition for his many accomplishments, including recognition as a MacArthur Foundation Fellow in 1984. His work has been highlighted in numerous publications on social change and in Bill Moyer's PBS series *A World of Ideas*.

Michael R. Darby is the Warren C. Cordner Professor of Money and Financial Markets and the Director of the John M. Olin Center for Policy in the John E. Anderson Graduate School of Management at UCLA. He is also Research Associate with the National Bureau of Economic Research and Adjunct Scholar with the American Enterprise Institute for Public Policy Research. From July 1986 to January 1992, he served in a number of senior positions in the Reagan and Bush administrations, including Assistant Secretary of the Treasury for Economic Policy, member of the National Commission on Superconductivity, Undersecretary of Commerce for Economic Affairs, and Administrator of the Economics and Statistics Administration. He is the author of eight books and monographs and numerous other professional publications.

Judith M. Gueron is President of the Manpower Demonstration Research Corporation (MDRC), a nonprofit research organization that designs and rigorously evaluates programs aimed at improving the self-sufficiency and life prospects of low-income Americans. The author (with Edward Pauly) of *From Welfare to Work* and many other publications in the areas of welfare reform and job training, she regularly presents the lessons from MDRC's research to policy audiences and government officials. She has served on numerous advisory panels to the U.S. Department of Labor and the National Academy of Sciences.

David Hayes-Bautista is Director of the Center for the Study of Latino Health at UCLA. He also serves on the National Advisory Committee for the Agency of Health Care Policy and Research, the California Tobacco Oversight Committee, and the Carnegie Commission on Adolescent Development, as well as on many other committees that emphasize health and public policy. He has written numerous articles and books on public health and policy.

Christopher Jencks is John D. MacArthur Professor of Sociology and Urban Affairs at Northwestern University. Before coming to Northwestern in 1979, he was a faculty member at Harvard University, a Fellow of the Institute of Policy Studies in Washington, D.C., and an editor of the *New Republic*. His recent work has dealt with changes in the material standard of living during the past generation, the effects of living in a poor neighborhood, welfare reform, and income measurement. His books include *The Academic Revolution* (with David Riesman), *Inequality* (with seven coauthors), *Who Gets Ahead?* (with eleven coauthors), *The Urban Underclass* (with Paul Peterson), *Rethinking Social Policy,* and, most recently, *The Homeless.*

James H. Johnson, Jr., is the E. Maynard Adams Distinguished Professor of Business, Geography, and Sociology and Director of the Urban Investment Strategies Center at the University of North Carolina at Chapel Hill. His research interests include the study of interregional black migration, interethnic minority conflict in advanced industrial societies, and urban poverty and social welfare policy in America. He has published more than 100 research articles and one research monograph and has coedited four theme issues of scholarly journals on these and related topics. Prior to joining the UNC faculty, he was Professor of Geography and Director of the Center for the Study of Urban Poverty at UCLA.

Leslie Lenkowsky is President of the Hudson Institute in Indianapolis. Prior to joining the Hudson Institute, he was President of the Institute for Educational Affairs in Washington, D.C. He is also an Adjunct Fellow of the American Enterprise Institute of Public Policy Research. He is the author of numerous articles in such publications as *Commentary,* the *Public Interest,* the *Wall Street Journal, This World, Fortune,* the *American Spectator,* and *Public Opinion* and is a regular contributor to the *Chronicle of Philanthropy.*

Glenn C. Loury is Professor of Economics at Boston University. He has published many articles in the fields of microeconomic theory, industrial organization, natural resource economics, and the economics of income distribution. In addition to his work as an academic theorist, he has been actively involved in public debate and analysis of the problems of racial inequality and social policy toward people who are poor in the United States. His articles and commentaries on these topics have been featured in the *New York Times,* the *Wall Street Journal,* the *Public Interest, Commentary,* the *New Republic,* and many other publications.

Lawrence M. Mead is Professor of Politics at New York University, where he teaches public policy and American government. Currently, he is a Visiting Fellow at the Woodrow Wilson School of Public and International Affairs at Princeton University. He has also been a Visiting Professor at Princeton, Harvard, and the University of Wisconsin—Madison, and a Visiting Scholar at the Hoover Institution at Stanford University. He is the author of two widely reviewed books on poverty, *Beyond Entitlement* and *The New Politics of Poverty,* and has written many articles on welfare and employment policy.

Terry M. Moe is Professor of Political Science at Stanford University and Senior Fellow at the Hoover Institution. He is author (with John E. Chubb) of *A Lesson in School Reform From Great Britain* and *Politics, Markets, and America's Schools*. He also writes extensively on bureaucracy, regulation, and political economy.

Charles Murray is the Bradley Fellow at the American Enterprise Institute. From 1974 to 1981, he was a Senior Scientist at the American Institutes of Research, one of the largest private social science research organizations, eventually rising to the position of Chief Scientist. He is perhaps best known as author of *Losing Ground*, the influential and controversial analysis of the reforms of the 1960s. He has also written widely in the *Public Interest, Commentary,* the *Atlantic,* the *New Republic, Political Science Quarterly, National Review, American Spectator,* the *Wall Street Journal,* the *Washington Post,* the *Los Angeles Times,* and the *New York Times.*

Albert Shanker has been President of the American Federation of Teachers, AFL-CIO, since 1974. He is a Vice President of the American Federation of Labor and Congress of Industrial Organizations (AFL-CIO) and Chair of its International Affairs Committee. Among the numerous boards and committees on which he serves are the National Academy of Education, the National Board for Professional Teaching Standards, and the A. Philip Randolph Institute.

Margaret C. Simms is Director of Research Programs for the Joint Center for Political and Economic Studies, Washington, DC. Her work has focused on economic analysis and public policy. She has also served as a consultant to a number of organizations, including the National Urban League, the National Institute of Education, the National Urban Coalition, and the Rockefeller Foundation. She was editor of the *Review of Black Political Economy* and is currently a member of the *Black Enterprise Magazine* Board of Economists.

Sally J. Styfco is Associate Director of the Head Start Unit at the Yale University Bush Center in Child Development and Social Policy. She is a writer and policy analyst specializing in issues pertaining to children and families, particularly early childhood and later educational intervention and child care. She has authored several scholarly articles and chapters. Recent works include *Head Start and Beyond: A National Plan for Extended Childhood Intervention,* coedited with Edward Zigler, and their *Social Policy Report,* "Using Research and Theory to Justify and Inform Head Start Expansion."

Ben Wattenberg is Senior Fellow at the American Enterprise Institute. He has written numerous books and articles on social issues and writes a weekly newspaper column that appears in 200 newspapers. His most recent book is *Values Matter*

Most. He has been the host of several public affairs television series including *Ben Wattenberg at Large* and *In Search of the Real America* and is moderator of the weekly public television program Think Tank. He has also been a member of President Carter's Advisory Board for Ambassadorial Appointments, President Reagan's Board for International Broadcasting, and President Bush's Task Force on U.S. Government International Broadcasting.

John C. Weicher is Senior Fellow at the Hudson Institute. From 1989 to 1993, he was Assistant Secretary for Policy Development and Research at the U.S. Department of Housing and Urban Development. He has also served as the Chief Economist at HUD and at the U.S. Office of Management and Budget. He has held the F. K. Weyerhaeuser Chair in Public Policy Research at the American Enterprise Institute and has served on the Committee on Urban Policy of the National Academy of Sciences. He is the author or editor of nine books and the author of numerous popular and scholarly articles on housing, urban problems, and the federal budget.

James Q. Wilson is the James Collins Professor of Management at UCLA. He is the author or coauthor of 12 books, including several books on the topics of crime and public policy. He has served on a number of national commissions concerned with public policy. He was chair of the White House Task Force on Crime in 1966, chair of the National Advisory Commission on Drug Abuse Prevention in 1972-1973, a member of the Attorney General's Task Force on Violent Crime in 1981, and a member of the President's Foreign Intelligence Advisory Board from 1985 to 1990. He is currently chair of the Board of Academic Advisors of the American Enterprise Institute.

Robert L. Woodson, Sr. is Founder and President of the National Center for Neighborhood Enterprise. He was formerly a Resident Fellow at the American Enterprise Institute, where he served as Director of the Institute's Neighborhood Revitalization Project. He has written extensively on the social issues of urban neighborhoods and minority progress. He is frequently interviewed by the news media on issues concerning minority and low-income populations.

Edward Zigler is Sterling Professor of Psychology, head of the Psychology Section of the Yale Child Study Center, and Director of Yale University Bush Center in Child Development and Social Policy. He was the first Director of the Office of Child Development and was an architect of our nation's Head Start program and succeeding efforts such as Project Follow Through, Home Start, the Child and Family Resource program, and the Child Development Associate program. He frequently testifies before Congress and has served as a consultant to a number of cabinet-rank officers.